Fashion Sketching

Online Services

Delmar Online
To access a wide variety of Delmar products and services on the World Wide Web, point your browser to:
> **http://www.delmar.com**
> or email: info@delmar.com

thomson.com
To access International Thomson Publishing's home site for information on more than 34 publishers and 20,000 products, point your browser to:
> **http://www.thomson.com**
> or email: findit@kiosk.thomson.com

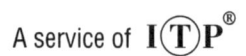

Fashion Sketching

ALFRED D. D'ORTENZIO

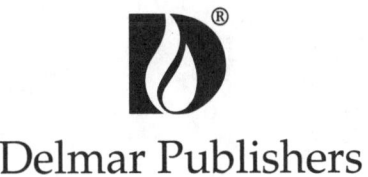

Delmar Publishers

I(T)P® an International Thomson Publishing company

Albany • Bonn • Boston • Cincinnati • Detroit • London • Madrid
Melbourne • Mexico City • New York • Pacific Grove • Paris • San Francisco
Singapore • Tokyo • Toronto • Washington

NOTICE TO THE READER

Publisher does not warrant or guarantee any of the products described herein or perform any independent analysis in connection with any of the product information contained herein. Publisher does not assume, and expressly disclaims, any obligation to obtain and include information other than that provided to it by the manufacturer.

The reader is expressly warned to consider and adopt all safety precautions that might be indicated by the activities herein and to avoid all potential hazards. By following the instructions contained herein, the reader willingly assumes all risks in connection with such instructions.

The publisher makes no representation or warranties of any kind, including but not limited to, the warranties of fitness for particular purpose or merchantability, nor are any such representations implied with respect to the material set forth herein, and the publisher takes no responsibility with respect to such material. The publisher shall not be liable for any special, consequential, or exemplary damages resulting, in whole or part, from the readers' use of, or reliance upon, this material.

Cover Design: Publisher's Studio

Delmar Staff
Acquisitions Editor: Christopher Anzalone
Editorial Assistant: Judy A. Roberts
Developmental Editor: Jeffrey D. Litton
Project Editor: Eugenia L. Orlandi
Art & Design Coordinator: Douglas J. Hyldelund

COPYRIGHT © 1998
By Delmar Publishers
an International Thomson Publishing Inc.

The ITP logo is a trademark under license.

Printed in the United States of America

For more information, contact:

Delmar Publishers
3 Columbia Circle, Box 15015
Albany, New York 12212-5015

International Thomson Editores
Campos Eliseos 385, Piso 7
Col Polanco
11560 Mexico D F Mexico

International Thomson Publishing–Europe
Berkshire House
168–173 High Holborn
London WC1V 7AA
England

International Thomson Publishing GmbH
Konigswinterer Strasse 418
53227 Bonn
Germany

Thomas Nelson Australia
102 Dodds Street
South Melbourne, 3205
Victoria, Australia

International Thomson Publishing–Asia
221 Henderson Road
#05–10 Henderson Building
Singapore 0315

Nelson Canada
1120 Birchmount Road
Scarborough, Ontario
Canada M1K 5G4

International Thomson Publishing–Japan
Hirakawacho Kyowa Building, 3F
2-2-1 Hirakawacho
Chiyoda-ku, Tokyo 102
Japan

All rights reserved. No part of this work covered by the copyright hereon may be reproduced or used in any form or by any means—graphic, electronic, or mechanical, including photocopying, recording, taping, or information storage and retrieval systems—without the written permission of the publisher.

1 2 3 4 5 6 7 8 9 10 XXX 03 02 01 00 99 98 97

Library of Congress Cataloging-in-Publication Data

D'Ortenzio, Alfred D.
   Fashion sketching   /   Alfred D. D'Ortenzio.
     p.   cm.
   ISBN 0-8273-7650-2
    1. Fashion drawing   2. Costume design   I. Title.
TT509.D63   1998
741.6'72—dc20

96-42410
CIP

DEDICATION

To my parents, Raney and Agnes D'Ortenzio

Contents

PREFACE	ix
ACKNOWLEGMENTS	x
ABOUT THE AUTHOR	x
INTRODUCTION	1
CHAPTER 1 *Proportion and Movement*	13
CHAPTER 2 *The Gesture Sketch*	23
CHAPTER 3 *The Head*	33
CHAPTER 4 *Hands, Arms, Legs, and Feet*	57
CHAPTER 5 *Solidifying the Figure*	75
CHAPTER 6 *Clothing the Figure*	86
CHAPTER 7 *Clothing Details I: Folds and Drapery*	101
CHAPTER 8 *Clothing Details II: Jackets and Hats*	114
CHAPTER 9 *Clothing Details III: Prints and Patterns*	125
CHAPTER 10 *Clothing Details IV: Practical Tips and Techniques*	140
CHAPTER 11 *Men's Figures*	147
CHAPTER 12 *Clothing the Male Figure*	164

Preface

Drawing the human figure with any degree of competence is often a lengthy process, but competency enables an artist to draw virtually anything. Over the years, well-meaning authors and teachers developed many formulas and charts to aid students in their attempts to illustrate the human form. Of course, some of these devices are very helpful, and at the beginning stages of learning, it is a good idea to get help wherever one can find it.

After using several approaches, I find the "old way" to be the best, producing the most gratifying results. It is simply a modified classical approach to drawing. Generally, this is a longer process since it is freehand drawing. However, the rewards are greater. The artist is master of what he wishes to portray in whatever size, shape, figure gesture, or view.

No one book or class will teach all there is to know of this subject. It is the duty of every serious student to search every possible venue. As a student, I was taught to explore the techniques of the old masters as well as current artists and illustrators. I strongly suggest that students study books and material covering all of the following areas: fashion history, current fashion, periodicals, human anatomy, basic drawings (still life), flats and specs, and fashion dictionaries. After studying clothing and its construction, one will quickly recognize unusual patterns and seam placements.

This book does not attempt to teach the illustration of every conceivable garment detail and construction. This subject matter covers an extensive range. To illustrate every garment variation, texture, and pattern with new ones being introduced daily is an impossibility.

With regard to the drawings in this book, the purpose of this book is to instruct and encourage drawing skills. Pencil techniques are the best choice for this kind of study, being the best tool when one is tentative. I strongly urge students to be secure in drawing before proceeding to other techniques. It is a great temptation for students to jump ahead and ink-in or color before they have reached a competent level of drawing.

I have allowed my struggle with freehand drawing to be visible; other than for production purposes, the drawings in this book are not touched up. Students must know that it is all right to make mistakes. All drawings were executed in charcoal pencils HB, B, or Prismacolor black on bond, tracing, or marker paper.

Acknowledgments

I wish to thank the following people who were extremely supportive and provided important suggestions and advice: May Sancibrian, Peter Constandy, Fern Mitchell, my beleaguered studio assistant, George Szentesi, who kept track of my numerous drawings, and my editors at Delmar, Christopher Anzalone, Jeff Litton, Doug Hydelund, and Judy Roberts. Also, those instructors who reviewed my work, for their valuable insights and suggestions.

Steven Miller
Art Institute of Chicago
Chicago, IL

Diane DeMers
Fashion Institute of Technology
New York, NY

Laurie Hoffman
Rhode Island School of Design
Providence, RI

Clare Podemski
The University of Alabama
College of Human Environmental Sciences
Tuscaloosa, AL

About the Author

Alfred D'Ortenzio is a graduate of Parsons School of Design, New York and Paris, France. His prior experience includes illustration for Macy's Department Store, New York and fashion advertising illustration for Warnaco. Mr. D'Ortenzio has received numerous awards including the Connecticut Advertising Society's First Prize and Best of Show awards for his illustration materials. He is currently a freelance artist and private art instructor. Mr. D'Ortenzio also conducts workshops at various colleges and universities.

Introduction

TOOLS AND MATERIALS

Tote board 23" x 26"
Newsprint 14" x 17" (Newsprint is good to begin with because it is inexpensive and you will use great quantities of it. Do not use colored pencils on newsprint—this will turn them gray.)
Bond or layout paper pad 14" x 17" (White is best for charcoal pencil or colored pencils)
Soft pencils (RITMO-B® [2] #B or B or other brand charcoal; PRISMACOLOR® [2] Black #935)
Kneaded eraser (Form in half and work in your hand. Avoid a fistfull ball.)
X-ACTO® knife (for pencil sharpening)
Tackle box (for transporting materials from home to class, and so on.)

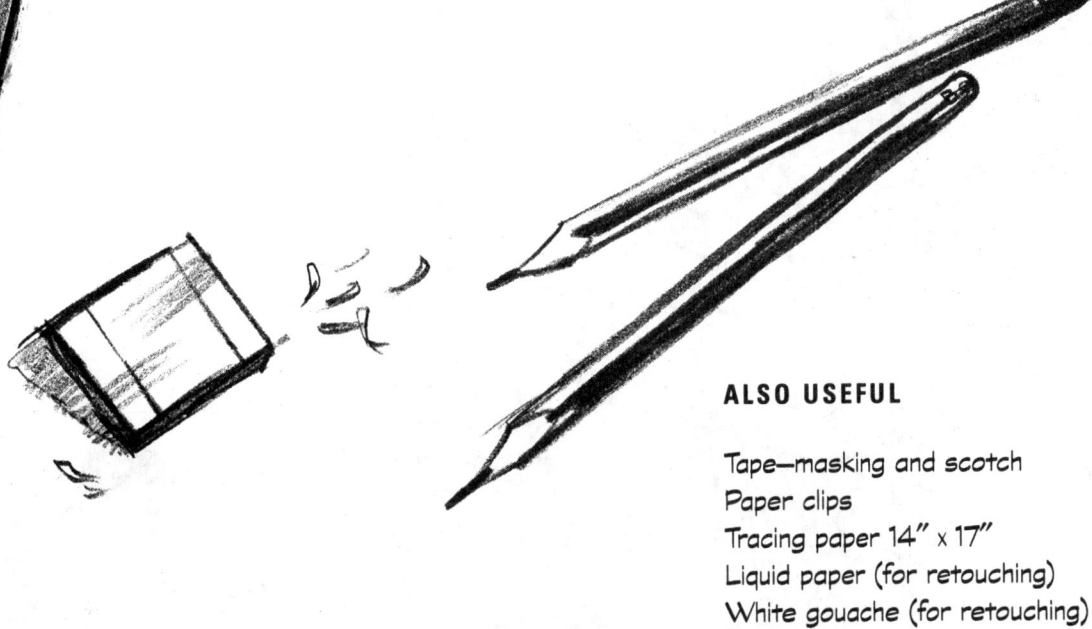

ALSO USEFUL

Tape—masking and scotch
Paper clips
Tracing paper 14" x 17"
Liquid paper (for retouching)
White gouache (for retouching)
Small brush, #2

STUDIO CLASSROOM SETUP

Whenever one begins to work, whether in class, a studio, or at home, the position one begins to work in is important. Always work on a hard-surfaced board. The back of a drawing pad is not adequate. The board must be propped up at a 45-degree angle.

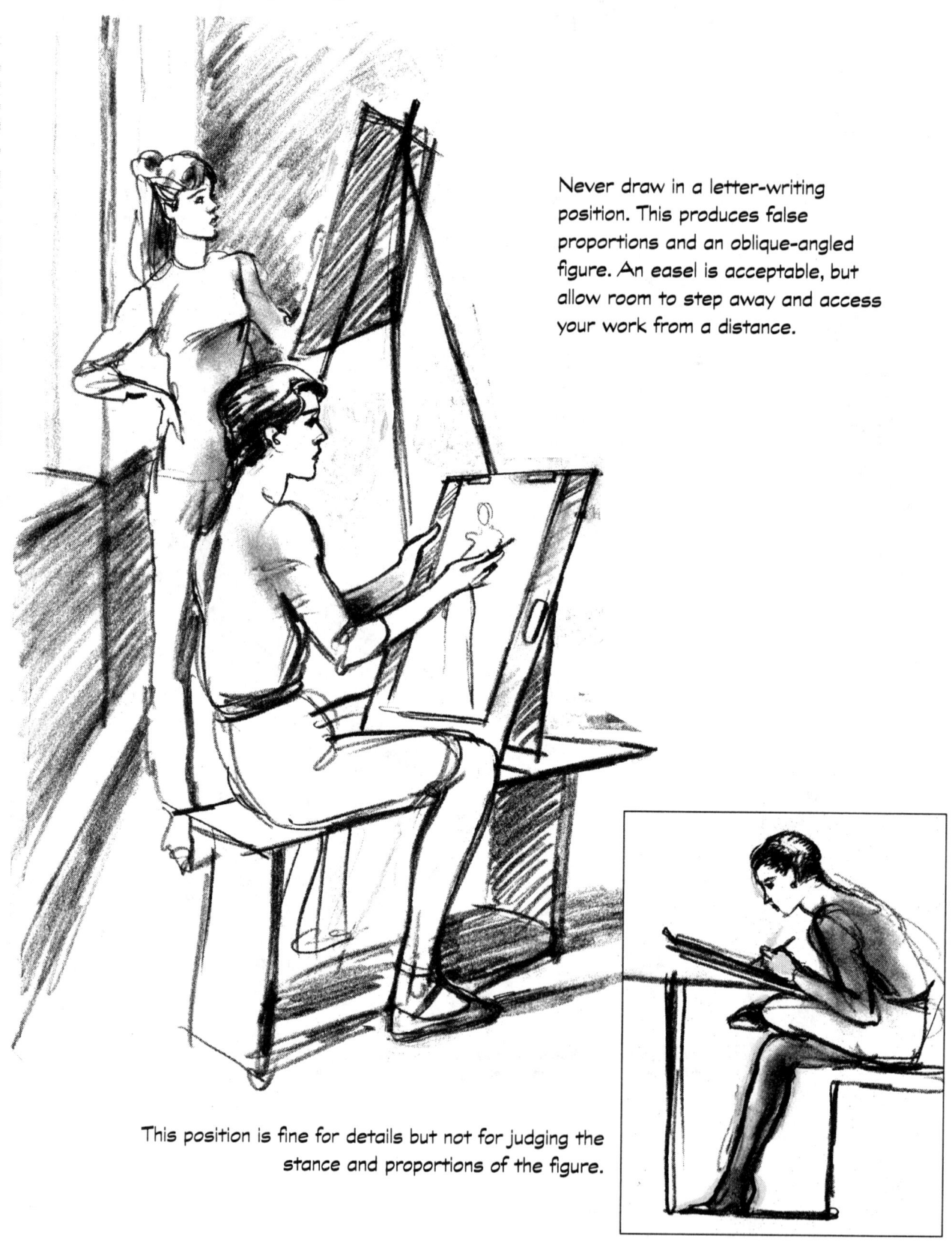

Never draw in a letter-writing position. This produces false proportions and an oblique-angled figure. An easel is acceptable, but allow room to step away and access your work from a distance.

This position is fine for details but not for judging the stance and proportions of the figure.

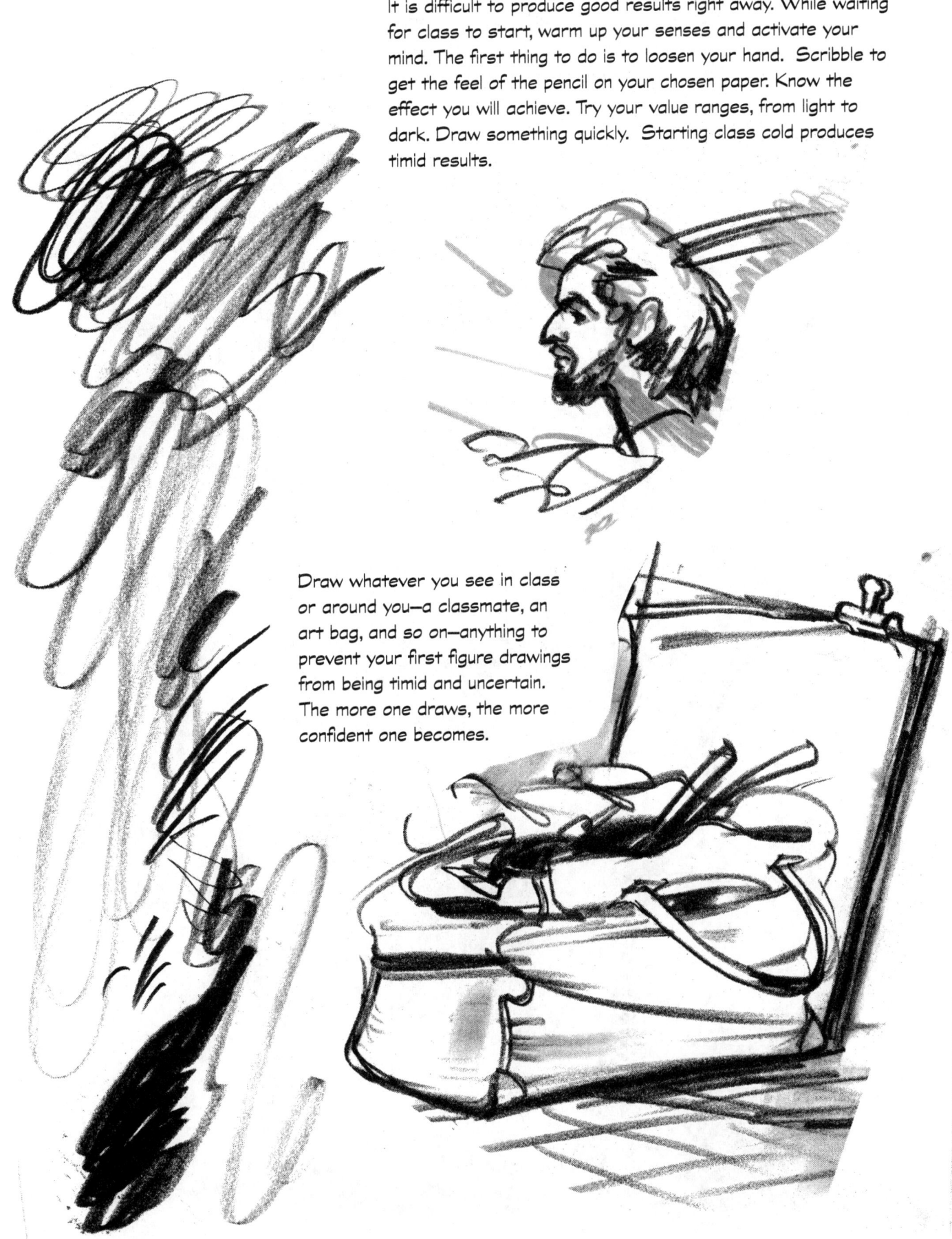

It is difficult to produce good results right away. While waiting for class to start, warm up your senses and activate your mind. The first thing to do is to loosen your hand. Scribble to get the feel of the pencil on your chosen paper. Know the effect you will achieve. Try your value ranges, from light to dark. Draw something quickly. Starting class cold produces timid results.

Draw whatever you see in class or around you—a classmate, an art bag, and so on—anything to prevent your first figure drawings from being timid and uncertain. The more one draws, the more confident one becomes.

PHOTOGRAPHIC RESEARCH

Considerations for collecting photographic research:

- Prepare and label a folder for each figure category.
- Avoid seated or reclining poses.
- Collect bathing suits or intimate apparel in all views.
- Lingerie catalogs are a good source, but make sure the entire figure can be seen.
- Look for figures wearing form-fitting garments, revealing most of the figure's outlines.
- Add more clothed figures in all categories.
- Avoid difficult or complicated hand views.

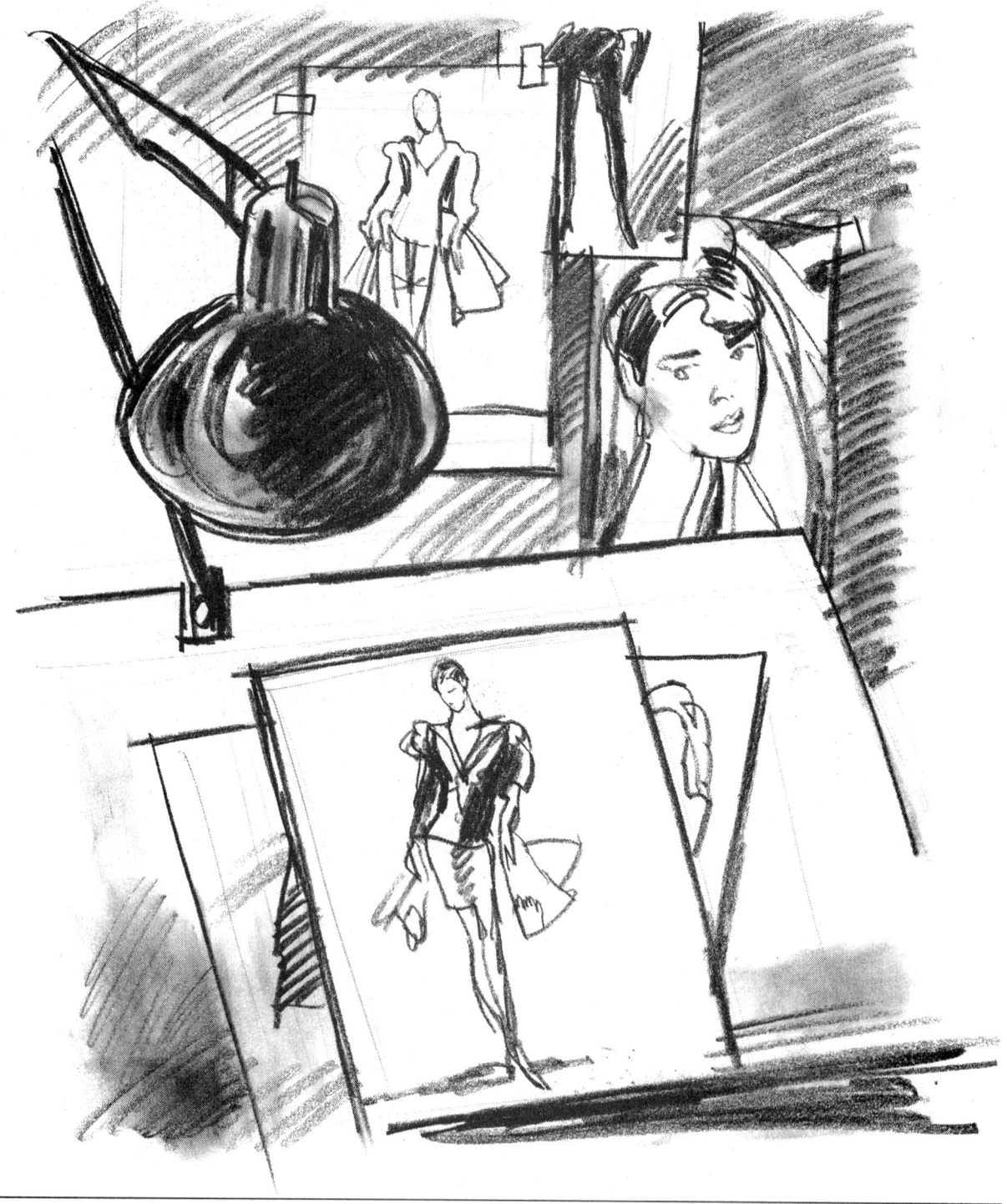

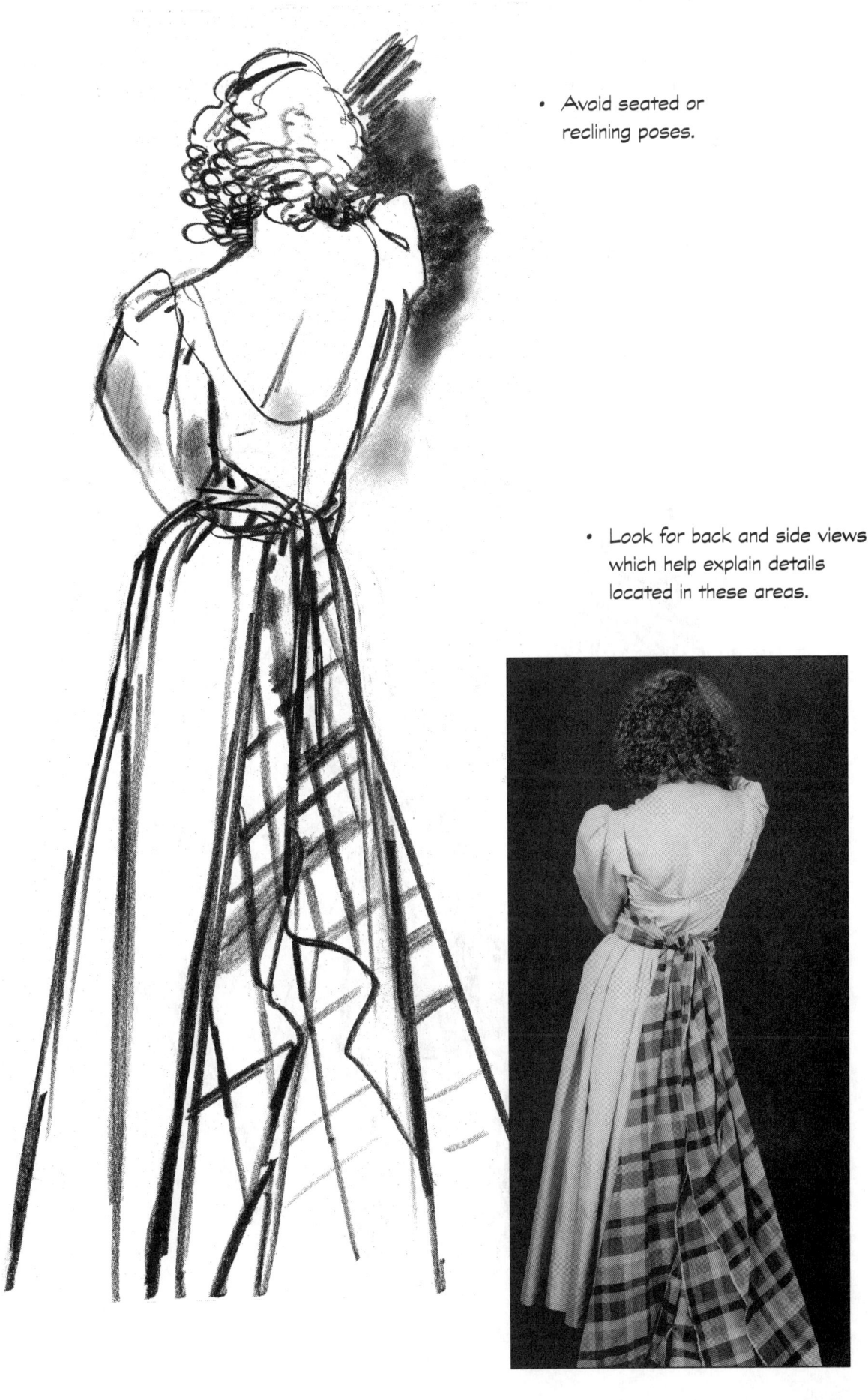

- Avoid seated or reclining poses.

- Look for back and side views which help explain details located in these areas.

INTRODUCTION 5

PHOTOGRAPHS TO AVOID

A. It is popular to photograph models from below eye level to elongate the figure. This causes the legs to appear too large and the head too small. What works in a photograph does not translate well to a drawing.
B. An excellent photograph, but the feet and legs are cut. The proportion and stance are uncertain.
C. This photograph is too small to use as a reference. The photograph must be at least 5" x 7".
D. This figure is tilted for layout excitement, but does not work for a design sketch.

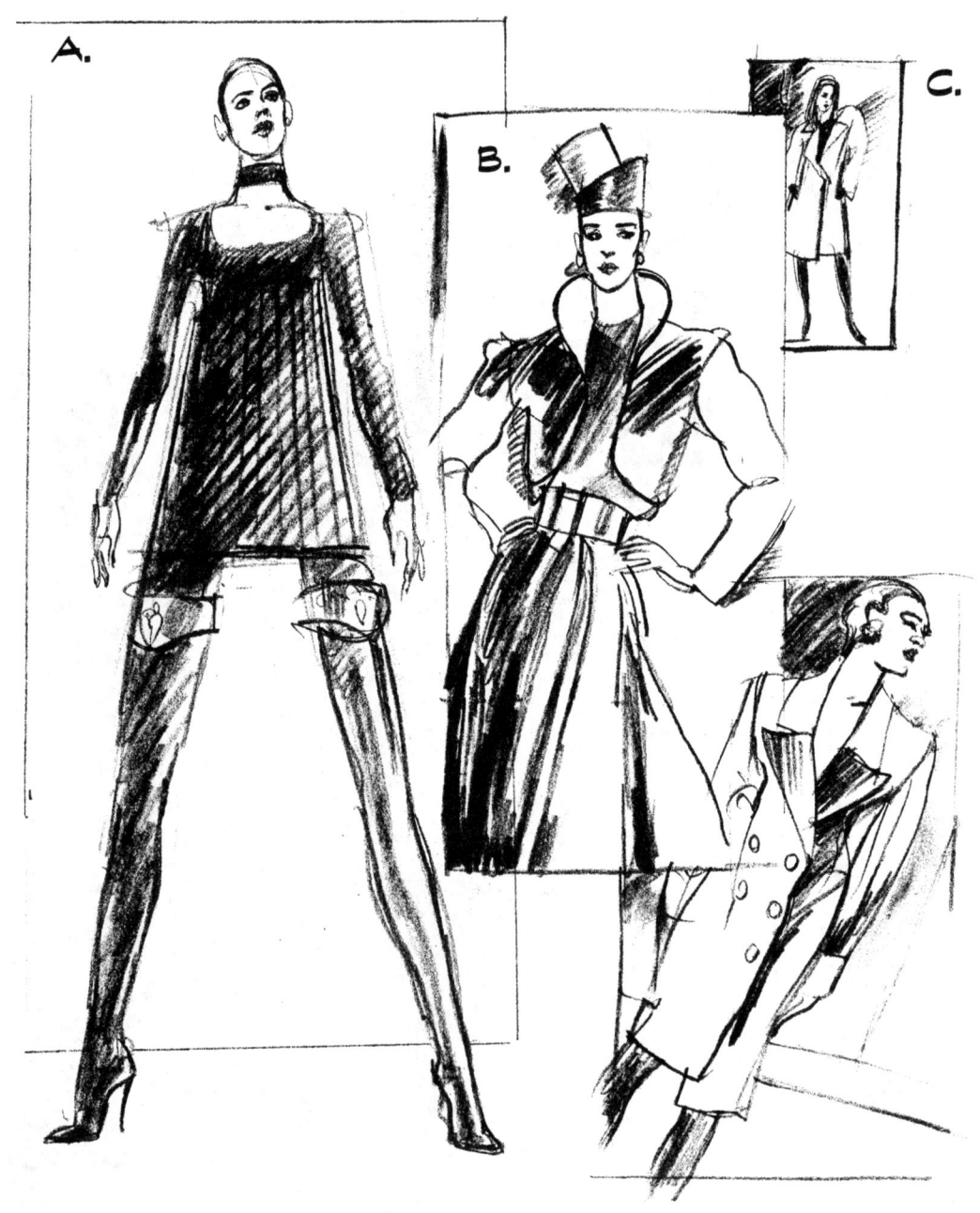

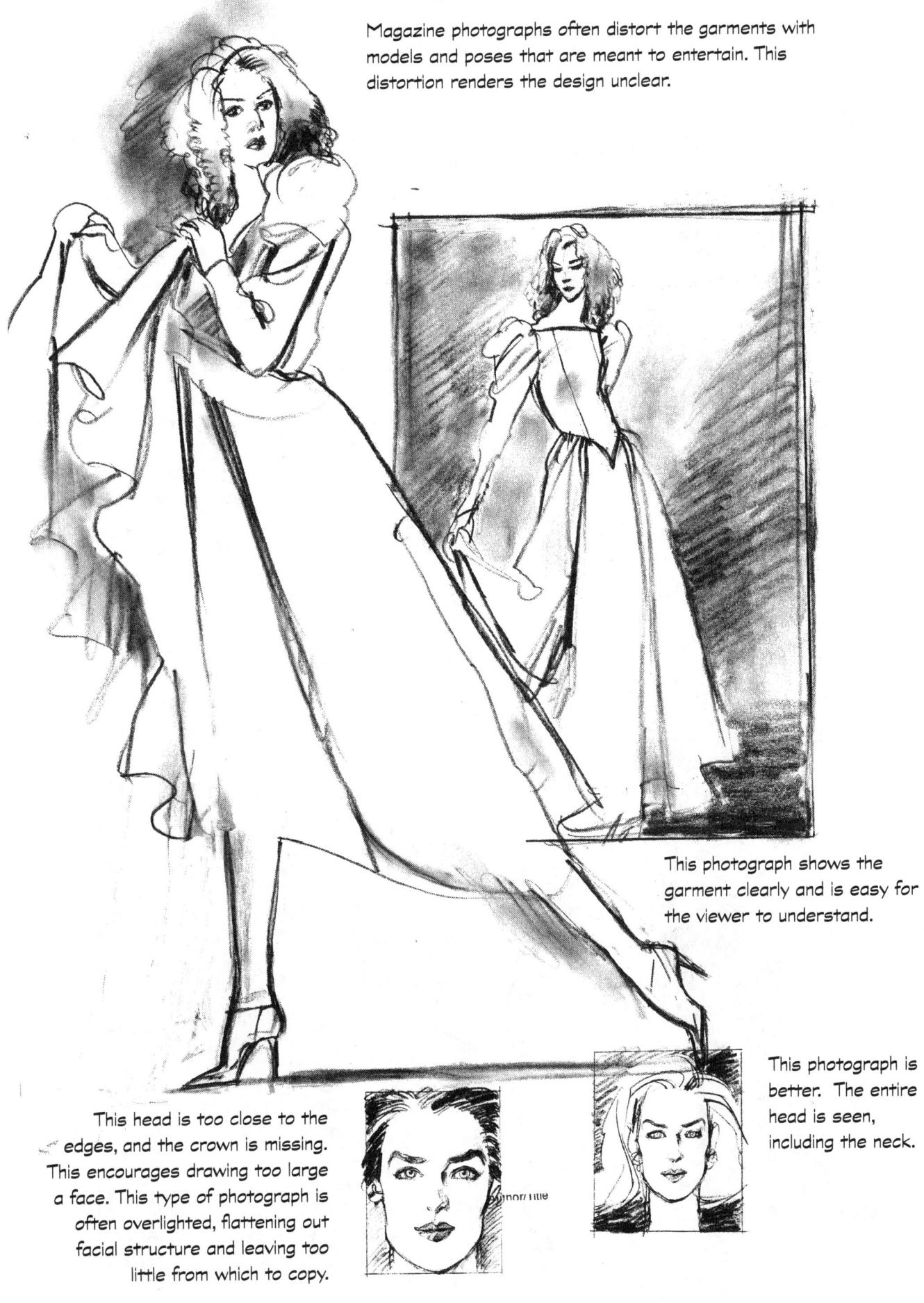

Magazine photographs often distort the garments with models and poses that are meant to entertain. This distortion renders the design unclear.

This photograph shows the garment clearly and is easy for the viewer to understand.

This head is too close to the edges, and the crown is missing. This encourages drawing too large a face. This type of photograph is often overlighted, flattening out facial structure and leaving too little from which to copy.

This photograph is better. The entire head is seen, including the neck.

INTRODUCTION 7

USING A PHOTOGRAPH AS A CLOTHING GUIDE AND SKETCHING A DESIGN

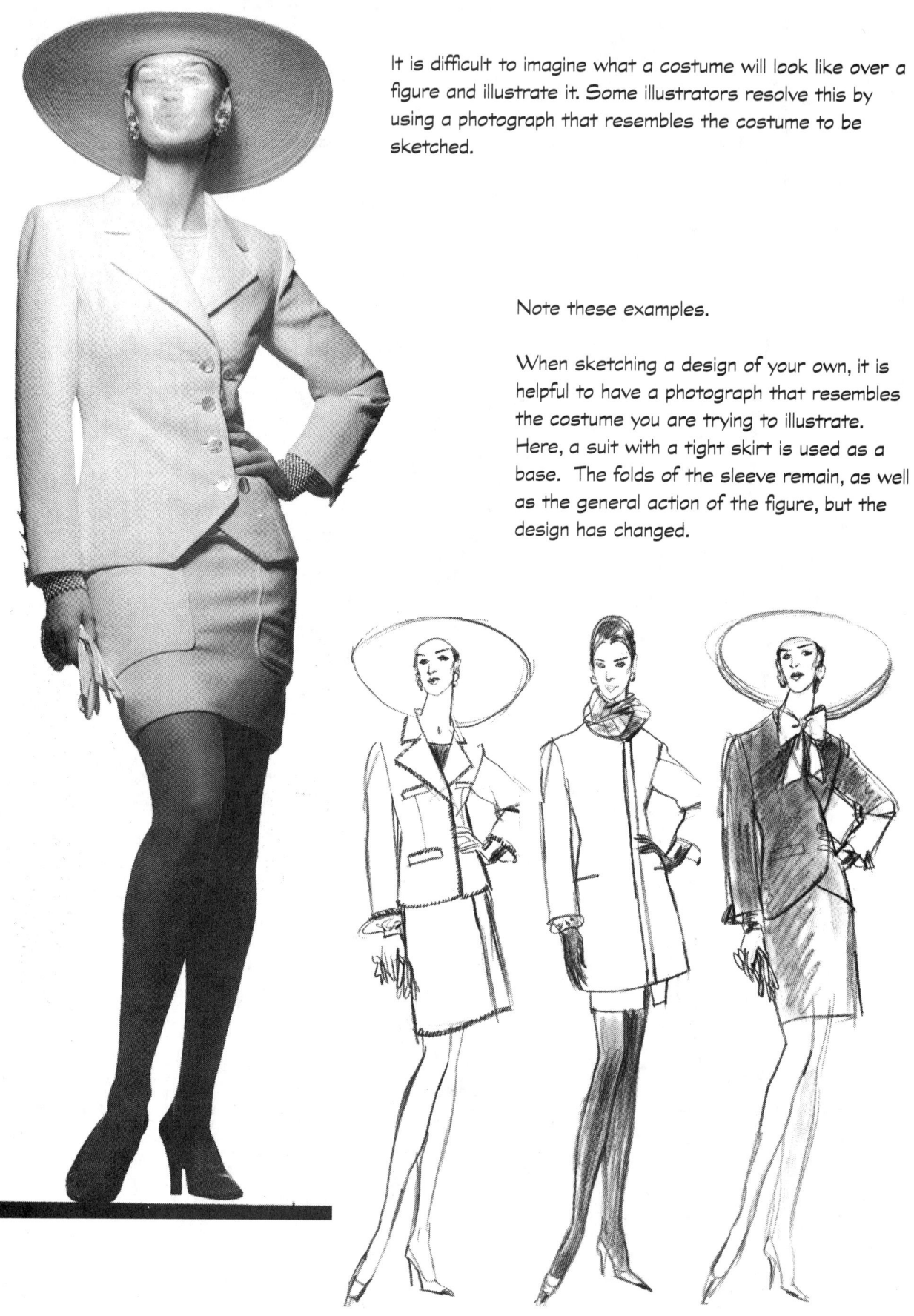

It is difficult to imagine what a costume will look like over a figure and illustrate it. Some illustrators resolve this by using a photograph that resembles the costume to be sketched.

Note these examples.

When sketching a design of your own, it is helpful to have a photograph that resembles the costume you are trying to illustrate. Here, a suit with a tight skirt is used as a base. The folds of the sleeve remain, as well as the general action of the figure, but the design has changed.

THE SKETCHBOOK

Perhaps in no other place does an artist think and observe more keenly than in his or her sketchbook. Made to be carried about to record observations or jot down ideas, every artist uses a sketchbook for these purposes. Every drawing does not have to be a finished drawing. Take this sketchbook out and about, especially shopping. Fashion windows acquaint us with design and fabric challenges we would not ordinarily encounter.

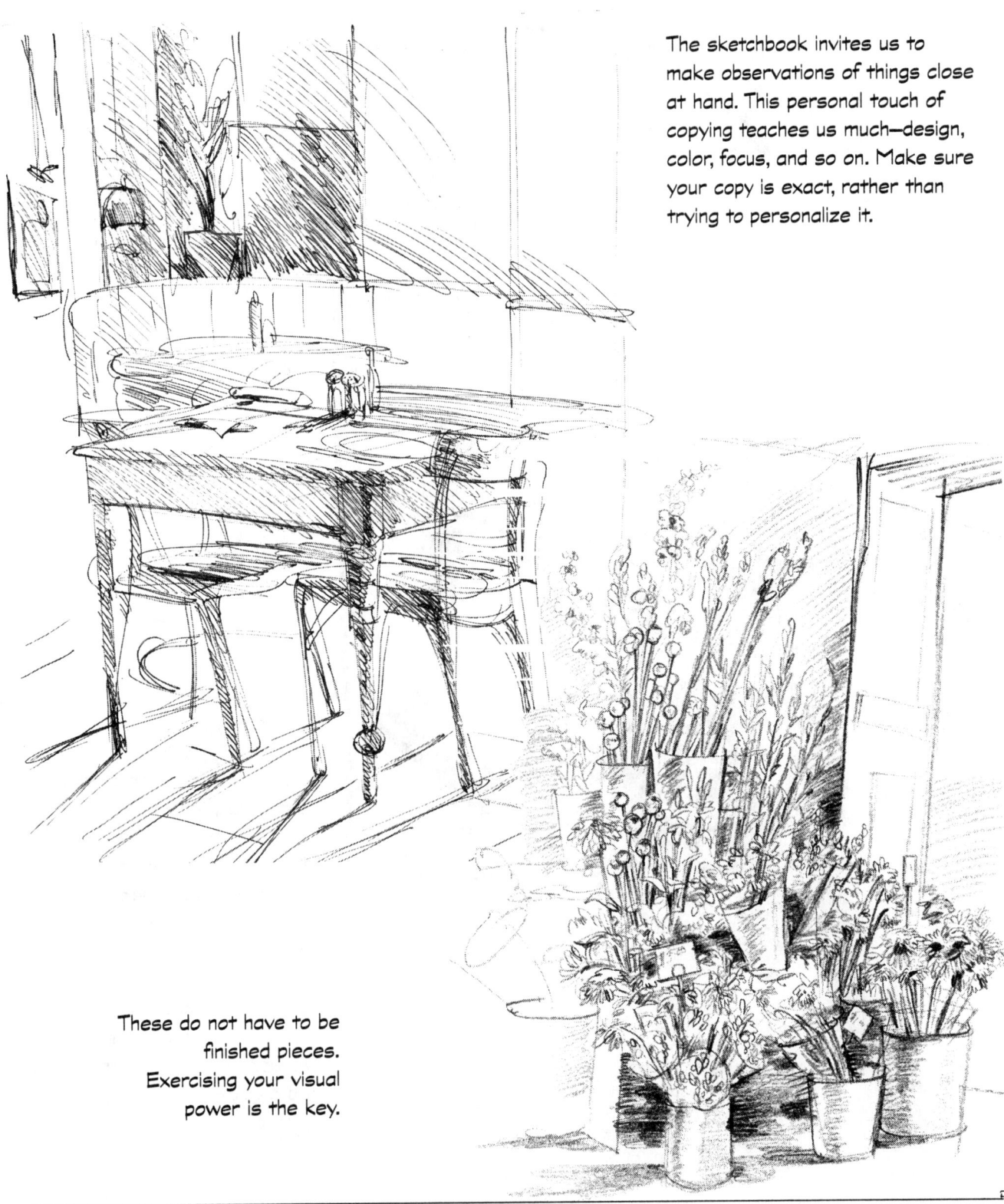

The sketchbook invites us to make observations of things close at hand. This personal touch of copying teaches us much—design, color, focus, and so on. Make sure your copy is exact, rather than trying to personalize it.

These do not have to be finished pieces. Exercising your visual power is the key.

WORKING UP A DRAWING

Tracing over a drawing is a good way to correct and finish a figure.

If a finished effect is needed and your present drawing is overworked or contains patchup work, tape the original art on a light table or window. The light must be strong enough so that the drawing is visible. Place a blank sheet of paper over the original. Redraw the figure on the new sheet of paper.

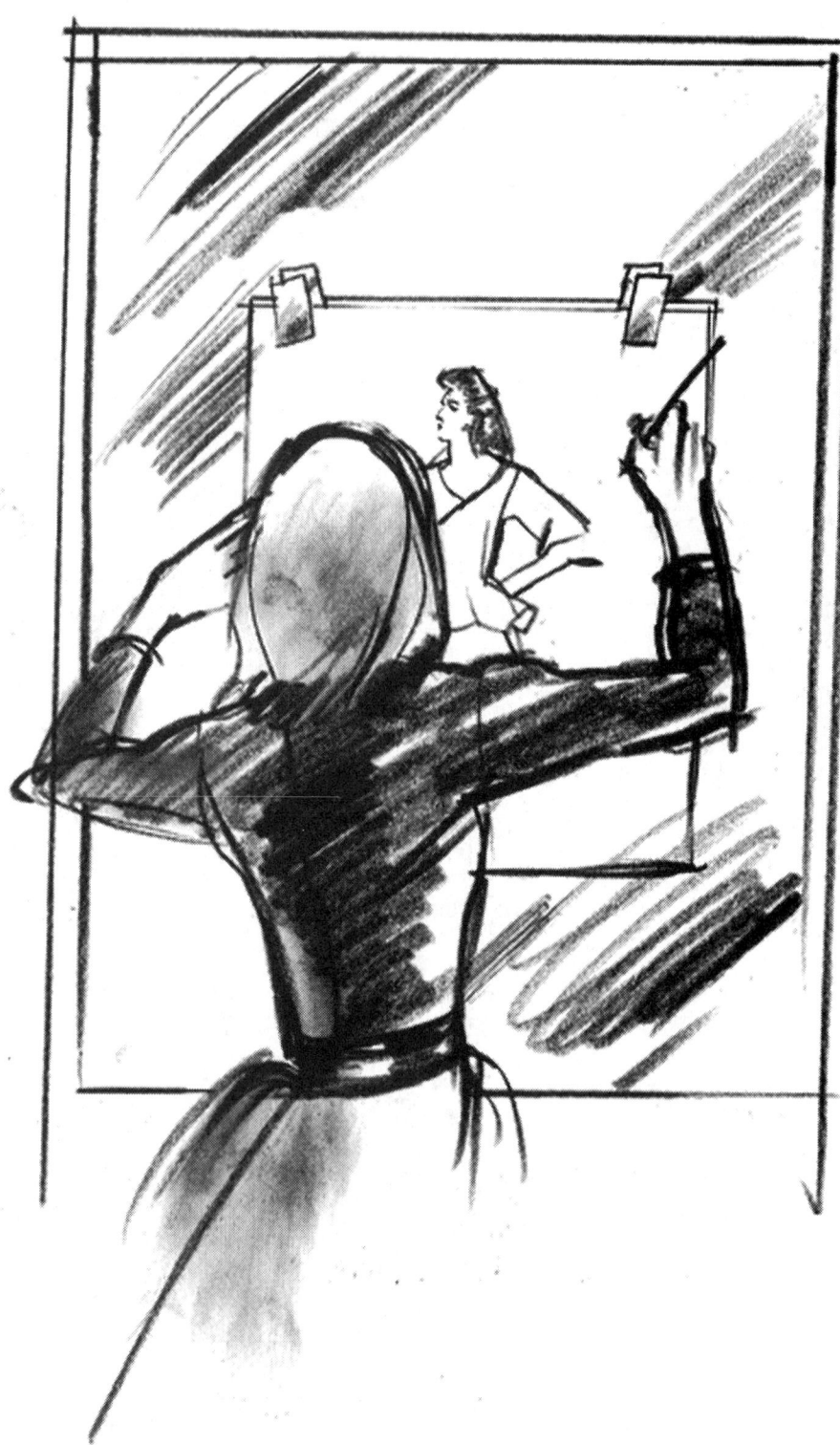

Do not outline or trace the art. This produces a stiff and monotonous drawing. Draw over the figure in a spontaneous manner. This makes the drawing look original.

Other techniques, such as watercolor or gouache, may be used with the underdrawing as a guide.

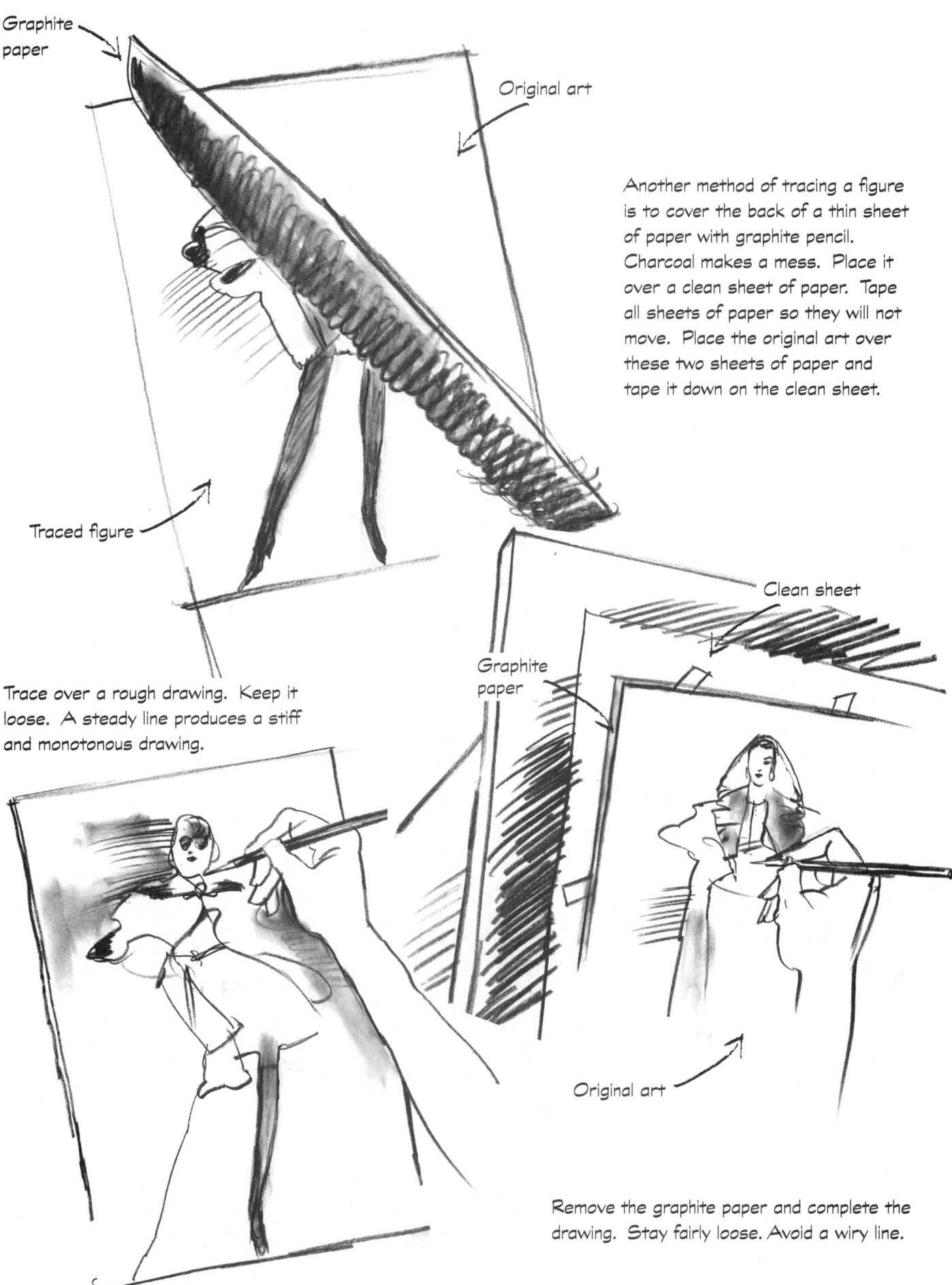

Another method of tracing a figure is to cover the back of a thin sheet of paper with graphite pencil. Charcoal makes a mess. Place it over a clean sheet of paper. Tape all sheets of paper so they will not move. Place the original art over these two sheets of paper and tape it down on the clean sheet.

Trace over a rough drawing. Keep it loose. A steady line produces a stiff and monotonous drawing.

Remove the graphite paper and complete the drawing. Stay fairly loose. Avoid a wiry line.

INTRODUCTION 11

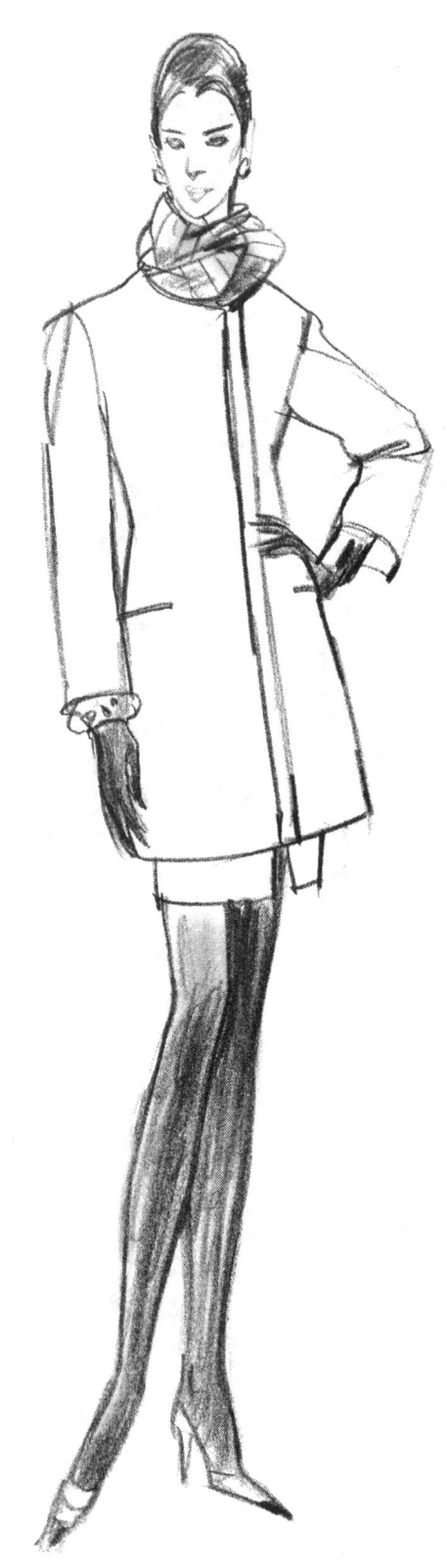

CHAPTER 1
Proportion and Movement

Proportions are a matter of taste and style. The proportions illustrated are meant as a guide and are intended to be changed.

Generally, to achieve a fashion effect or sketching for design purposes, lengthen these distances: chin to shoulders, waist to chest, and leg length. Check these distances on your figures.

Although our models and photographs are real people, we are trying to construct a fantasy figure. A good deal of imagination is helpful. Try not to be too literal when sketching figures, especially clothes, which can seem to appear as a mass of folds and wrinkles.

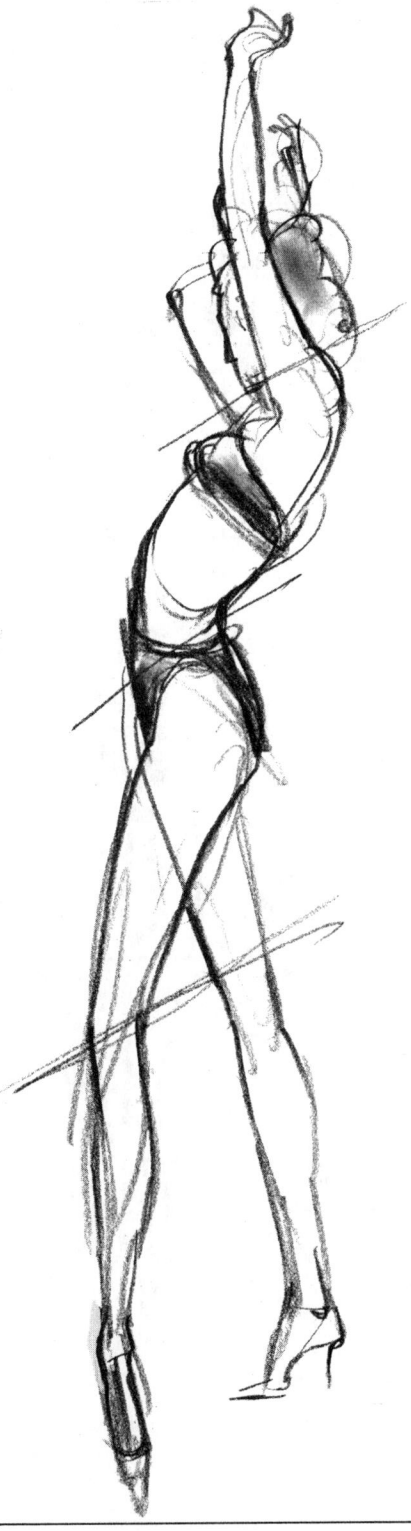

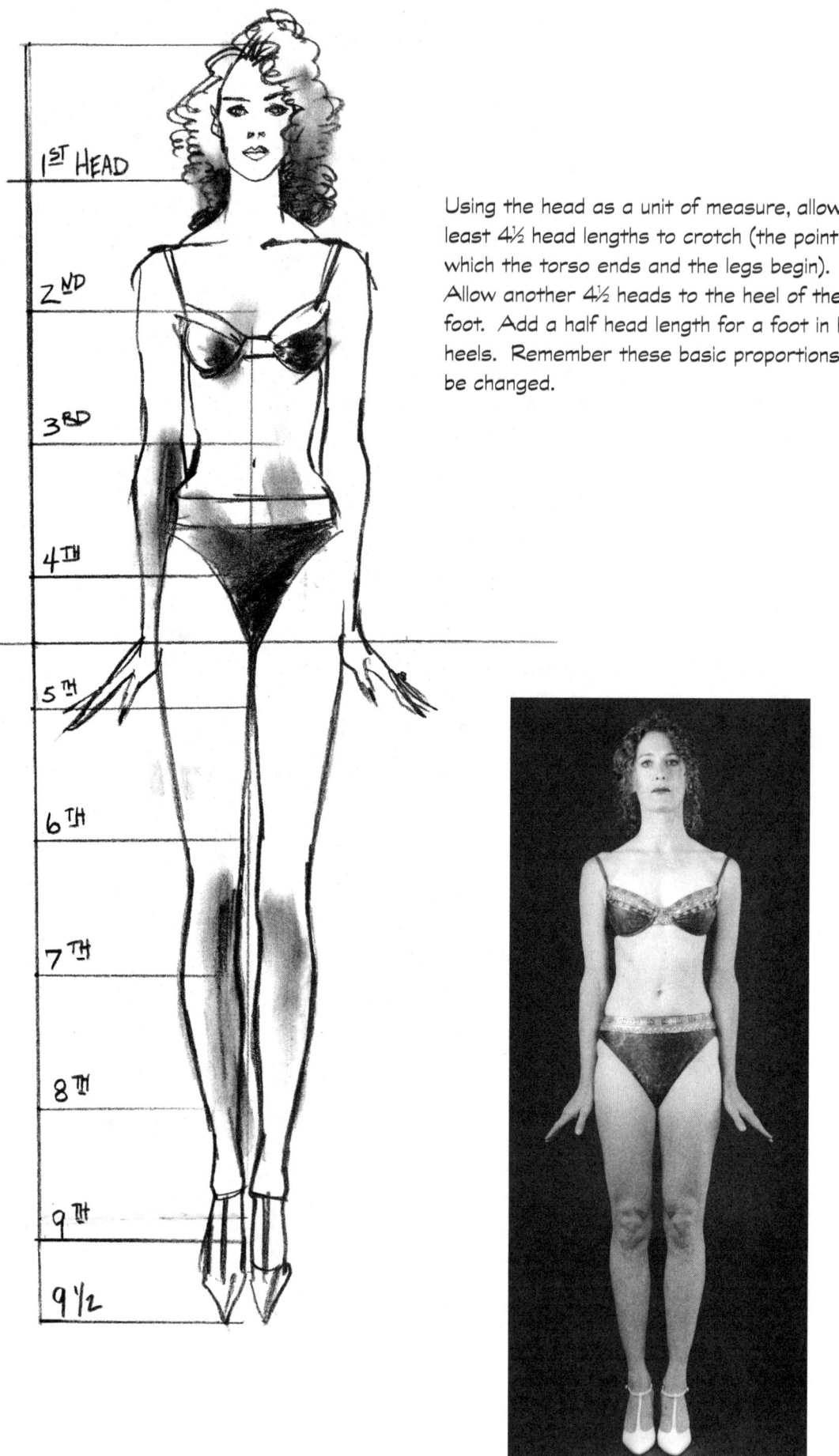

Using the head as a unit of measure, allow at least 4½ head lengths to crotch (the point at which the torso ends and the legs begin). Allow another 4½ heads to the heel of the foot. Add a half head length for a foot in high heels. Remember these basic proportions can be changed.

If you prefer to bypass the head count system, check your figure for these distances. Any fashion figure, including men, must be long from chin to shoulders, armpits to top of hips, and in the legs.

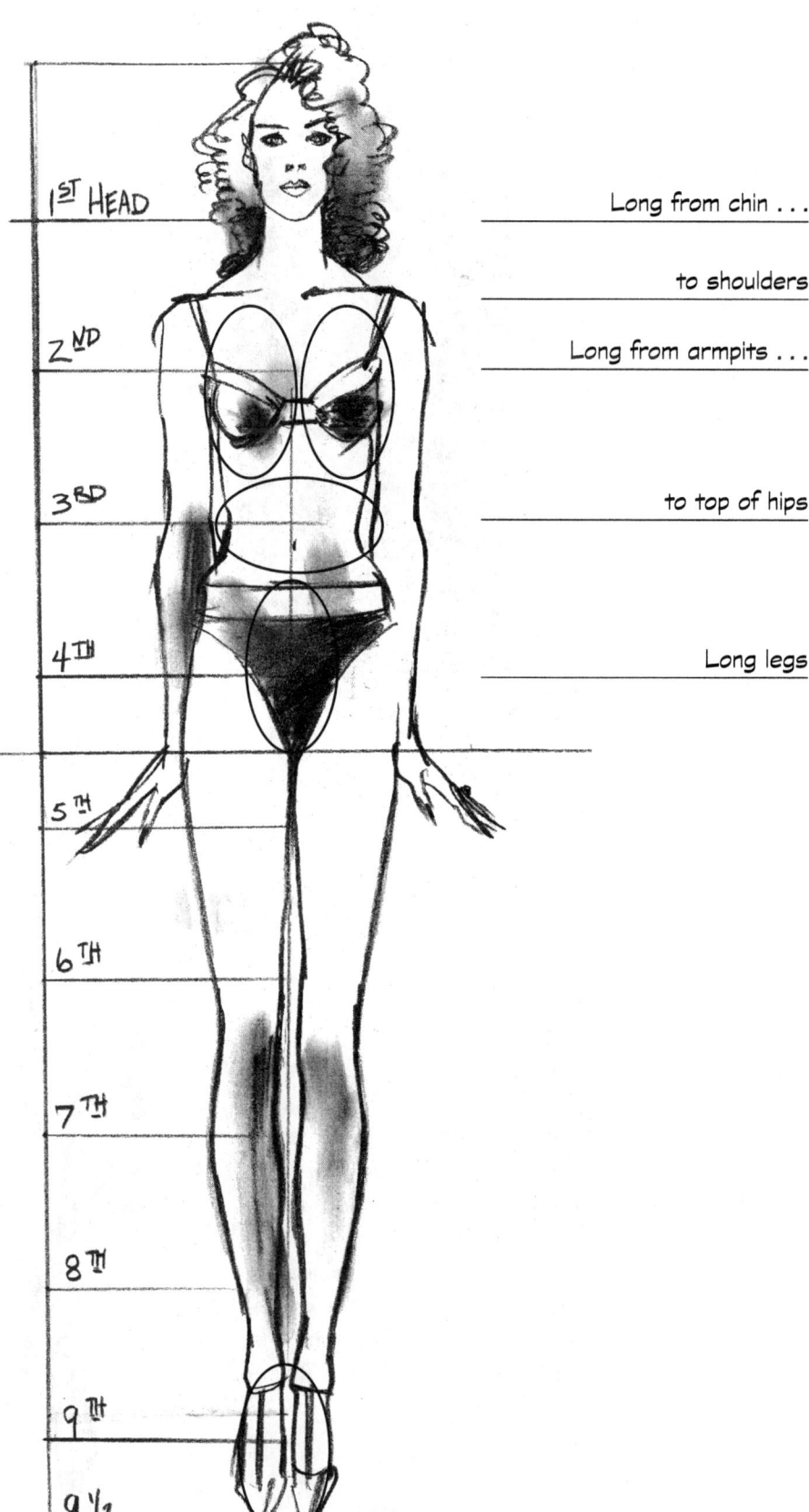

Long from chin . . .

to shoulders

Long from armpits . . .

to top of hips

Long legs

Use the head size to find proportion inside the figure. Two heads barely fit across the ribcage. Keep the figure narrow here. The waist occupies only ¾ of the head on its side. The pelvis is about one head. Do not use the bikini as a head length. The pelvis is longer.

To avoid fat, tiny feet, use a head length from the ankle to the toe area.

The wrist lines up with the crotch when the arms are down.

CHAPTER 1 PROPORTION AND MOVEMENT   15

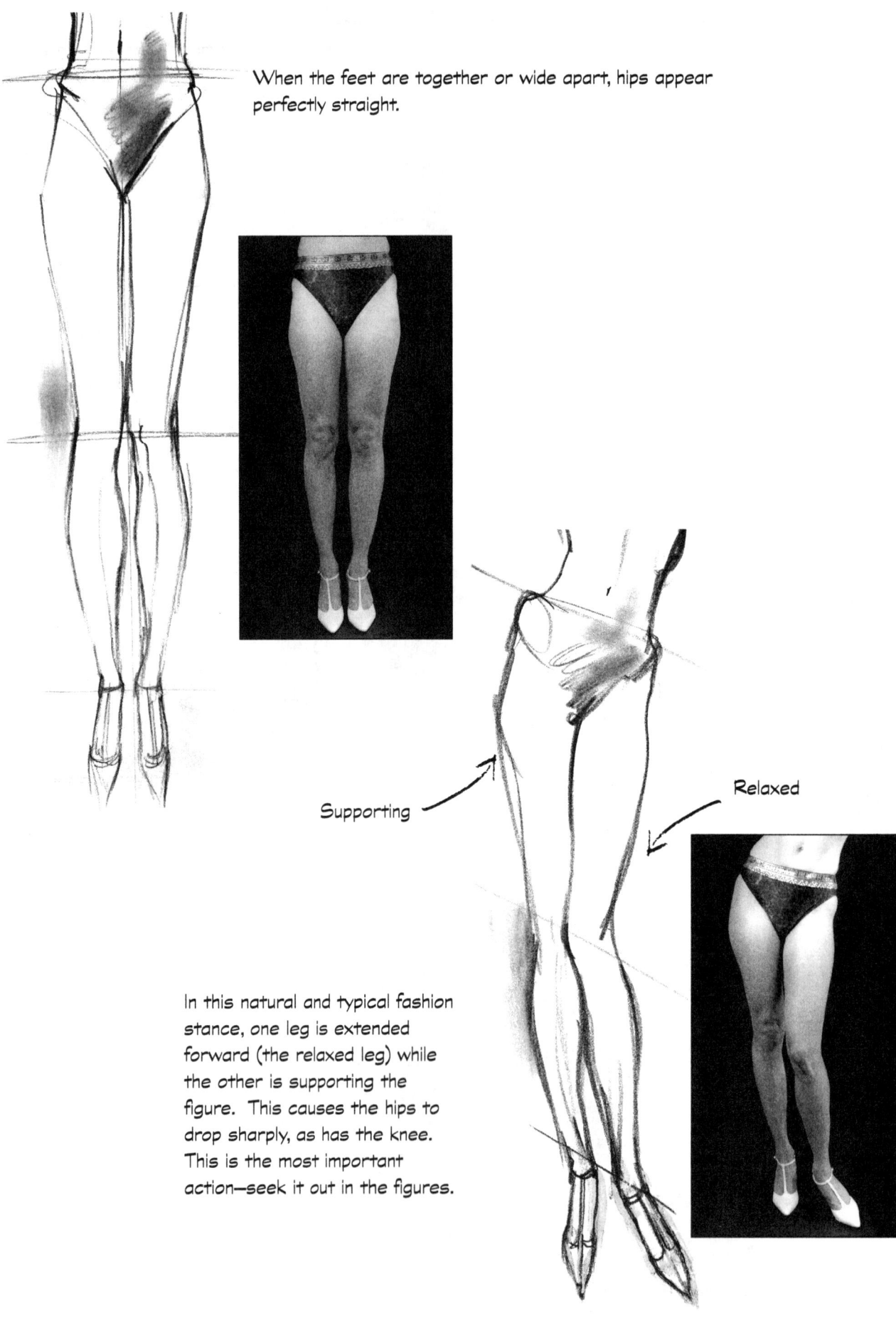

When the feet are together or wide apart, hips appear perfectly straight.

Supporting

Relaxed

In this natural and typical fashion stance, one leg is extended forward (the relaxed leg) while the other is supporting the figure. This causes the hips to drop sharply, as has the knee. This is the most important action—seek it out in the figures.

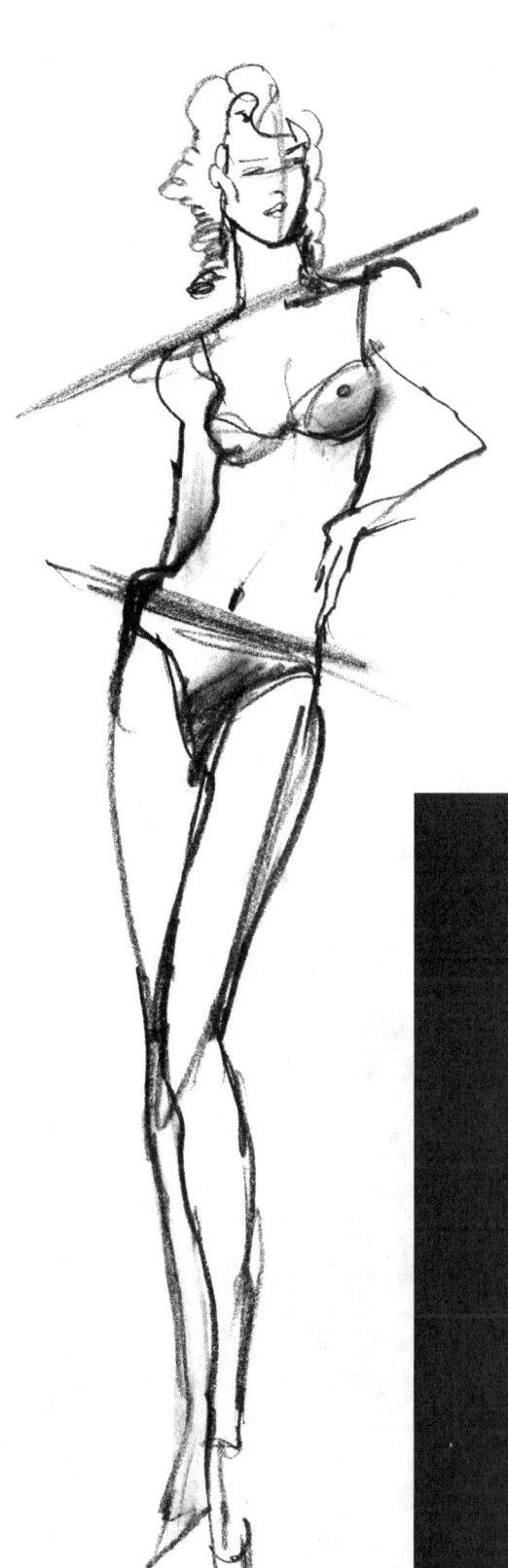

Often the figure will move the upper portion or shoulders as the figure relaxes even further. This causes the tube or torso to bend, causing the shoulders to move in the opposite direction of the hips. This is referred to as the opposing slants. Without keen observation, the figure will continue to have the appearance of a soldier at attention. Do not minimize this hip action. Exaggerate it!

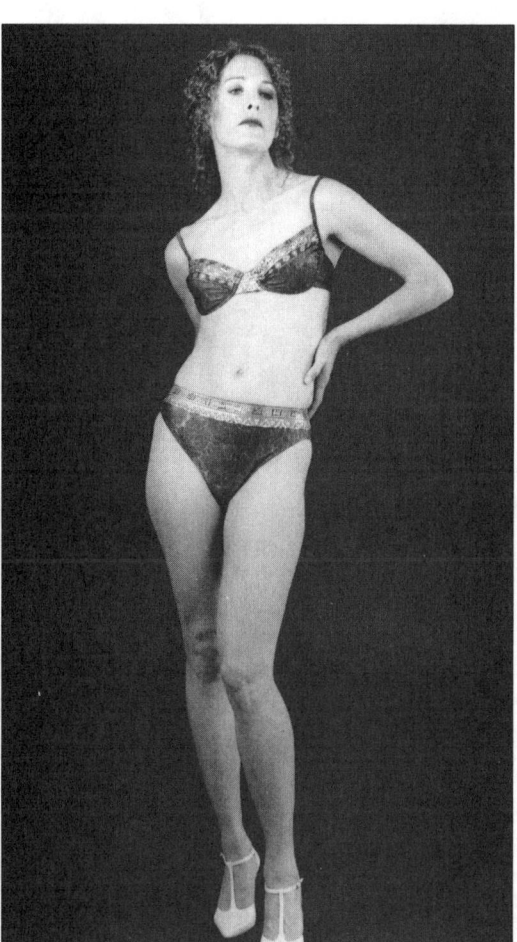

CHAPTER 1 PROPORTION AND MOVEMENT

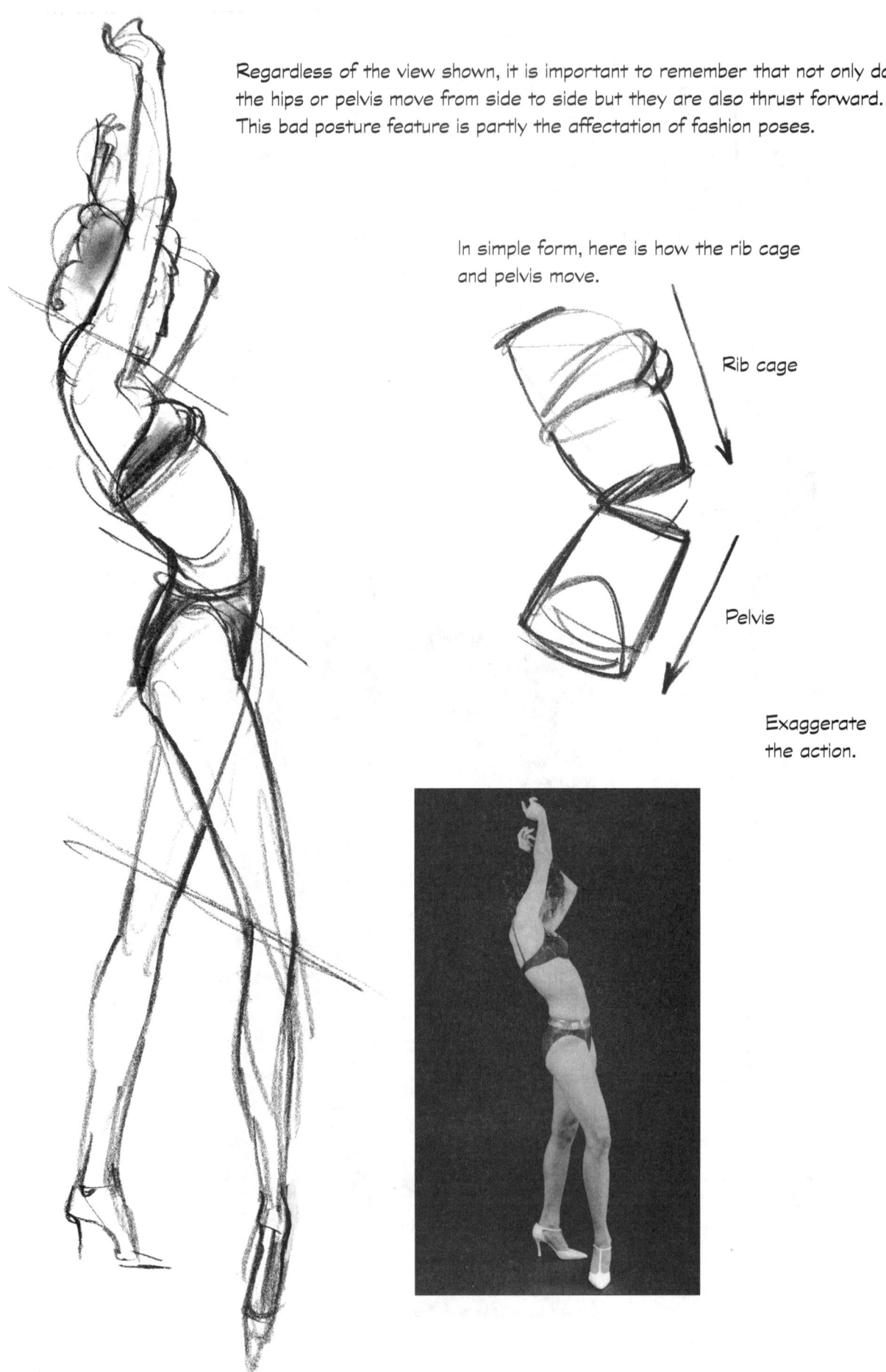

Regardless of the view shown, it is important to remember that not only do the hips or pelvis move from side to side but they are also thrust forward. This bad posture feature is partly the affectation of fashion poses.

In simple form, here is how the rib cage and pelvis move.

Rib cage

Pelvis

Exaggerate the action.

18 FASHION SKETCHING

It is useful to study this close-up of the side view figure in order to understand the construction of supporting and relaxed legs. The thigh of the supporting leg is hidden from view and causes great confusion. Draw it from the hip and right through the relaxed thigh. It may appear straight, but a curved leg suggests grace and youthfulness.

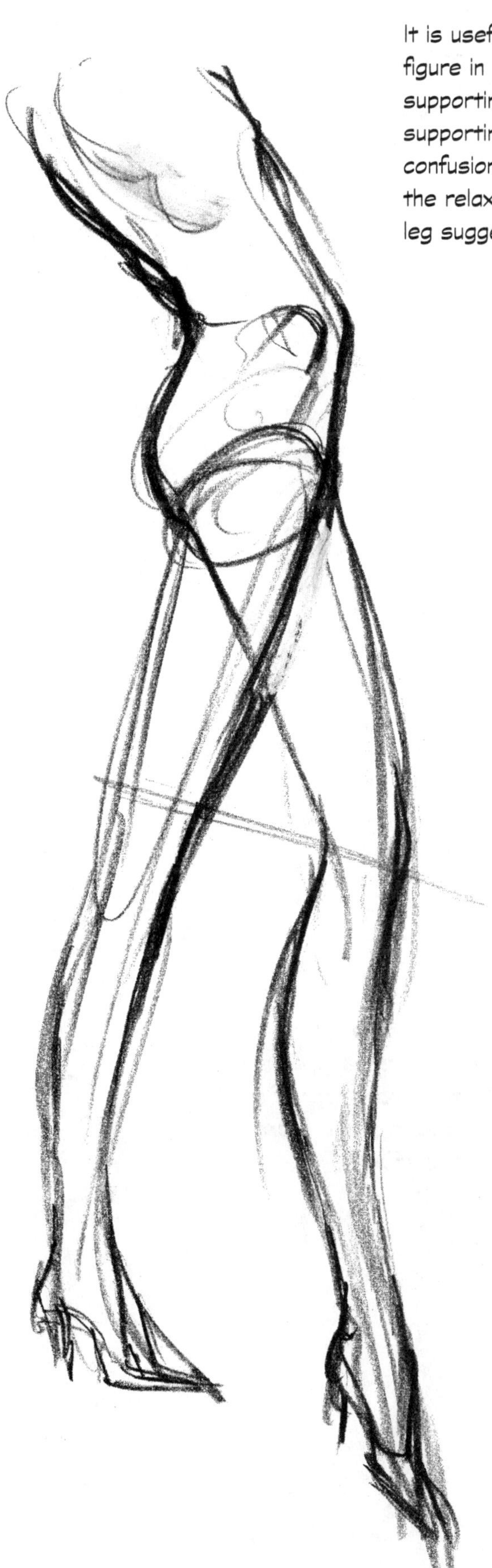

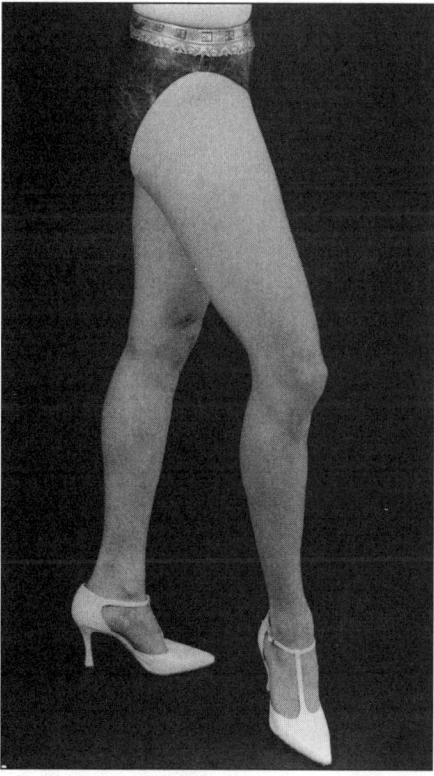

If you are having problems with proportions, mark the head lengths on each practice page, or check head lengths with a measuring device as you work. You can measure with your fingertips.

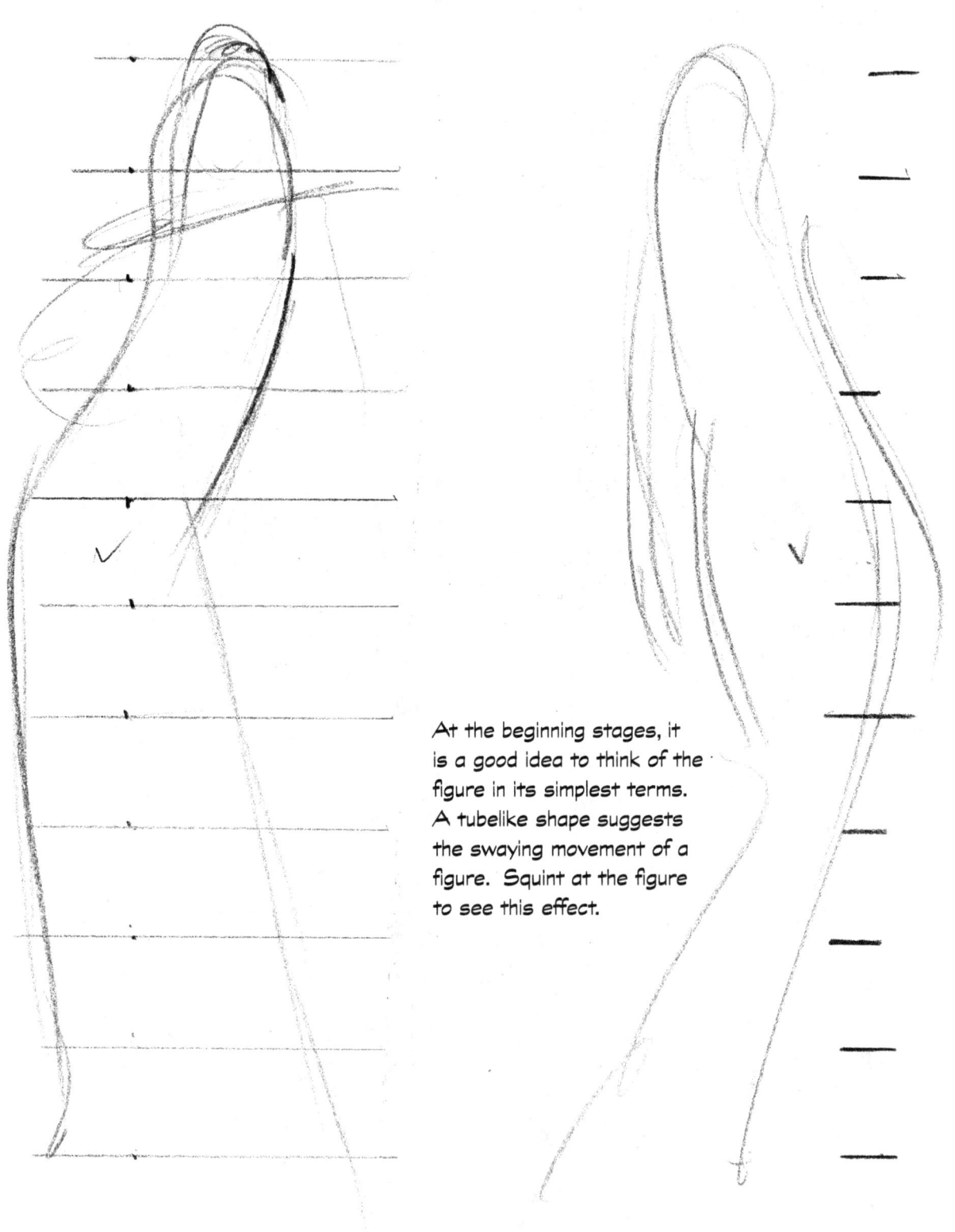

At the beginning stages, it is a good idea to think of the figure in its simplest terms. A tubelike shape suggests the swaying movement of a figure. Squint at the figure to see this effect.

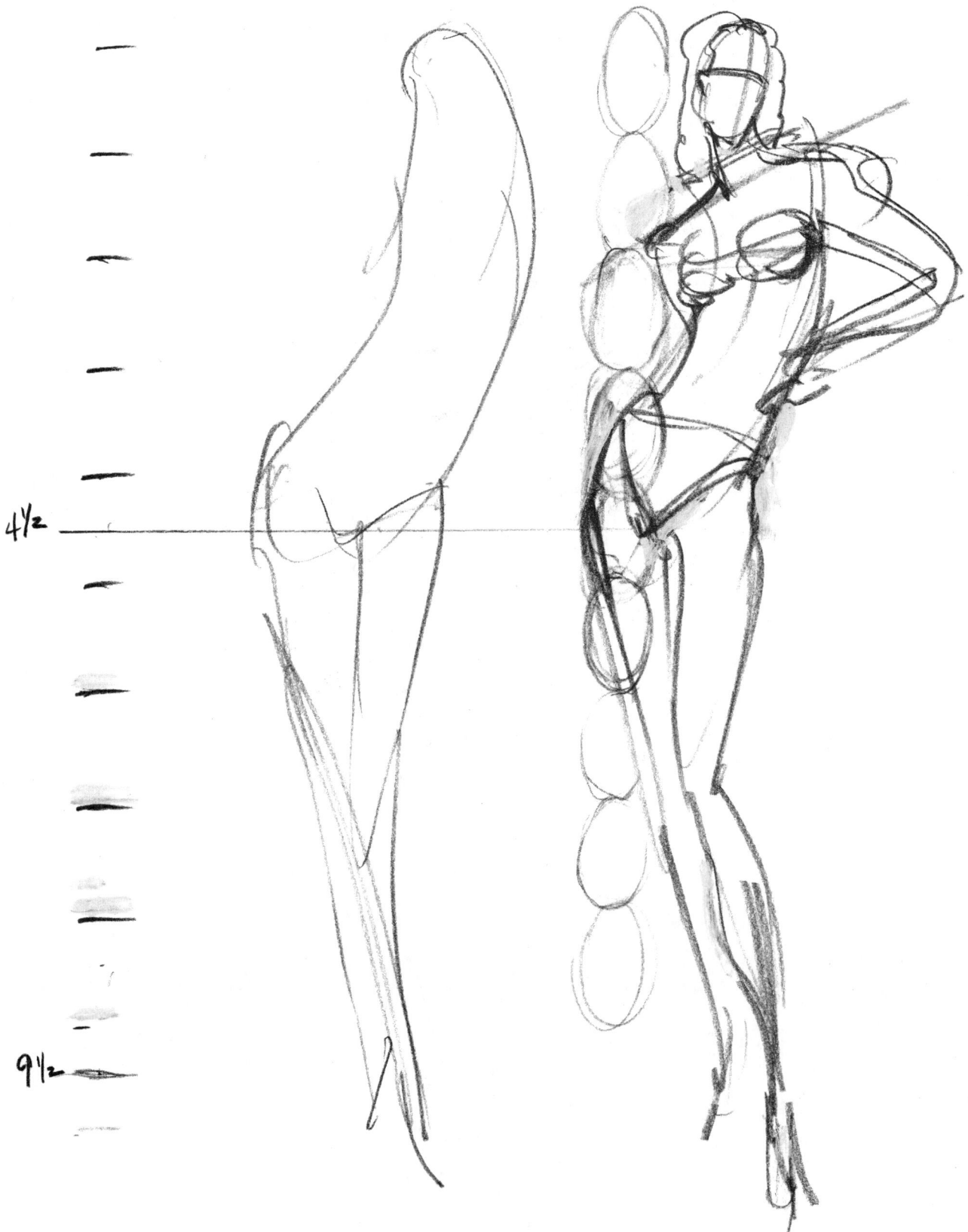

Draw practice figures over this until your eye becomes accustomed to where the head lengths will strike on the figure. For example, the second head length is level with the armpits.

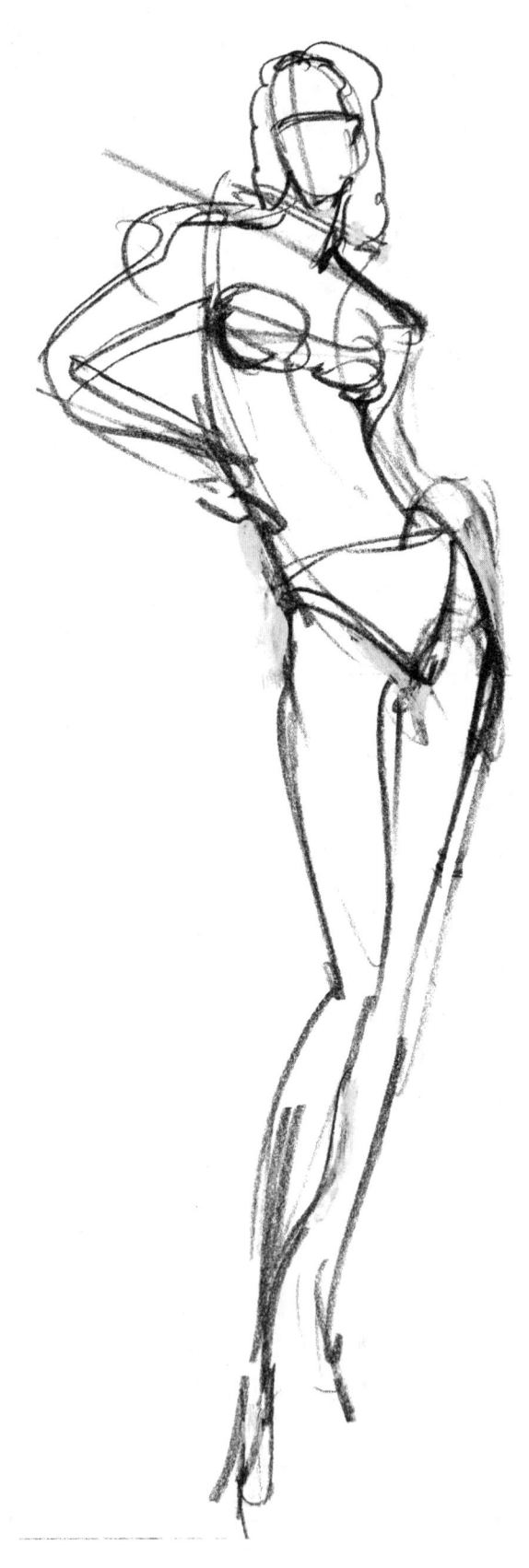

CHAPTER 2

The Gesture Sketch

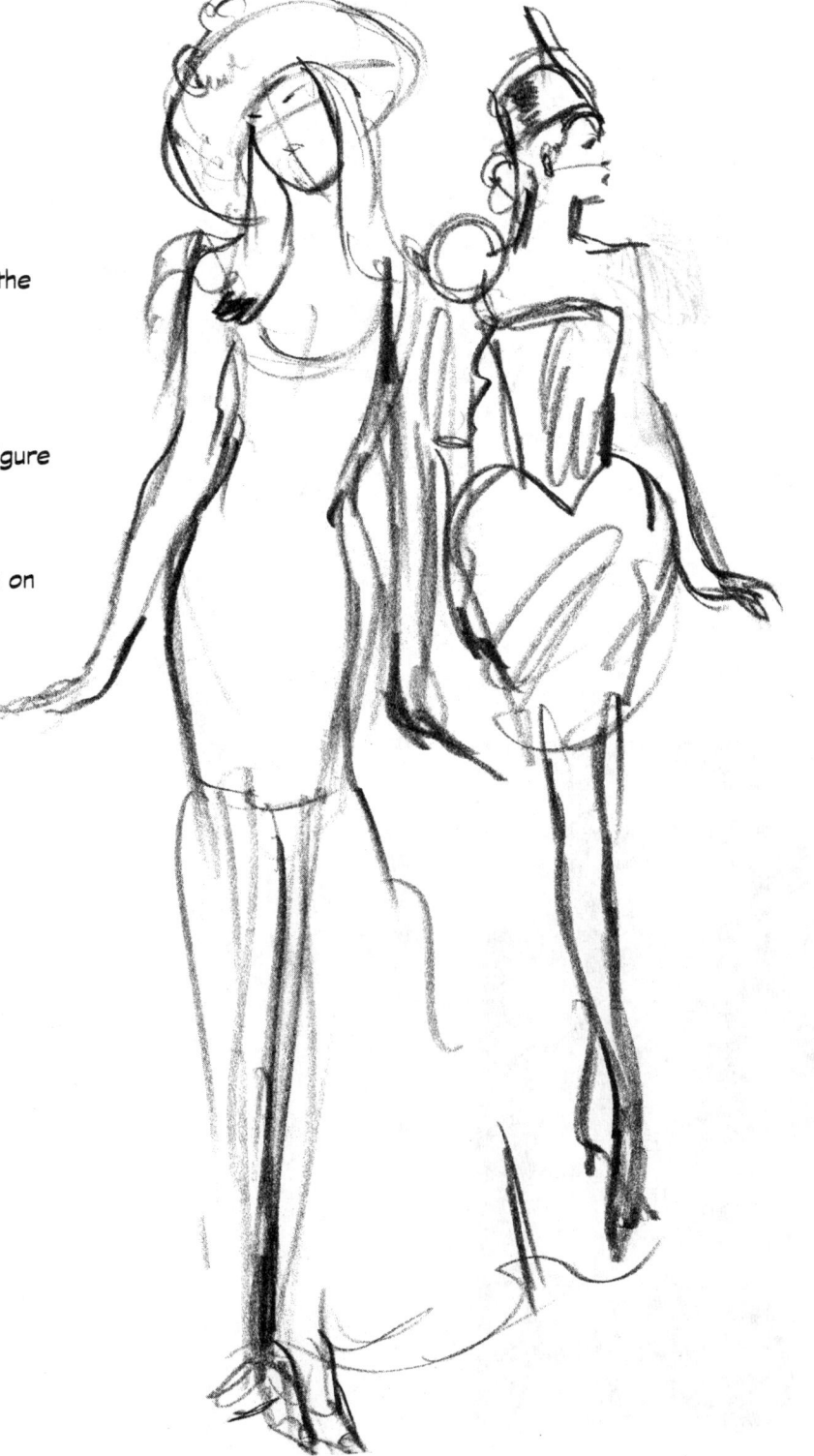

The gesture sketch is the most important first step. The uses of the gesture sketch are as follows:

1. To loosen up
2. To find proportions
3. To feel out the action of the figure
4. To plan or lay in the figure on the page
5. To sense or lay in the clothing on the figure

Do not overanalyze what the figure is doing. Give your impression of the action.

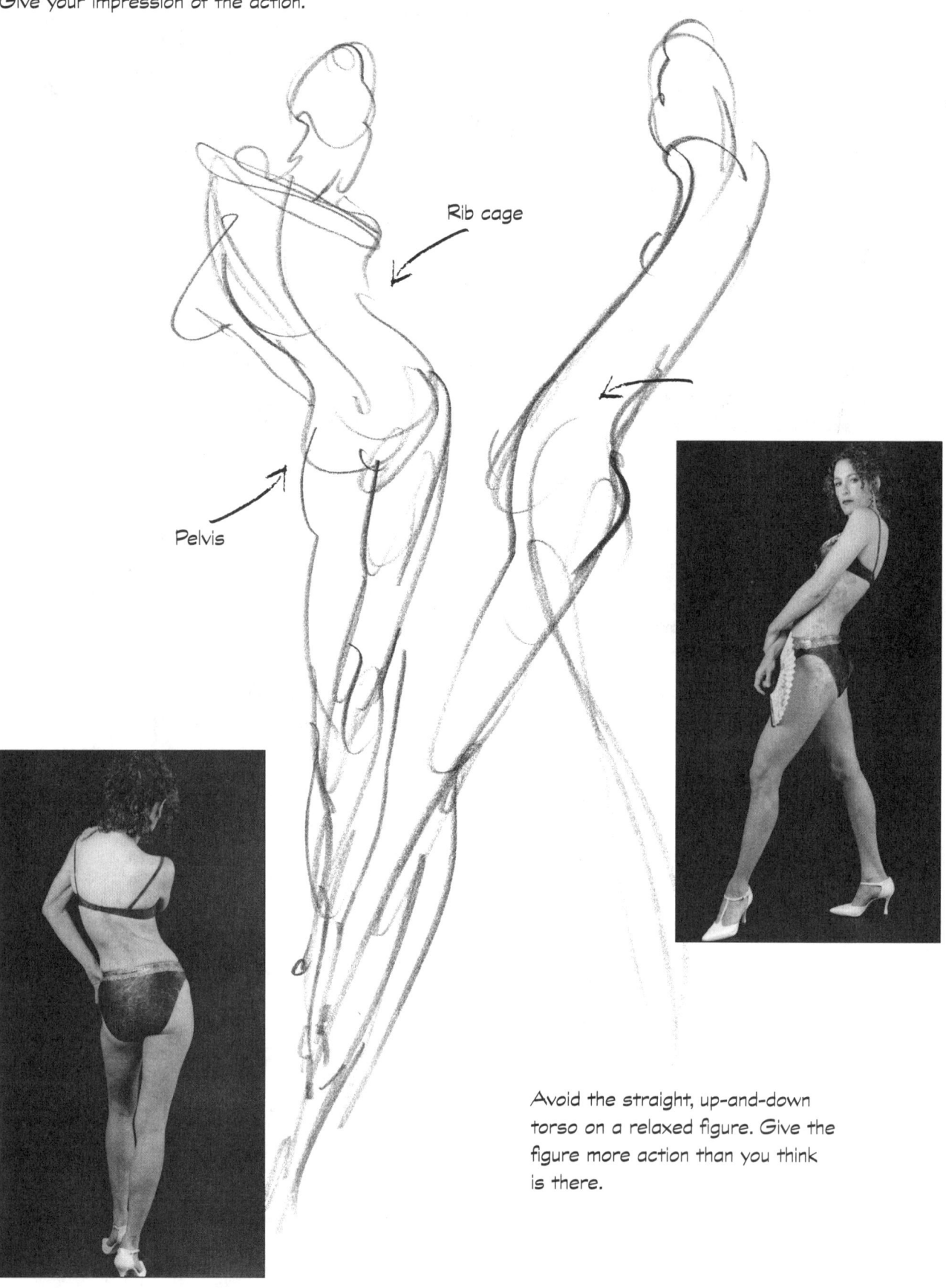

Rib cage

Pelvis

Avoid the straight, up-and-down torso on a relaxed figure. Give the figure more action than you think is there.

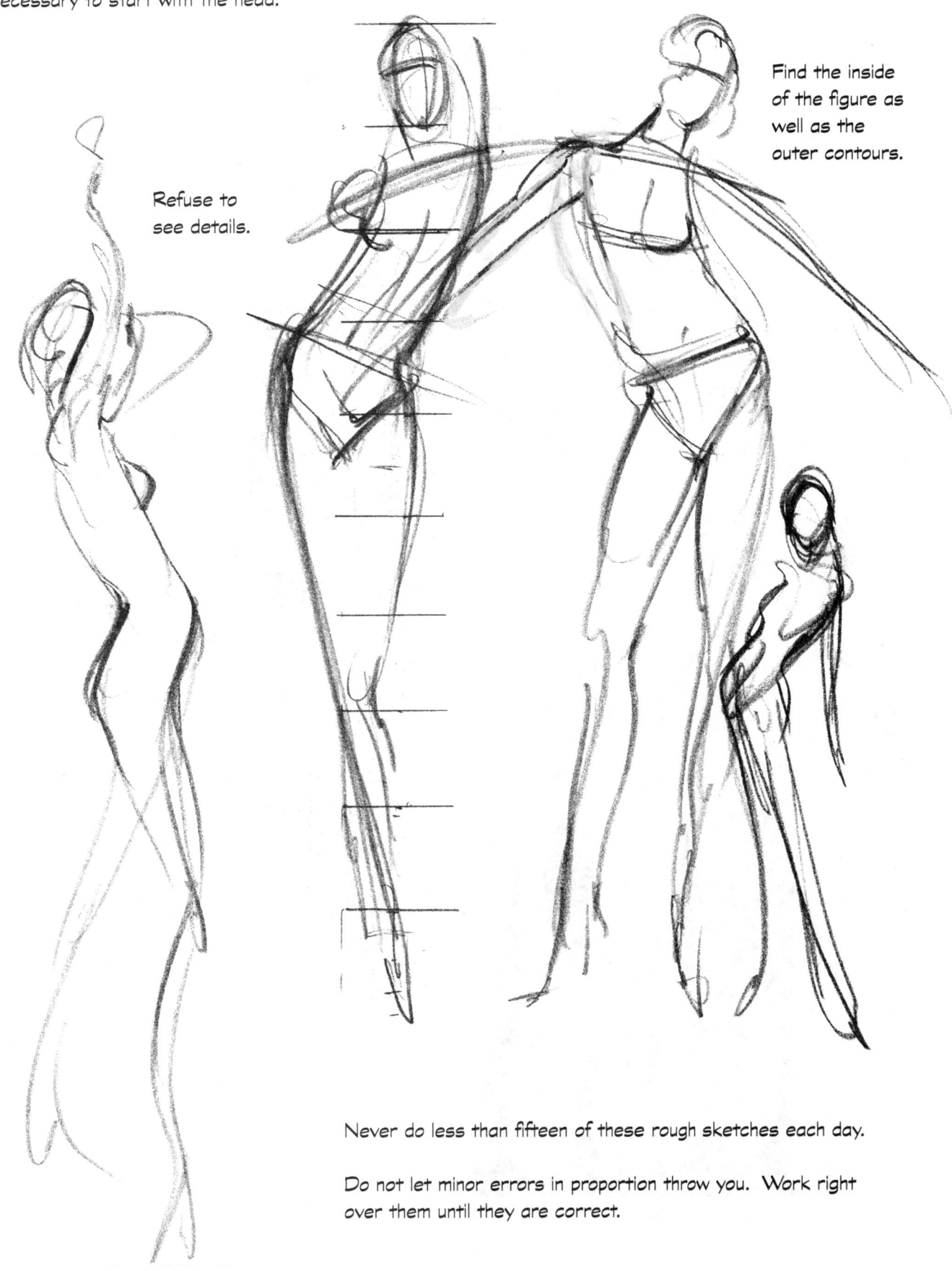

Try not to pick up your pencil too often. It is not necessary to start with the head.

Refuse to see details.

Find the inside of the figure as well as the outer contours.

Never do less than fifteen of these rough sketches each day.

Do not let minor errors in proportion throw you. Work right over them until they are correct.

CHAPTER 2 THE GESTURE SKETCH

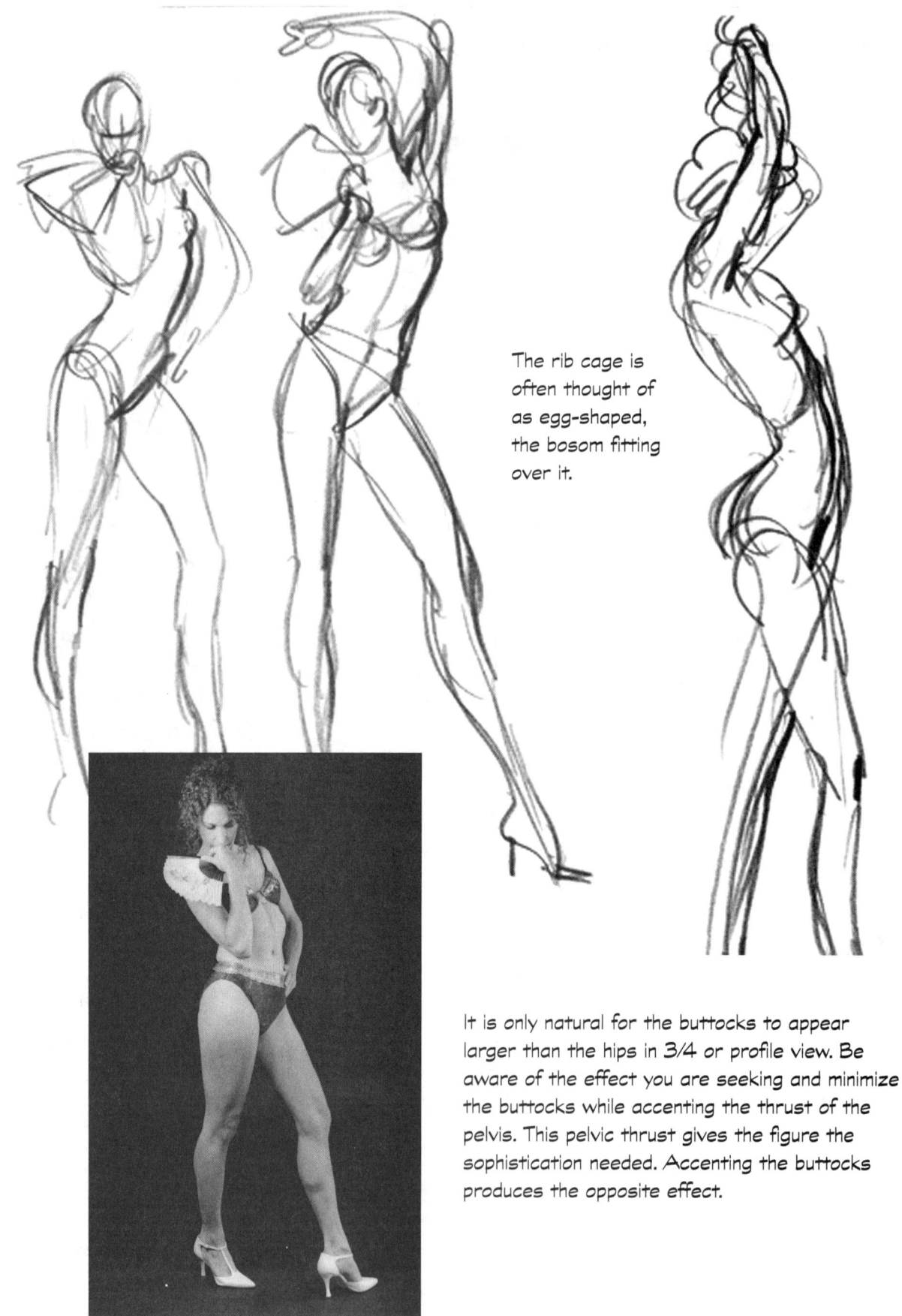

The rib cage is often thought of as egg-shaped, the bosom fitting over it.

It is only natural for the buttocks to appear larger than the hips in 3/4 or profile view. Be aware of the effect you are seeking and minimize the buttocks while accenting the thrust of the pelvis. This pelvic thrust gives the figure the sophistication needed. Accenting the buttocks produces the opposite effect.

Exaggerate the side thrust of the hip, rather than lessen it.

A common error is trying to finish edges or contours too quickly. This creates a hard and mechanical edge around the figure.

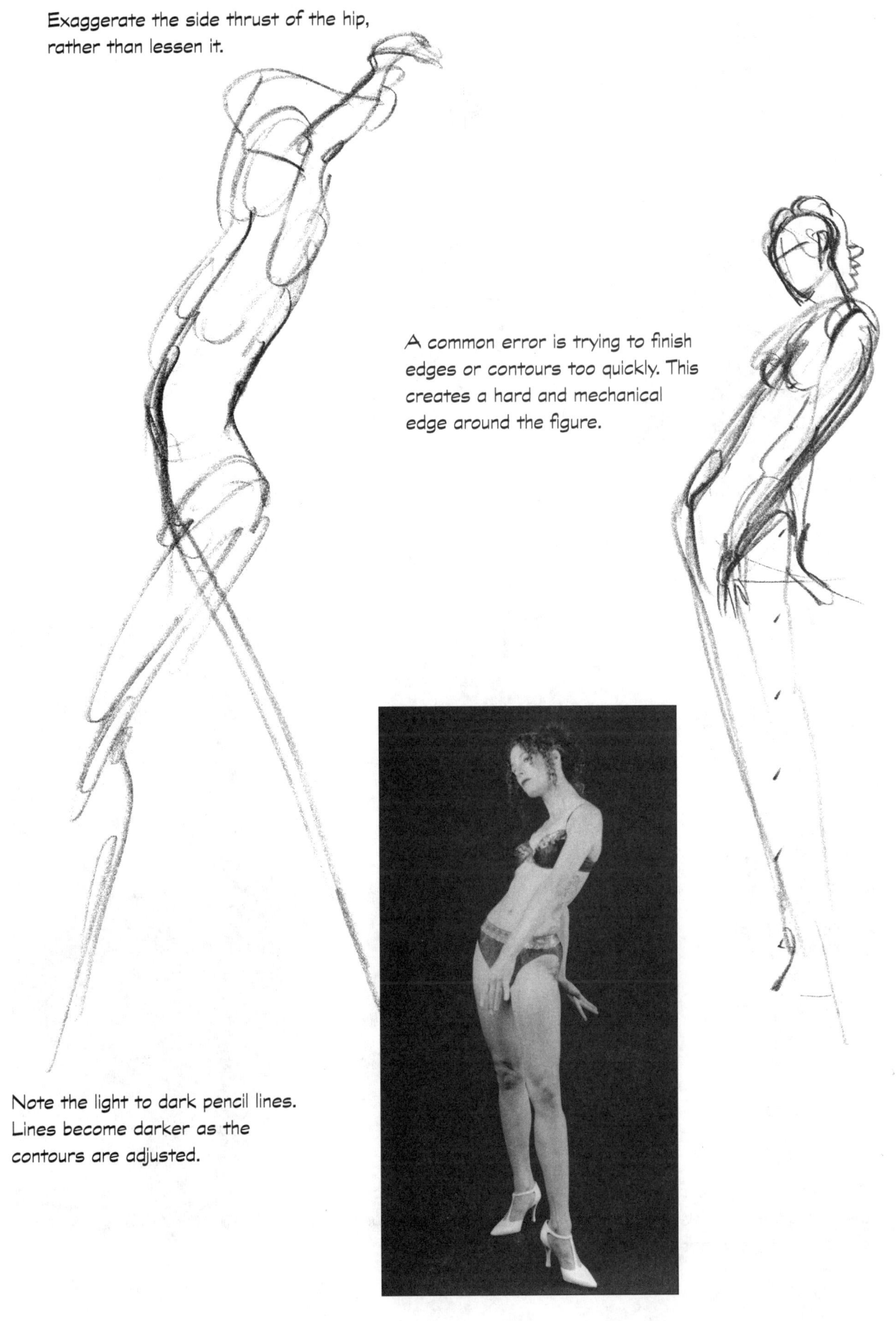

Note the light to dark pencil lines. Lines become darker as the contours are adjusted.

CHAPTER 2 THE GESTURE SKETCH

3-MINUTE POSES

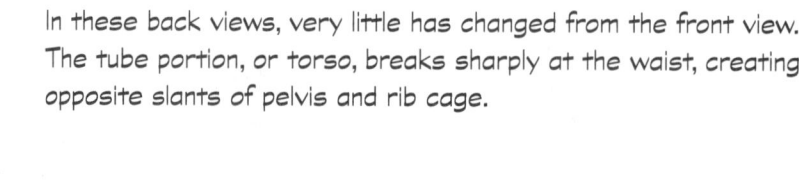

In these back views, very little has changed from the front view. The tube portion, or torso, breaks sharply at the waist, creating opposite slants of pelvis and rib cage.

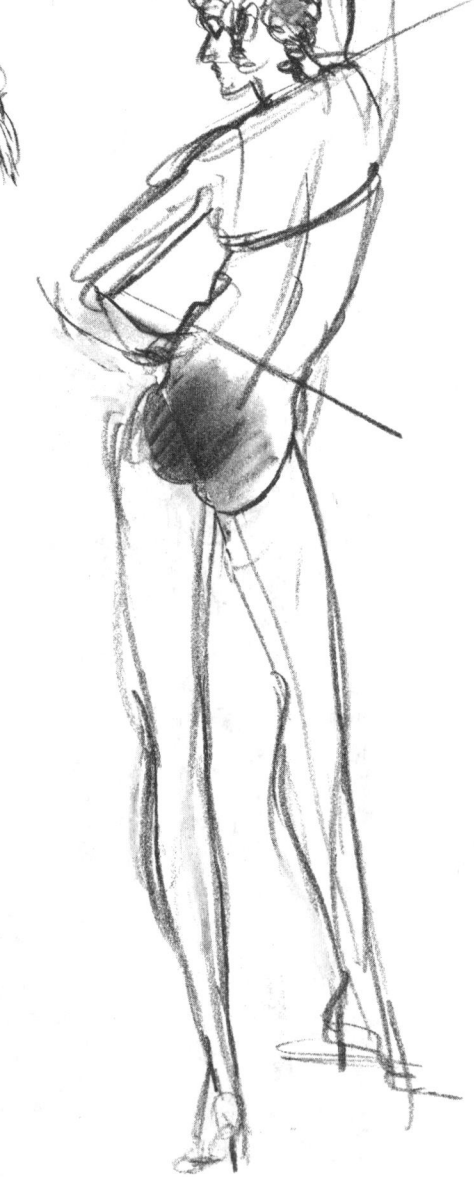

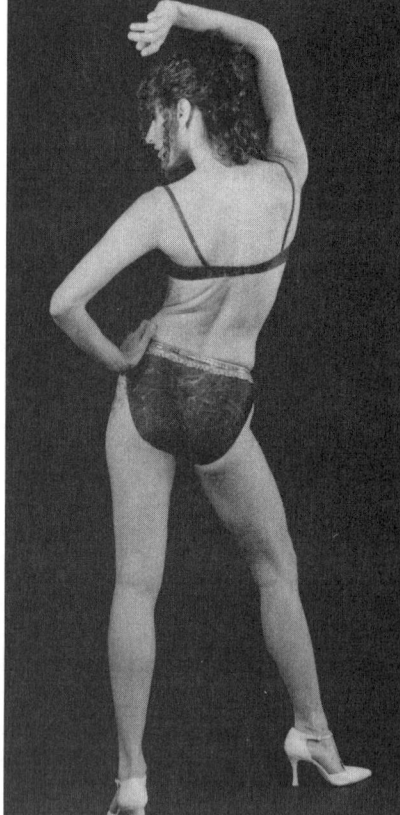

After completing a successful gesture sketch, do not trace over its edges, as doing so creates a harsh and monotonous contour. For now, maintain light to dark lines.

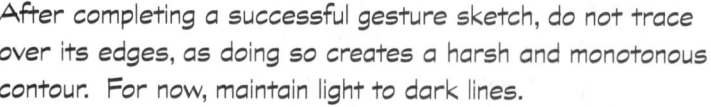

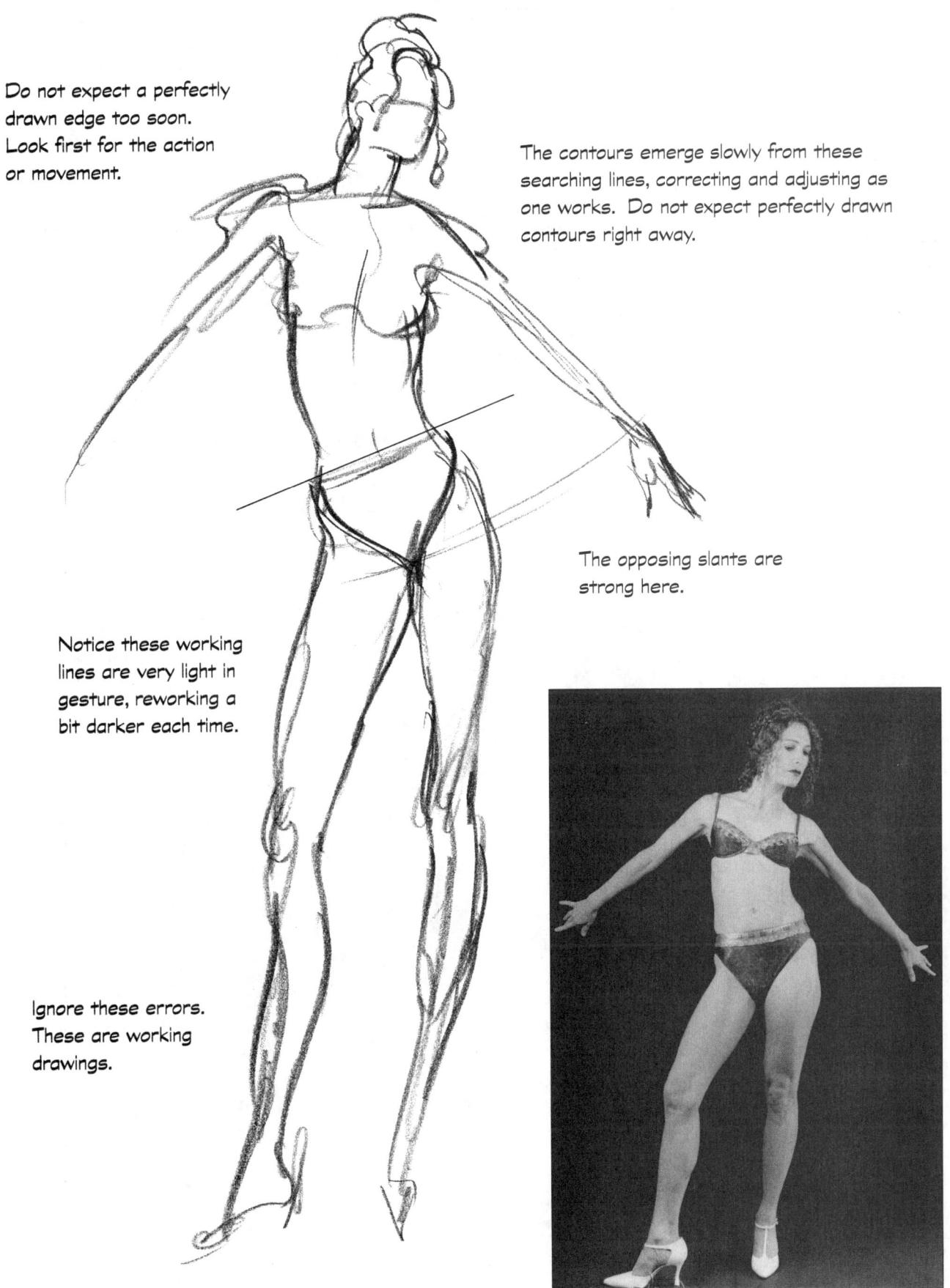

The opposing slants are recognizable in this drawing. Notice that the bikini top and bottom take on these slants as well.

Do not expect a perfectly drawn edge too soon. Look first for the action or movement.

The contours emerge slowly from these searching lines, correcting and adjusting as one works. Do not expect perfectly drawn contours right away.

The opposing slants are strong here.

Notice these working lines are very light in gesture, reworking a bit darker each time.

Ignore these errors. These are working drawings.

CHAPTER 2 THE GESTURE SKETCH

LONGER POSES—3 TO 5 MINUTES

Always begin a drawing of any duration with a gesture sketch. This is the very foundation of the figure. The gesture sketch captures the movement, no matter how slight or subtle. This is how the proportions can be rearranged if needed.

The classical artists have taught us to create a foundation on which to build a drawing. This is the gesture or foundation sketch.

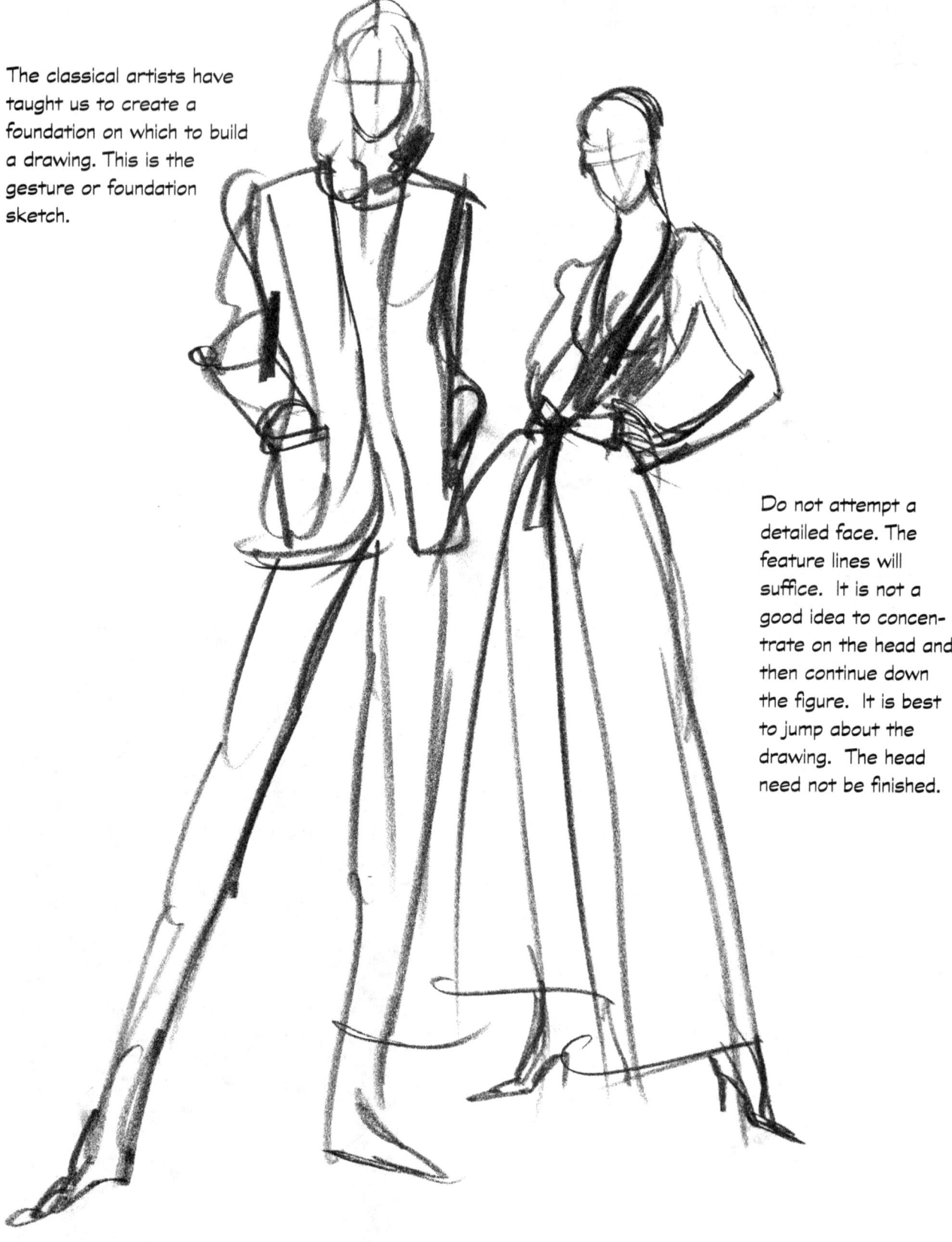

Do not attempt a detailed face. The feature lines will suffice. It is not a good idea to concentrate on the head and then continue down the figure. It is best to jump about the drawing. The head need not be finished.

When working from photographs, do not overdo the anatomy: muscles around the neck, bulging elbows, knees, and ankles. The sculptors of department store mannequins know to eliminate this in fashion figures.

Always indicate the head and its action, but do not tack it on at the end or after the figure has been completed.

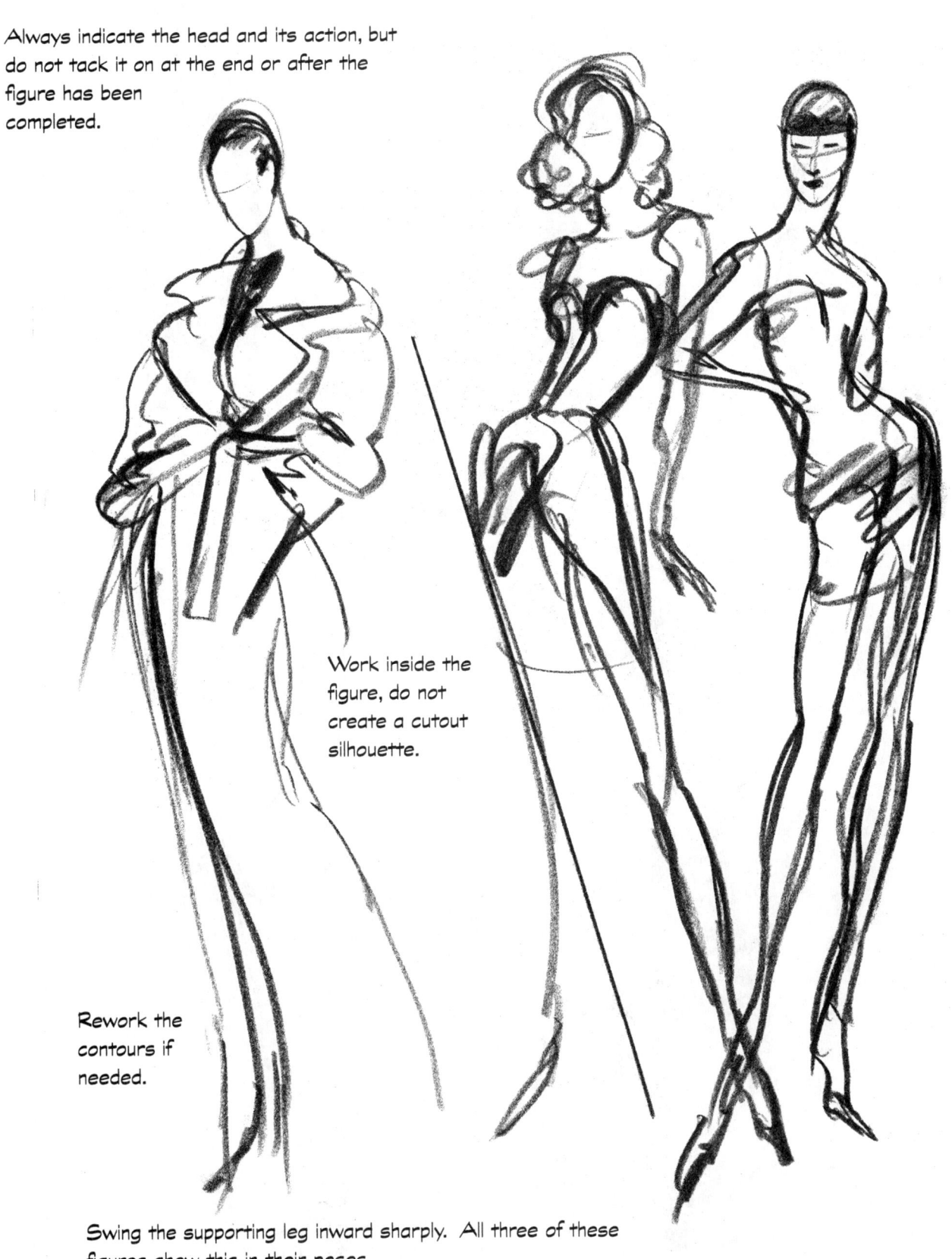

Work inside the figure, do not create a cutout silhouette.

Rework the contours if needed.

Swing the supporting leg inward sharply. All three of these figures show this in their poses.

STUDENT EXAMPLES

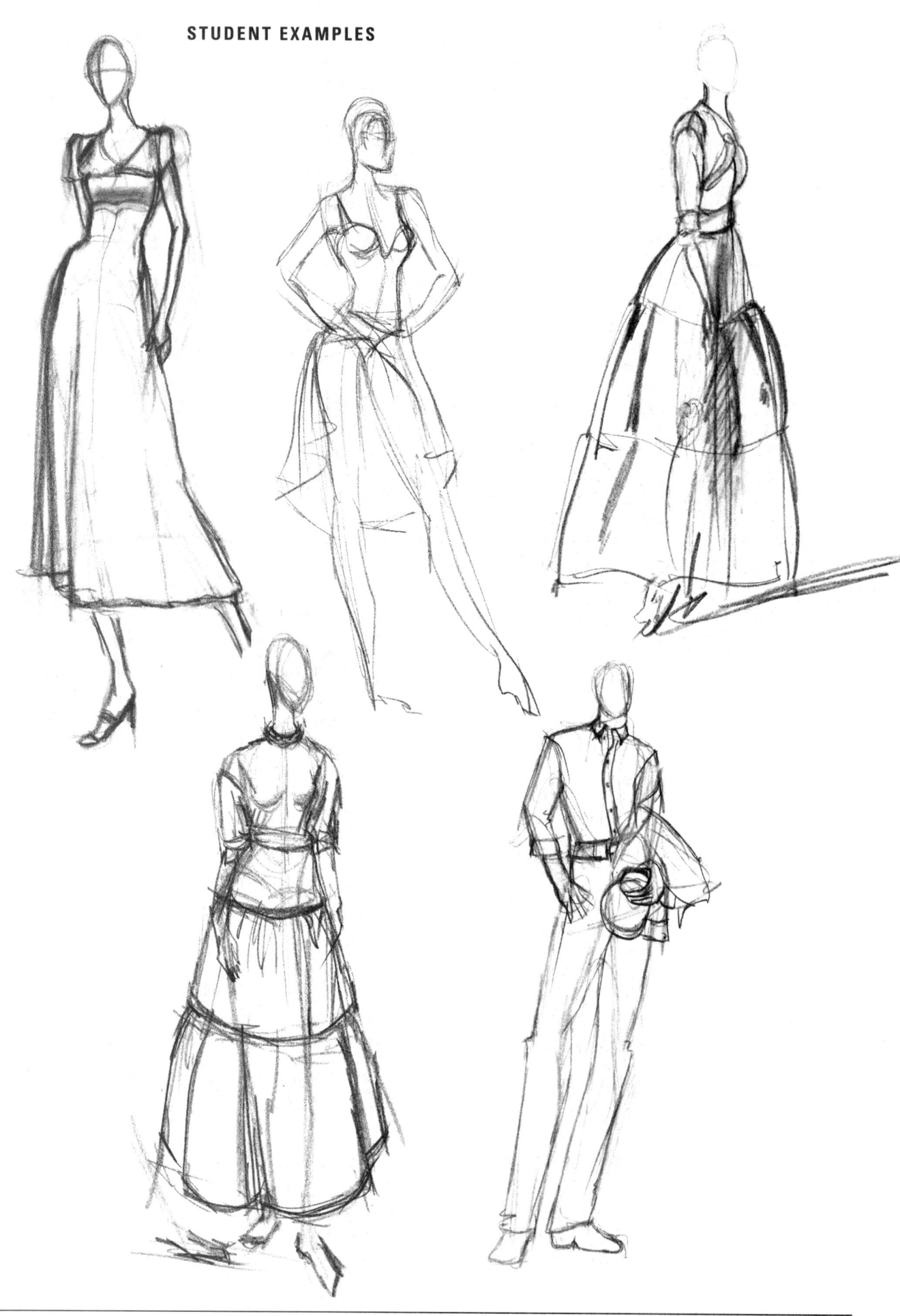

CHAPTER 3

The Head

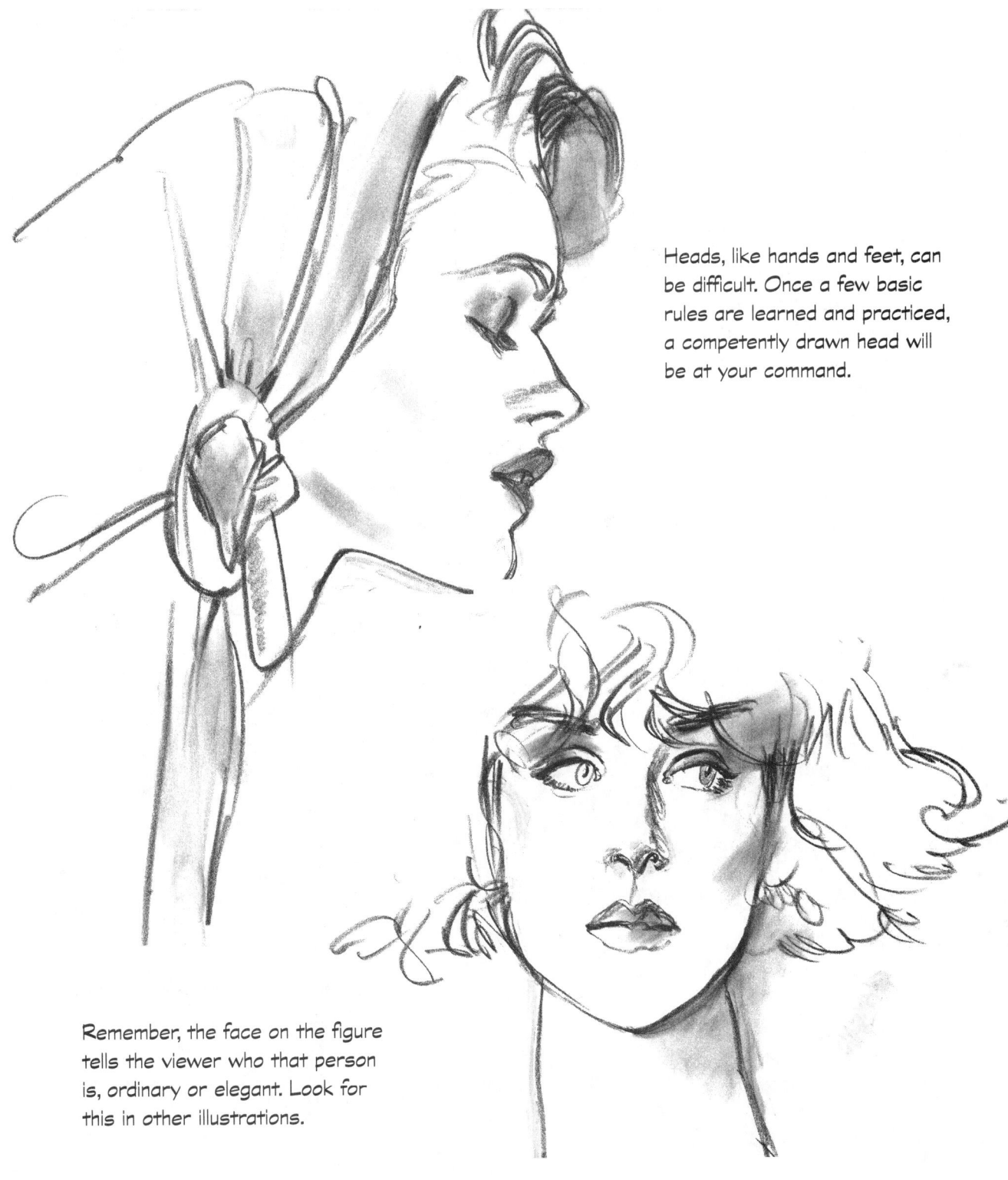

Heads, like hands and feet, can be difficult. Once a few basic rules are learned and practiced, a competently drawn head will be at your command.

Remember, the face on the figure tells the viewer who that person is, ordinary or elegant. Look for this in other illustrations.

It is essential in the study stages of drawing the head that the egg shape is used in all views. Without these basic form and feature placement lines, errors and distortions begin to occur. Professional artists still continue to use this process.

Never draw the silhouette edge of the profile. Start with drawing the eye. This causes the nose to appear too large.

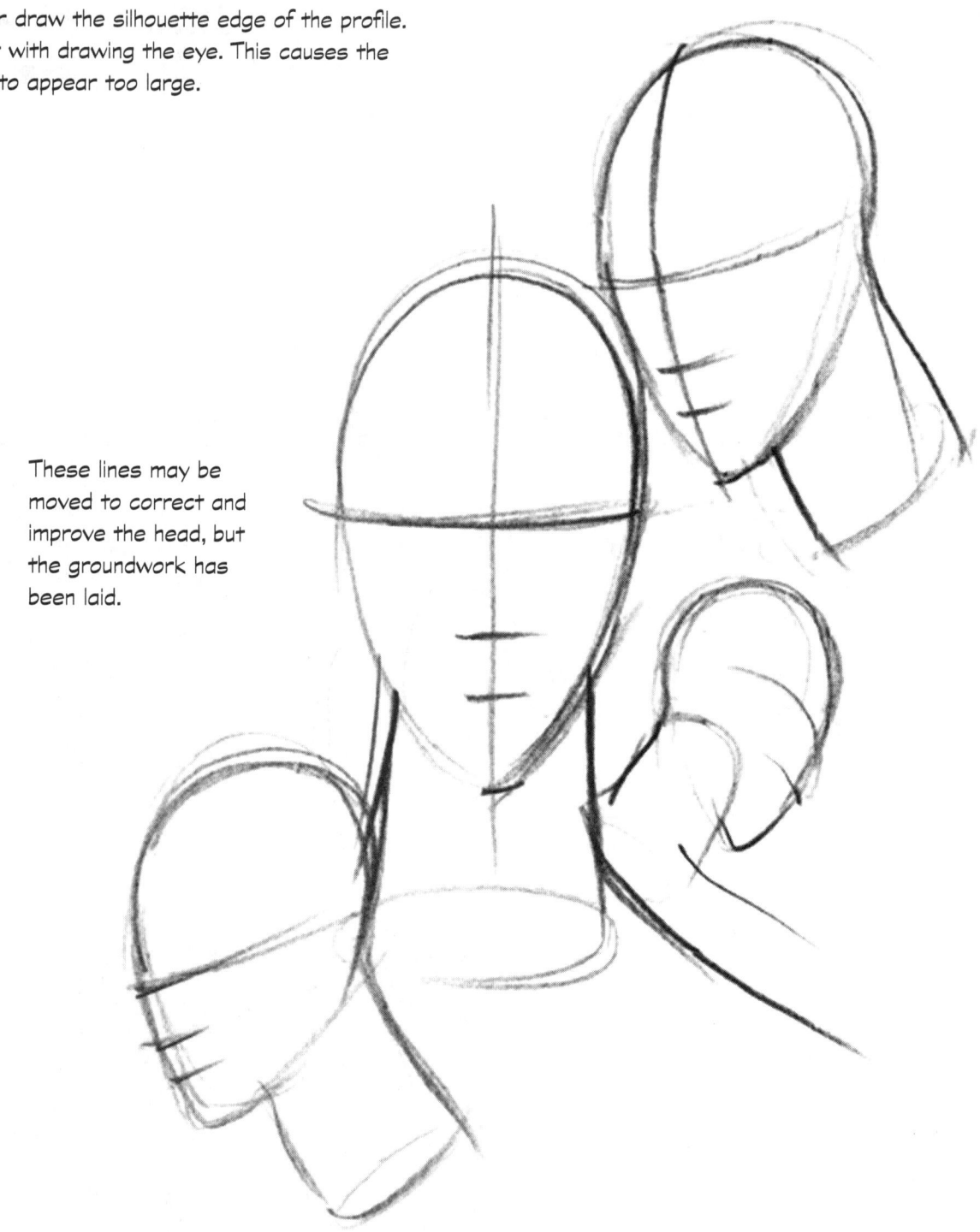

These lines may be moved to correct and improve the head, but the groundwork has been laid.

Often these feature-placement heads will pass as the face itself.

34 FASHION SKETCHING

USING THE EYE AS A GUIDE TO PLACE THE FEATURES

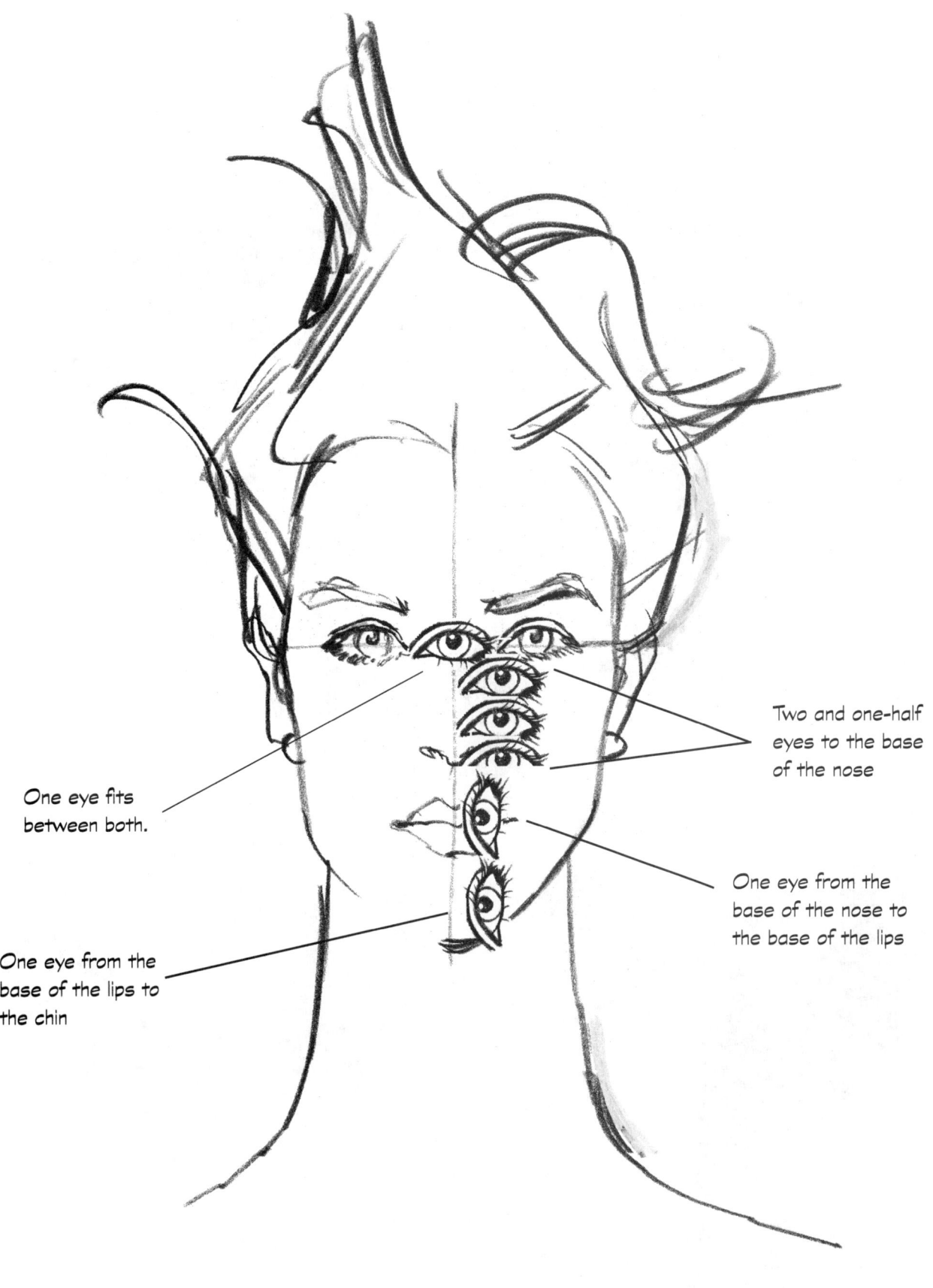

One eye fits between both.

Two and one-half eyes to the base of the nose

One eye from the base of the nose to the base of the lips

One eye from the base of the lips to the chin

CHAPTER 3 THE HEAD 35

THE EYE

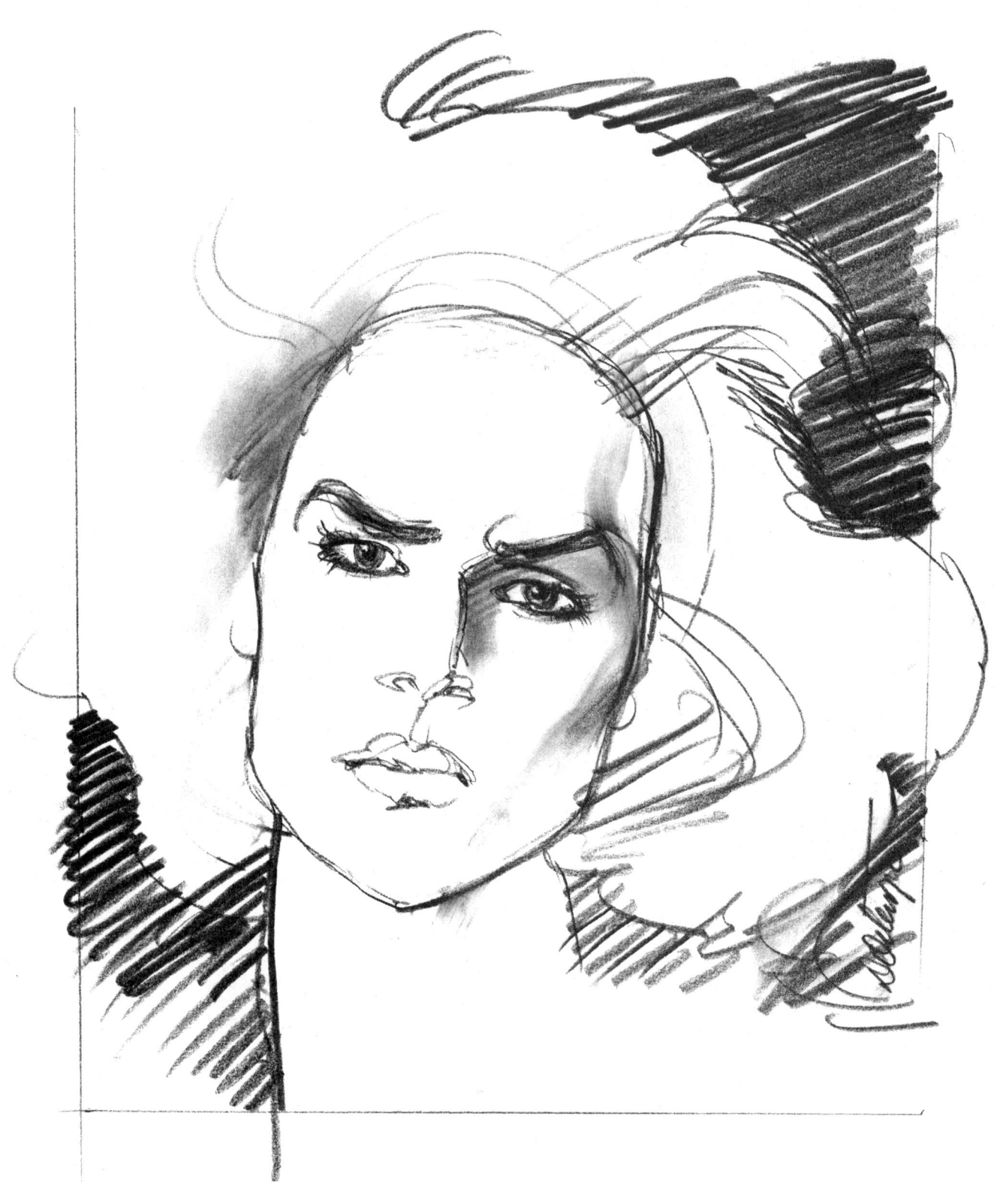

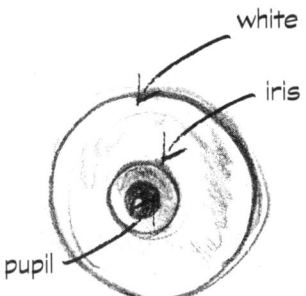

Seen without the lids, the eye looks quite different. However, this is a clue to the lid shape.

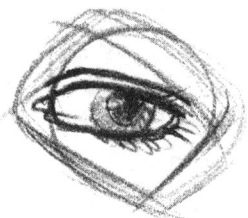

The white of the eye is set into the orbits of the skull.

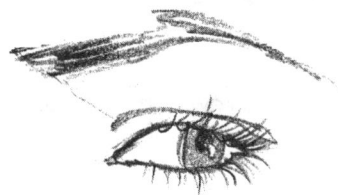

The peak of the eyebrow is at an angle.

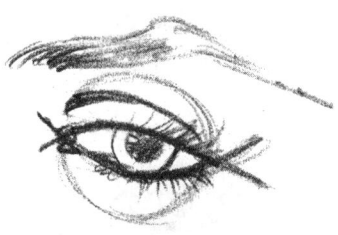

Both upper and lower lids wrap around the spherical white.

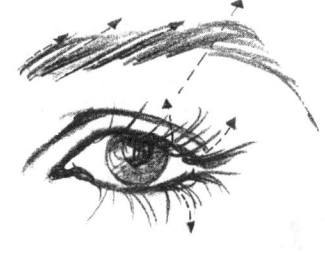

Hairs grow in an oblique angle over the eye. The eyelashes of the top lid grow down, then up. Lower lid eyelashes curl down.

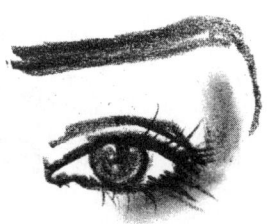

Eyelashes are heaviest at the ends. Heavy makeup enlarges the eye.

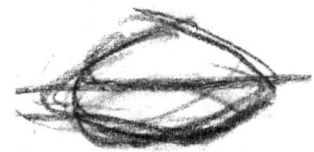

Rather than draw hard edges quickly, feel out their placement as a gesture drawing.

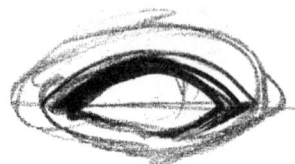

The eye is not a definable shape, as almond or spade, but turned corners resembling a football.

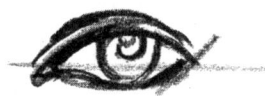

One-quarter of the iris is tucked under the upper lid. The iris touches the lower lid also.

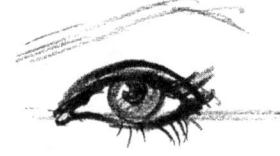

Draw in the eyelid.

SOME COMMON FAULTS:

- Pupil is not touching the upper lid—the eye is staring.
- Iris is too large.
- Iris is too small.
- Eyelashes are too straight and evenly placed.
- The eyebrow is often drawn too short. When in full view, penciled eyebrow should be longer than the eye.

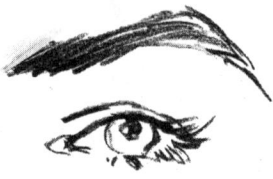

Do not place the hairs of the eyebrow too close to the eye. This coarsens the face.

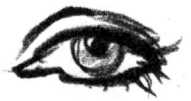

Eyelashes are heaviest at the ends of the lid.

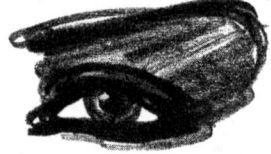

Heavy makeup creates drama and closes up the white.

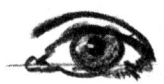
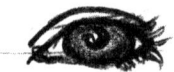
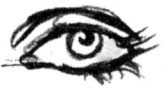
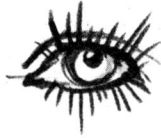
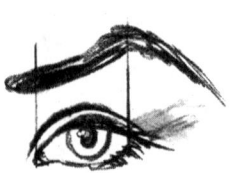

THE NOSE AND ITS PLANES

For study purposes, think of the nose as a series of planes: Plane #1, one down the center; Plane #2, one on both sides; and Plane #3, on the bottom at the nostrils, the wing of the nose.

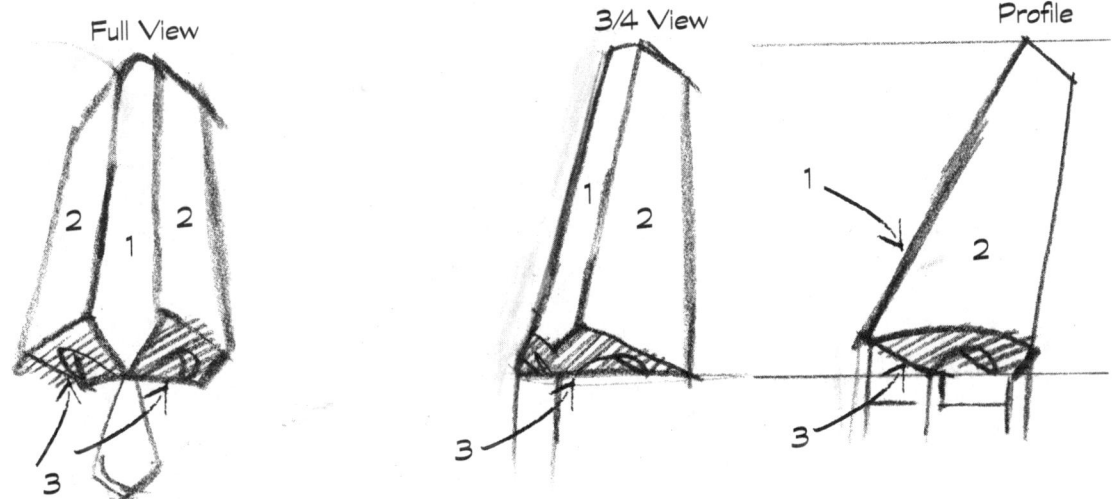

Full View 3/4 View Profile

It is not necessary to draw these plane edges every time, but think about them as you work. Without this plane knowledge, this difficult 3/4 view will be impossible to think out.

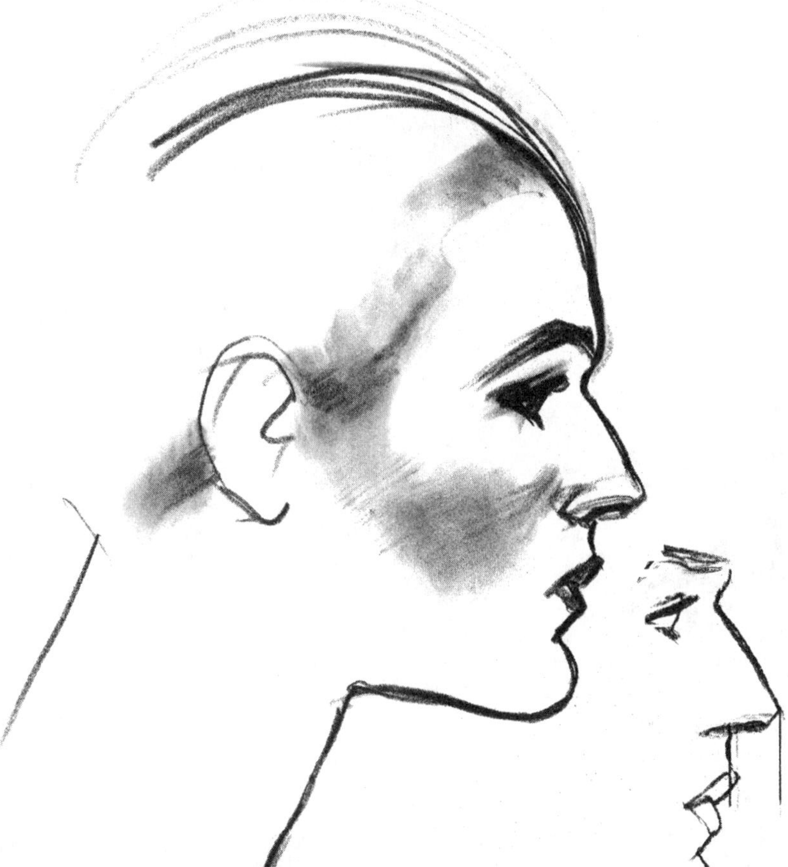

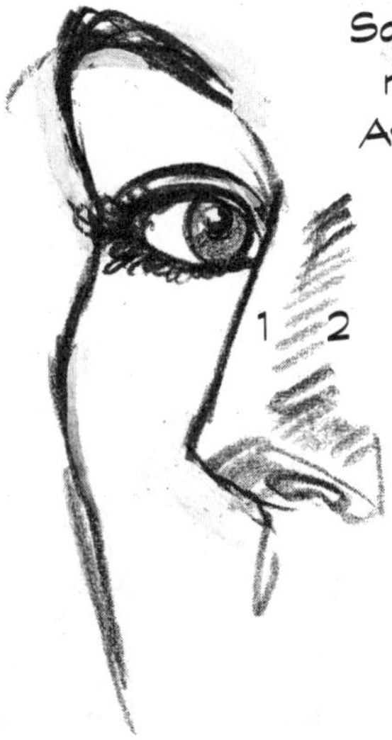

Nostrils differ from person to person. Some nostrils are not visible at all. Avoid too black a spot, which creates a hole in the face.

Very little of the eye is seen in profile. A clean (no hint of fat) and long jawline adds to the elegance and slimness of the head. Allow for space between the tip of nose and the lips. Do not crush Plane #1.

Lip shapes vary, but generally they are diamond shaped.

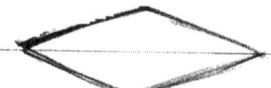 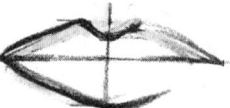 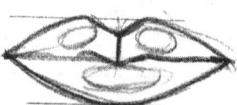 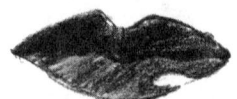

Here is the basic diamond shape.

"Cupid Bow" is placed in the center.

Always draw the center of the mouth. This gives expression to the face. Painted lips flatten out fat forms. Cracks have disappeared. Outer shape remains sharp.

Lipstick shine often appears here, catching light from above. Velvetlike smoothness is achieved by makeup.

Cupid Bow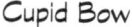

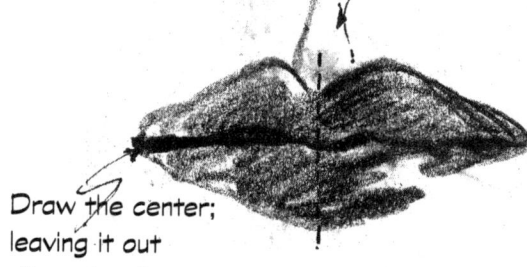

Draw the center; leaving it out altogether has a strange effect.

In 3/4 view, . . .

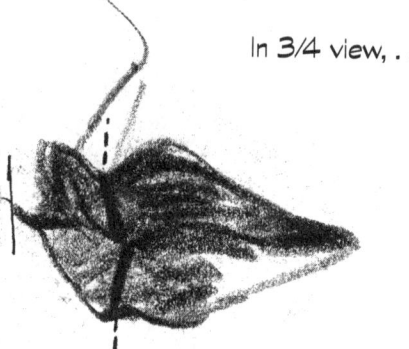

. . . the turned-side is very short, . . .

. . . and, the center has moved to the side.

In profile, leave room for an open V at the center. Without this inward dent, female lips take on a swollen effect.

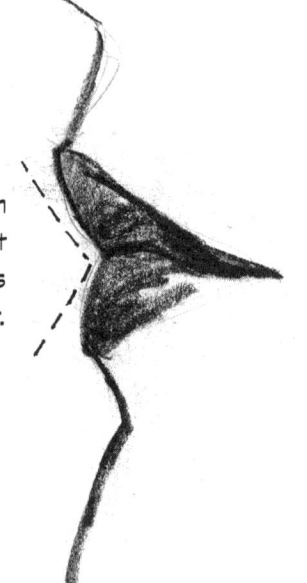

40 FASHION SKETCHING

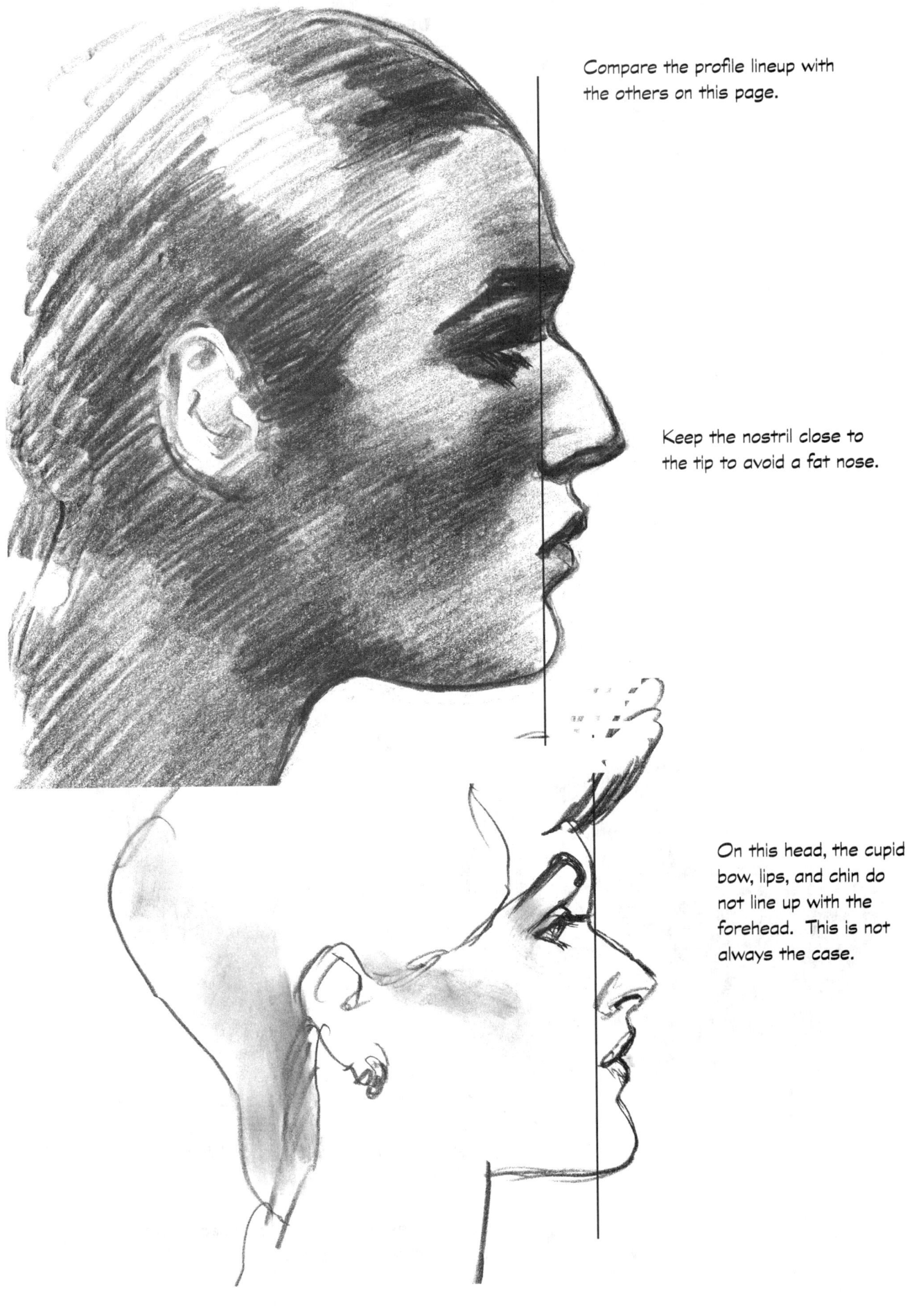

Compare the profile lineup with the others on this page.

Keep the nostril close to the tip to avoid a fat nose.

On this head, the cupid bow, lips, and chin do not line up with the forehead. This is not always the case.

CHAPTER 3 THE HEAD 41

DRAWING HAIR

A question asked often is, "How do you draw hair?" There is no set way, but do not draw every strand. This produces a confused and heavy look. The design of the hair is important.

Remember, this is a very small area on the figure. Treat it simply to avoid overworking.

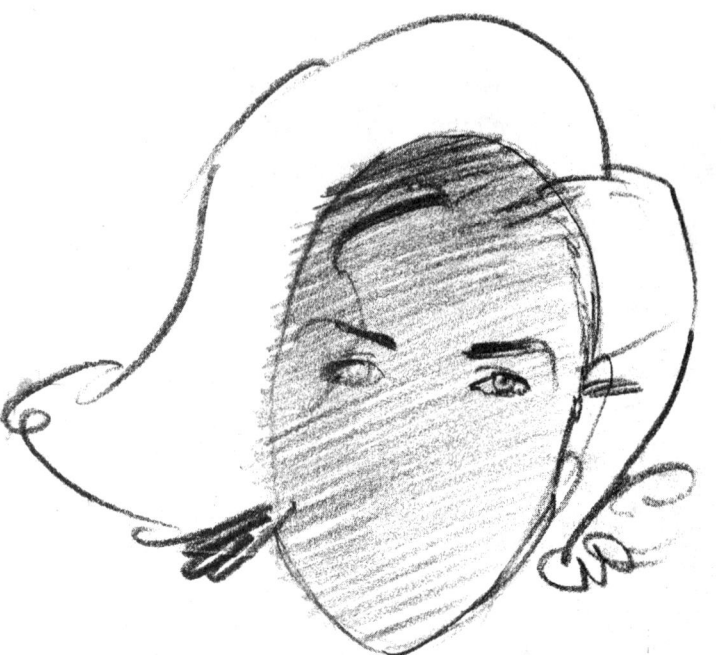

Here is the same hairstyle treated in different ways.

The cut is suggested by a few strands. This is the kind of simplicity for which to aim. Strands may overlap.

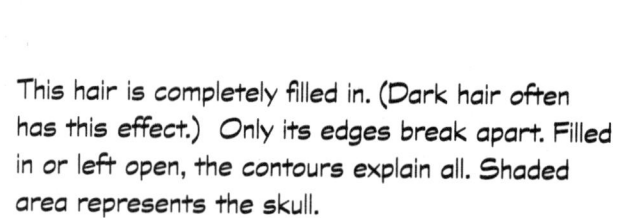

This hair is completely filled in. (Dark hair often has this effect.) Only its edges break apart. Filled in or left open, the contours explain all. Shaded area represents the skull.

Note the extra volume of hair needed to fit comfortably over the skull.

Hair combed closely over the crown still has volume.

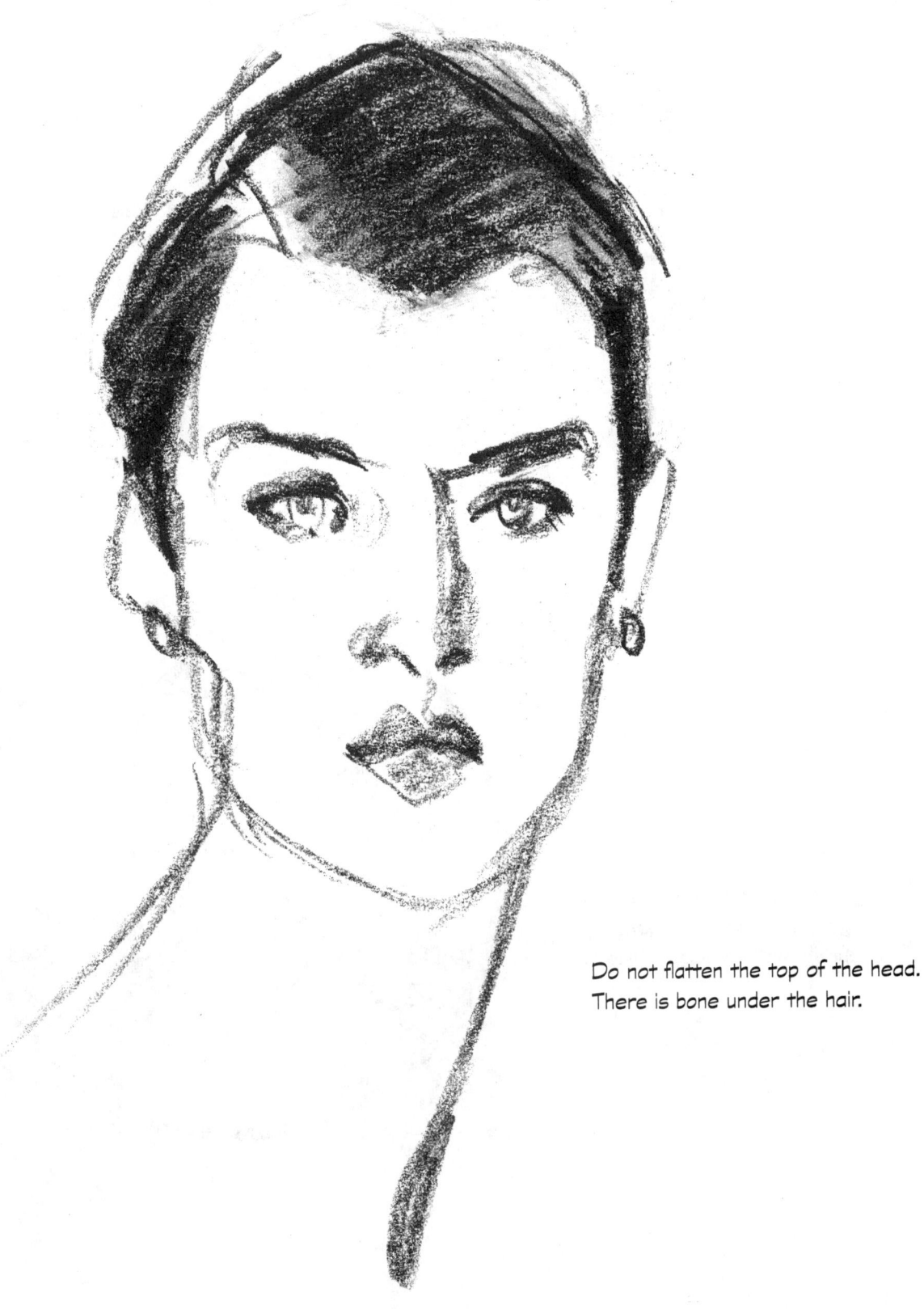

Do not flatten the top of the head. There is bone under the hair.

CHAPTER 3 THE HEAD 43

No allowance has been made for the crown—a common fault. The face appears too large and heavy.

Filling in circles to suggest curls is not a good solution. This looks amateurish and only vaguely like hair.

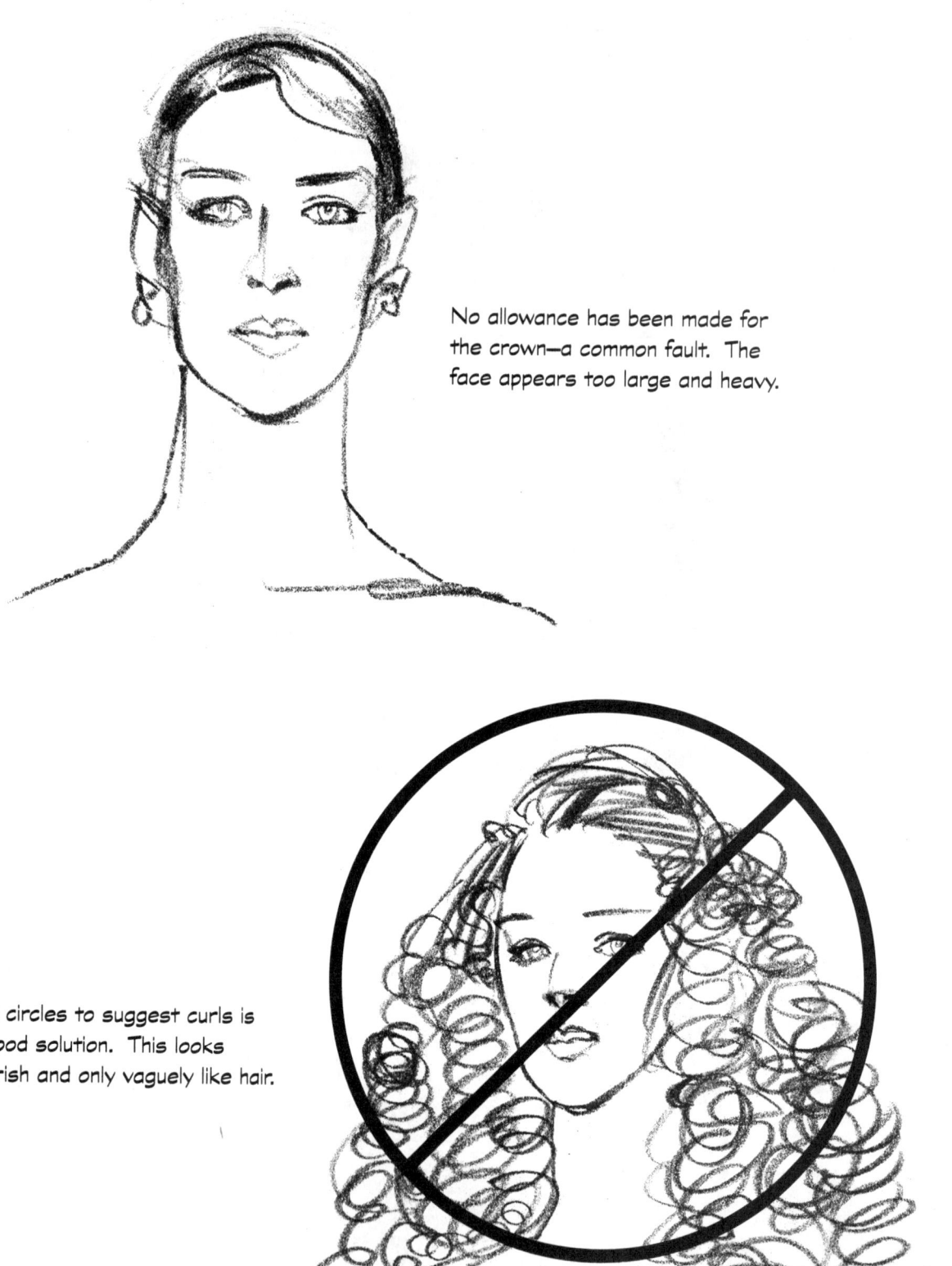

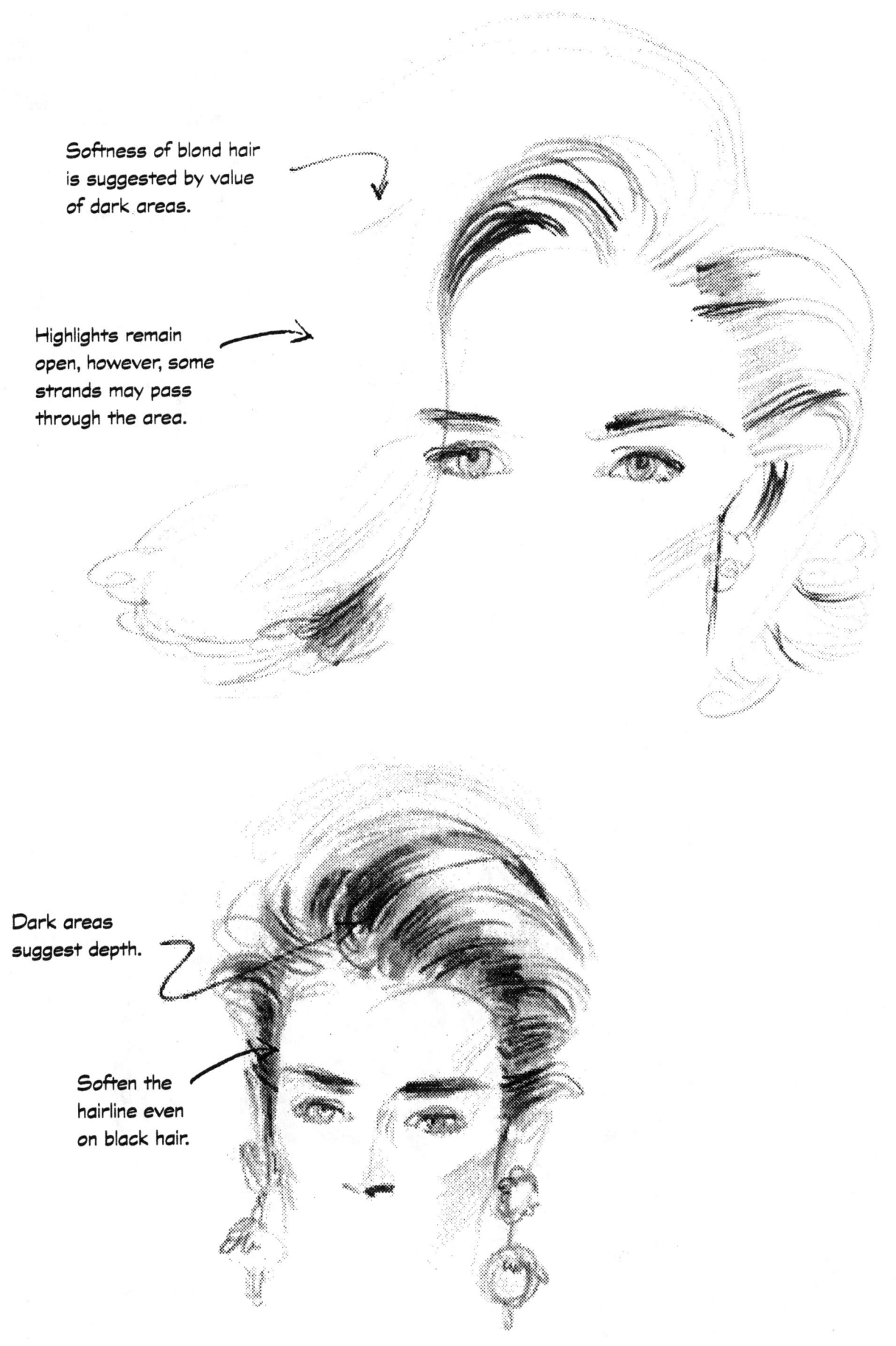

Softness of blond hair is suggested by value of dark areas.

Highlights remain open, however, some strands may pass through the area.

Dark areas suggest depth.

Soften the hairline even on black hair.

Try to capture the feeling of the hairstyles without drawing in every strand.

Only wet hair will be flat and close to the skull—as if painted on.

Keep it simple.

Think of the skull when blocking in the hair.

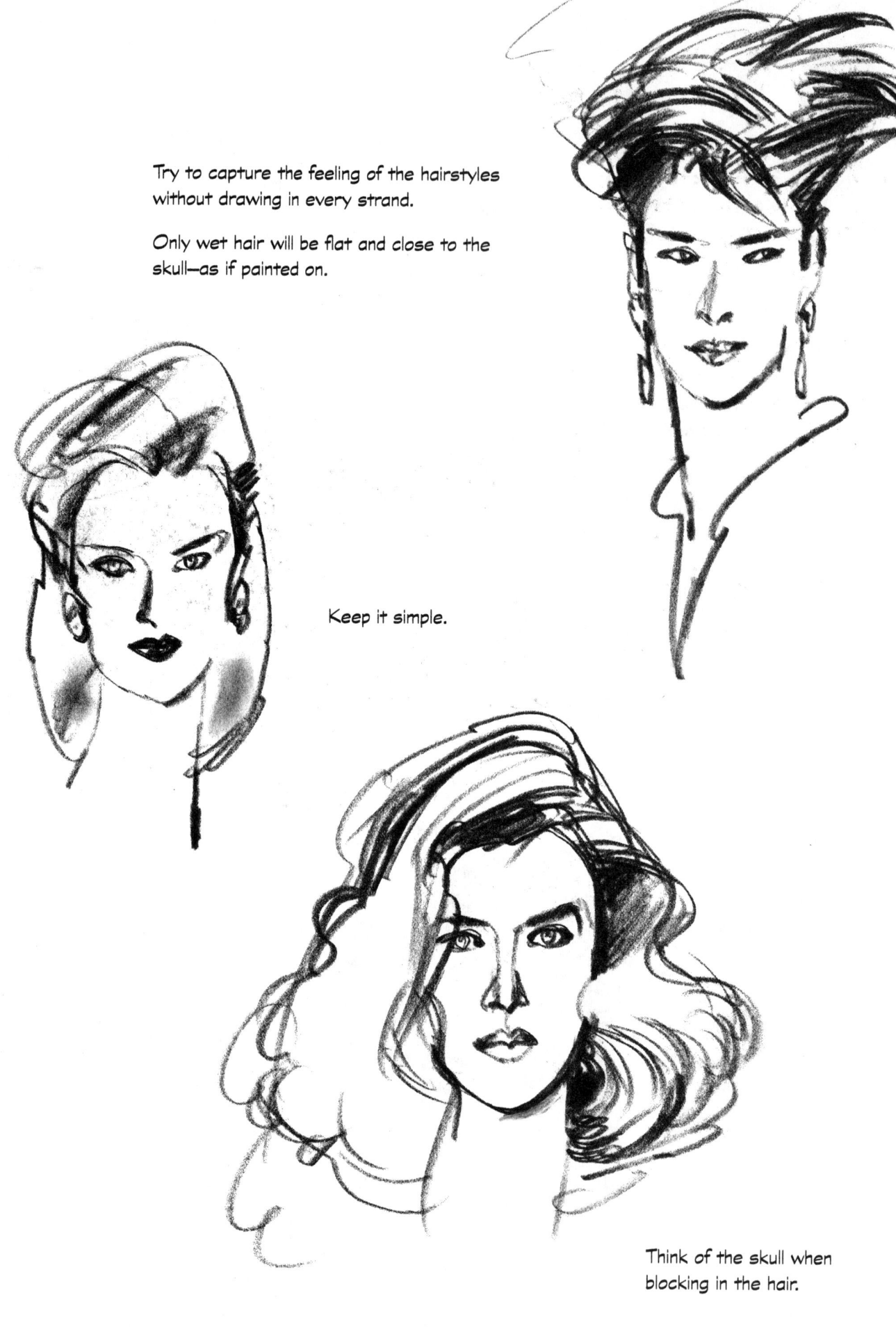

46 FASHION SKETCHING

THE FEATURES IN 3/4 VIEW

The 3/4 view is a difficult angle to draw and completely different from the full view.

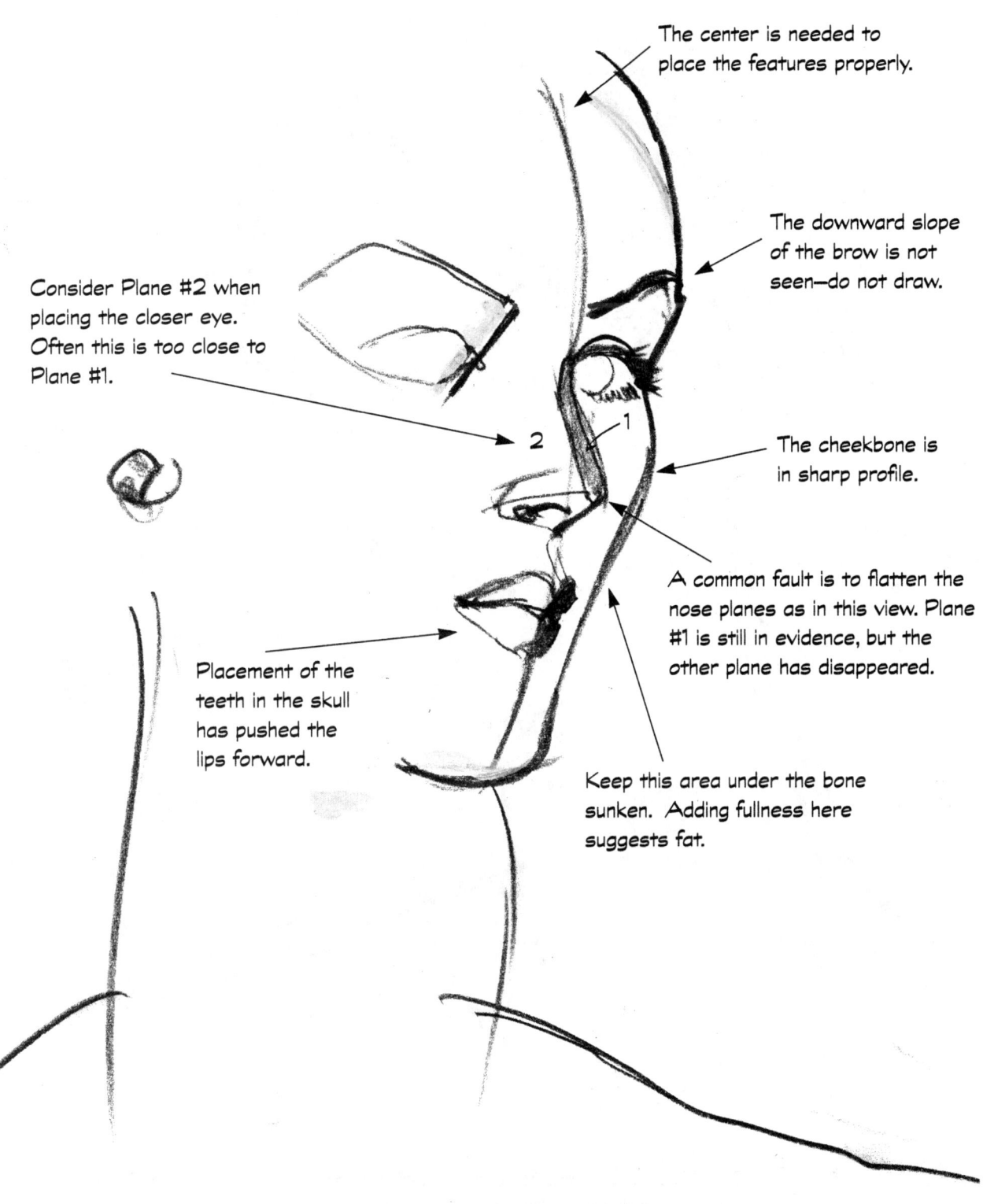

The center is needed to place the features properly.

The downward slope of the brow is not seen—do not draw.

Consider Plane #2 when placing the closer eye. Often this is too close to Plane #1.

The cheekbone is in sharp profile.

A common fault is to flatten the nose planes as in this view. Plane #1 is still in evidence, but the other plane has disappeared.

Placement of the teeth in the skull has pushed the lips forward.

Keep this area under the bone sunken. Adding fullness here suggests fat.

CHAPTER 3   THE HEAD   47

The far eye seems to be growing out of the nose. Appearing this way, students refuse to draw the iris close to Plane #1 as a result.

If you do not see the pink of the eye, do not draw it. The eye will appear pulled out of its socket.

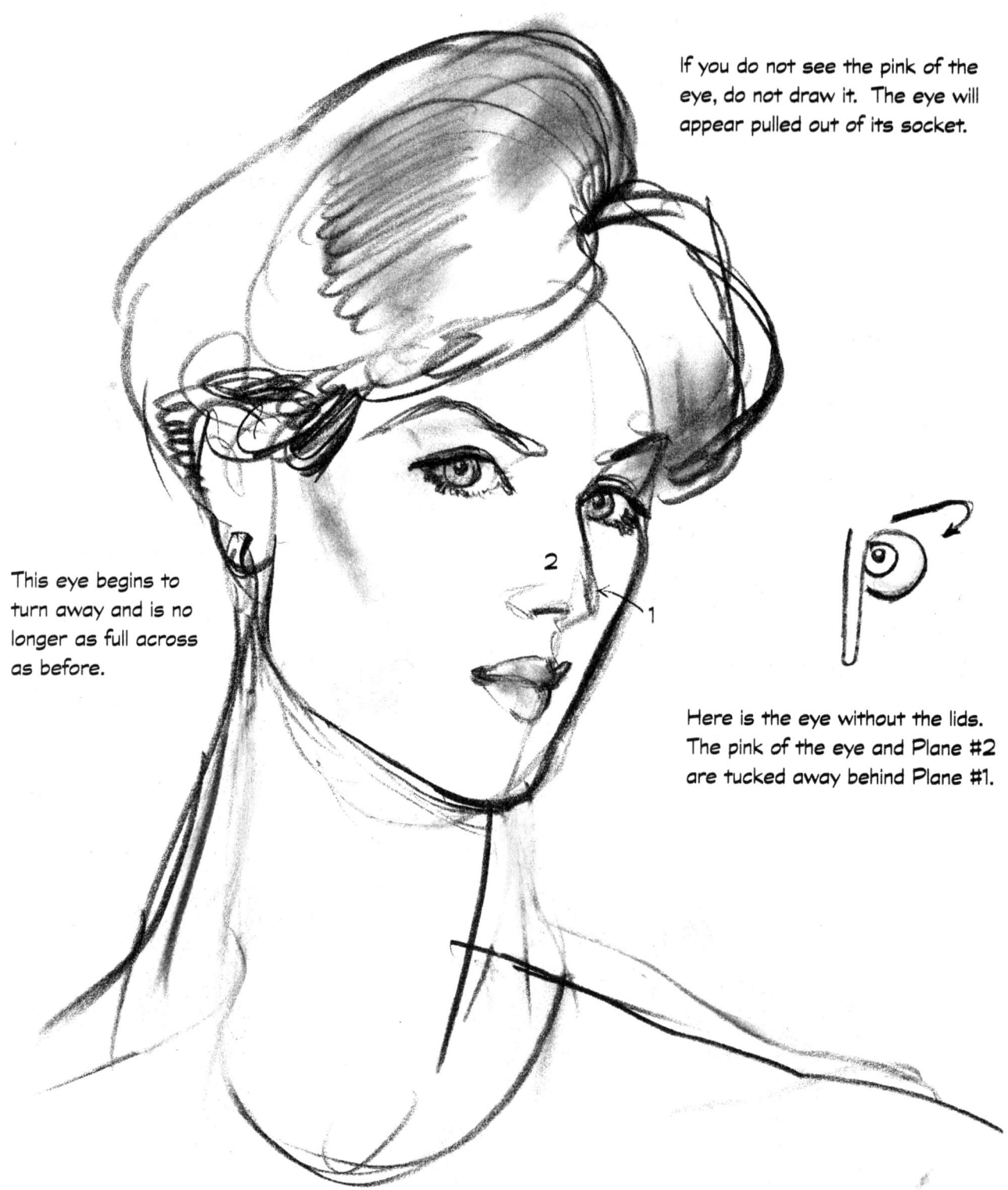

This eye begins to turn away and is no longer as full across as before.

Here is the eye without the lids. The pink of the eye and Plane #2 are tucked away behind Plane #1.

REMEMBER: Use the foundation sketch to think this out. It is difficult to contour or draw in with dark lines in the beginning.

THE EYE IN PROFILE

The white or eyeball is set far back into the orbit.

Study these details carefully but always start the head with a complete egg shape, otherwise the face appears too large.

Do not place the eye too close to Plane #1. Note the oblique angle.

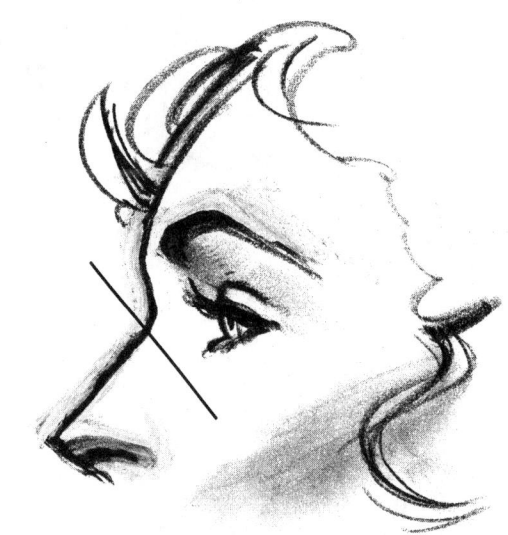

Iris seen as an ellipse

Makeup areas

Eyes in profile have a V shape.

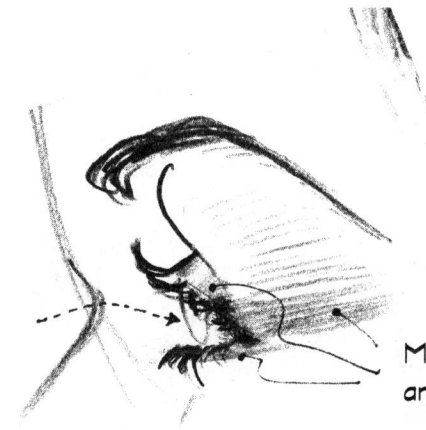

Side view skull—notice how small the actual face area is in profile.

CHAPTER 3 THE HEAD 49

THE NECK

The neck is seen as a column or a rounded cylinder.

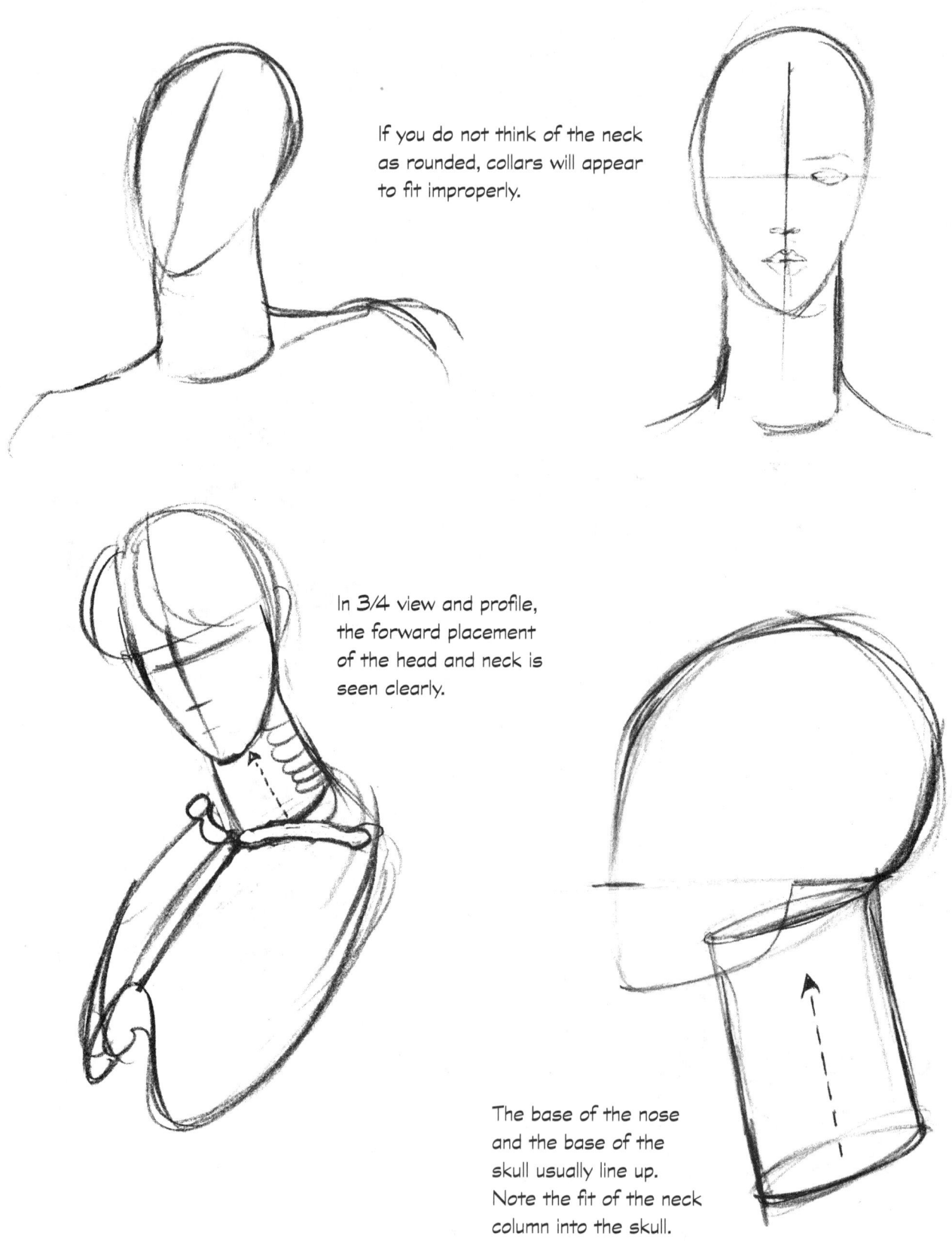

If you do not think of the neck as rounded, collars will appear to fit improperly.

In 3/4 view and profile, the forward placement of the head and neck is seen clearly.

The base of the nose and the base of the skull usually line up. Note the fit of the neck column into the skull.

Although the neck may not be seen due to hair or collars, draw the neck and head thrust forward. Otherwise, the neck appears to be growing straight up, out of the shoulders.

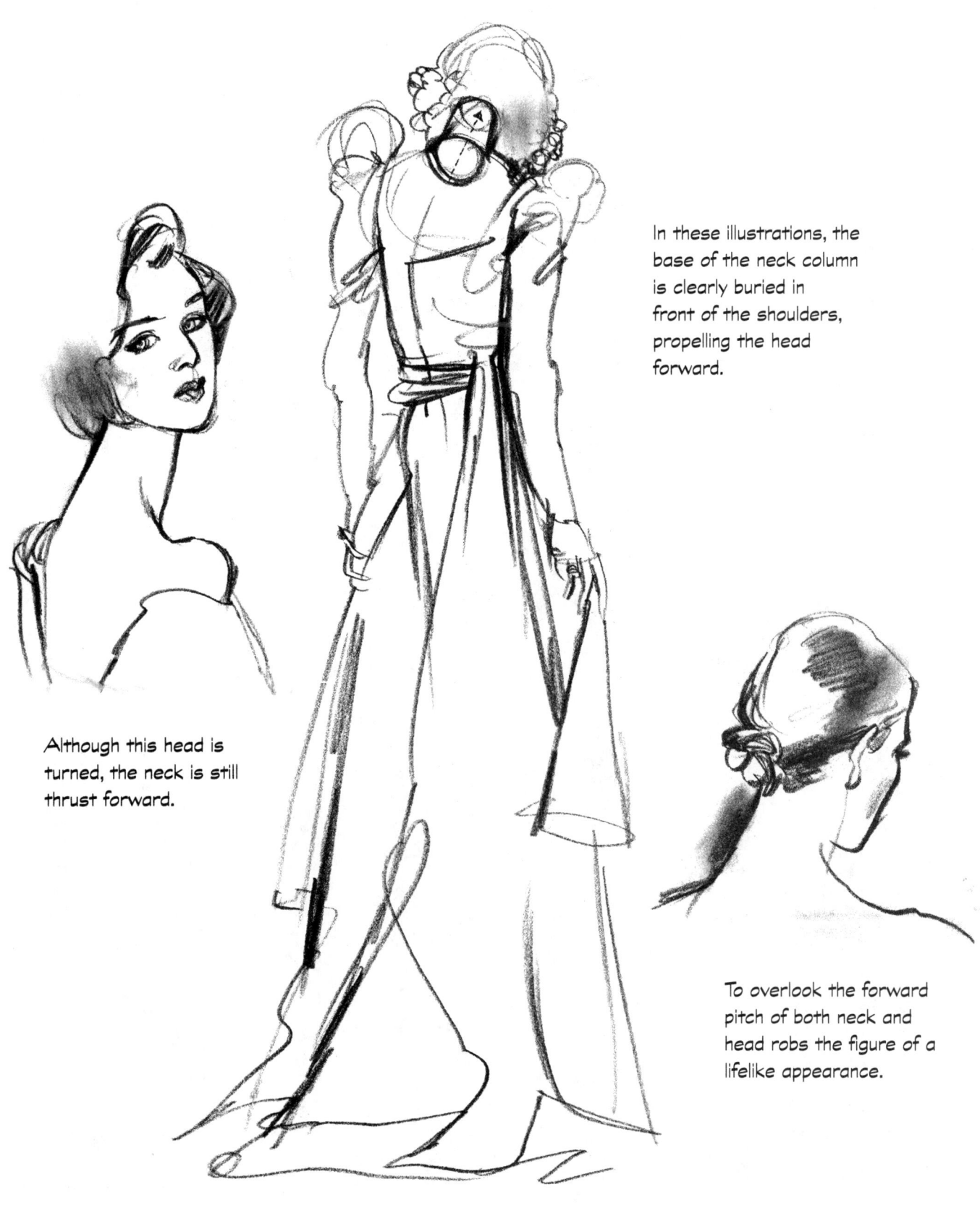

In these illustrations, the base of the neck column is clearly buried in front of the shoulders, propelling the head forward.

Although this head is turned, the neck is still thrust forward.

To overlook the forward pitch of both neck and head robs the figure of a lifelike appearance.

CHAPTER 3 THE HEAD

THE EAR

The ear is a complicated shape. Treat the ear with great simplicity, or a swollen mass will result. The ear is best drawn with earrings, which serve to dress and glamorize the head.

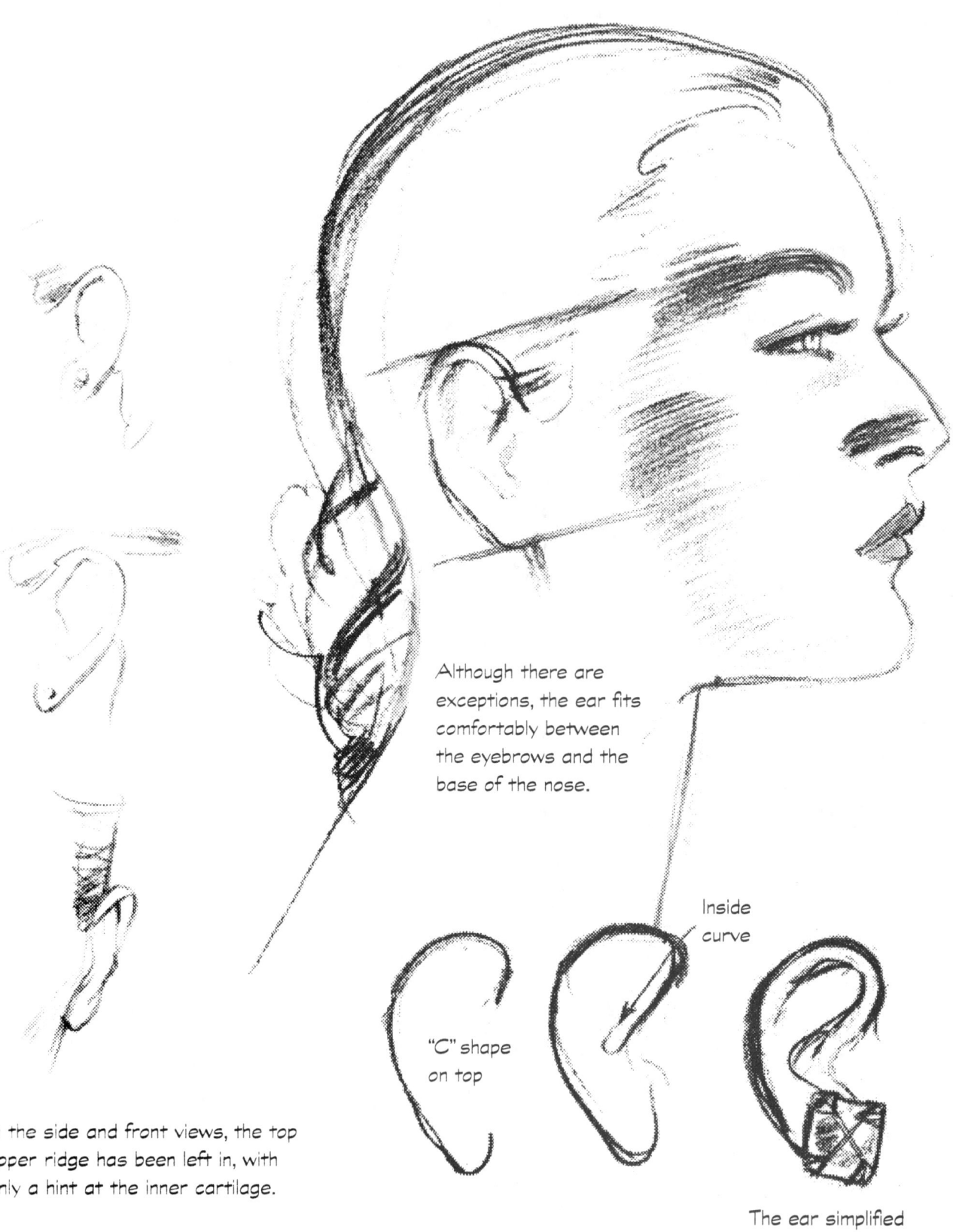

Although there are exceptions, the ear fits comfortably between the eyebrows and the base of the nose.

"C" shape on top

Inside curve

In the side and front views, the top upper ridge has been left in, with only a hint at the inner cartilage.

The ear simplified

STEP BY STEP, #1

Always sketch out the egg shape of the head first; then find the center of the egg both vertically and horizontally.

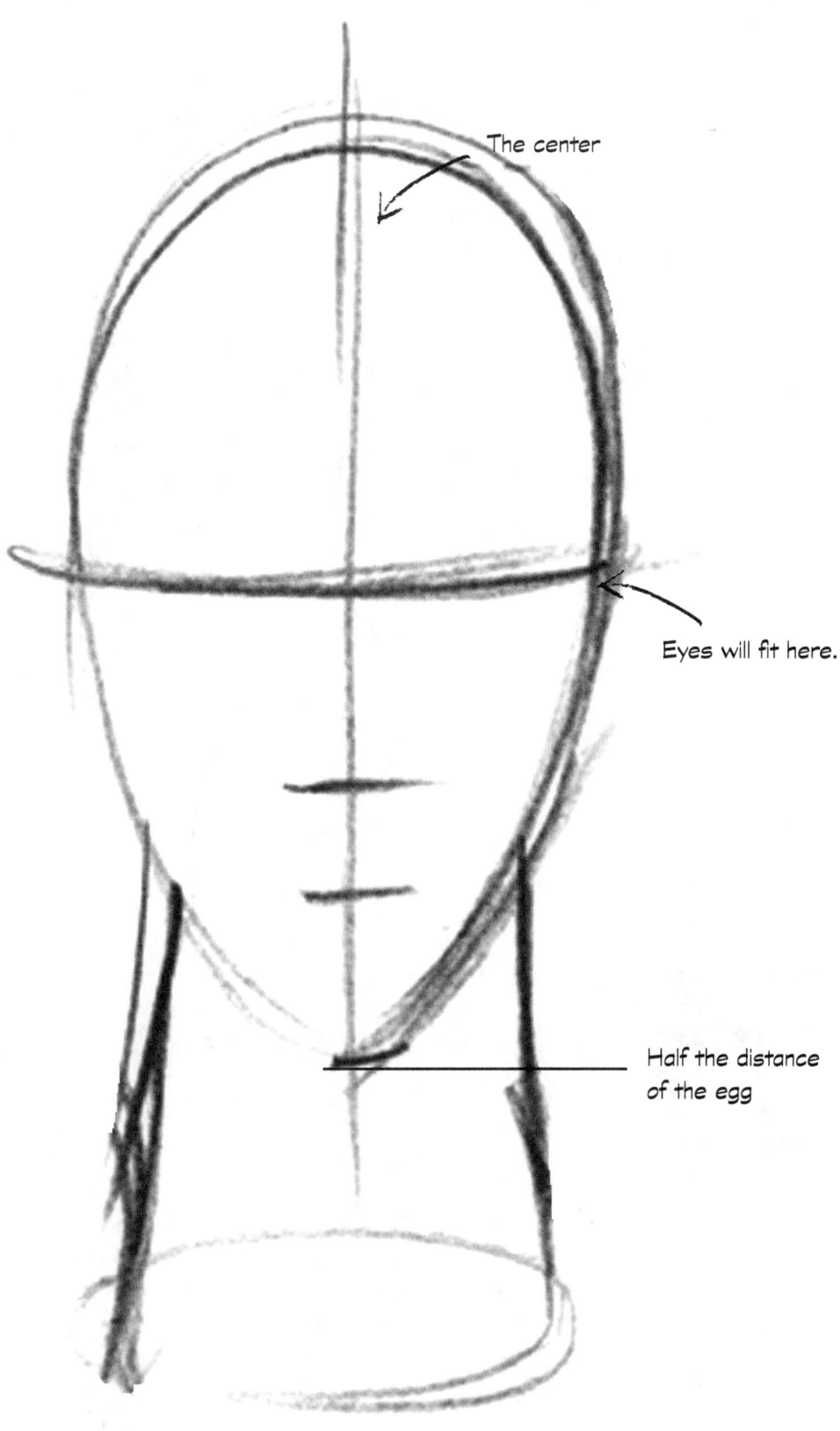

The center

Eyes will fit here.

Half the distance of the egg

CHAPTER 3 THE HEAD

STEP BY STEP, #2

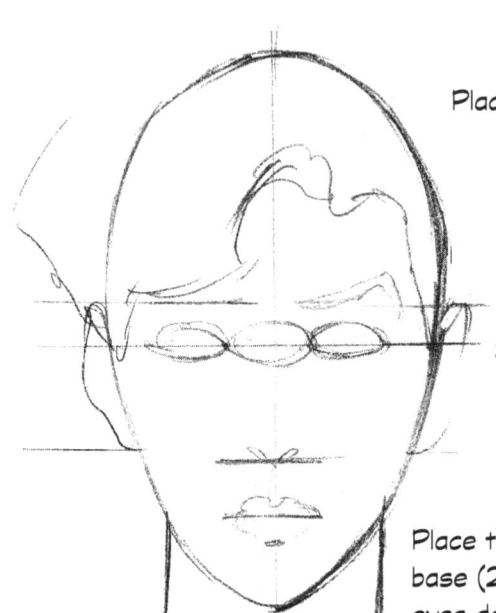

Place the hairline around the features.

Sketch in all three eyes lightly.

Place the nose base (2 1/2 eyes down), then the lips.

Put in some indication of the neck. A floating head is difficult to judge.

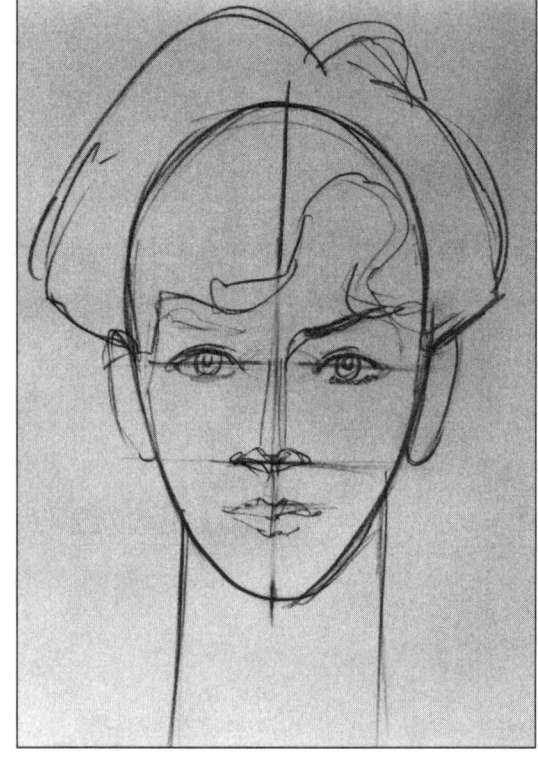

Fill out the hair over the skull.

Sketch in the eyes and irises and the rest of the features.

Keep sketchy at this point. You may need to correct some errors.

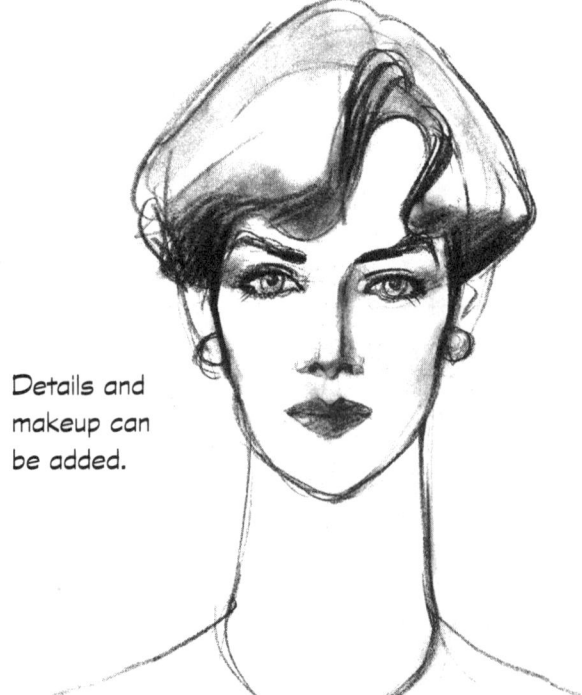

Details and makeup can be added.

Do not line up the corners of the mouth with the pupil of the eye, as in classical art. This is too heavy an effect for fashion. However, the lips can be larger and full. Face contours are adjusted to resemble the skeletal base rather than the egg. Note the sunken cheeks.

Balance darks—notice that the hair, eyes, and lips have dark areas. Filling in black lips only results in an out-of-balance drawing.

54 FASHION SKETCHING

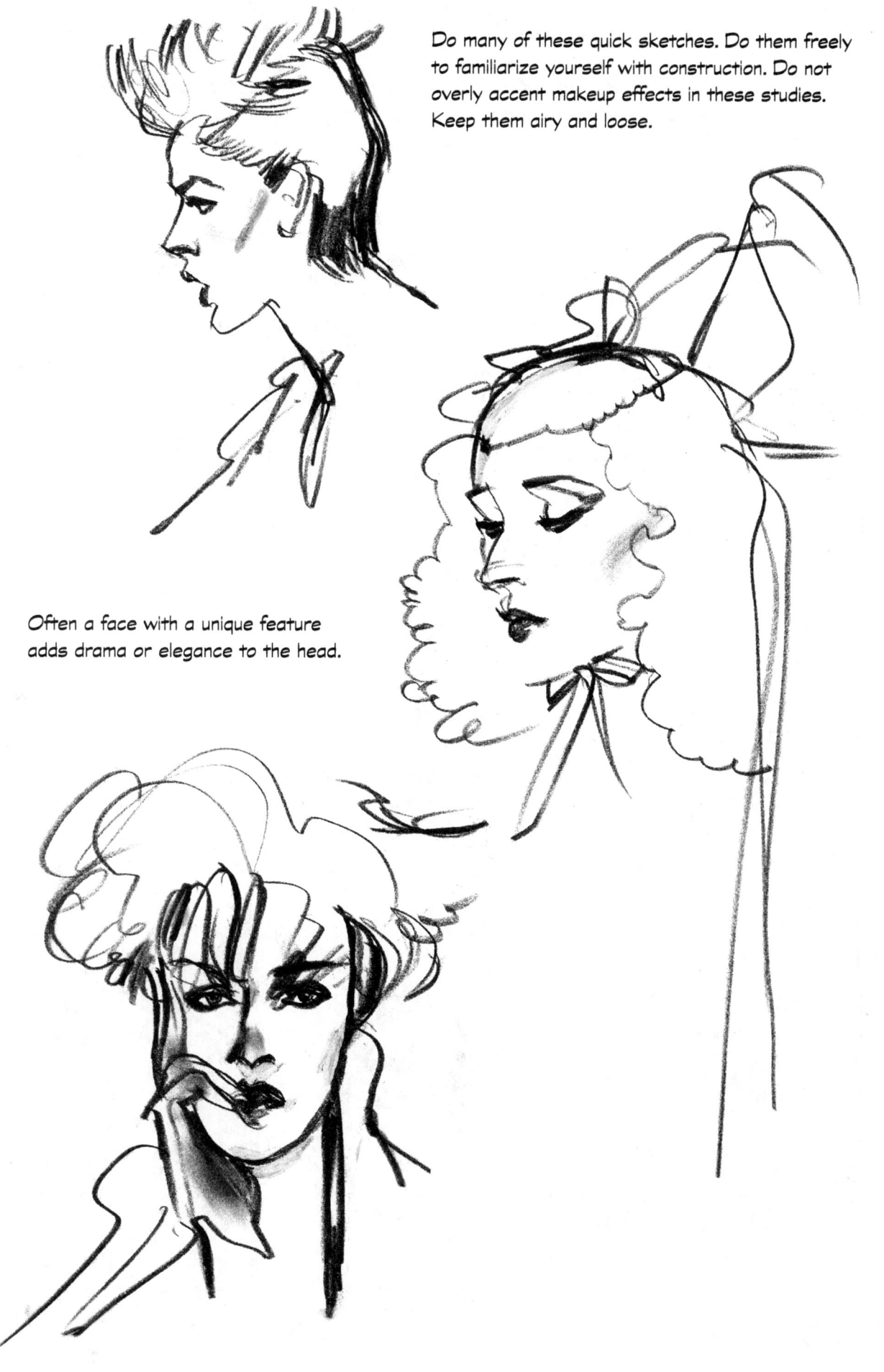

Do many of these quick sketches. Do them freely to familiarize yourself with construction. Do not overly accent makeup effects in these studies. Keep them airy and loose.

Often a face with a unique feature adds drama or elegance to the head.

STYLIZING THE FACE

Some artists and designers prefer not to draw the face, choosing instead to stylize the face and hair or merely suggest them.

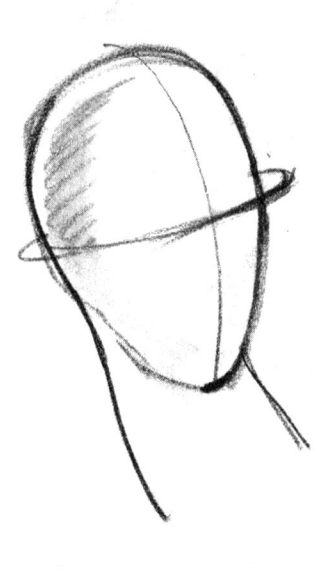
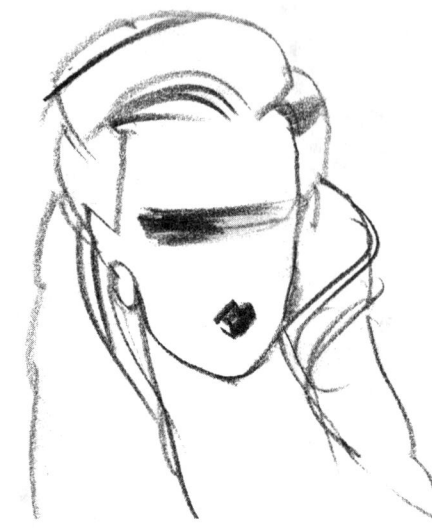

These are suggestions. Develop your own style, but make an attempt to learn how to draw the face and head.

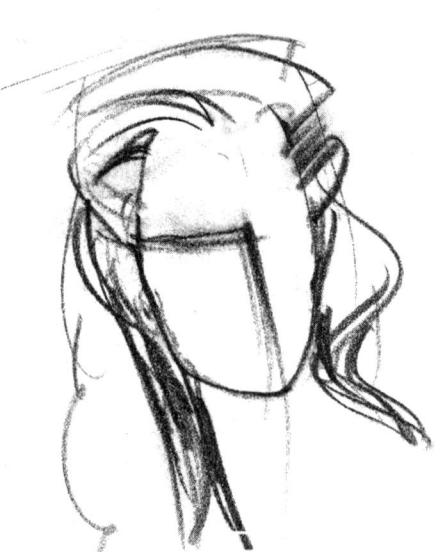
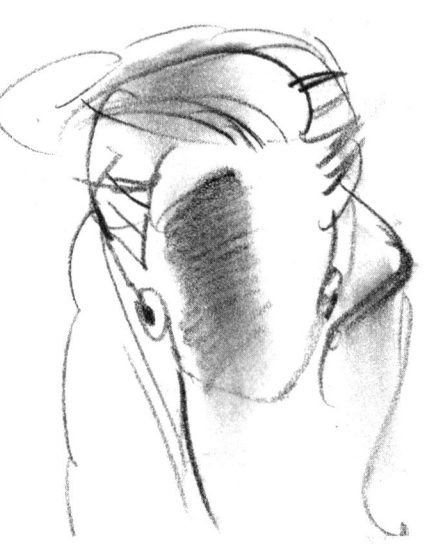

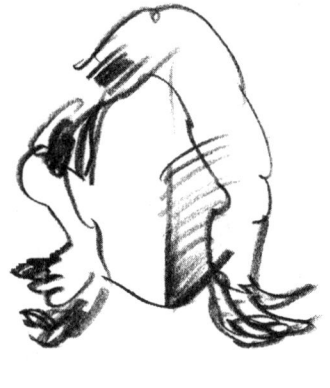
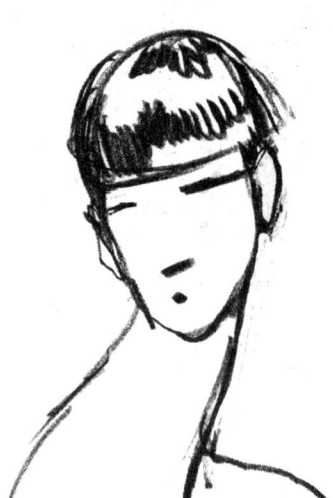
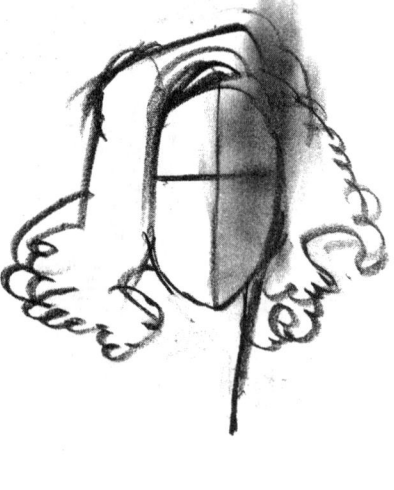

56 FASHION SKETCHING

CHAPTER 4
Hands, Arms, Legs, and Feet

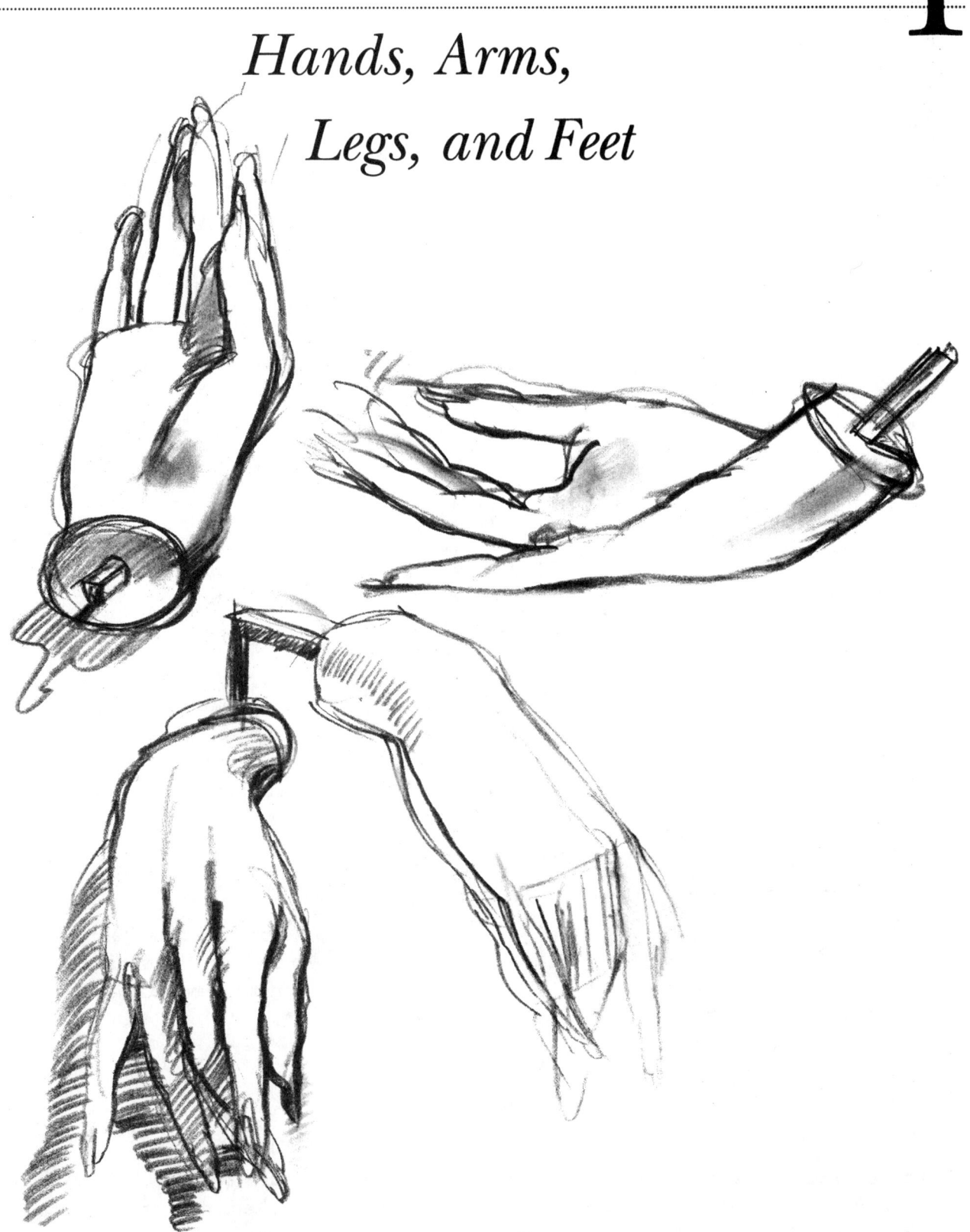

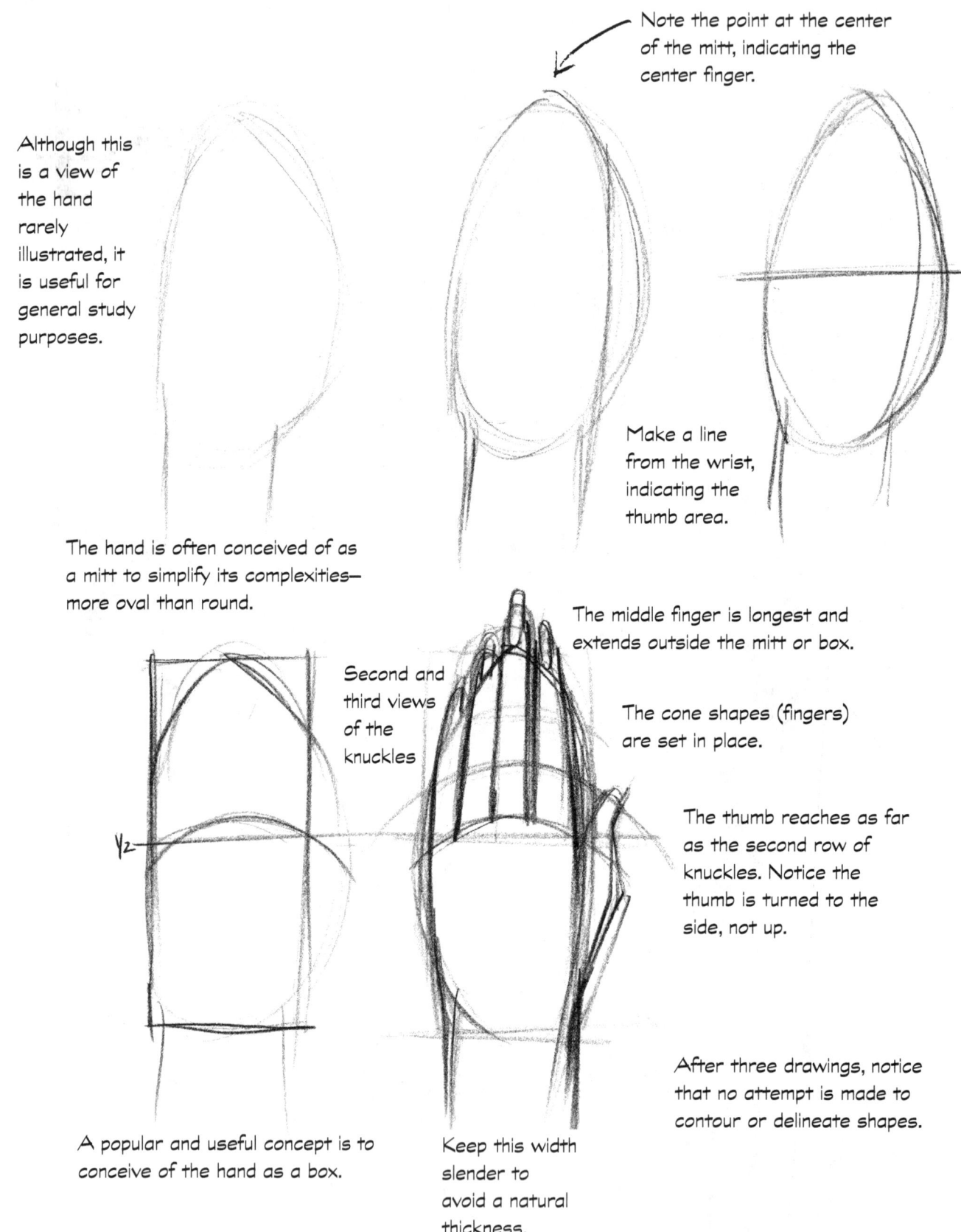

Although this is a view of the hand rarely illustrated, it is useful for general study purposes.

Note the point at the center of the mitt, indicating the center finger.

Make a line from the wrist, indicating the thumb area.

The hand is often conceived of as a mitt to simplify its complexities—more oval than round.

Second and third views of the knuckles

The middle finger is longest and extends outside the mitt or box.

The cone shapes (fingers) are set in place.

The thumb reaches as far as the second row of knuckles. Notice the thumb is turned to the side, not up.

A popular and useful concept is to conceive of the hand as a box.

Keep this width slender to avoid a natural thickness.

After three drawings, notice that no attempt is made to contour or delineate shapes.

With the exception of the thumb, the fingers are cone-shaped, wide at the base (or top of the palm) and narrow at the tips. The thumb is spade-shaped. Proportions must be correct. Keep this in mind for finger placement and full figure. Only after all the elements are put together can flesh contours be studied.

58 FASHION SKETCHING

Students often see hands and feet as being too small or too large for the figure.

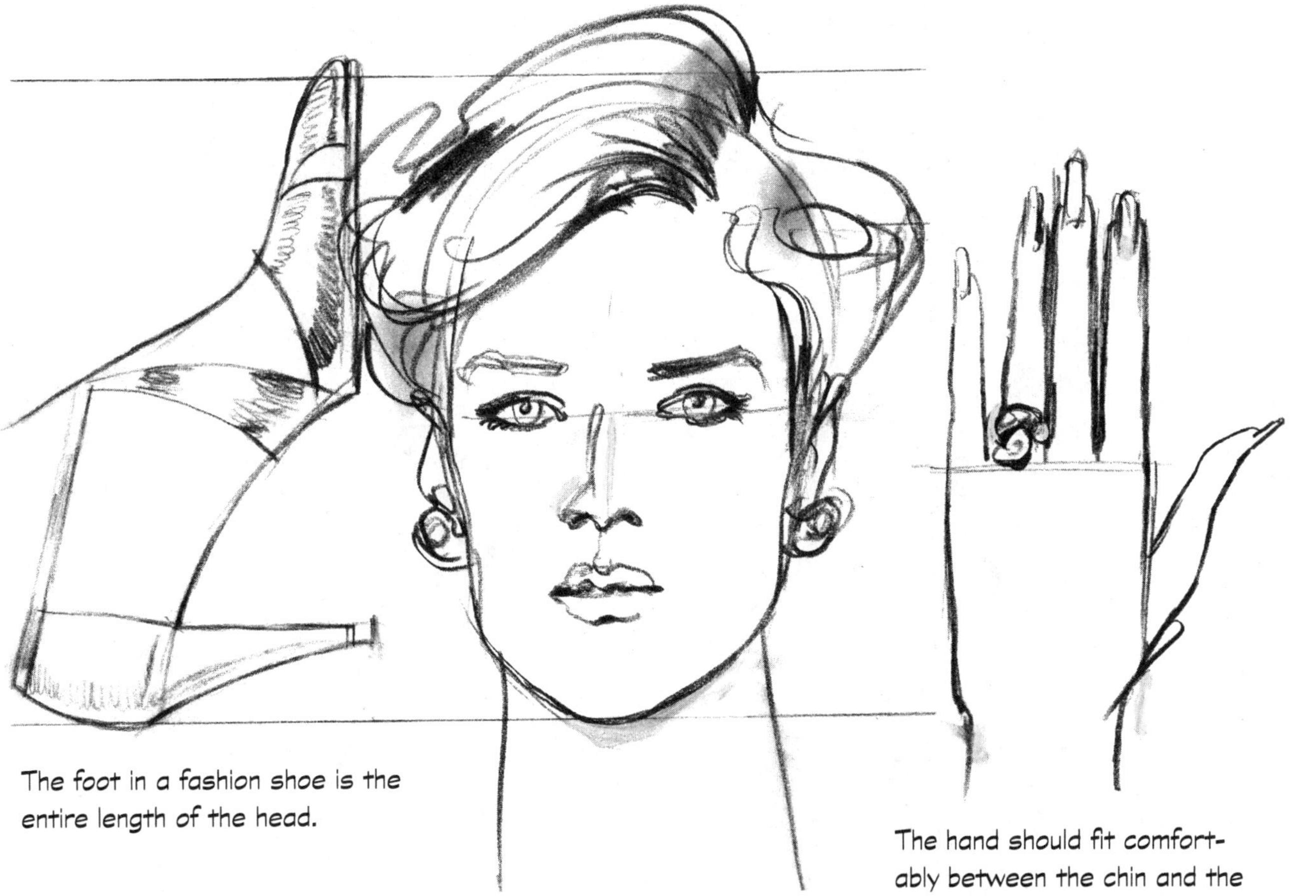

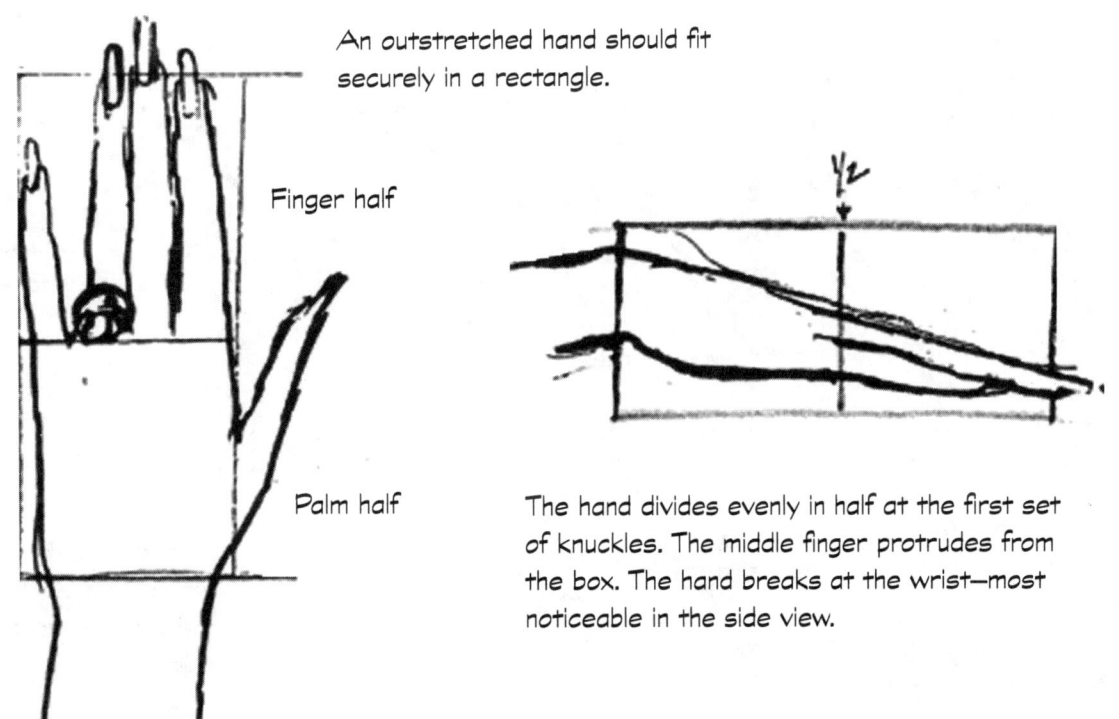

The foot in a fashion shoe is the entire length of the head.

The hand should fit comfortably between the chin and the forehead. Try this on yourself.

An outstretched hand should fit securely in a rectangle.

Finger half

Palm half

The hand divides evenly in half at the first set of knuckles. The middle finger protrudes from the box. The hand breaks at the wrist—most noticeable in the side view.

CHAPTER 4 HANDS, ARMS, LEGS, AND FEET

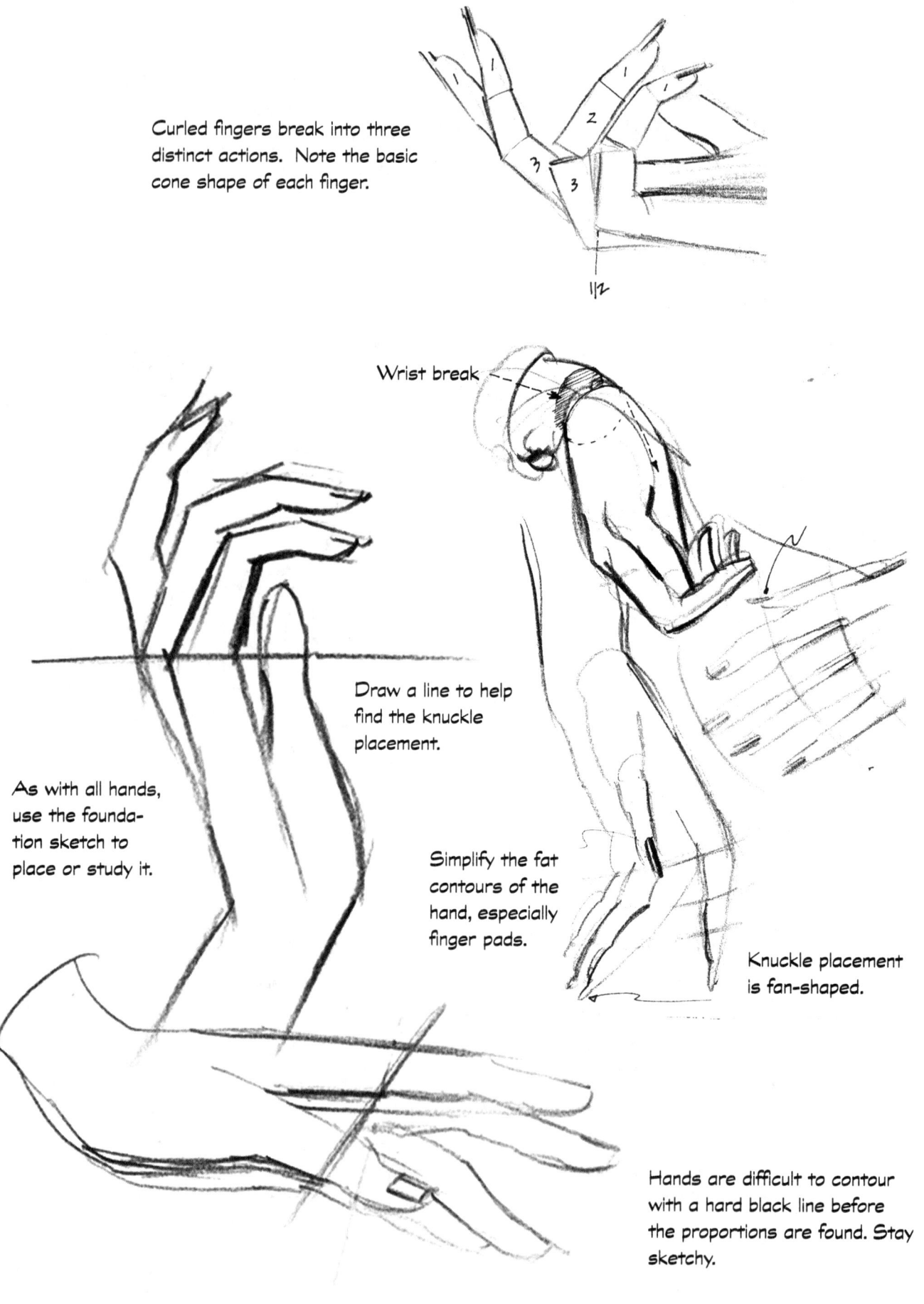

Curled fingers break into three distinct actions. Note the basic cone shape of each finger.

Wrist break

Draw a line to help find the knuckle placement.

As with all hands, use the foundation sketch to place or study it.

Simplify the fat contours of the hand, especially finger pads.

Knuckle placement is fan-shaped.

Hands are difficult to contour with a hard black line before the proportions are found. Stay sketchy.

In the side view of the hand, fingers are seen overlapping each other.

Unless the finger is lifted up and out, keep these areas slender. Remember, part of the finger is hidden.

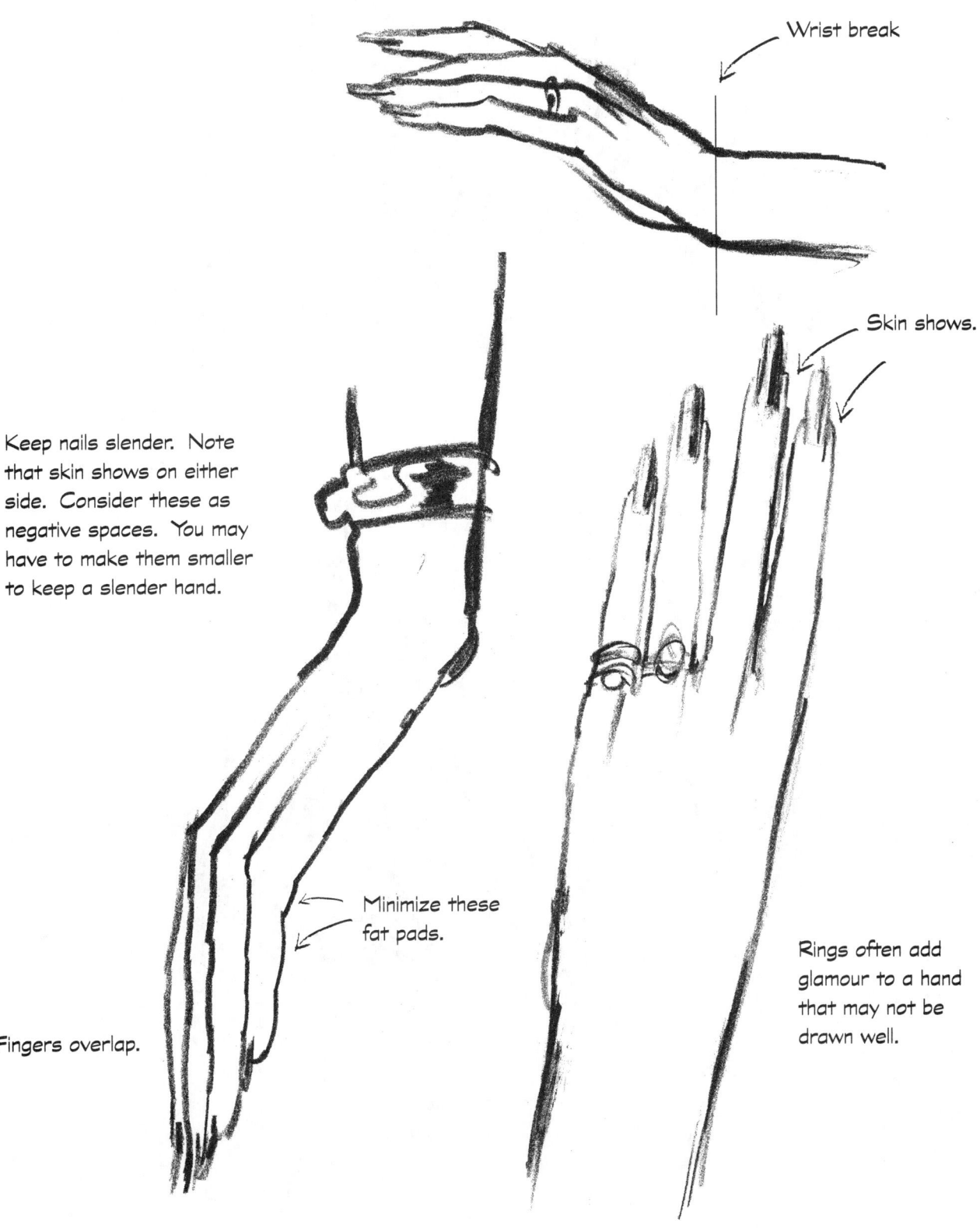

Wrist break

Skin shows.

Keep nails slender. Note that skin shows on either side. Consider these as negative spaces. You may have to make them smaller to keep a slender hand.

Minimize these fat pads.

Fingers overlap.

Rings often add glamour to a hand that may not be drawn well.

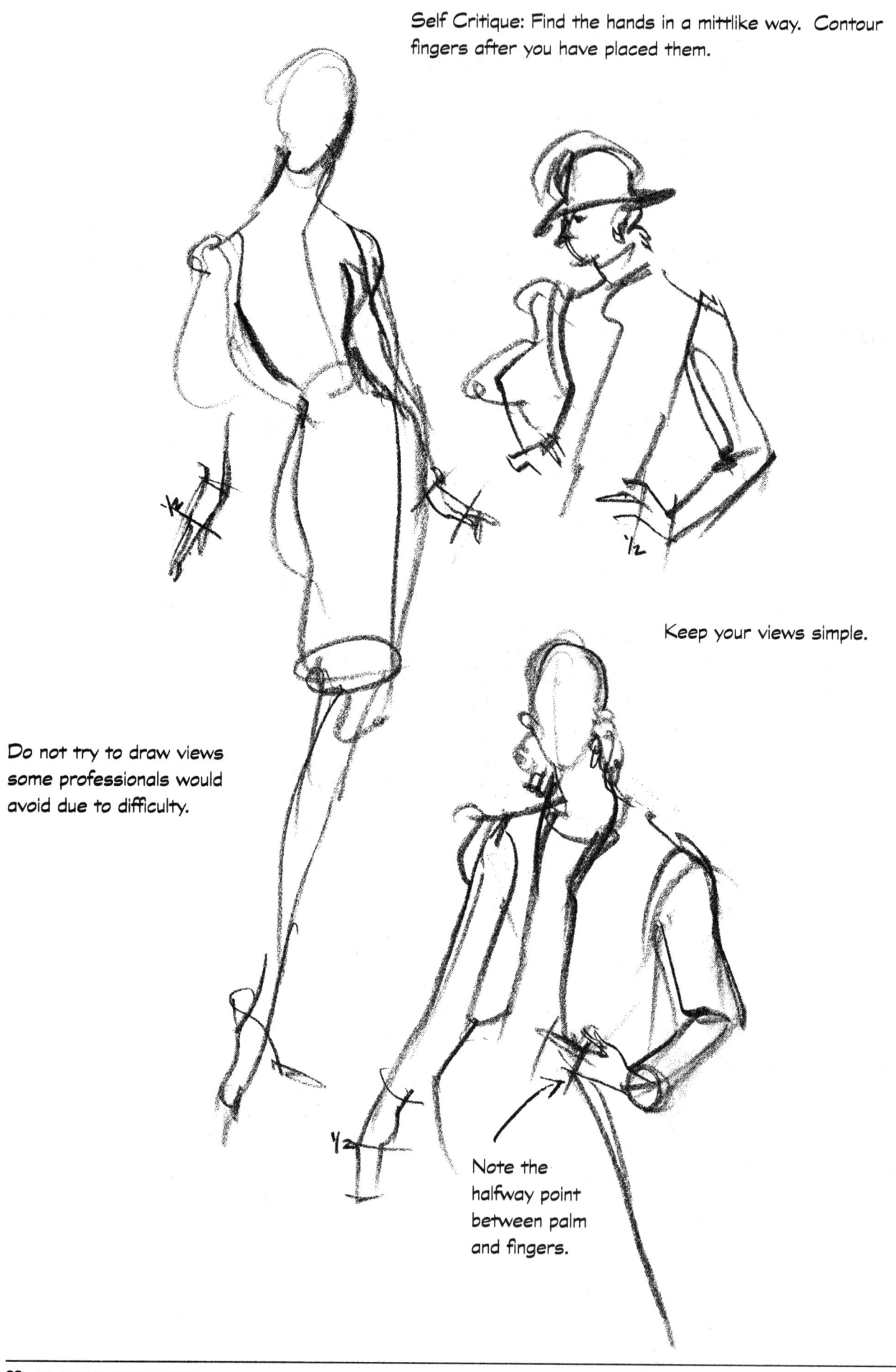

Self Critique: Find the hands in a mittlike way. Contour fingers after you have placed them.

Keep your views simple.

Do not try to draw views some professionals would avoid due to difficulty.

Note the halfway point between palm and fingers.

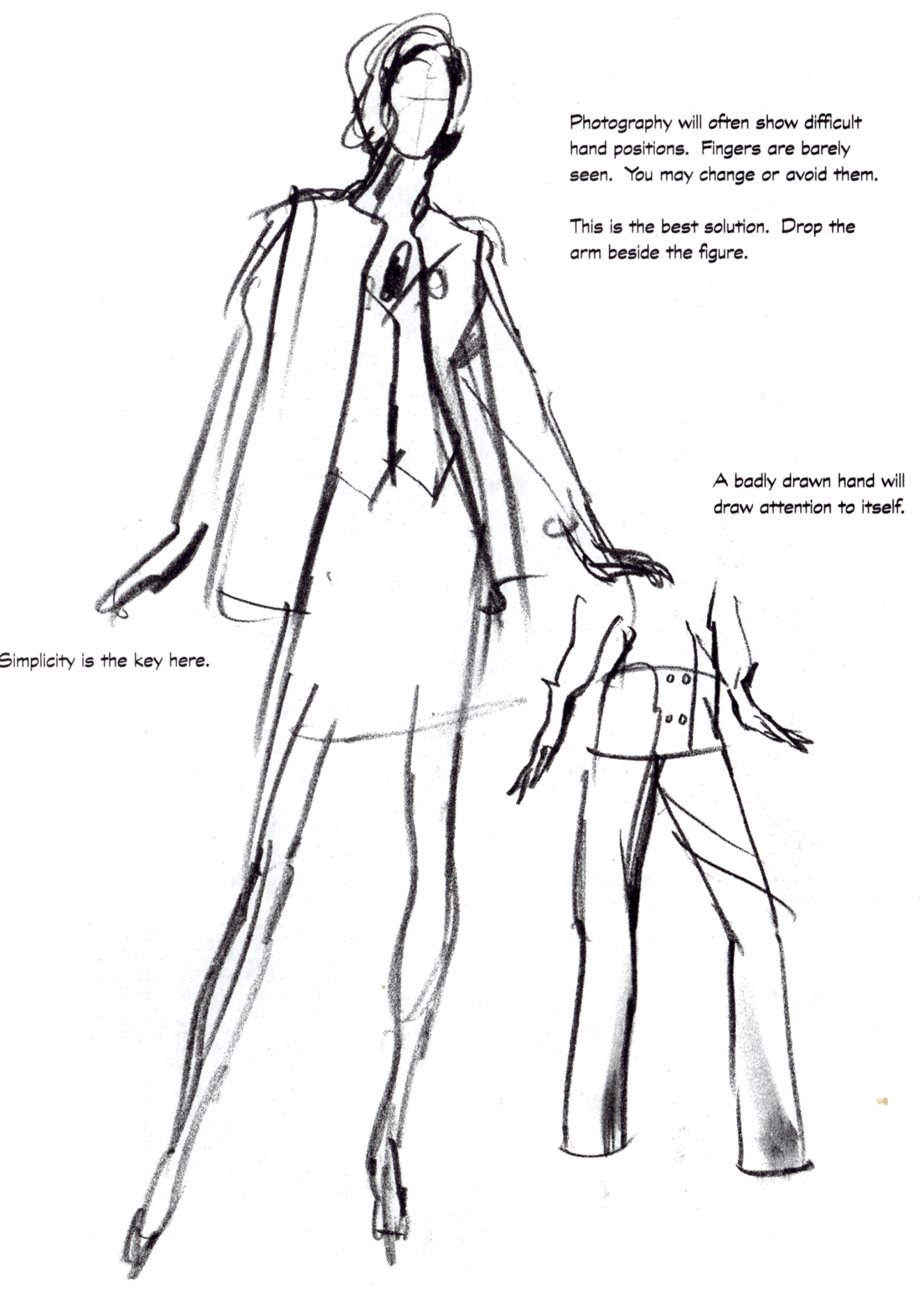

Photography will often show difficult hand positions. Fingers are barely seen. You may change or avoid them.

This is the best solution. Drop the arm beside the figure.

A badly drawn hand will draw attention to itself.

Simplicity is the key here.

CHAPTER 4   HANDS, ARMS, LEGS, AND FEET   63

BEST HAND VIEWS

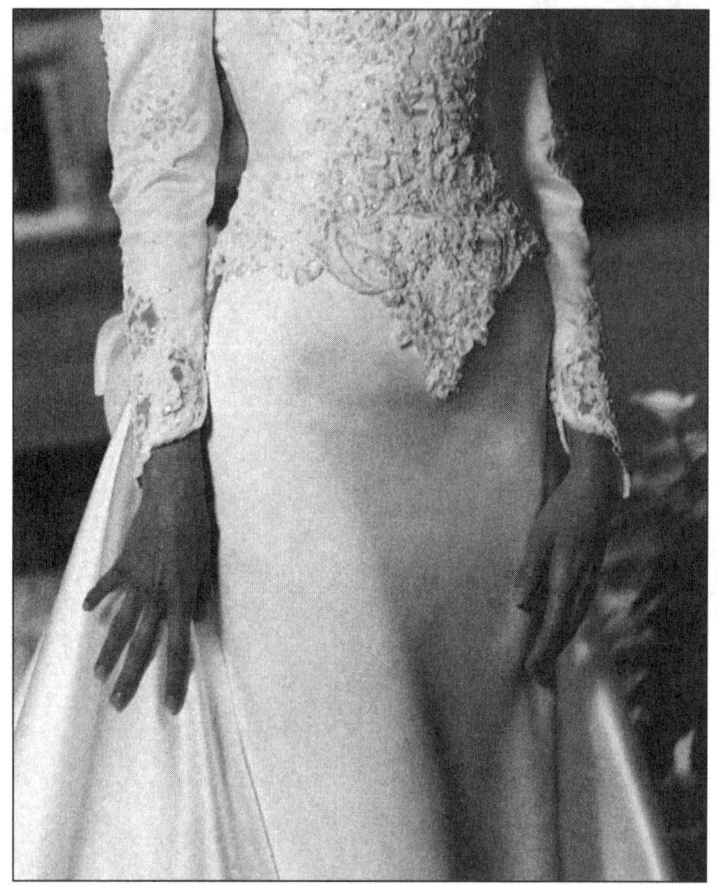
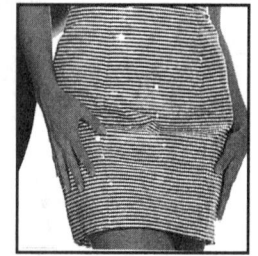
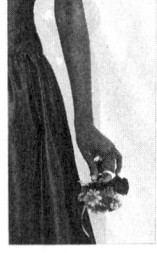
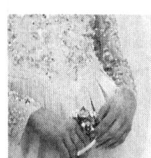
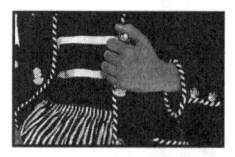
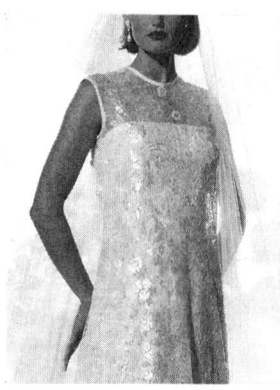
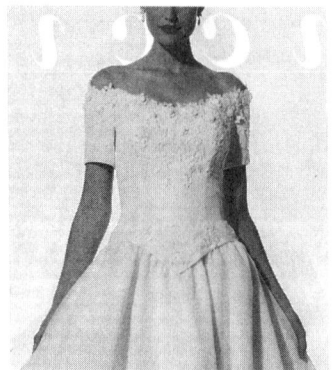
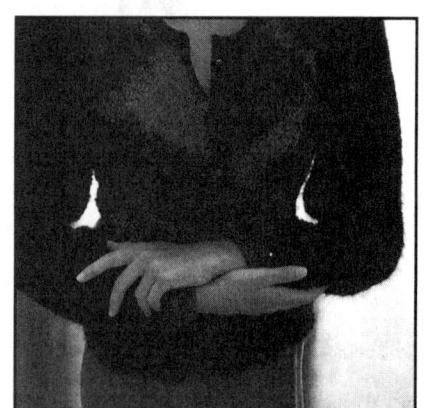

64　FASHION SKETCHING

ARMS

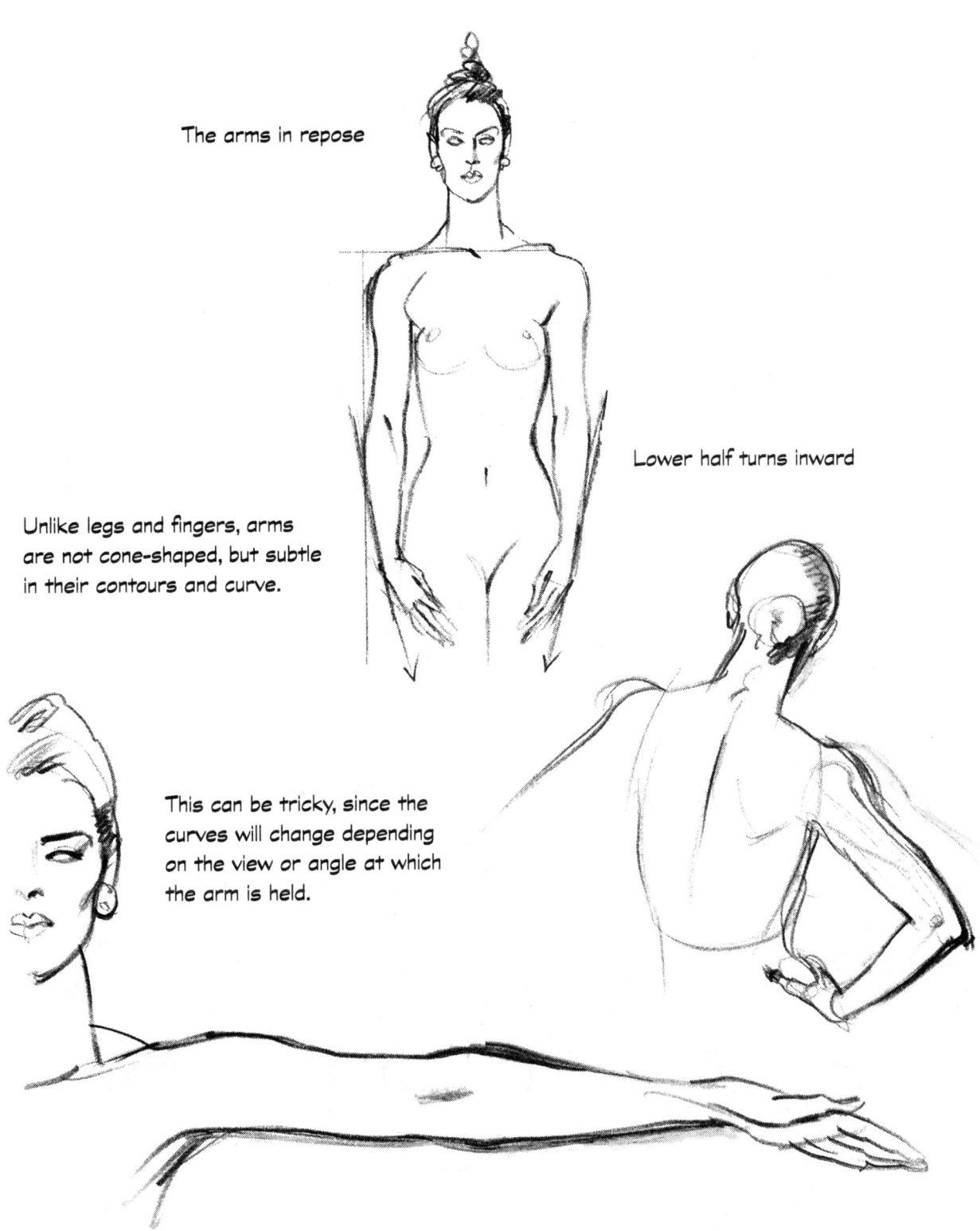

The arms in repose

Lower half turns inward

Unlike legs and fingers, arms are not cone-shaped, but subtle in their contours and curve.

This can be tricky, since the curves will change depending on the view or angle at which the arm is held.

Note the width at the elbow area, due to the addition of two bones in the lower arm. Only the lower arm will resemble the familiar cone shape.

Arms are turned out. Elbows are close to the sides.

Relaxed arms are curved inward, their most natural state.

Hands on hips create V-shaped curves.

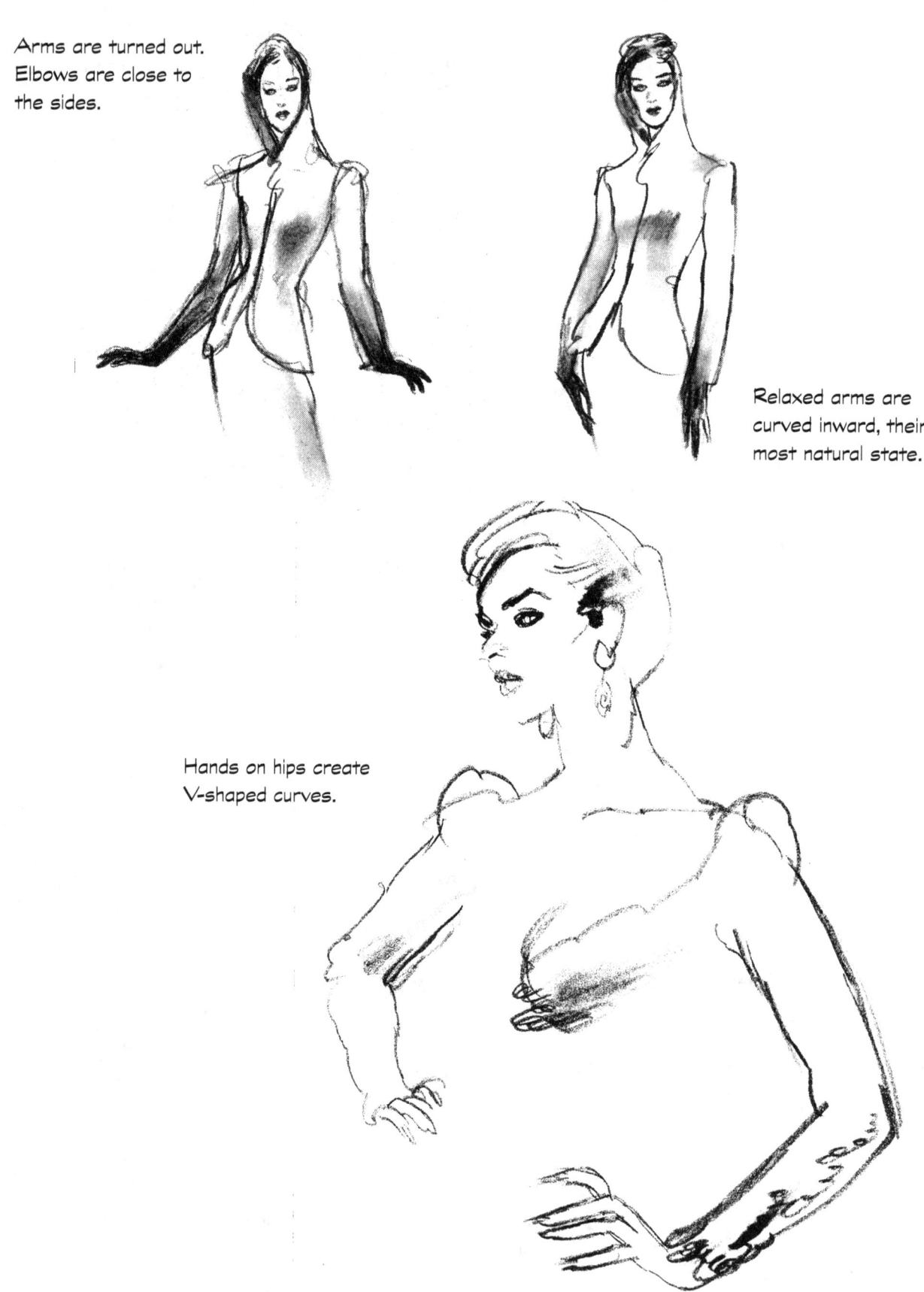

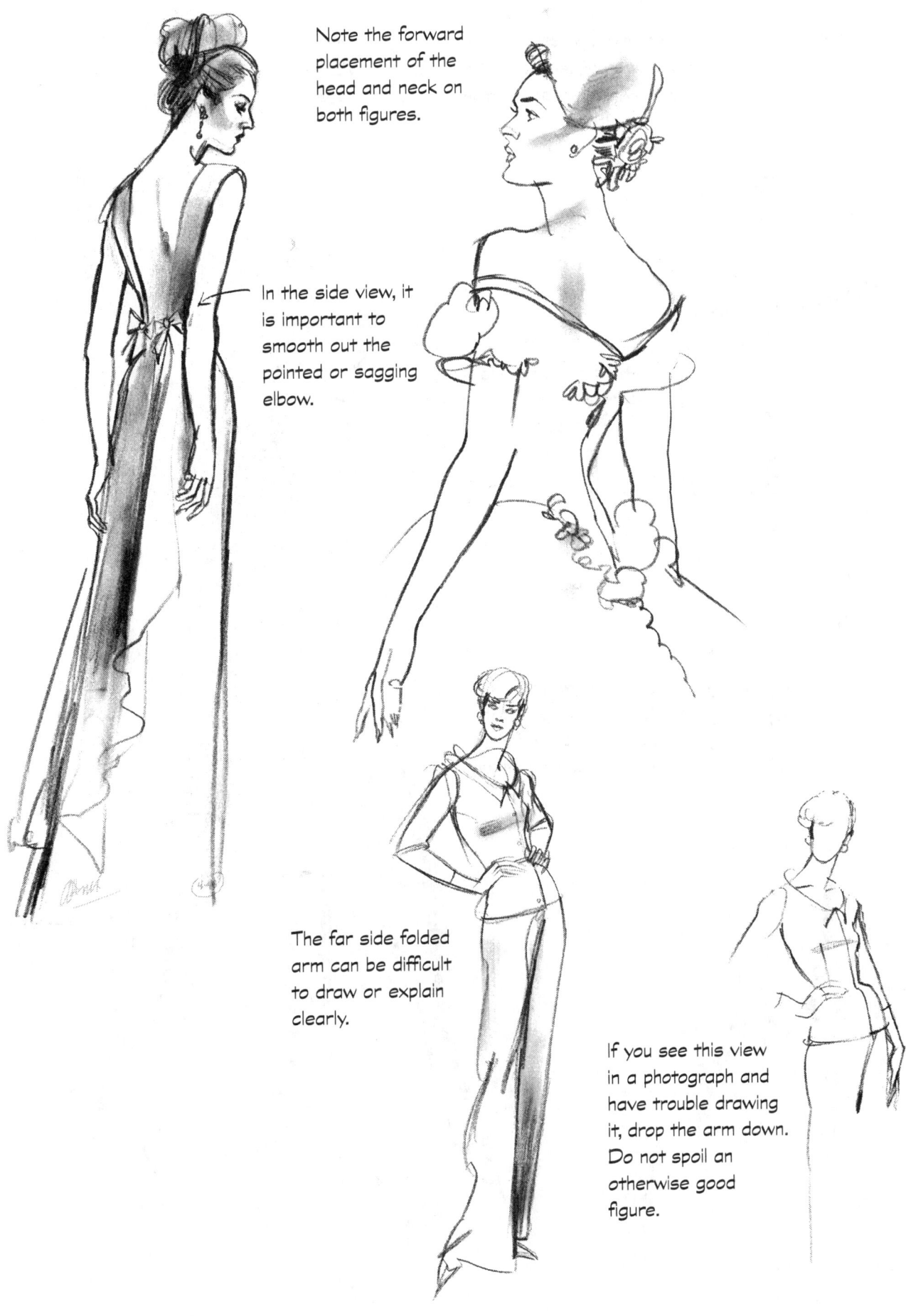

Note the forward placement of the head and neck on both figures.

In the side view, it is important to smooth out the pointed or sagging elbow.

The far side folded arm can be difficult to draw or explain clearly.

If you see this view in a photograph and have trouble drawing it, drop the arm down. Do not spoil an otherwise good figure.

LEGS

Unlike arms, which vary in width, legs are thought of as elongated cones—wide on top and narrow at the ankle. There will be variances from this basic shape.

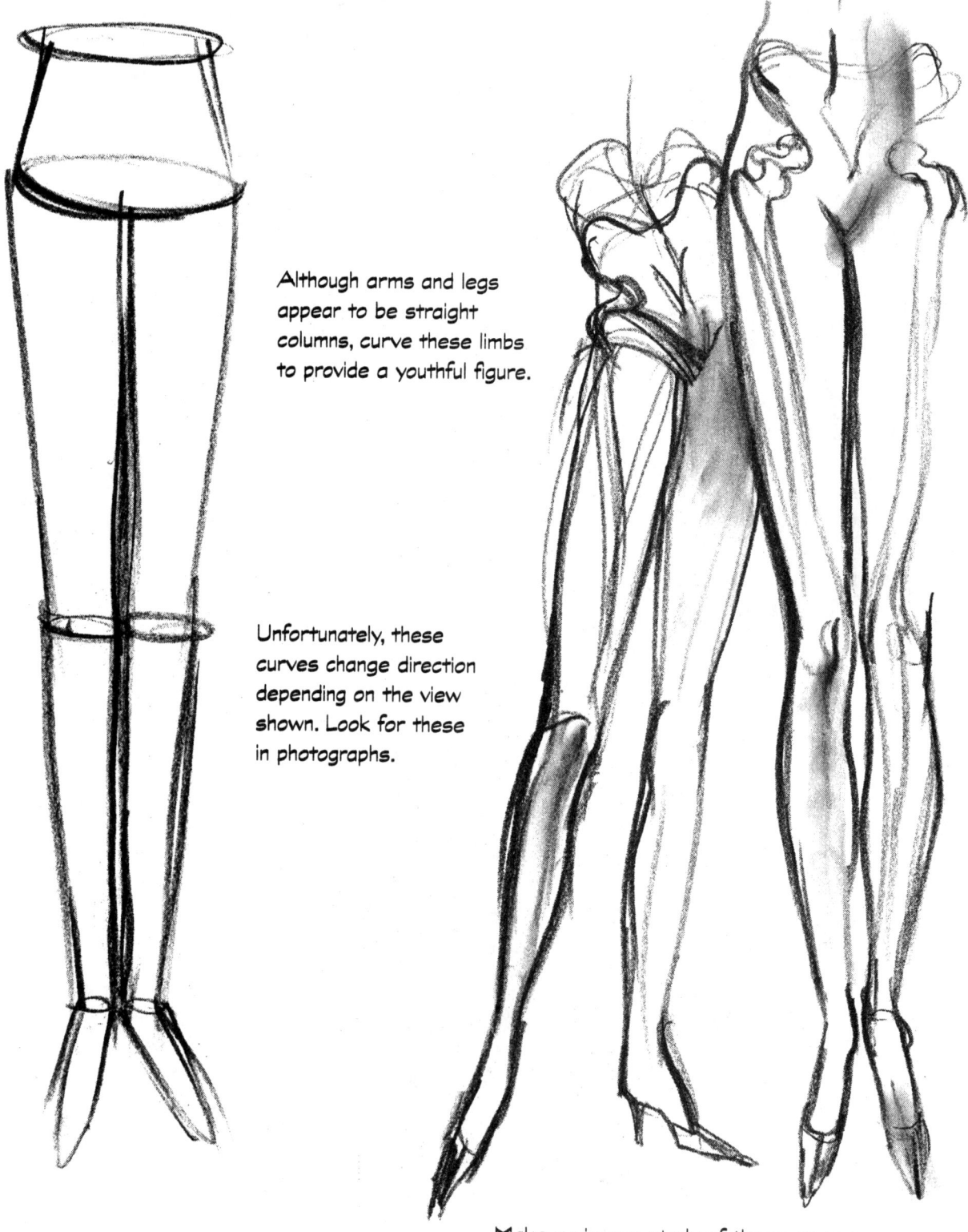

Although arms and legs appear to be straight columns, curve these limbs to provide a youthful figure.

Unfortunately, these curves change direction depending on the view shown. Look for these in photographs.

Make a sincere study of these curves.

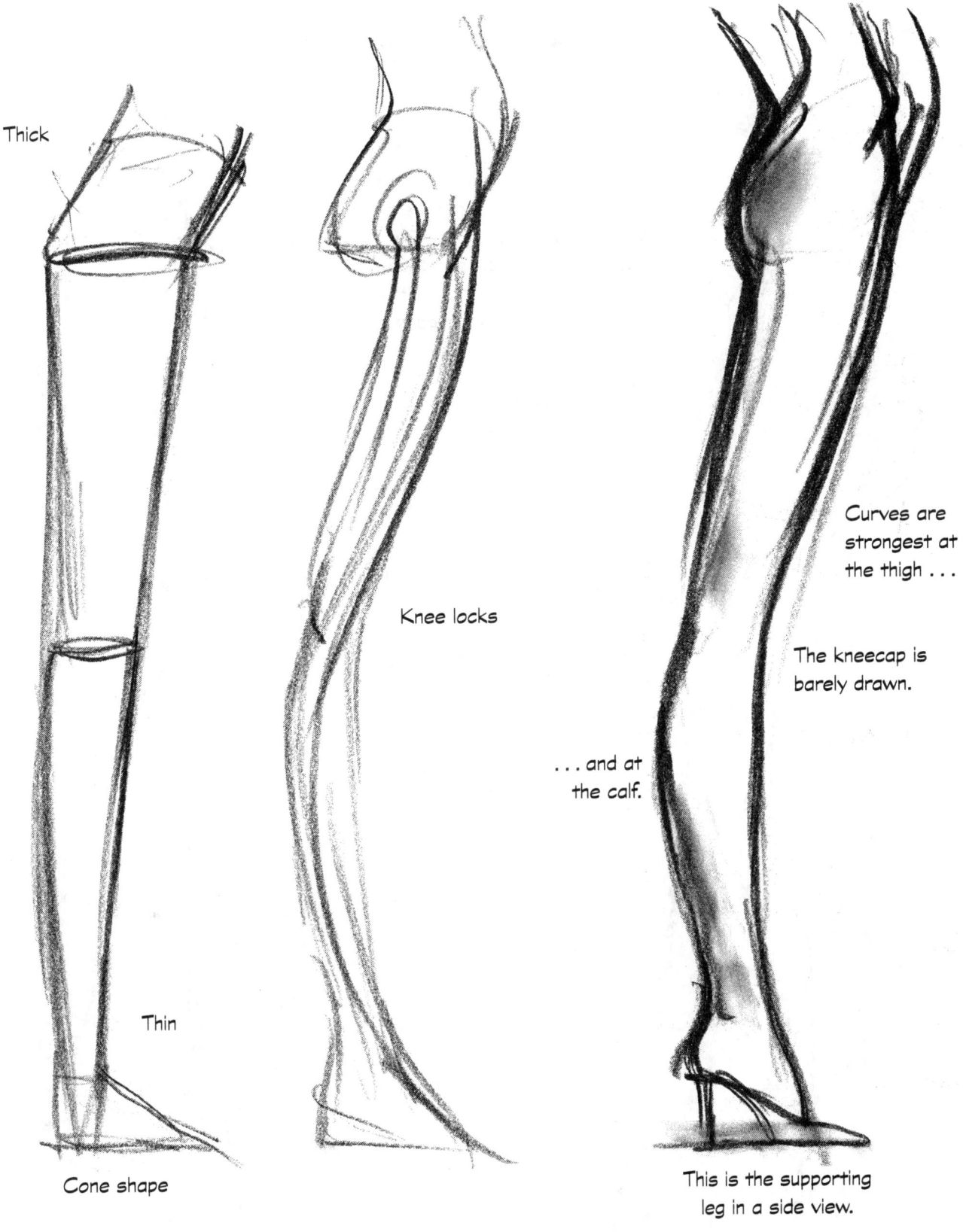

In profile, the leg has a strong back curve.

Thick

Thin

Cone shape

Knee locks

Curves are strongest at the thigh...

The kneecap is barely drawn.

...and at the calf.

This is the supporting leg in a side view.

CHAPTER 4 HANDS, ARMS, LEGS, AND FEET

Do not draw the anatomy of the knee. A stocking will smooth out this area. Look for this effect in a department store advertisement. Indicate this area with a shadow or a line.

The same is true for ankles. This can be a clumsy-looking area, especially the front view. Simply play them down or leave them out. In a side view, ankles may be drawn more naturally.

The ankle is the breaking point, as the wrist is for the hand. The ankle gives grace to a moving or turned-out foot. This action gives elegance to an otherwise clumsy foot seen in some photographs. It is all right to change what you see in order to improve it.

Back view legs have the same curve as the front, but the side view curves are different. Check the drawing to see that you have given the legs these movements, especially the lower half which often appears straight and stiff.

Note the flow of leg curve into the foot instep.

Tight-fitting slacks and jeans reveal the leg curves and contours (or silhouettes).

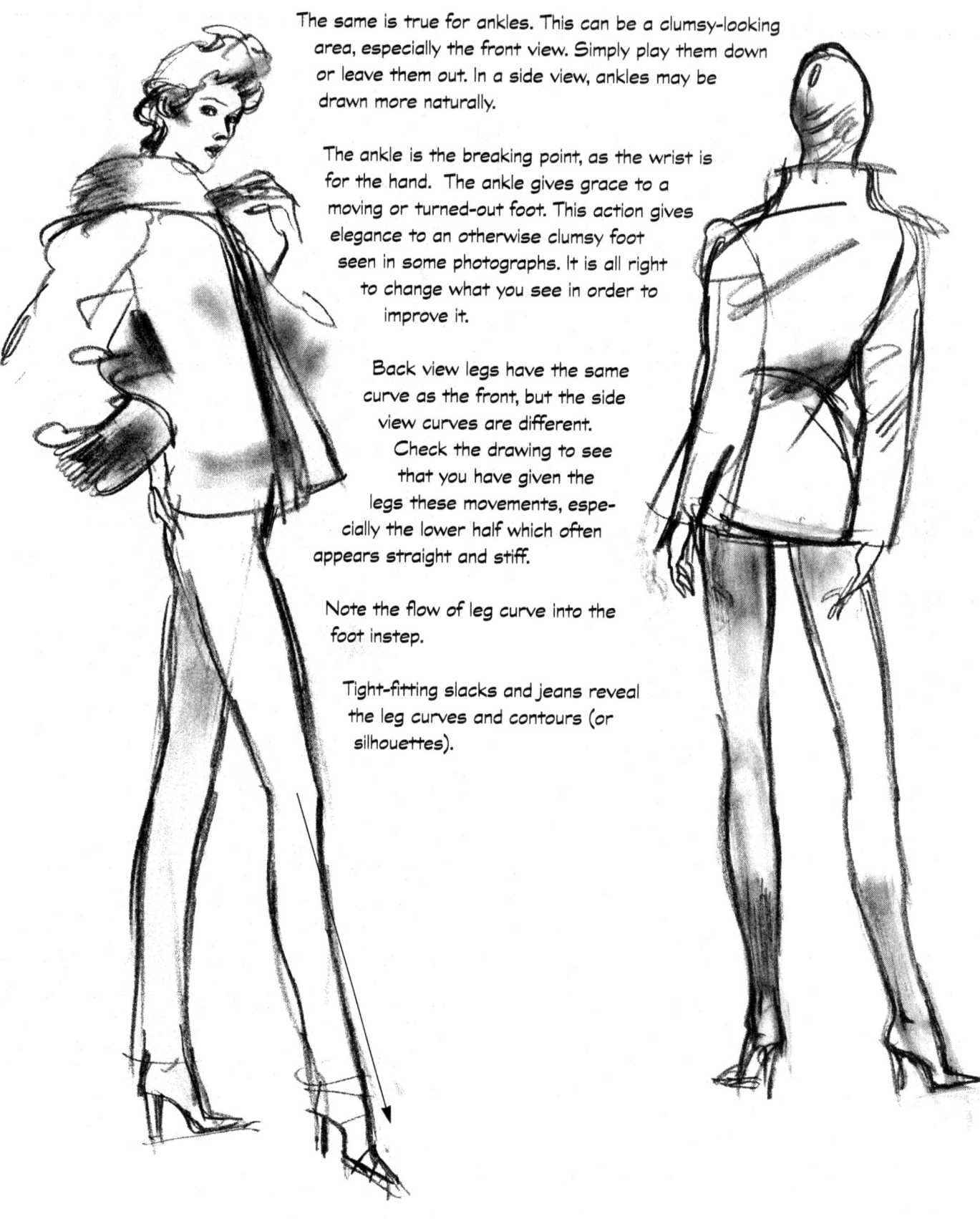

70 FASHION SKETCHING

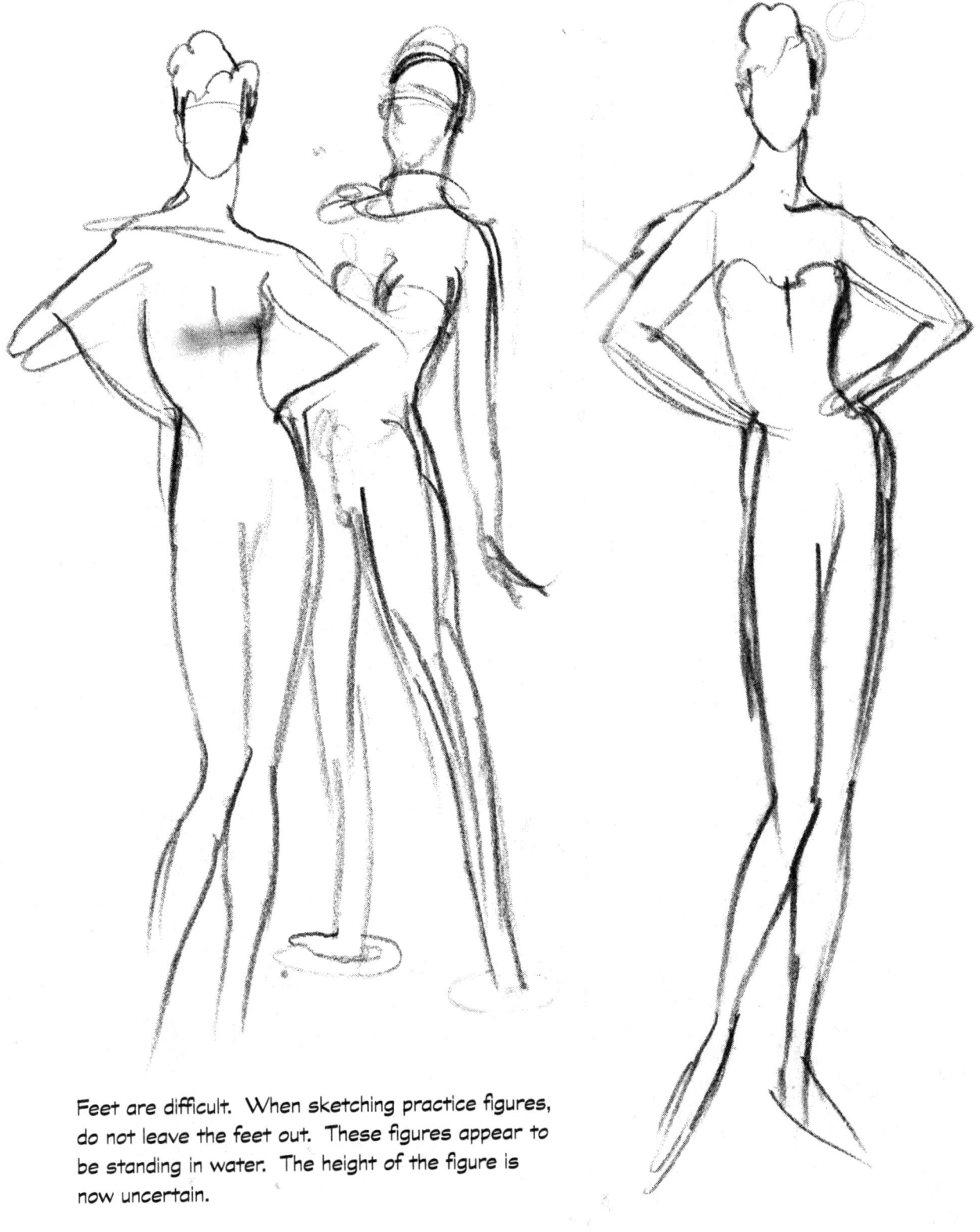

Feet are difficult. When sketching practice figures, do not leave the feet out. These figures appear to be standing in water. The height of the figure is now uncertain.

Attempt some indication of feet, no matter how simple. Now the figure seems complete. Its action is understood.

WOMEN'S SHOES

A good way to draw feet is to draw feet in shoes or to draw just shoes. This is a mechanical shape which only vaguely resembles the naked foot. Find different shoes and different views to draw. When drawing any shoe, remember to keep it new in appearance.

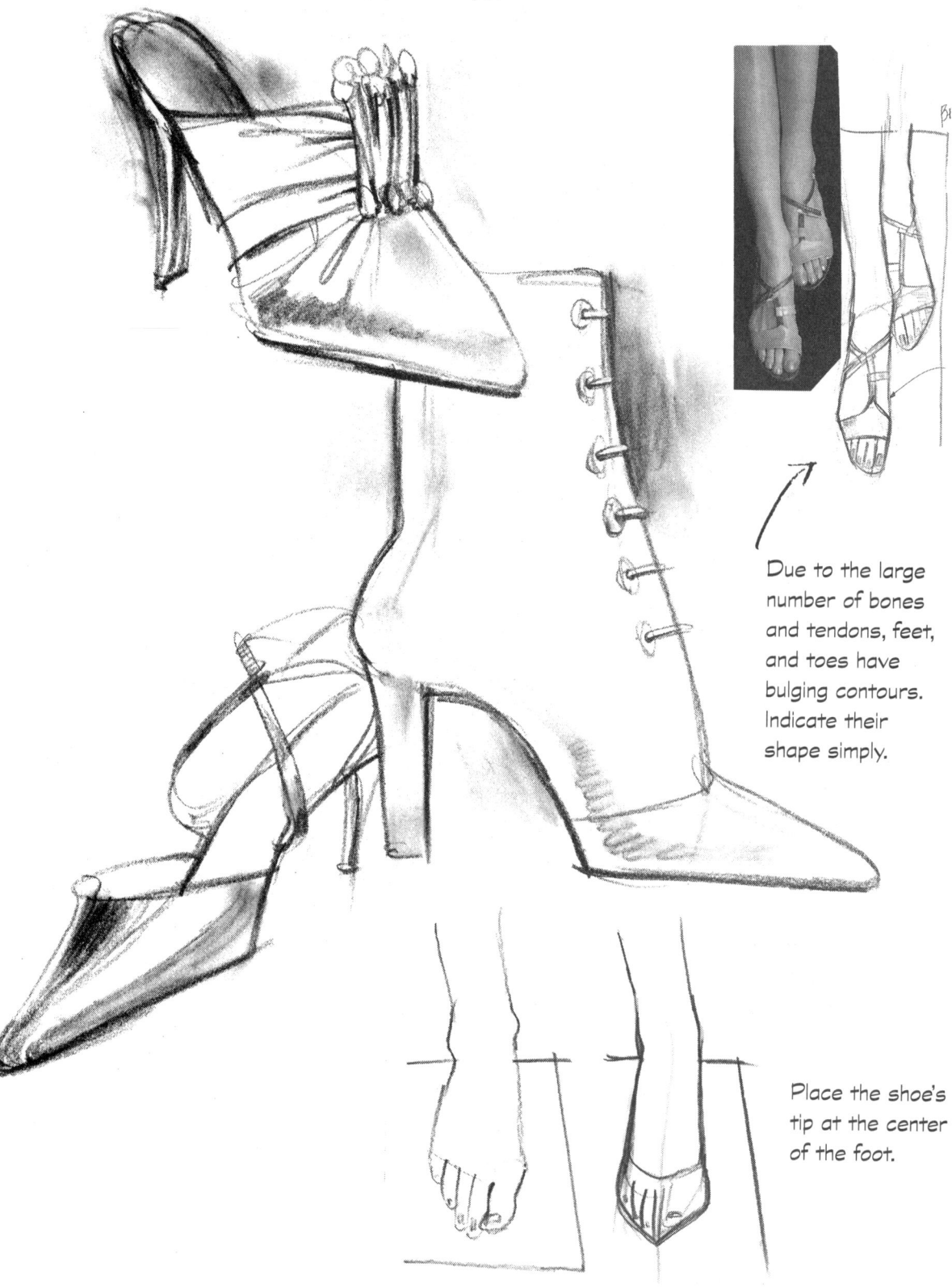

Due to the large number of bones and tendons, feet, and toes have bulging contours. Indicate their shape simply.

Place the shoe's tip at the center of the foot.

THE EFFECT OF THE INSTEP IN LOWER HEELS

The instep is lower.
Lower heels cause the instep to retain its normal bare-footed appearance.

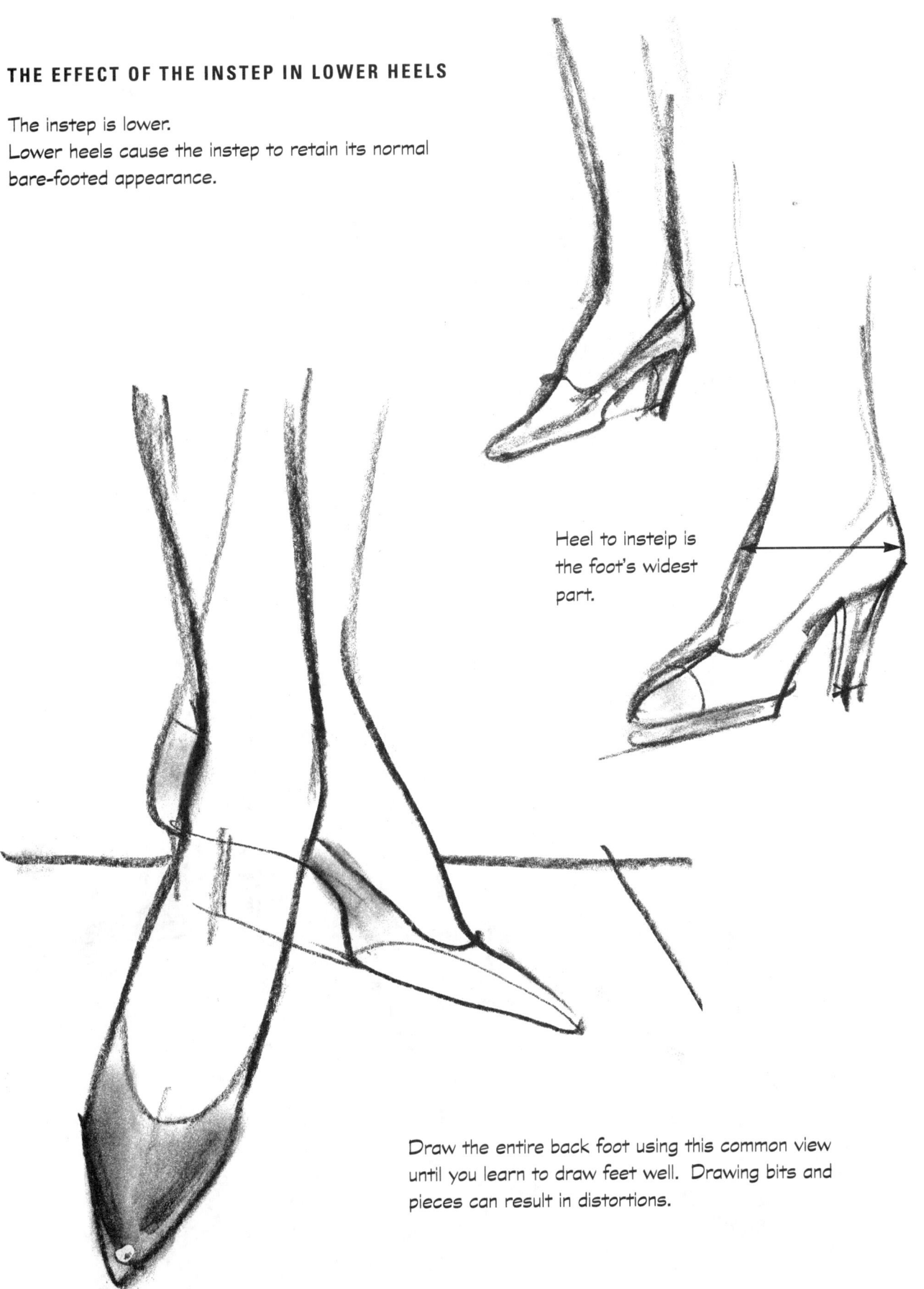

Heel to insteip is the foot's widest part.

Draw the entire back foot using this common view until you learn to draw feet well. Drawing bits and pieces can result in distortions.

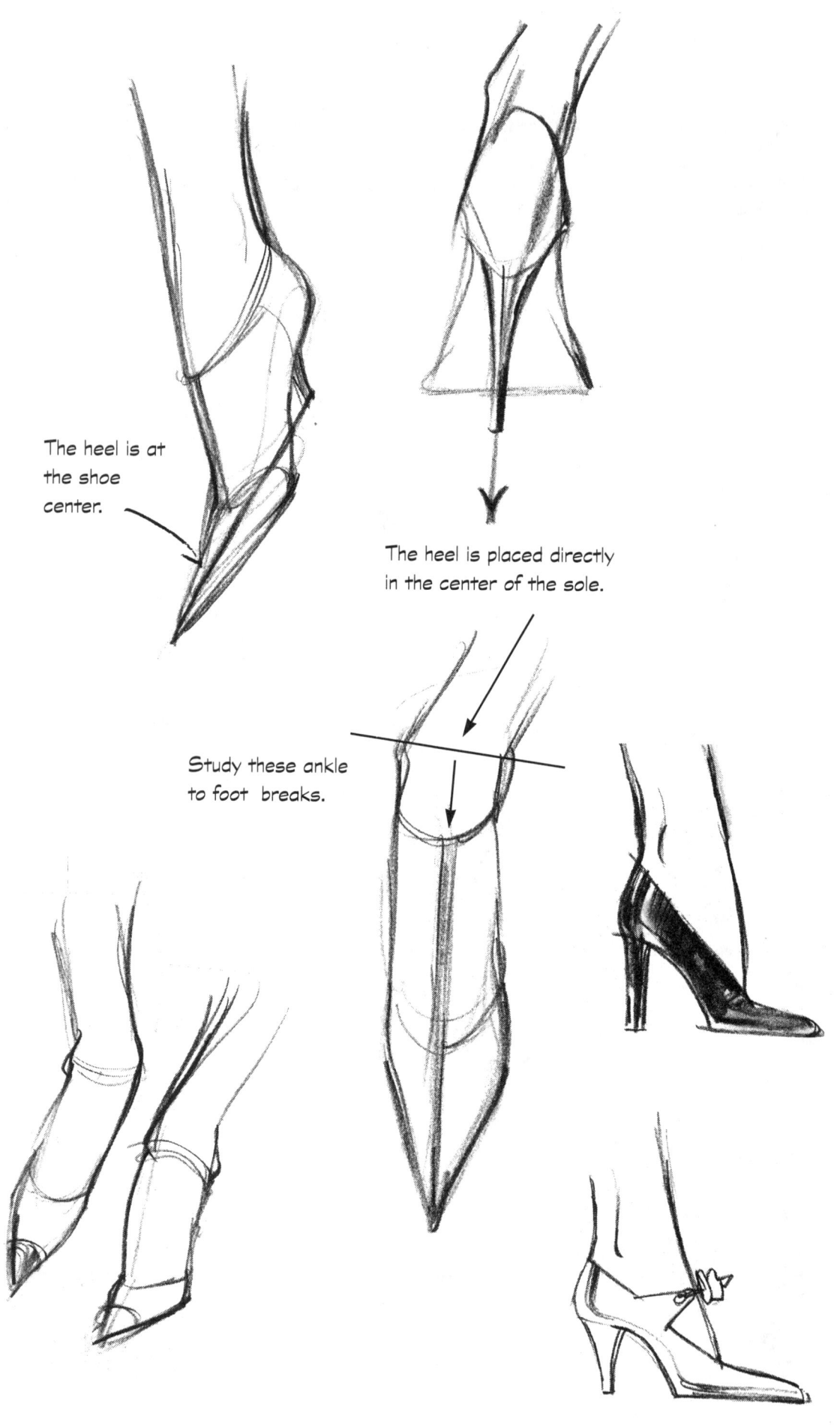

CHAPTER 5
Solidifying the Figure

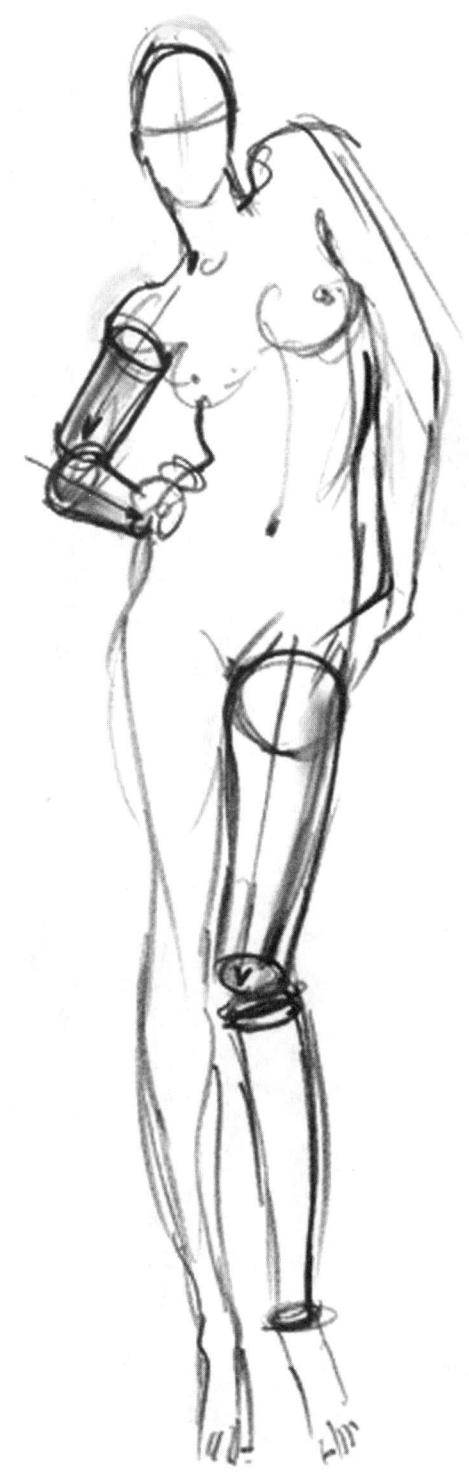

Study of the human skeleton is helpful. Human flesh often hides important information about the construction of the body.

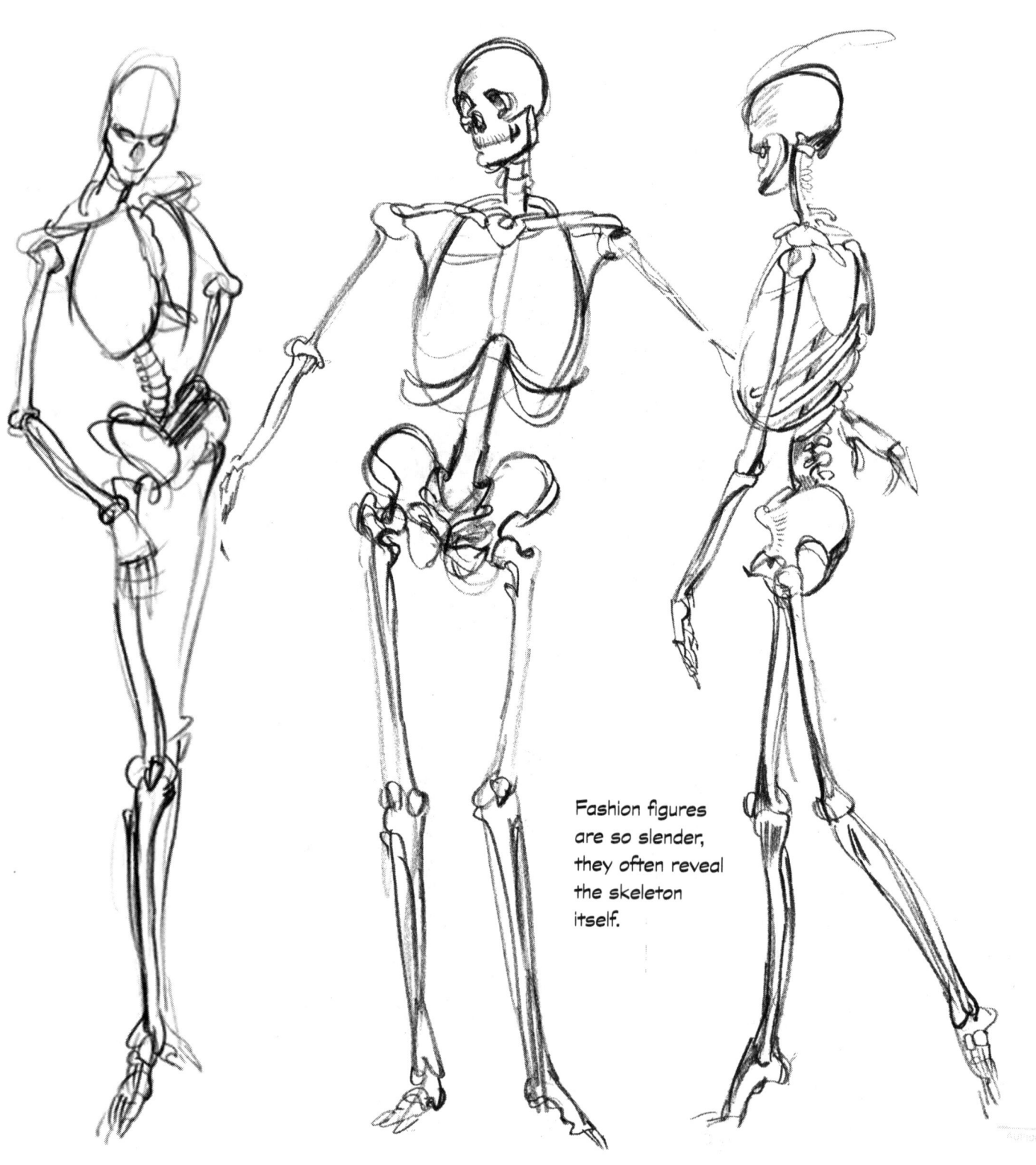

Fashion figures are so slender, they often reveal the skeleton itself.

It is helpful to think of the body and its parts as a series of cylinders or other shapes that suggest firmness and roundness. This will help prevent the figures from becoming rubbery or flat.

Work these forms into the gesture drawing. Draw through the ellipses whether you see them or not. As suggested previously, study the works of old and modern masters.

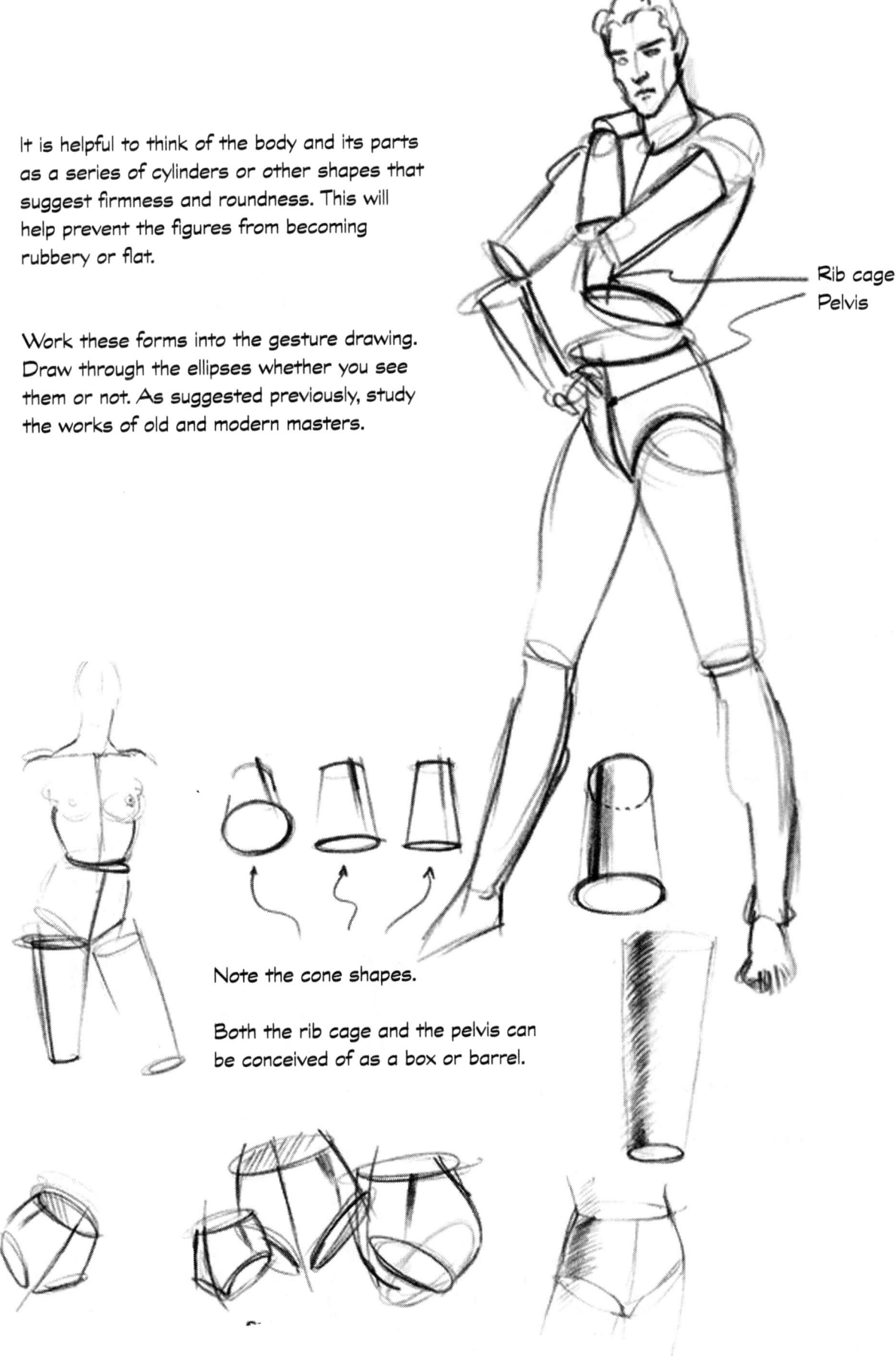

Rib cage
Pelvis

Note the cone shapes.

Both the rib cage and the pelvis can be conceived of as a box or barrel.

CHAPTER 5 SOLIDIFYING THE FIGURE

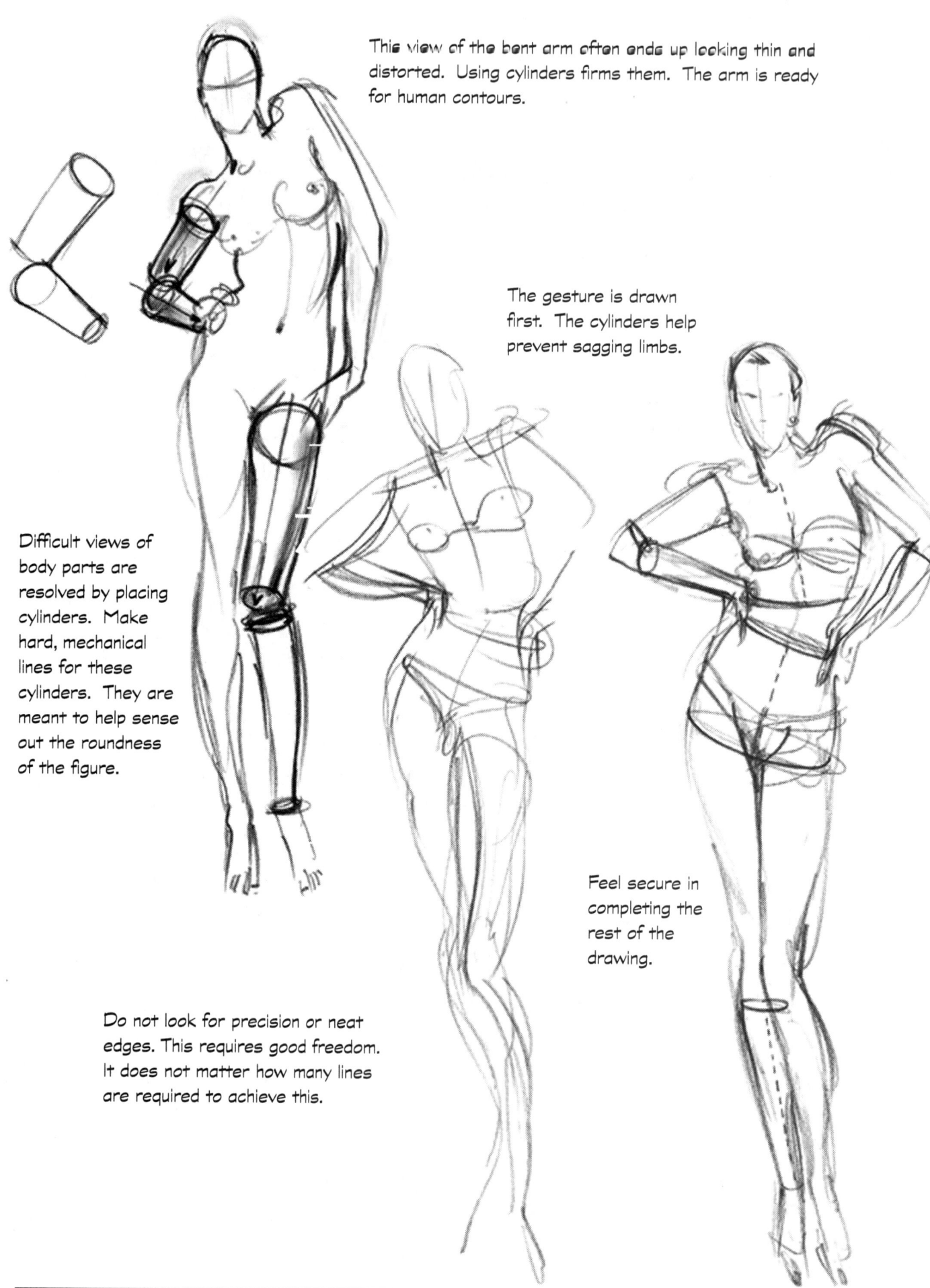

This view of the bent arm often ends up looking thin and distorted. Using cylinders firms them. The arm is ready for human contours.

The gesture is drawn first. The cylinders help prevent sagging limbs.

Difficult views of body parts are resolved by placing cylinders. Make hard, mechanical lines for these cylinders. They are meant to help sense out the roundness of the figure.

Feel secure in completing the rest of the drawing.

Do not look for precision or neat edges. This requires good freedom. It does not matter how many lines are required to achieve this.

POSITIVE AND NEGATIVE SPACES

Positive space is the subject. Negative space is the background.

Recognizing these spaces on and around the figure is helpful when deciding on the placement of the limbs. Showing a figure with arms or legs extended can result in distortions. One way to control distortion is to draw the space between the limbs or between the limb and the body.

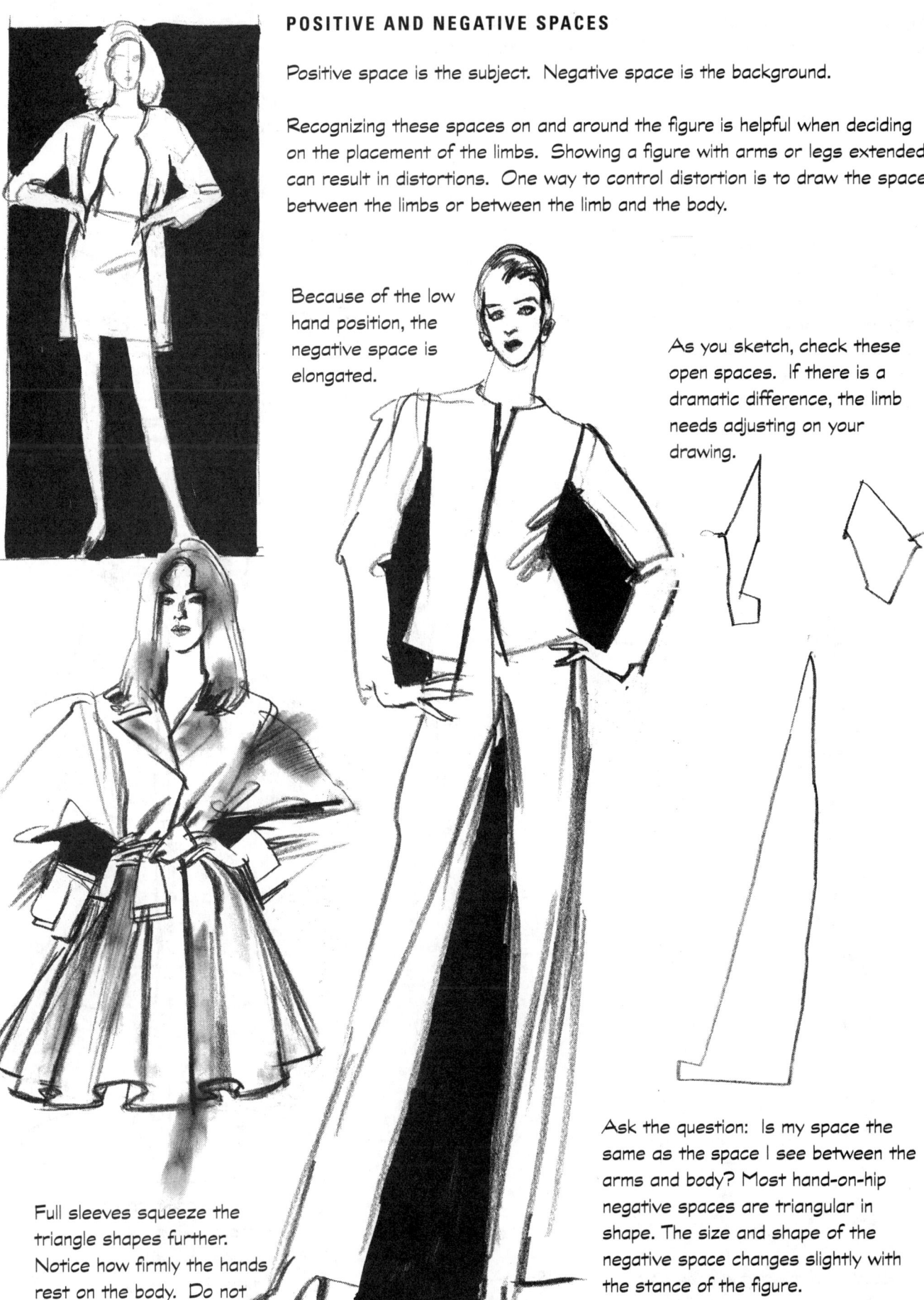

Because of the low hand position, the negative space is elongated.

As you sketch, check these open spaces. If there is a dramatic difference, the limb needs adjusting on your drawing.

Full sleeves squeeze the triangle shapes further. Notice how firmly the hands rest on the body. Do not allow hands to float.

Ask the question: Is my space the same as the space I see between the arms and body? Most hand-on-hip negative spaces are triangular in shape. The size and shape of the negative space changes slightly with the stance of the figure.

CHAPTER 5 SOLIDIFYING THE FIGURE

The ellipse is a circle seen in perspective. Circles and ellipses are everywhere on the clothed figure. Sensing these around the body gives well-fitting clothing as well as solid and convincing structure to drawings.

Imagine a plate on a wall, perfectly circular, suddenly falling to the floor. In stop action we see a series of ellipses as the plate falls. Notice that at eye level, the circle/ellipse appears to be straight across. This is the best view.

Where some typical ellipses are located:

Hats

Collars and necklines

Cuffs

Hemlines

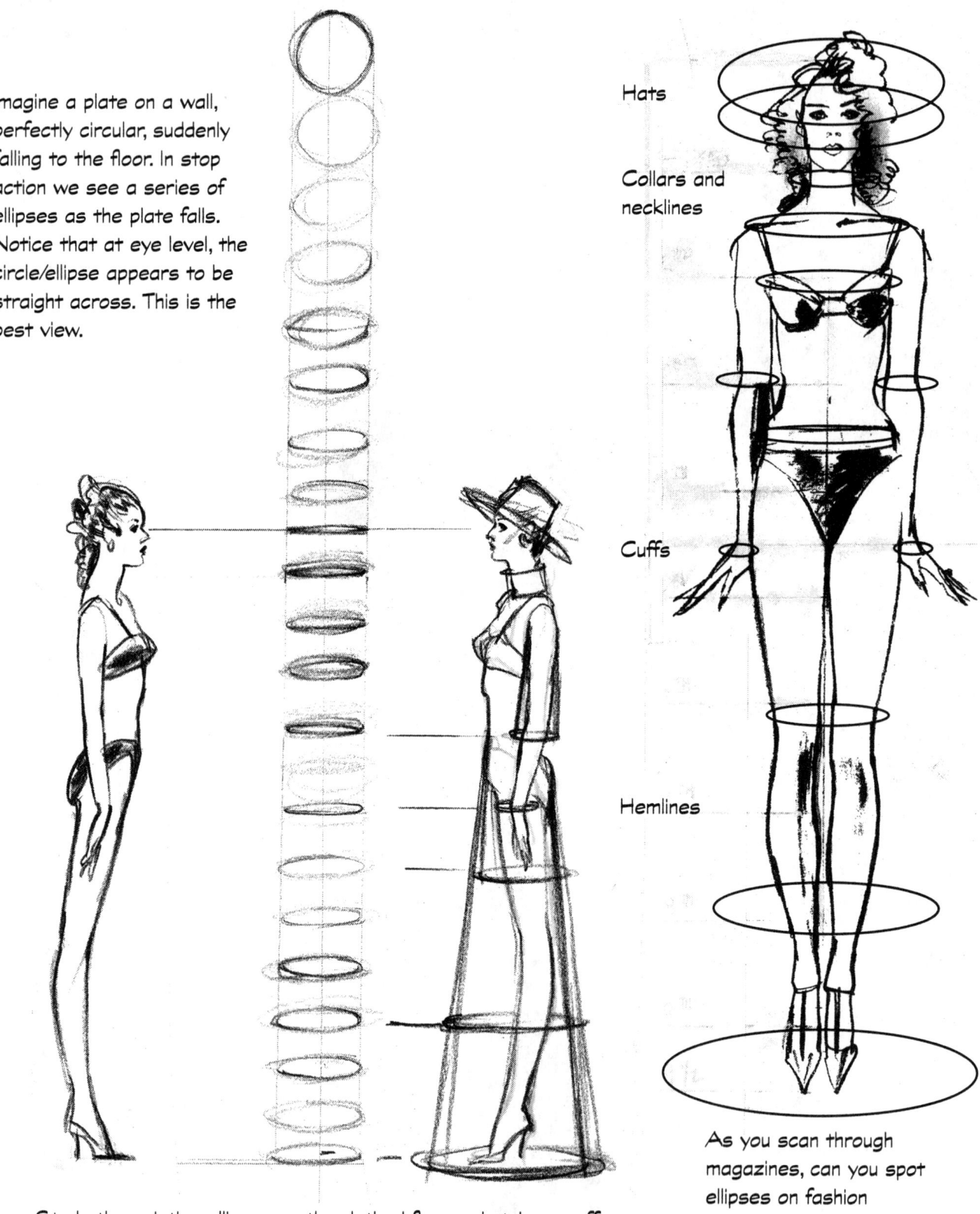

Study the existing ellipses on the clothed figure— hat, hem, cuffs, collars, and so on. Look for them as the work progresses.

As you scan through magazines, can you spot ellipses on fashion figures?

80 FASHION SKETCHING

Use the gesture sketch to sense out the figure and its ellipses.

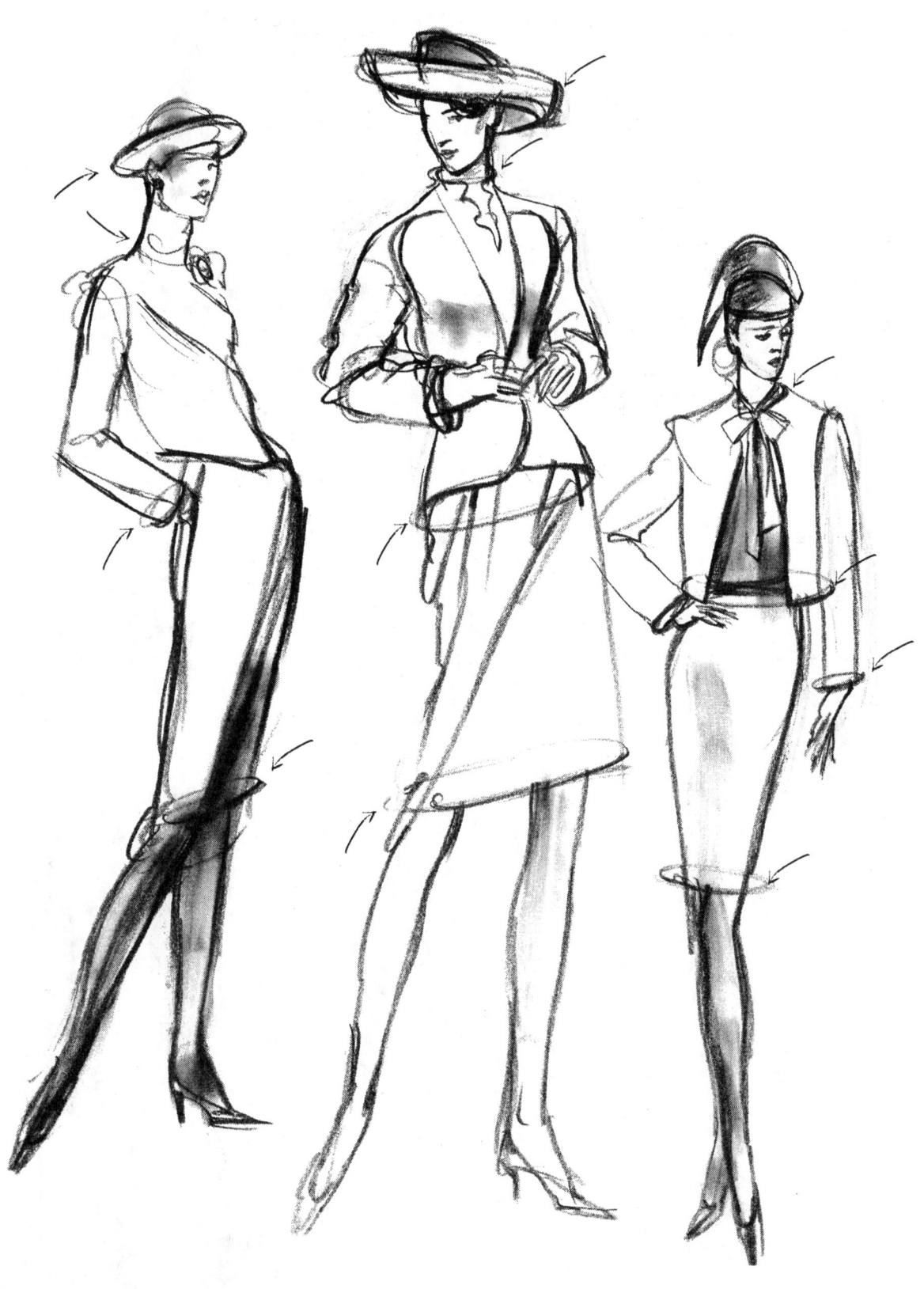

CHAPTER 5 SOLIDIFYING THE FIGURE

STEP-BY-STEP FIGURE DRAWING

- A light gesture sketch is used to lay out action and proportion. Observe opposing slants closely.
- Although not seen, try to understand the position of the legs.
- Next, block in the head, features, and hair.
- In this rough state, judge the costume. What are the design and proportion of the sleeves and skirt?
- The feet are correctly placed because they were drawn from the legs.
- Add details such as hair, seams, patterns, and so on toward the finish of the drawing.
- I have changed the head because I prefer it this way. It is all right to do this with any other area if done convincingly.

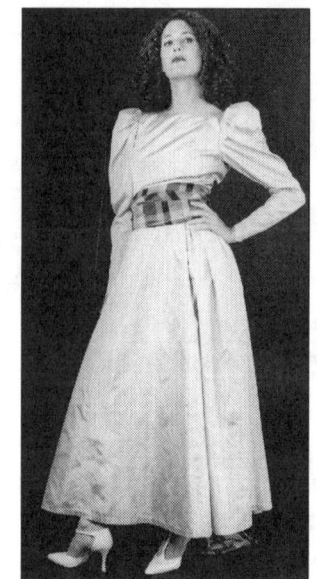

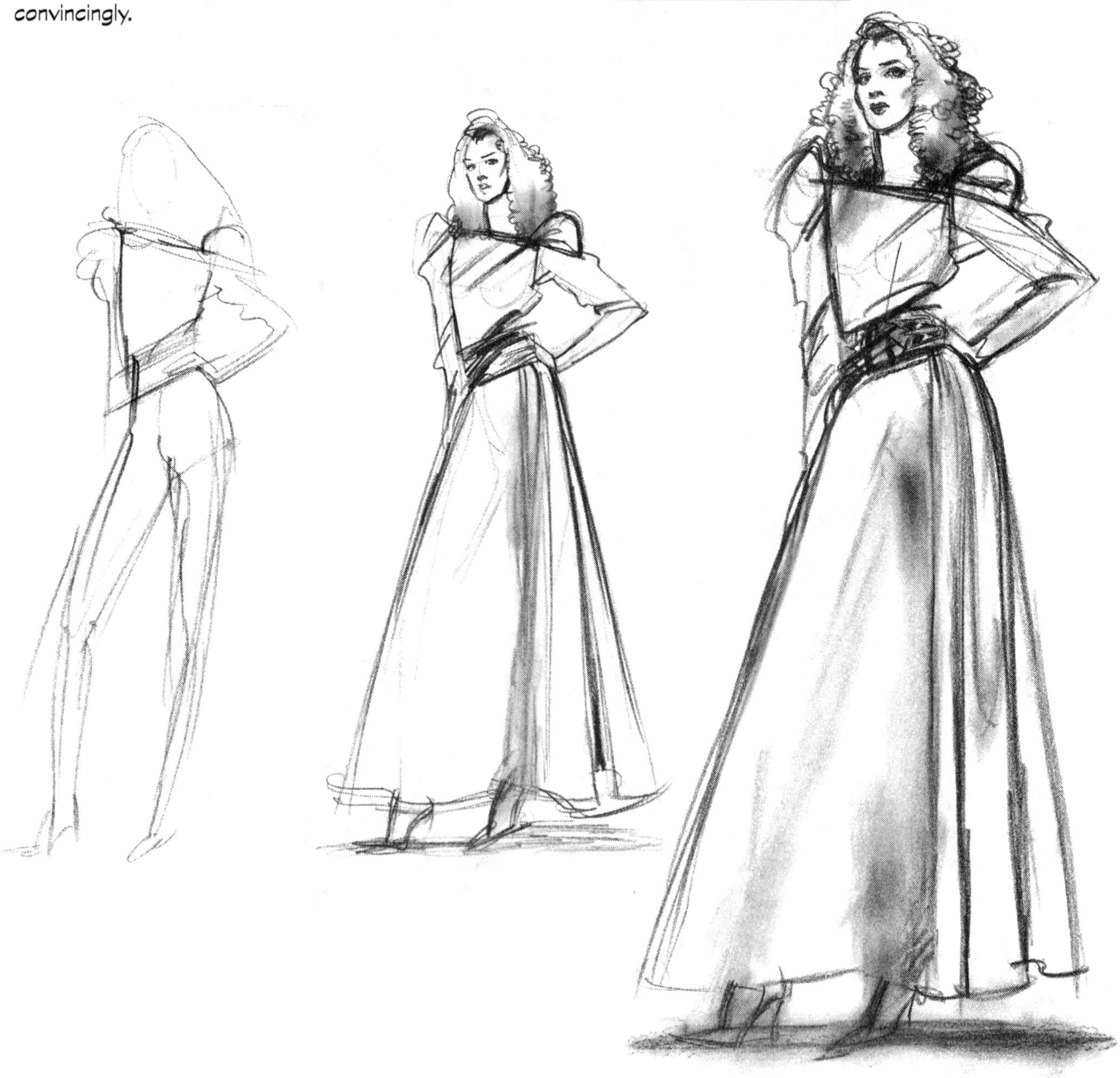

82 FASHION SKETCHING

Another method of sensing roundness is to suggest value on the sides of the forms.

Use only the flat side of a broken crayon or pastel.

Using ovals and circles, work around the forms to create the cylinders with value only, keeping a highlight area.

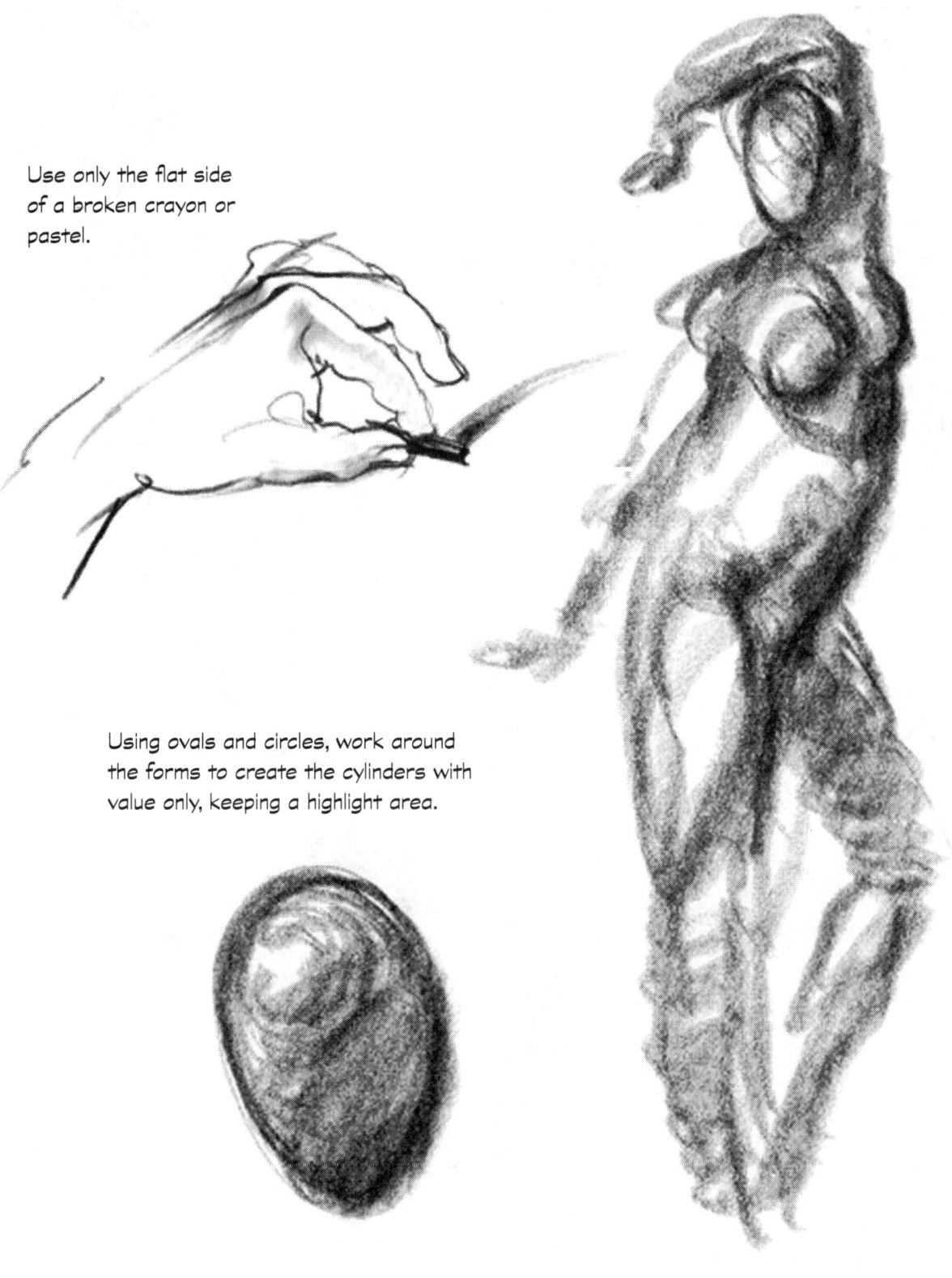

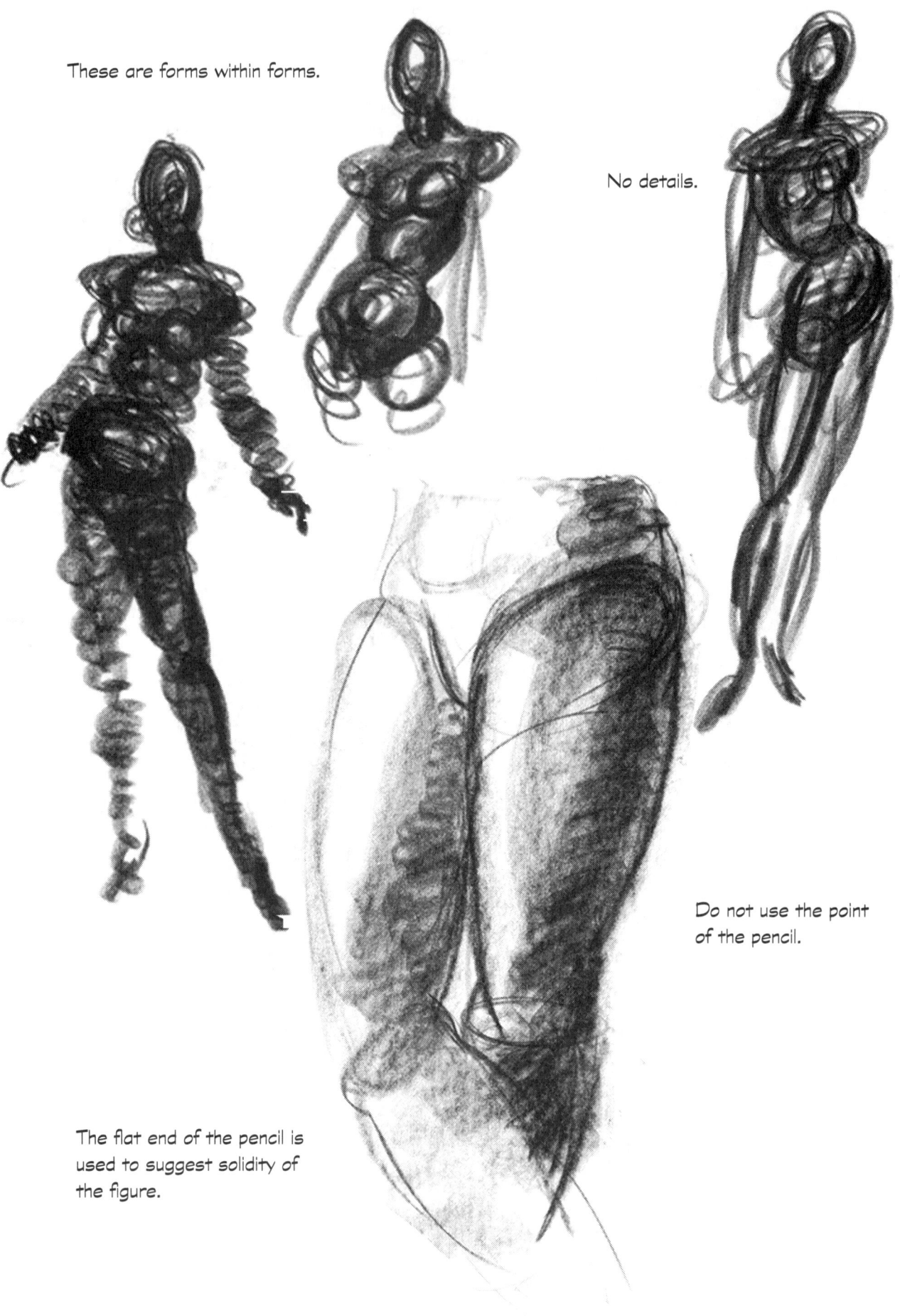

These are forms within forms.

No details.

Do not use the point of the pencil.

The flat end of the pencil is used to suggest solidity of the figure.

CONTOUR DRAWING

In nature, there are two kinds of lines: convex and concave. The shapes vary. It is the use of these lines that best depict the human form.

Contours or edges help describe what we wish to represent. It is important to understand and observe contours or edges in order to depict them. This is done by careful and slow observation of the object. For practice it can be anything: shoes, flowers, vegetables, and so on. The first attempts at contour studies will be highly detailed and faithful to the rounded forms of human flesh. Later, these edges are simplified and stylized to best suit the depiction of fashion.

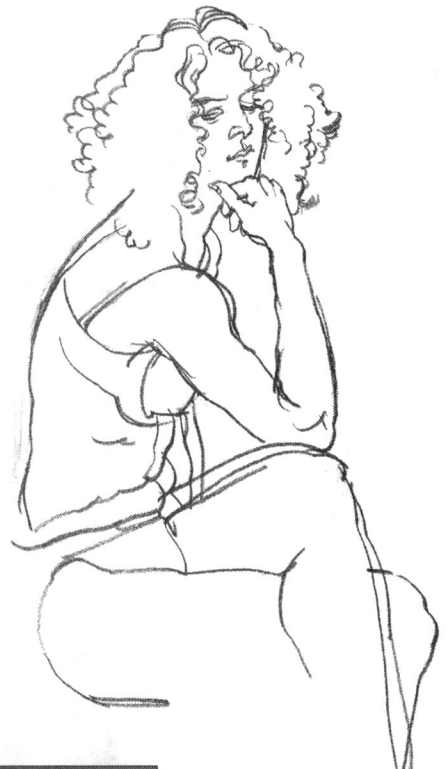

Think of the pencil actually touching the edges of the figure.

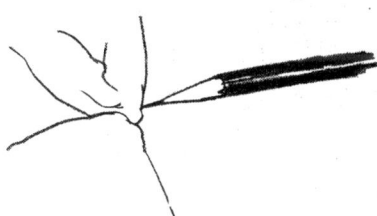

Study your own hand.

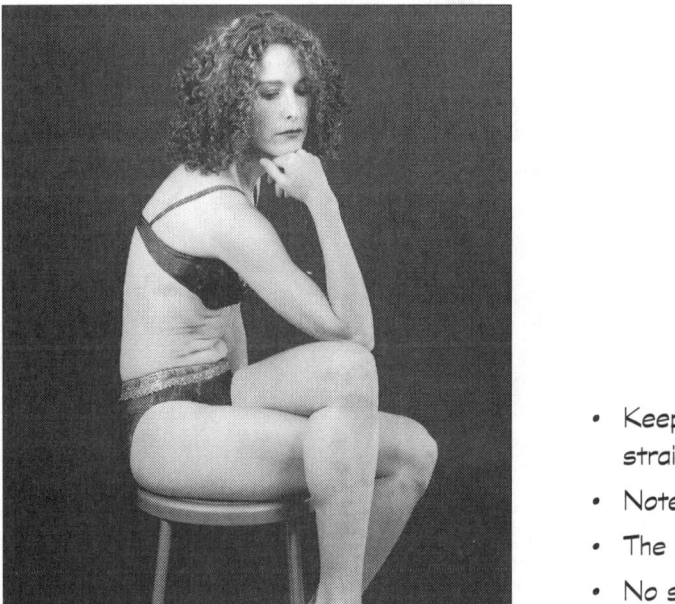

- Keep the contours rounded. Avoid lines that are too straight. This is often caused by drawing too quickly.
- Note overlapping forms.
- The pencil slowly traces the figure's edge.
- No sketching. Work very slowly. Look more at the body contours than at the art work.

CHAPTER 6

Clothing the Figure

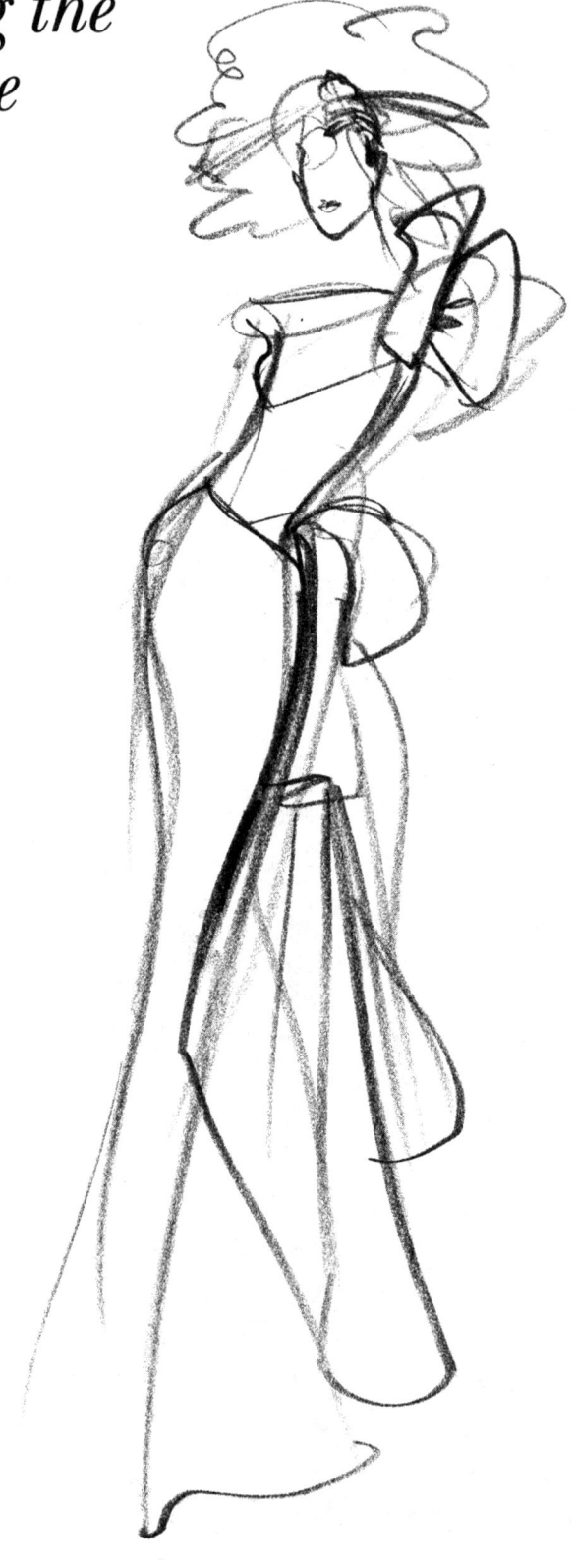

SEEING CLOTHING AS SIMPLE SHAPES

It is a common fault to see an article of clothing in bits and pieces, a mass of wrinkles and folds, before seeing its overall shape. Often students draw a garment, with the final result being a garment completely unlike the one set before them.

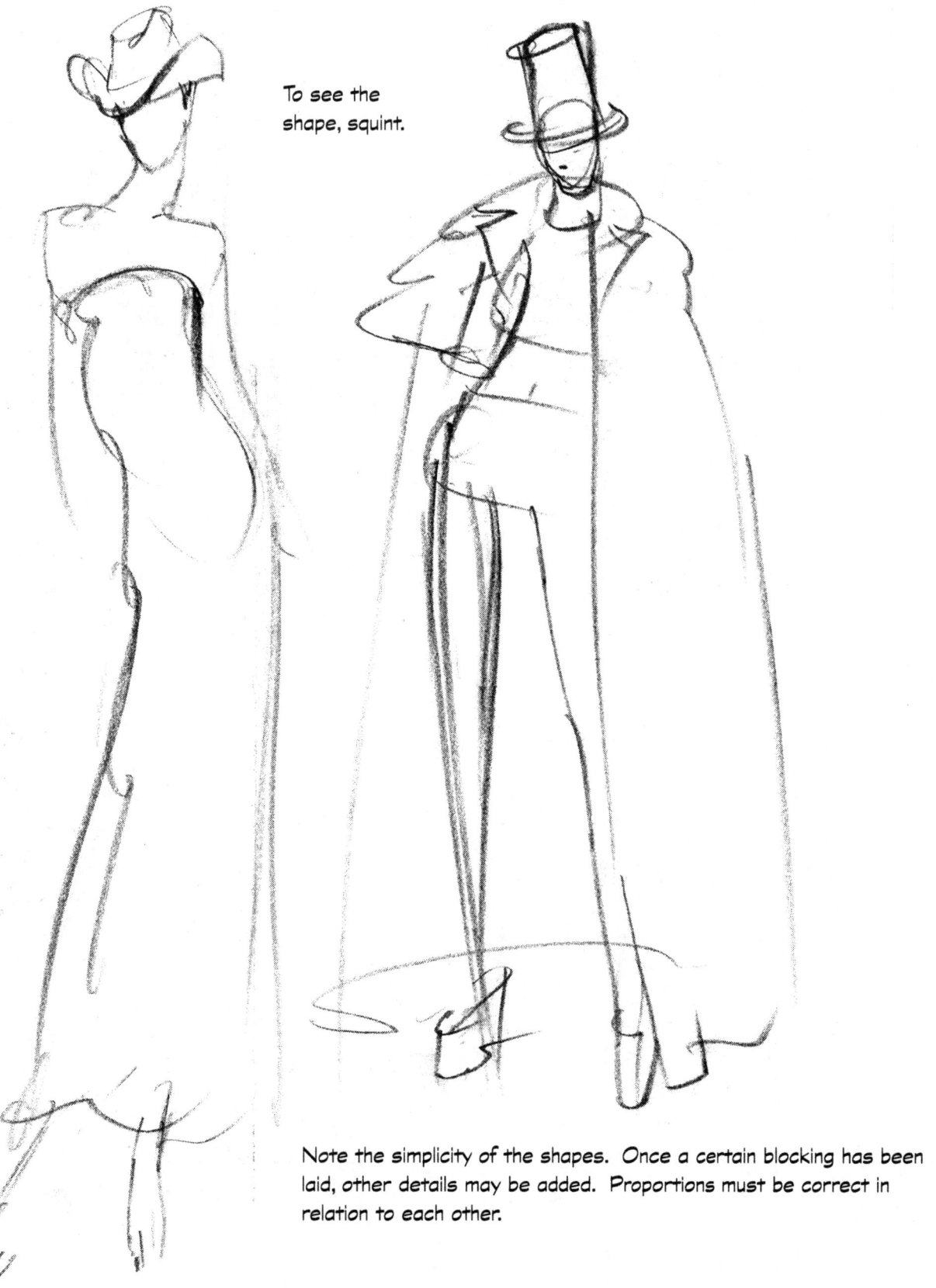

To see the shape, squint.

Note the simplicity of the shapes. Once a certain blocking has been laid, other details may be added. Proportions must be correct in relation to each other.

CHAPTER 6 CLOTHING THE FIGURE

This rough sketch has resulted in . . .

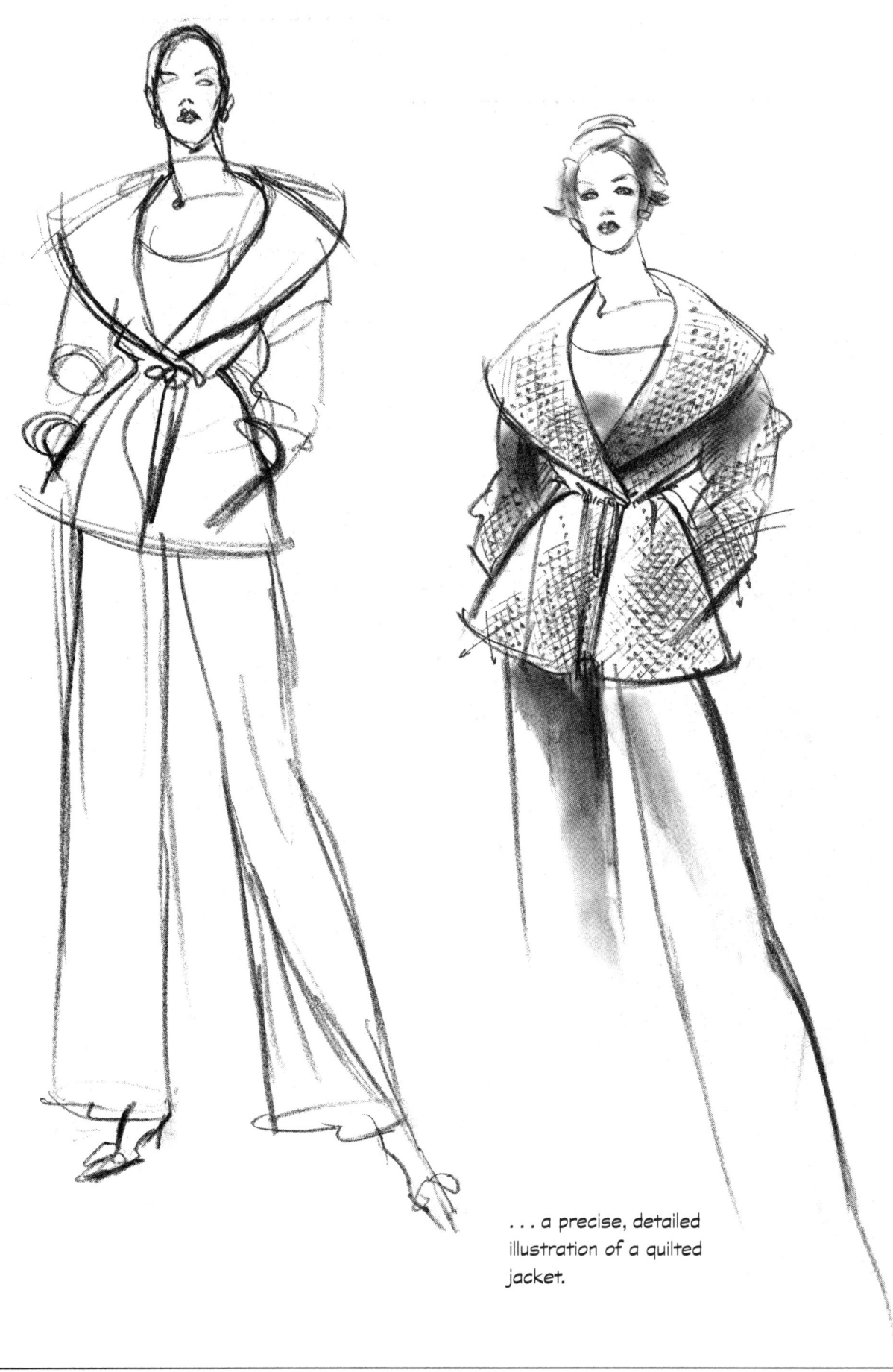

. . . a precise, detailed illustration of a quilted jacket.

88 FASHION SKETCHING

SUPPORTING THE STANDING FIGURE

- Concentrate on drawing the figure correctly: gesture, contour, and so on. Be sure to place the supporting leg and foot far enough back. This is often overlooked.

- Proof and correct your drawing if it contains this fault.

- Line up the pencil with the inside ankle of the model or photograph.

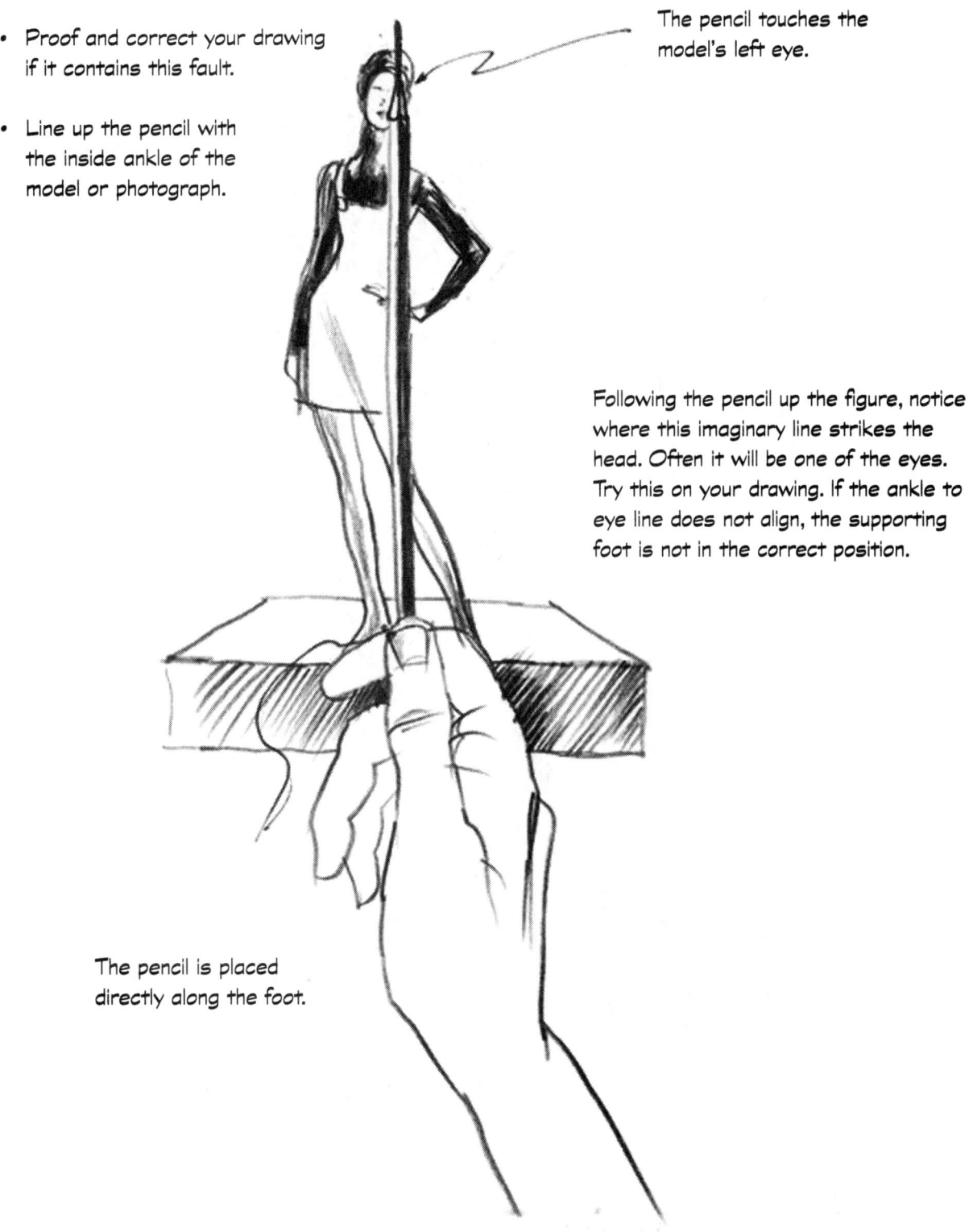

The pencil touches the model's left eye.

Following the pencil up the figure, notice where this imaginary line strikes the head. Often it will be one of the eyes. Try this on your drawing. If the ankle to eye line does not align, the supporting foot is not in the correct position.

The pencil is placed directly along the foot.

CHAPTER 6 CLOTHING THE FIGURE

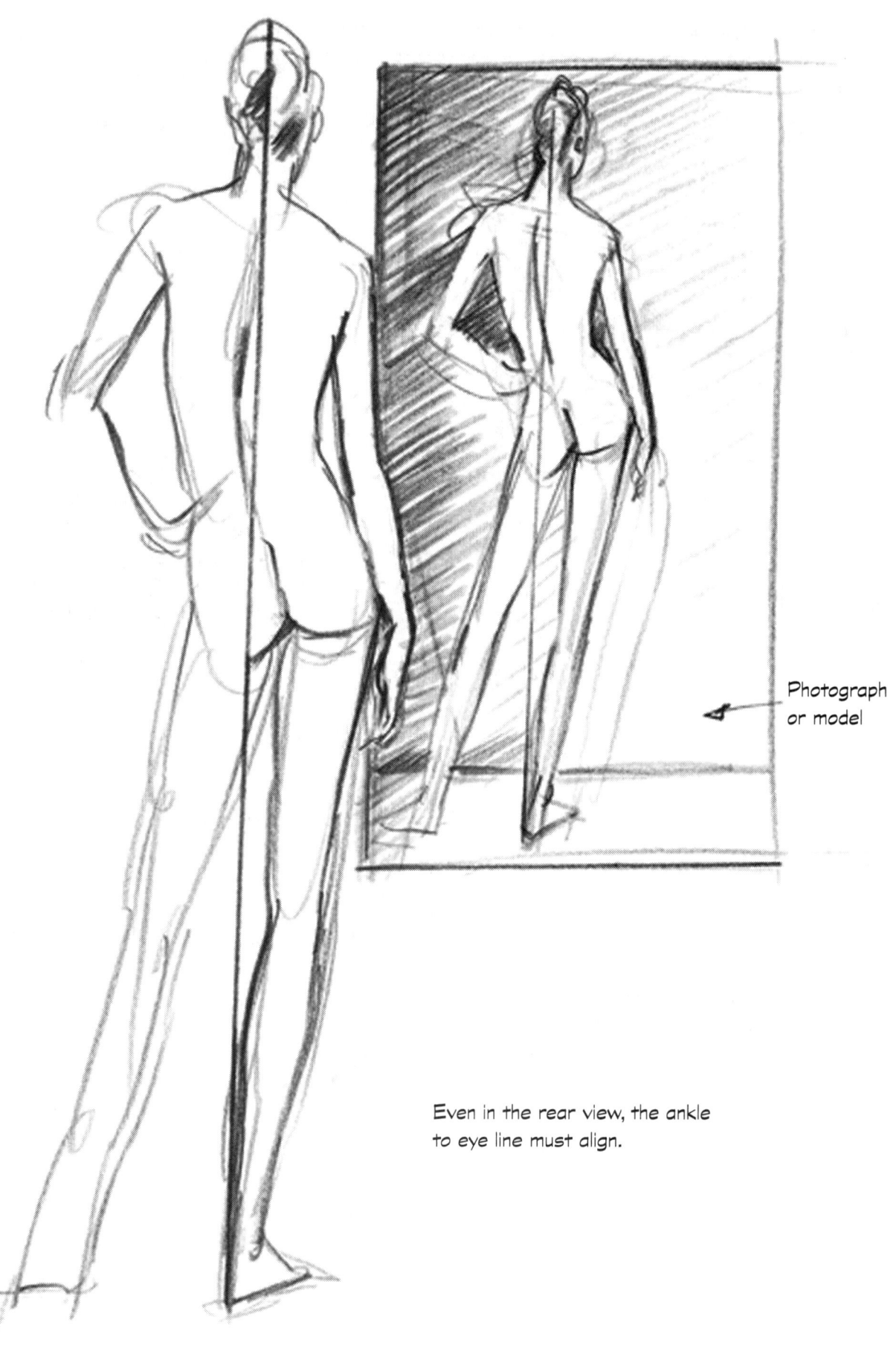

Photograph or model

Even in the rear view, the ankle to eye line must align.

A common fault is not pushing the supporting leg back far enough when drawing from the hip.

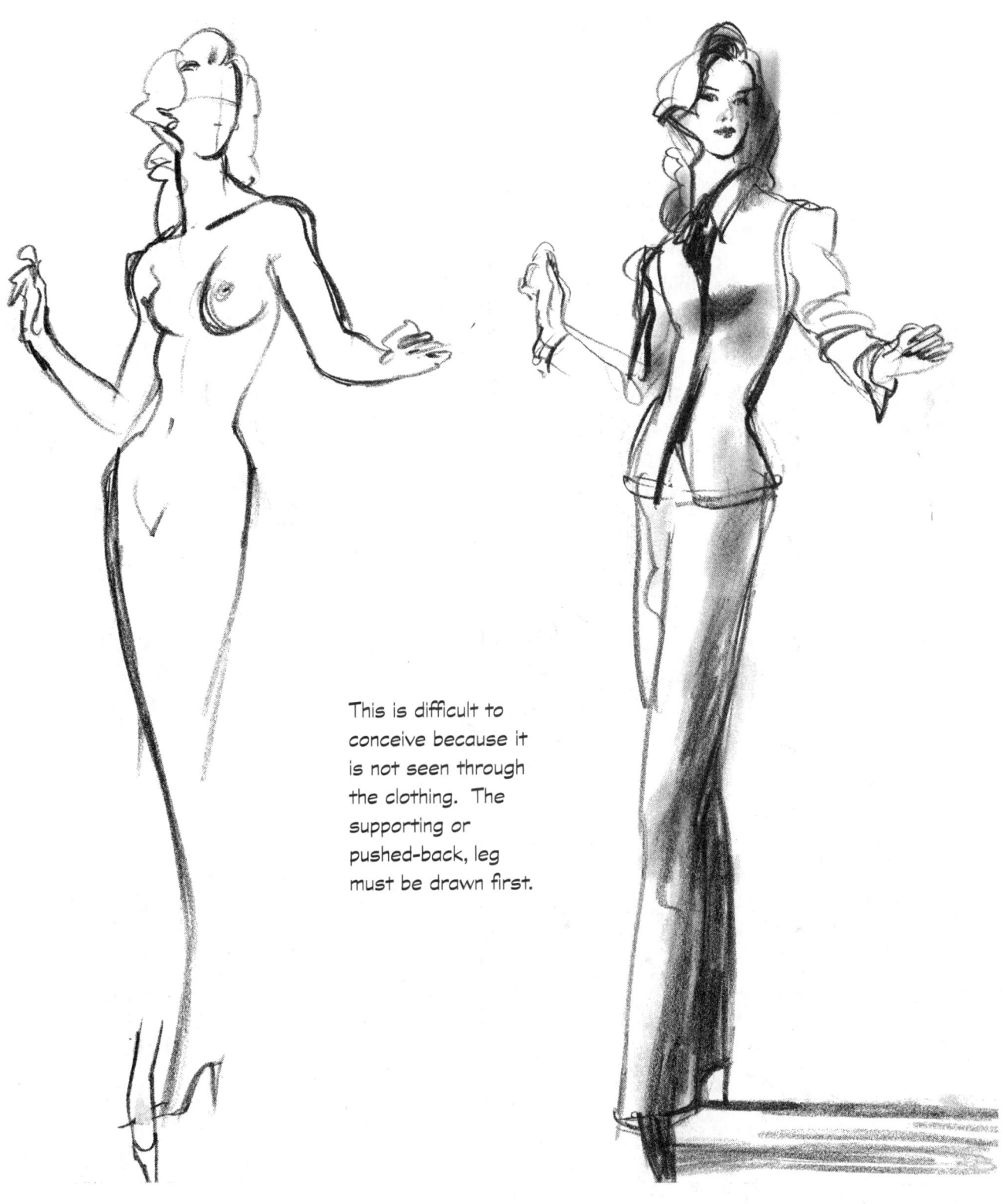

This is difficult to conceive because it is not seen through the clothing. The supporting or pushed-back, leg must be drawn first.

Avoid the falling effect of an unbalanced figure. This figure needs to lean on something, or it will fall to the floor.

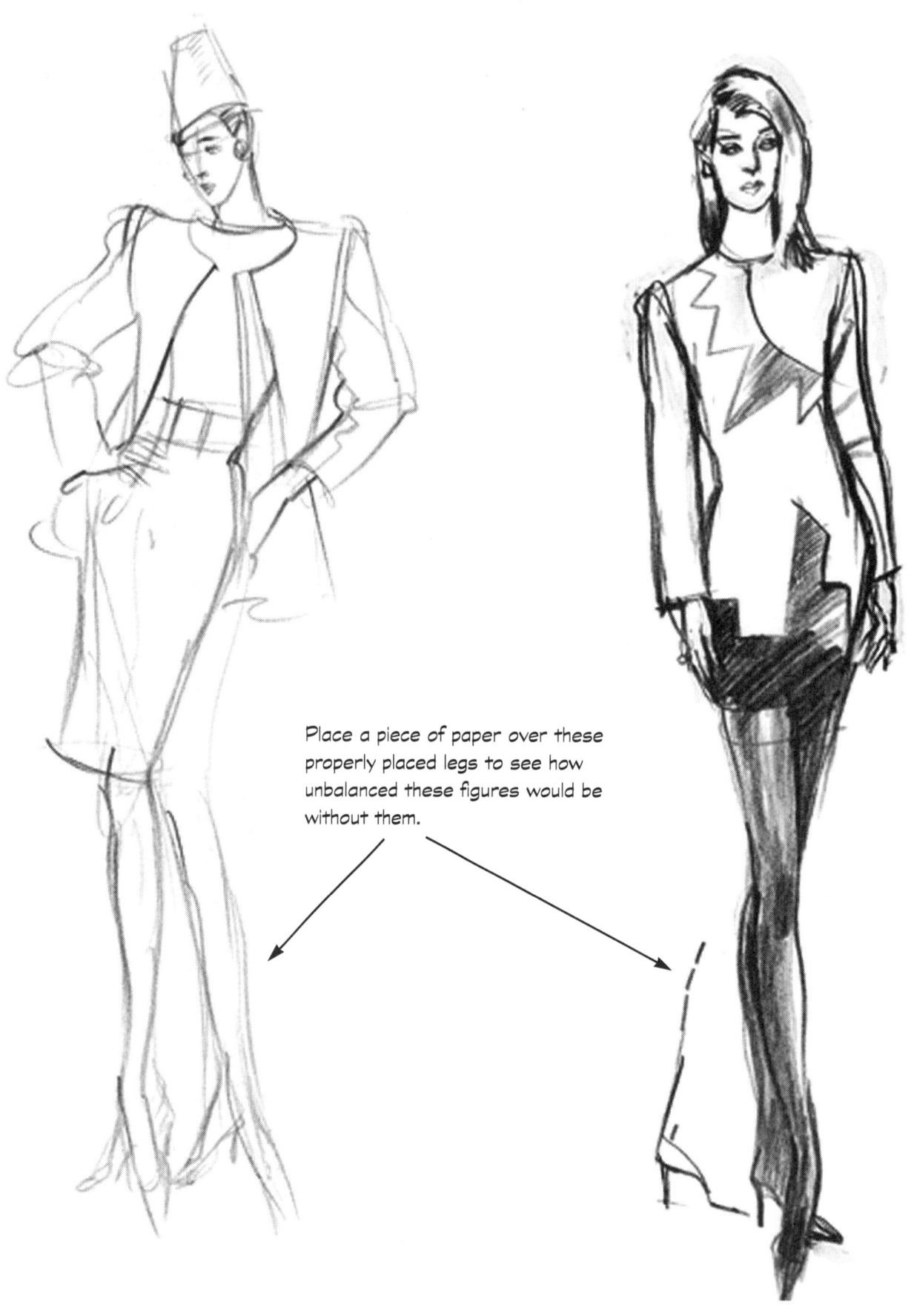

Place a piece of paper over these properly placed legs to see how unbalanced these figures would be without them.

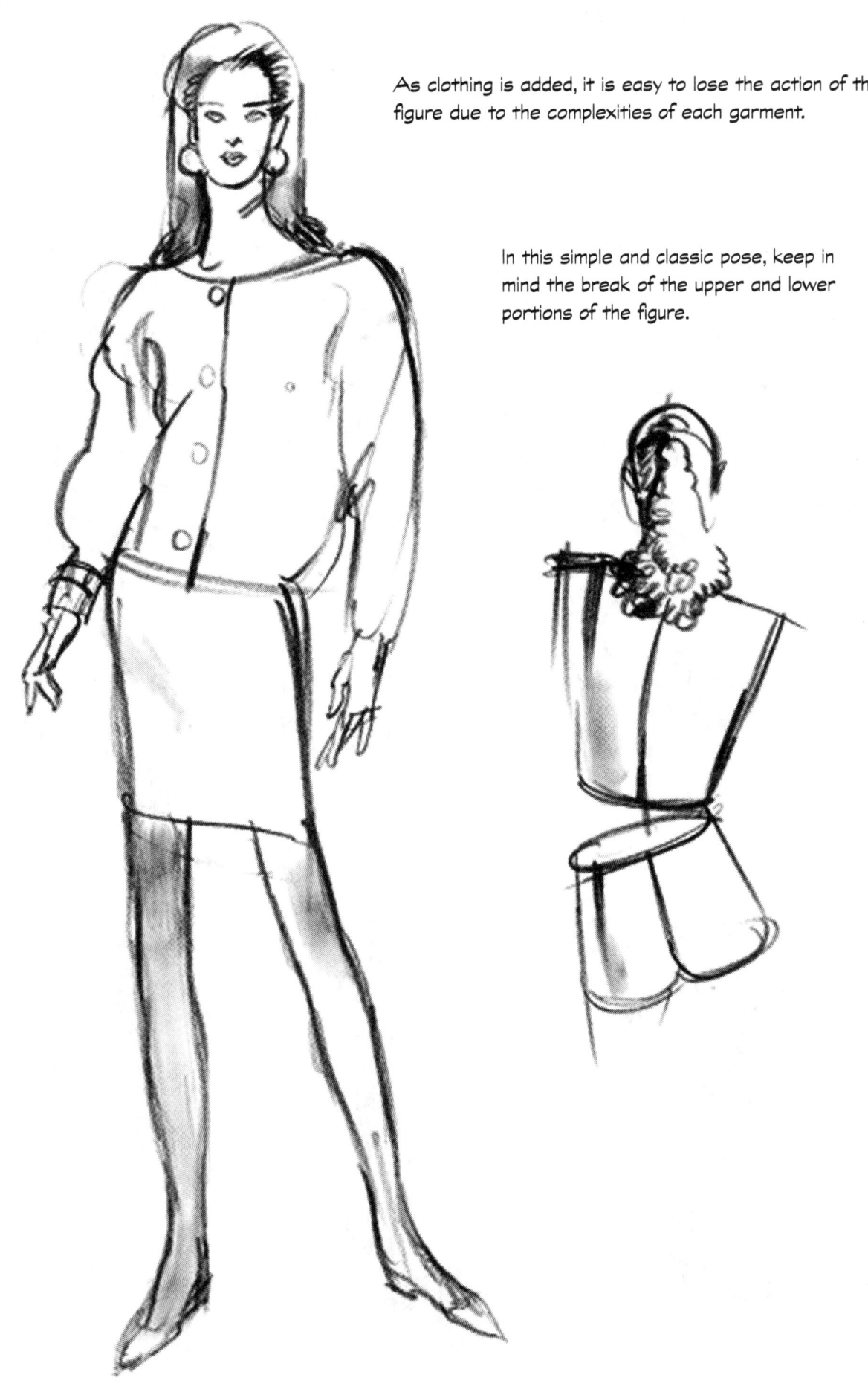

As clothing is added, it is easy to lose the action of the figure due to the complexities of each garment.

In this simple and classic pose, keep in mind the break of the upper and lower portions of the figure.

BODY CENTER

Keep the body center accurate when using a 3/4 view. In a 3/4 view, keep the center constant. Note the angle of jacket opening and consider both bosoms.

Check these points:
- Is the center truly between the bosoms?
- Is any waist detail, such as a belt buckle, directly under that center?
- Finding the crotch area is also helpful. It is not given much consideration in this turned figure.
- Are you checking the figure to be sure it is supporting itself? Is the supporting leg back far enough?

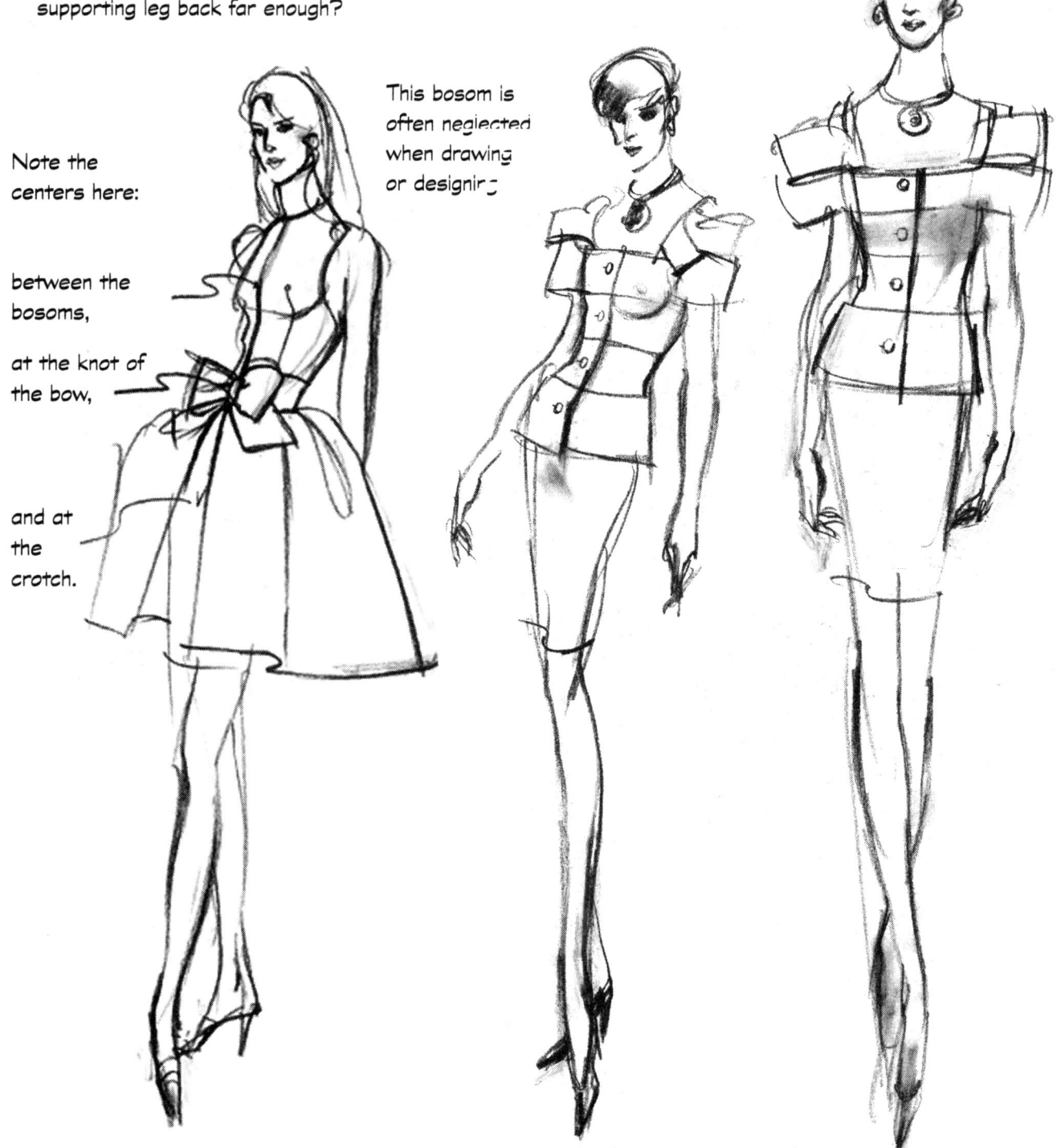

Note the centers here:

between the bosoms,

at the knot of the bow,

and at the crotch.

This bosom is often neglected when drawing or designing

FASHION SKETCHING

THE POSITION OF LEGS UNDER SKIRTS

Folds are affected by their placement. Look for this on your figure. It is especially important in order to place the feet.

The forward thrust of the foot and leg causes a break in the skirt. Notice how this affects the hemline.

Both skirts are now at an angle due to the side thrust of the hip.

The hip slants match the hemline slant.

The dress now hugs the body on this side.

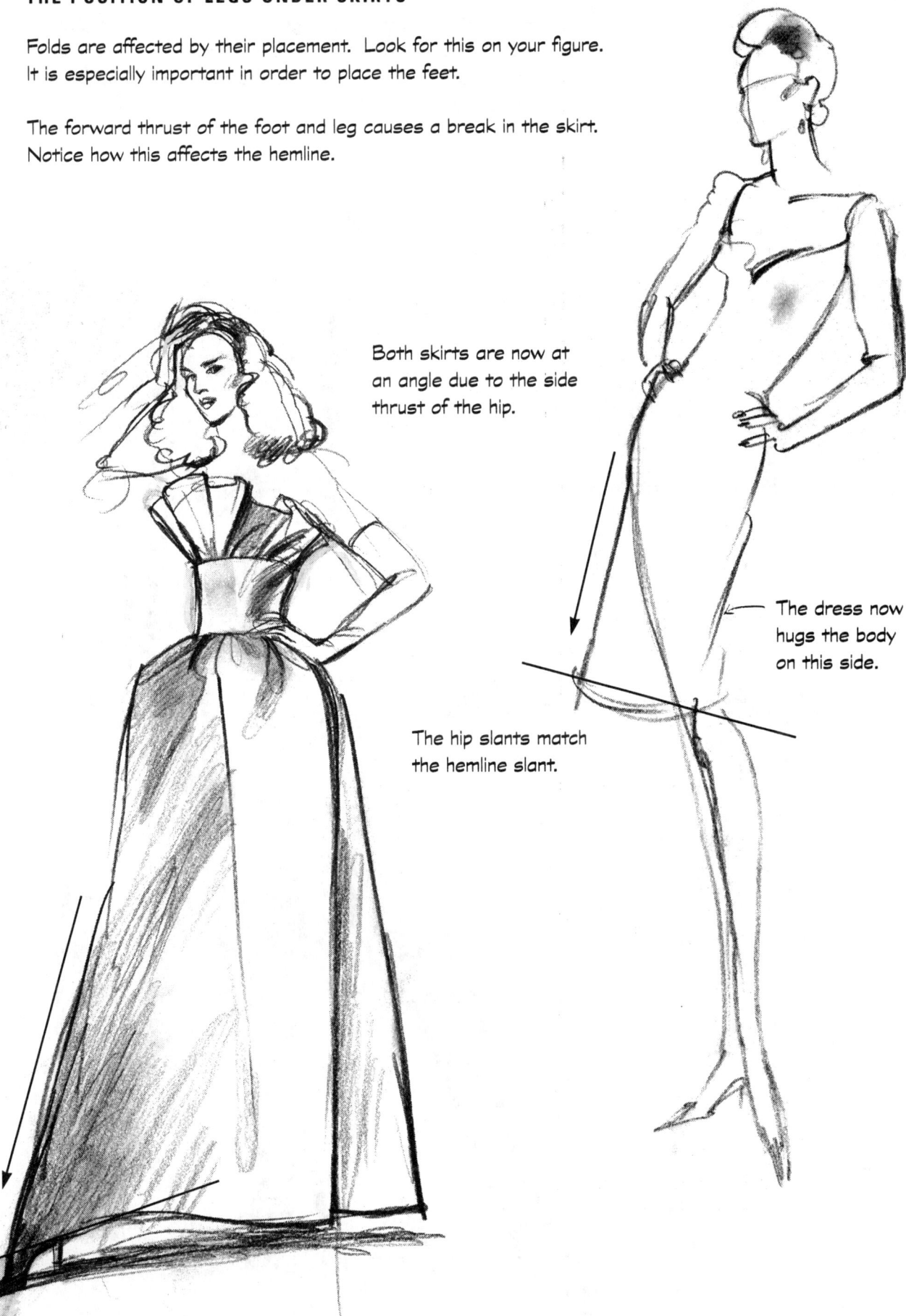

CHAPTER 6 CLOTHING THE FIGURE

Forward thigh breaks through the bell-shaped skirt. When drawing skirts, draw the entire leg, rather than from the hemline only. There is a risk of placing the legs incorrectly and losing the action.

The figure often has its relaxed foot extended forward, placing it on another plane than the supporting foot.

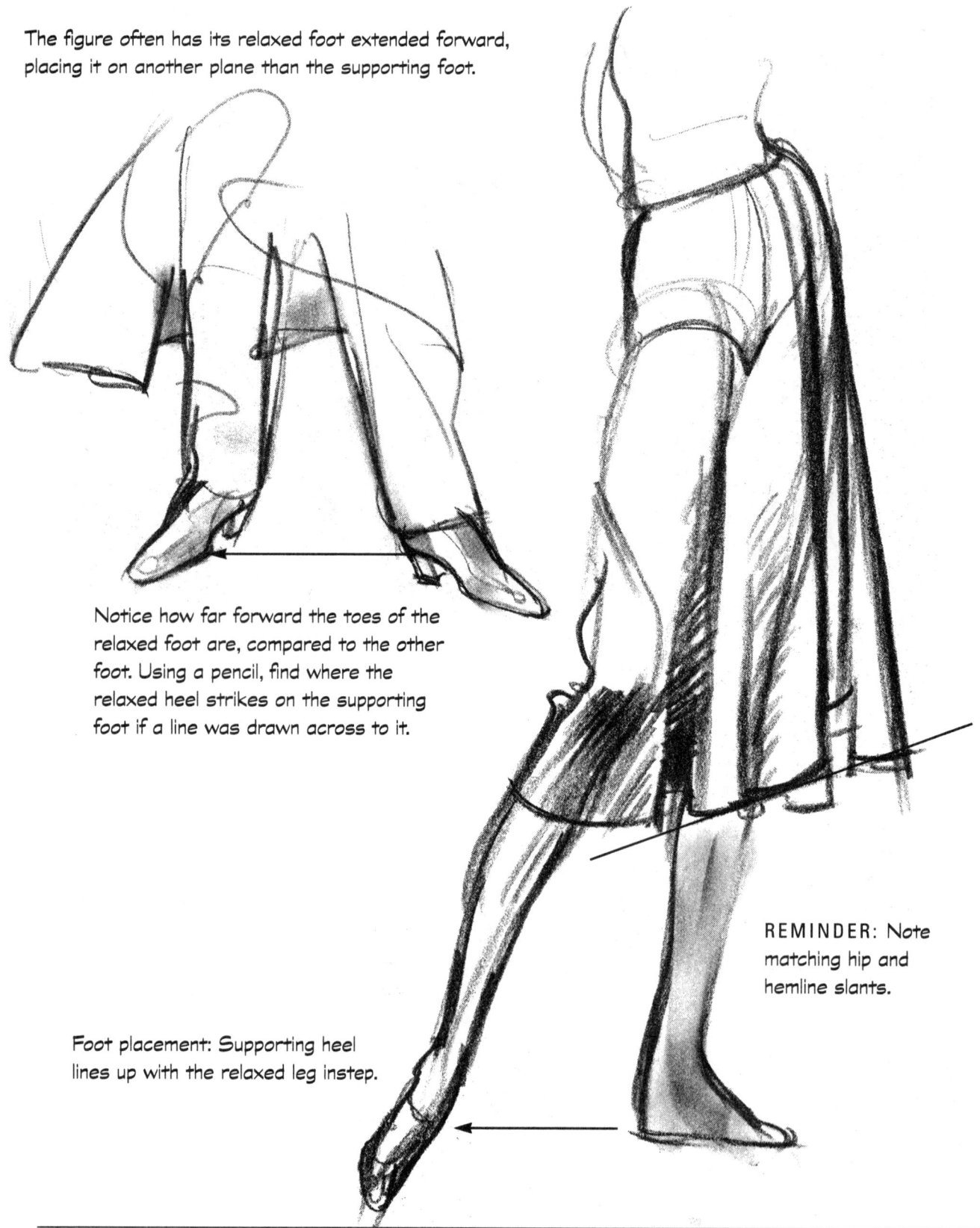

Notice how far forward the toes of the relaxed foot are, compared to the other foot. Using a pencil, find where the relaxed heel strikes on the supporting foot if a line was drawn across to it.

REMINDER: Note matching hip and hemline slants.

Foot placement: Supporting heel lines up with the relaxed leg instep.

96 FASHION SKETCHING

Leg and body positions affect slack folds.

The most common folds or tension pulls in women's slacks and men's trousers:

- from crotch to side or knee on the relaxed leg
- from hip to inner knee on the supporting leg

A leg extended forward breaks at the knee, causing one or two folds. Note the contours remain fairly straight, avoiding a rumpled look.

The fuller the slacks, the deeper the folds will be, especially at the hem.

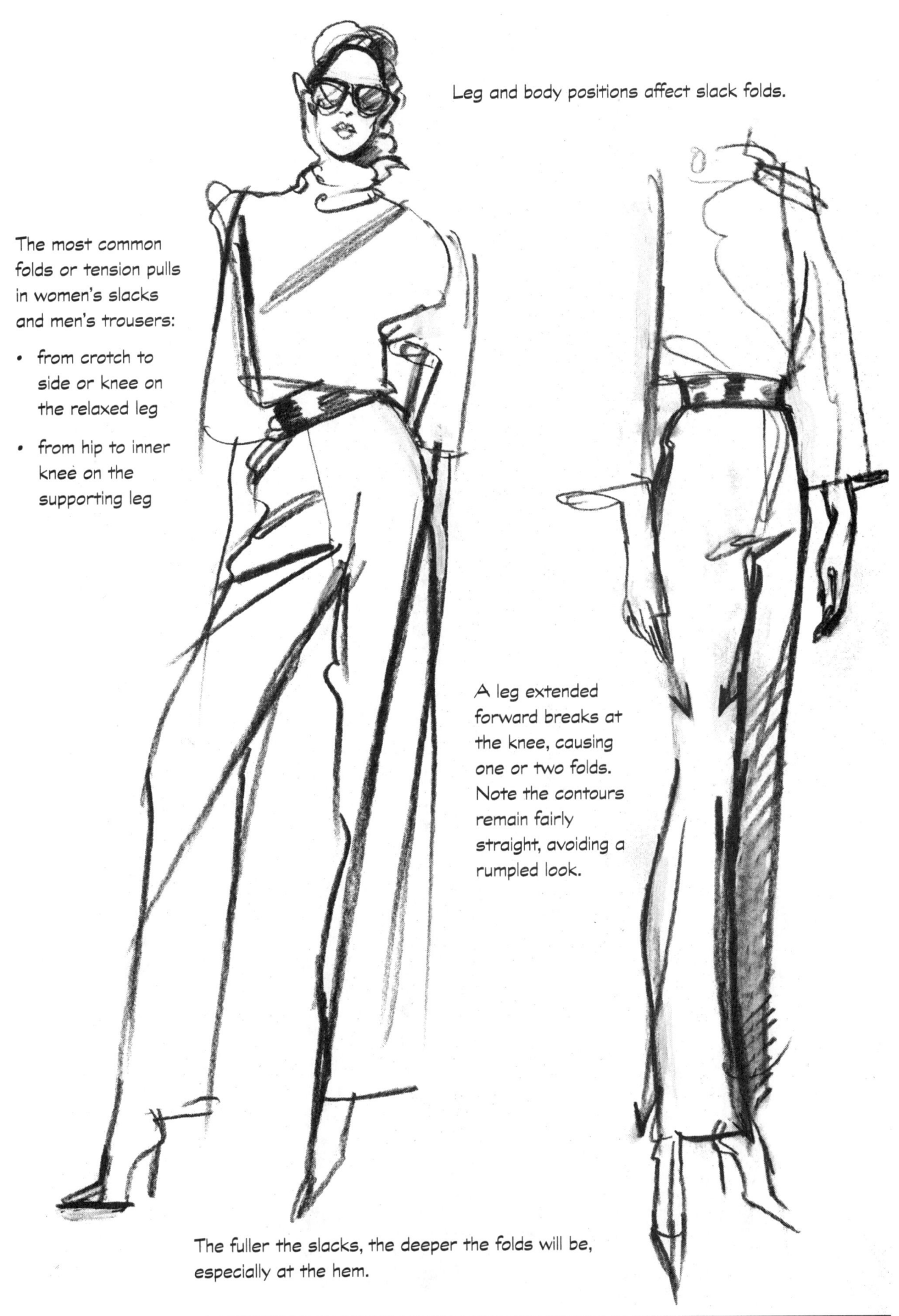

CHAPTER 6 CLOTHING THE FIGURE

Due to the raised arm, both the shoulder and hip slants are the same.

If it is necessary to show a figure leaning on something, indicate its means of support.

Check these back view key points: head is thrust forward, chin is often missing from view, and important design elements are placed at the center.

REMINDER: Push the hip of the supporting leg out.

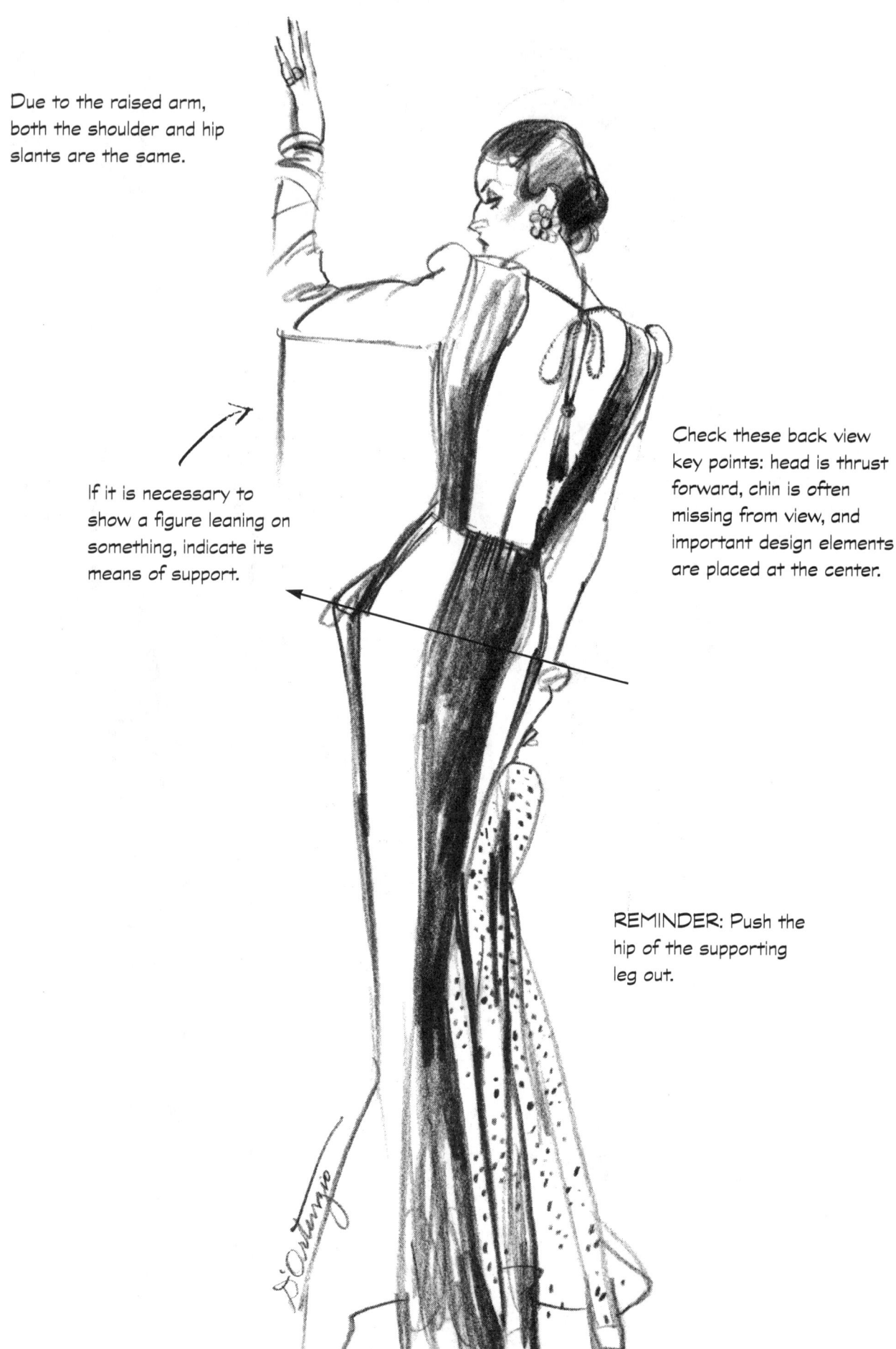

98 FASHION SKETCHING

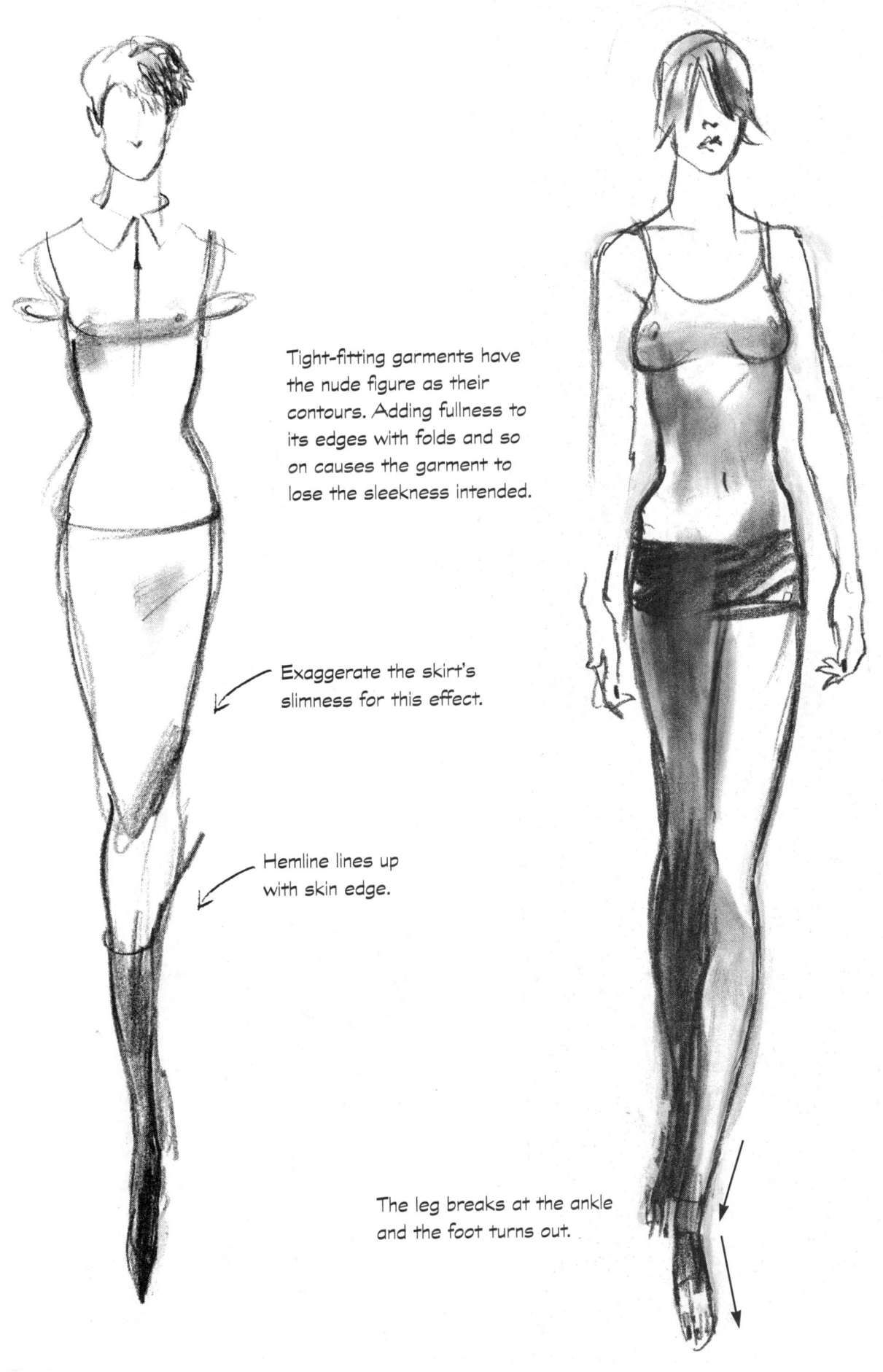

Tight-fitting garments have the nude figure as their contours. Adding fullness to its edges with folds and so on causes the garment to lose the sleekness intended.

Exaggerate the skirt's slimness for this effect.

Hemline lines up with skin edge.

The leg breaks at the ankle and the foot turns out.

CHAPTER 6 CLOTHING THE FIGURE

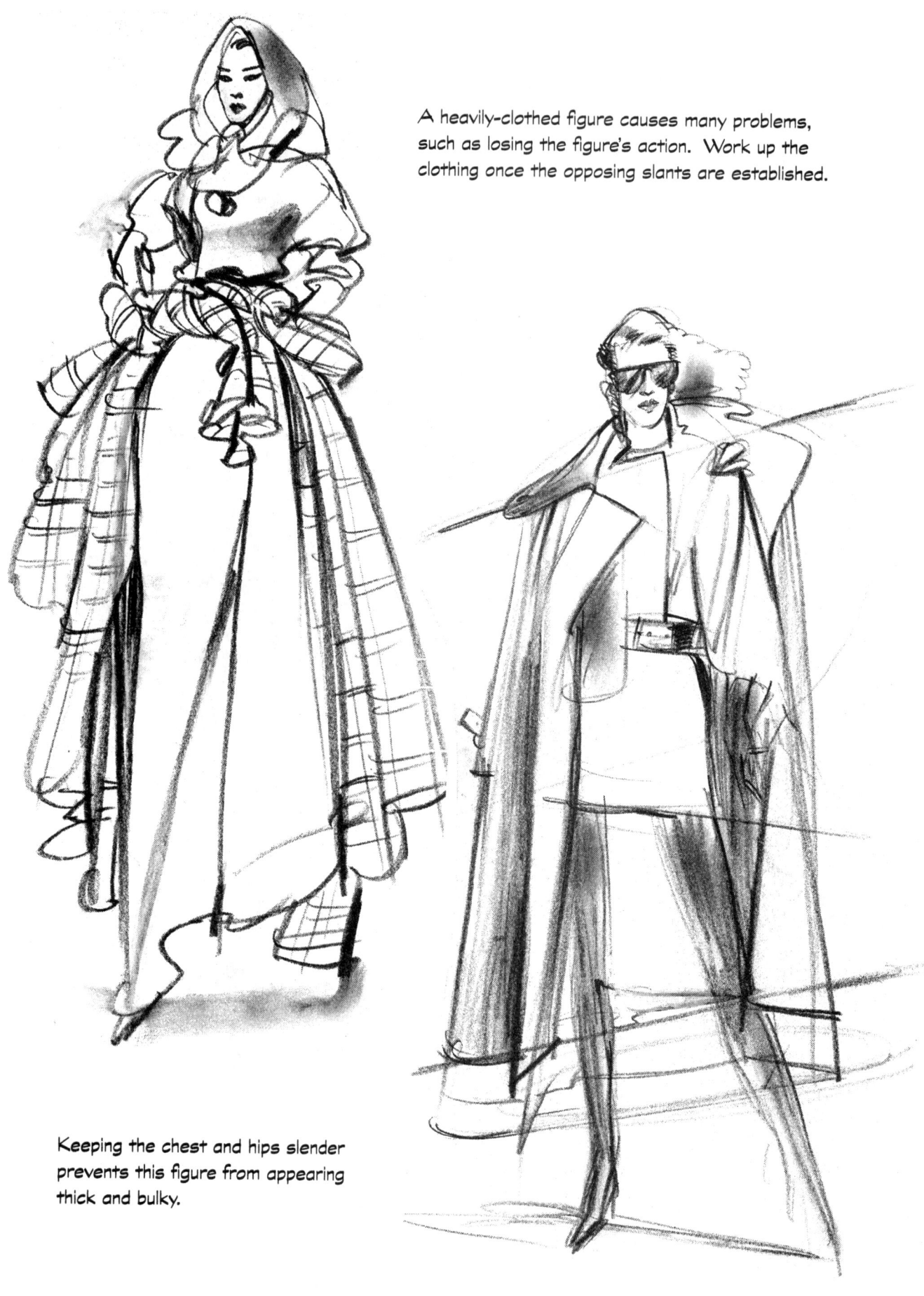

A heavily-clothed figure causes many problems, such as losing the figure's action. Work up the clothing once the opposing slants are established.

Keeping the chest and hips slender prevents this figure from appearing thick and bulky.

CHAPTER 7

Clothing Details I: Folds and Drapery

- Approach both folds and drapery the same way as clothing shapes since that is precisely what they are: shapes.

- Squinting is important. It is the only way to simplify the confusion that accompanies gathered and draped fabric. While squinting, the eyes block out small and unneeded wrinkles and folds. All that remains is the darkest and most important folds.

- Contours also tell a great deal about the fabric. The problem to be solved is to make the fabric look new. It is not necessary to draw razor-sharp edges, but a certain firmness to the contour is important to suggest the body of the fabric.

- Tightly squeezed fabric spreads out from its seam.

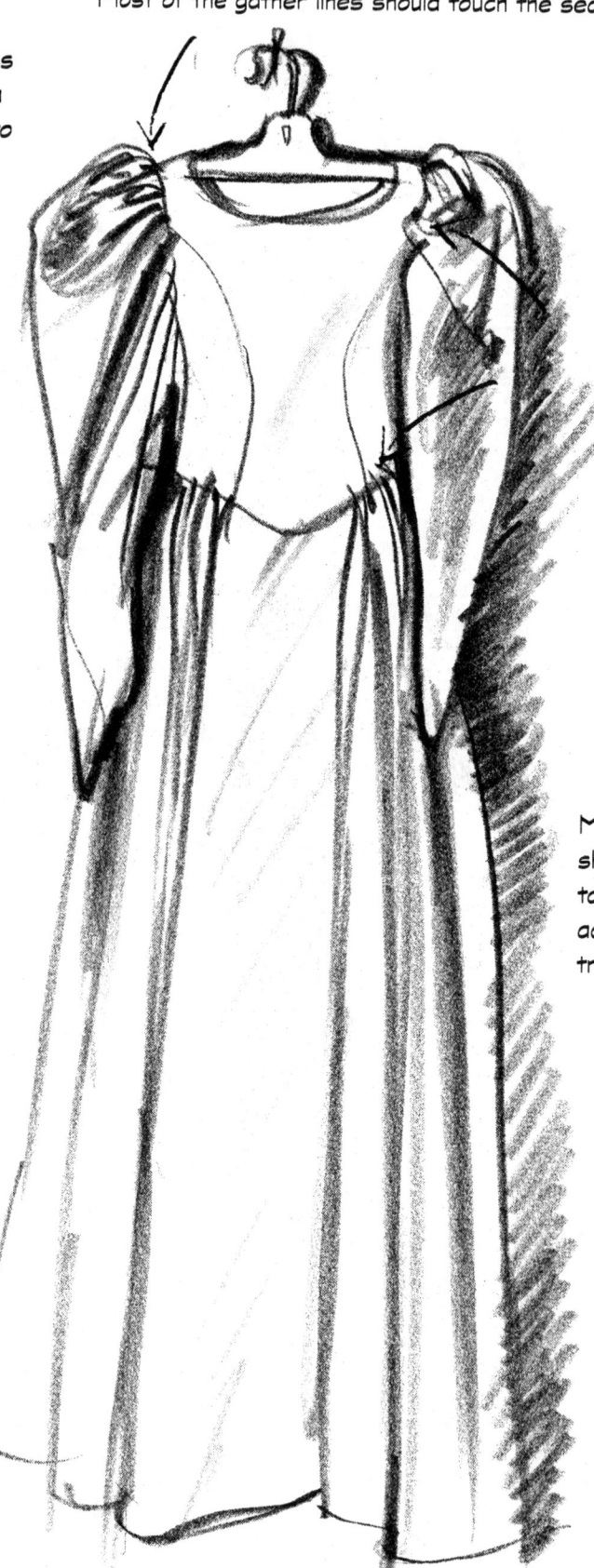

Place a costume on a dress form. Draping fabric over a dress form and fitting it into a design also works.

Wrinkles are not folds.

Most of the gather lines should touch the seam.

Gathers are placed firmly into the seam.

Make sure the dress shapes are correct. (Think to yourself: What is the actual skirt shape? Bell, triangle, and so on?)

Break up the hemline into uneven folds.

Tight gathers open into wide folds before becoming a hemline.

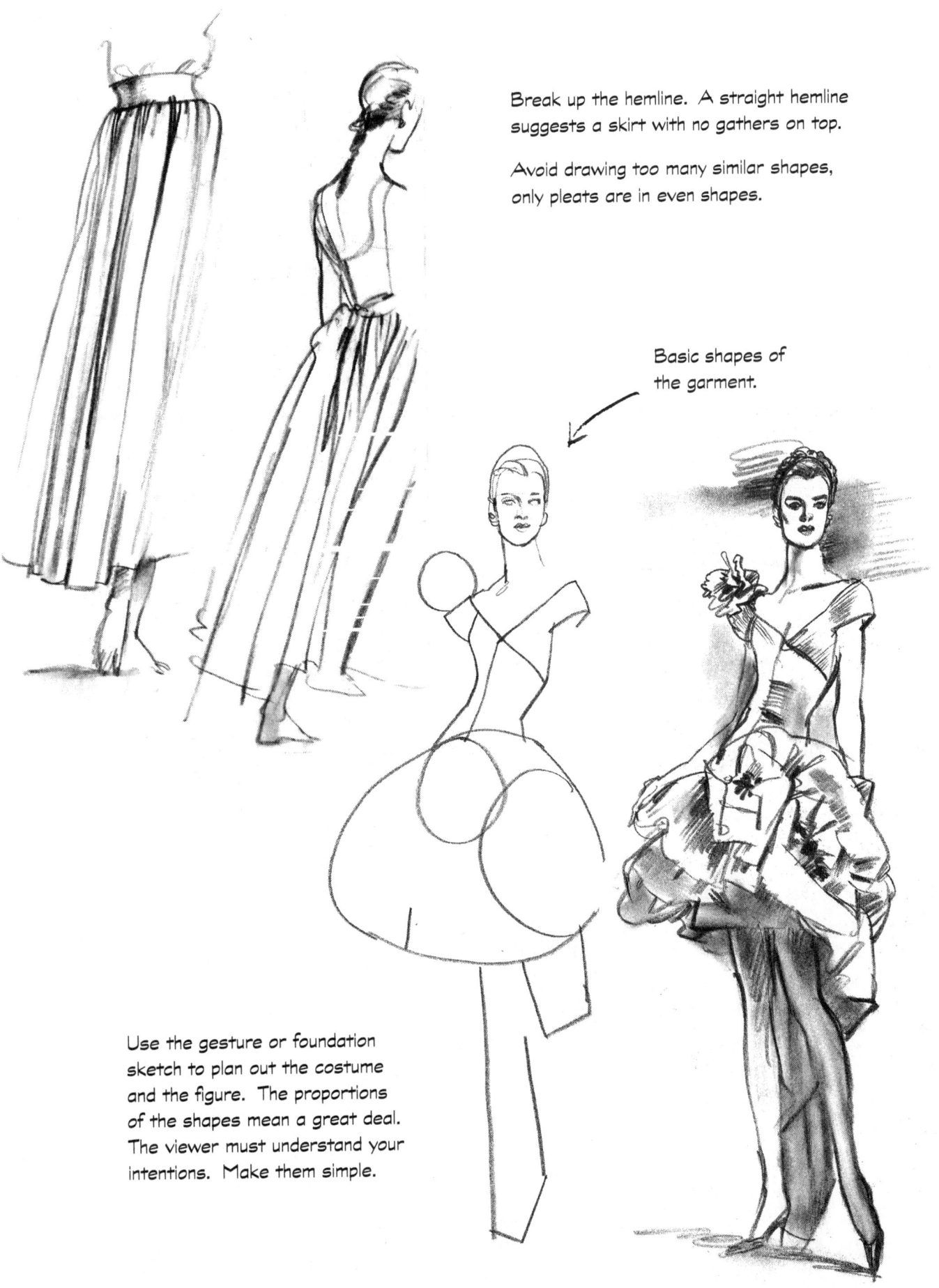

Break up the hemline. A straight hemline suggests a skirt with no gathers on top.

Avoid drawing too many similar shapes, only pleats are in even shapes.

Basic shapes of the garment.

Use the gesture or foundation sketch to plan out the costume and the figure. The proportions of the shapes mean a great deal. The viewer must understand your intentions. Make them simple.

CHAPTER 7 CLOTHING DETAILS I: FOLDS AND DRAPERY

Squinting helps eliminate many of the smaller folds. A crisp, new-looking garment is depicted.

Extremely tight bunching creates elongated teardrop shapes.

These pushed-up sleeves create many small folds. Not all of these are necessary to show this effect.

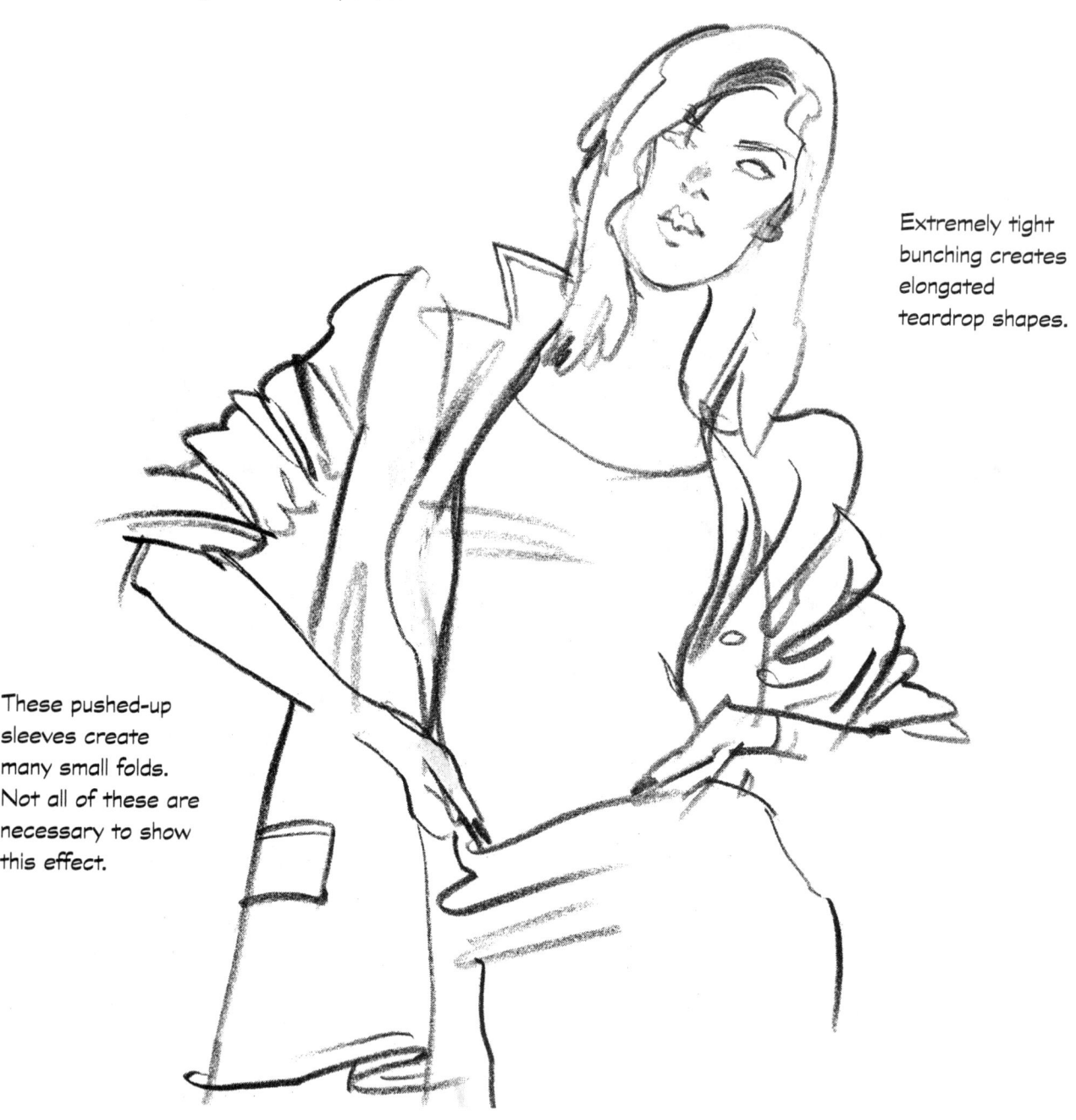

104 FASHION SKETCHING

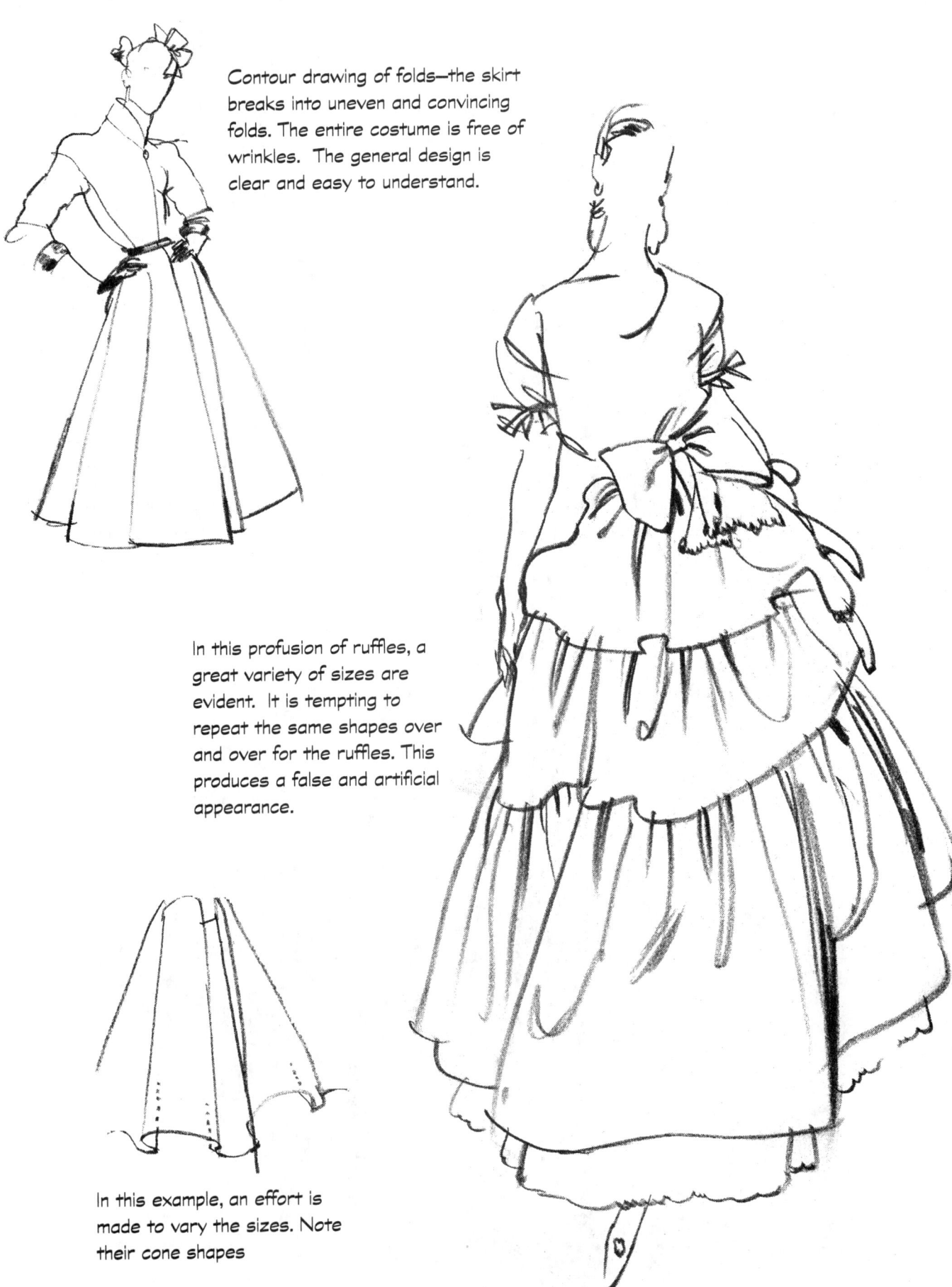

Contour drawing of folds—the skirt breaks into uneven and convincing folds. The entire costume is free of wrinkles. The general design is clear and easy to understand.

In this profusion of ruffles, a great variety of sizes are evident. It is tempting to repeat the same shapes over and over for the ruffles. This produces a false and artificial appearance.

In this example, an effort is made to vary the sizes. Note their cone shapes

When drawing tiers or flounces, keep a good distance between tier layers. This gives crispness to the contours.

Flattening these tiers gives a limp or crushed look to them.

Now shapes within shapes can be added. The hems of each layer are changed to match added details.

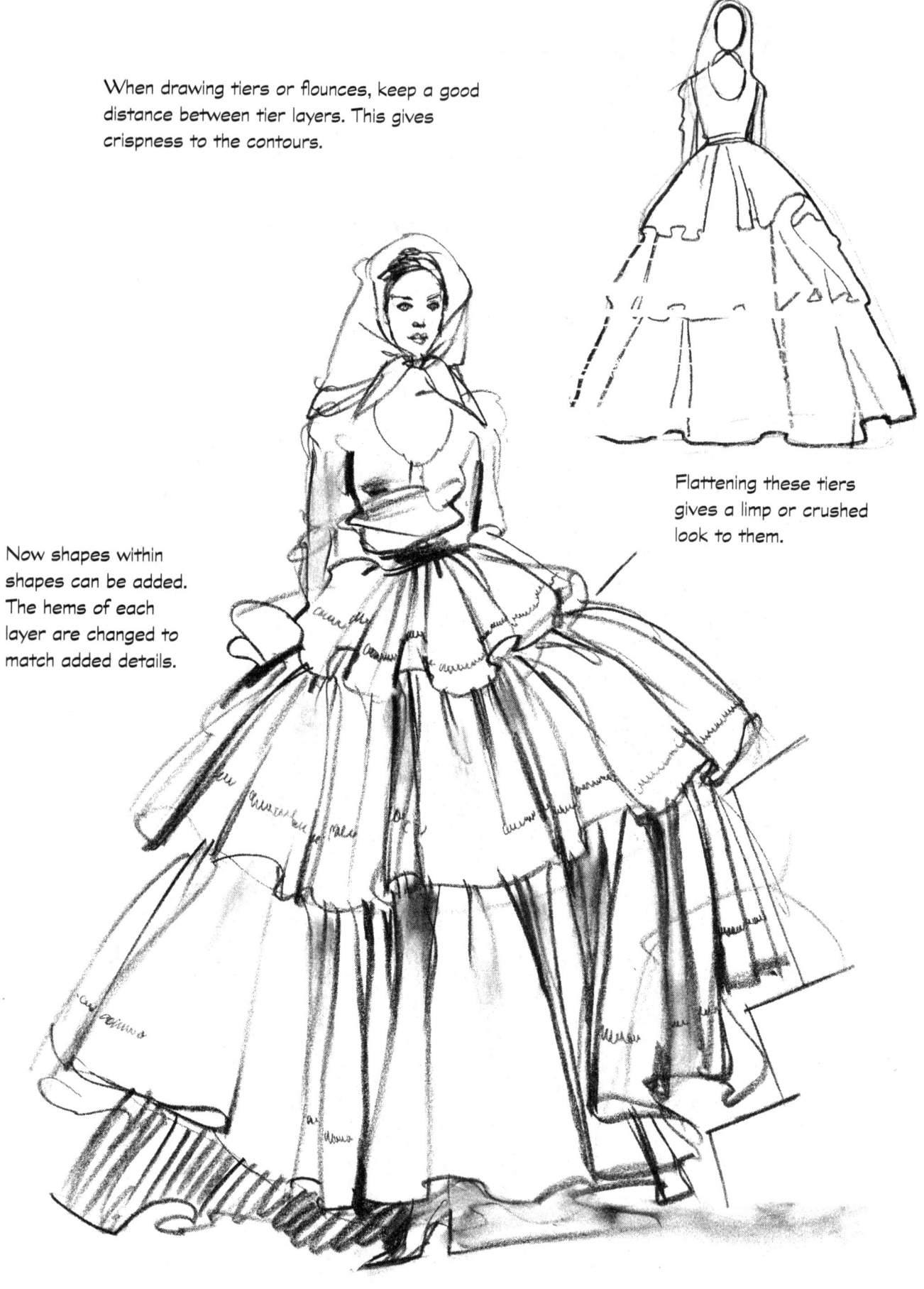

106 FASHION SKETCHING

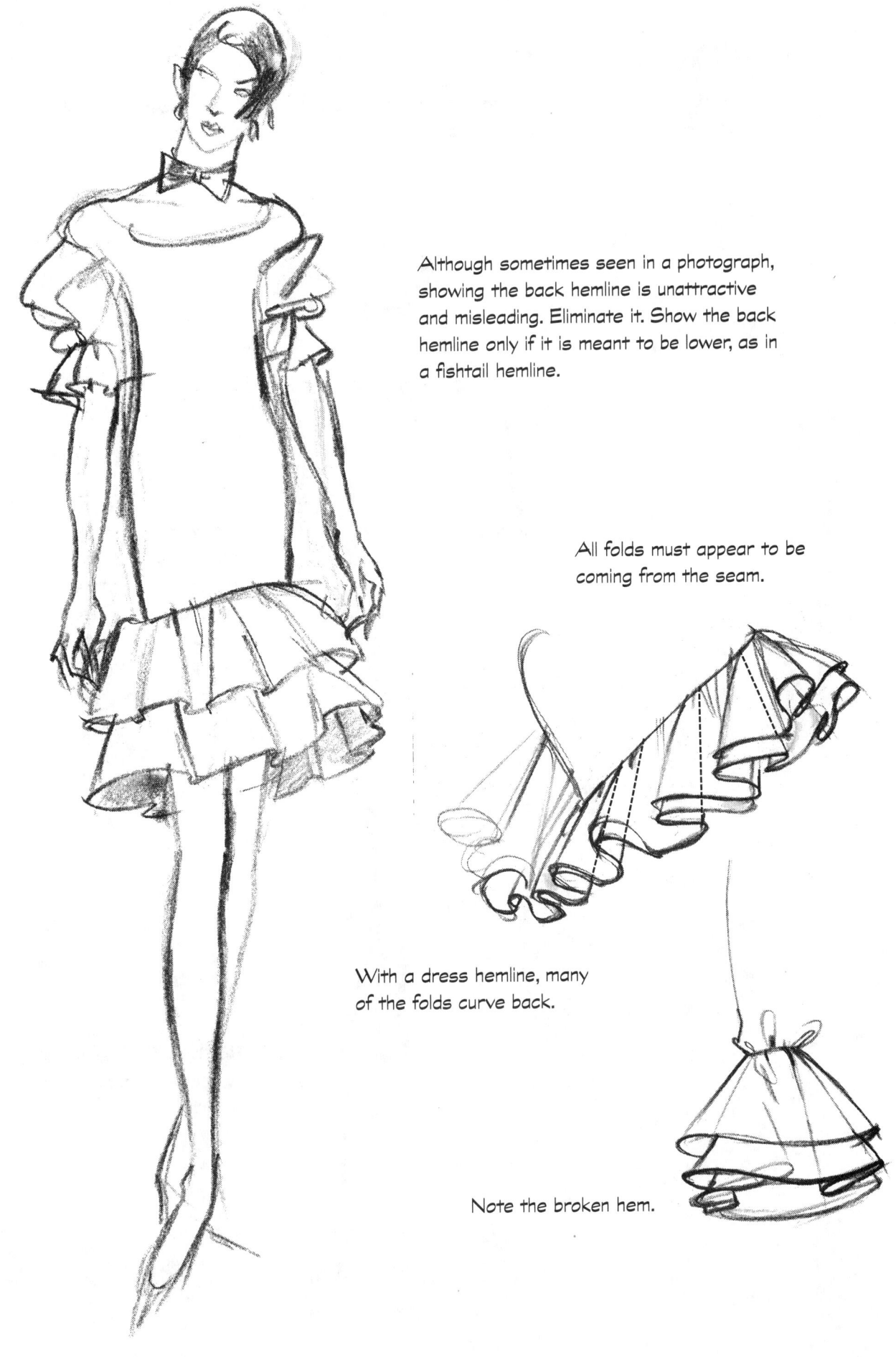

Although sometimes seen in a photograph, showing the back hemline is unattractive and misleading. Eliminate it. Show the back hemline only if it is meant to be lower, as in a fishtail hemline.

All folds must appear to be coming from the seam.

With a dress hemline, many of the folds curve back.

Note the broken hem.

CHAPTER 7 CLOTHING DETAILS I: FOLDS AND DRAPERY

SEAMS

Seams are seen as thin, sharp lines curving to follow the contours of the body.

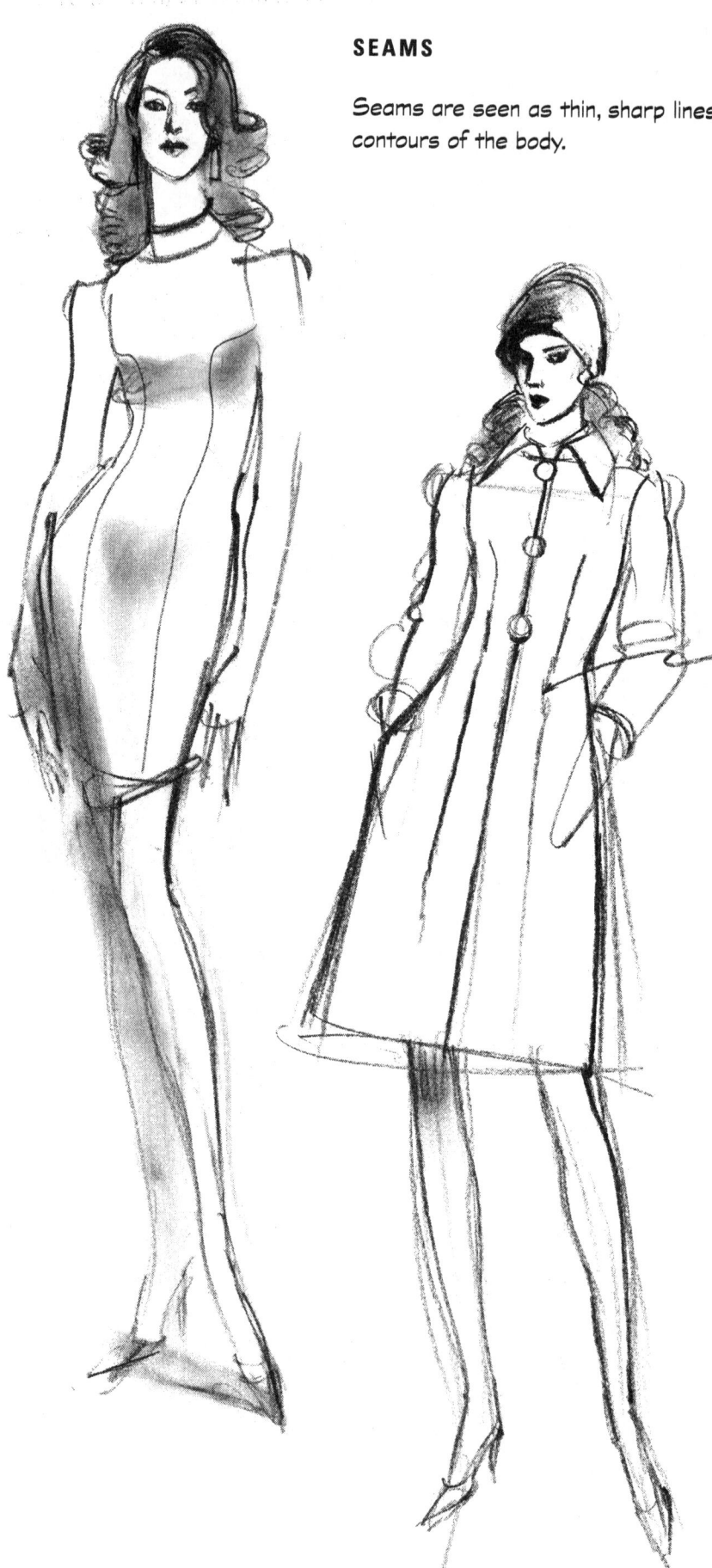

These thick and broken lines suggest piping or ripped-open seams. Keep the line steady. Use a sharpened pencil point to help produce these wire-like lines.

REMINDER: Use the ellipse to find cuffs, hemlines, and collars.

PLEATS

Pleats are seen as rows of creased fabric.

Although pleats are meant to be even, full sleeves or skirts will sometimes overlap.

The hemline continues in a zigzag fashion.

Side A   Crease   Side B

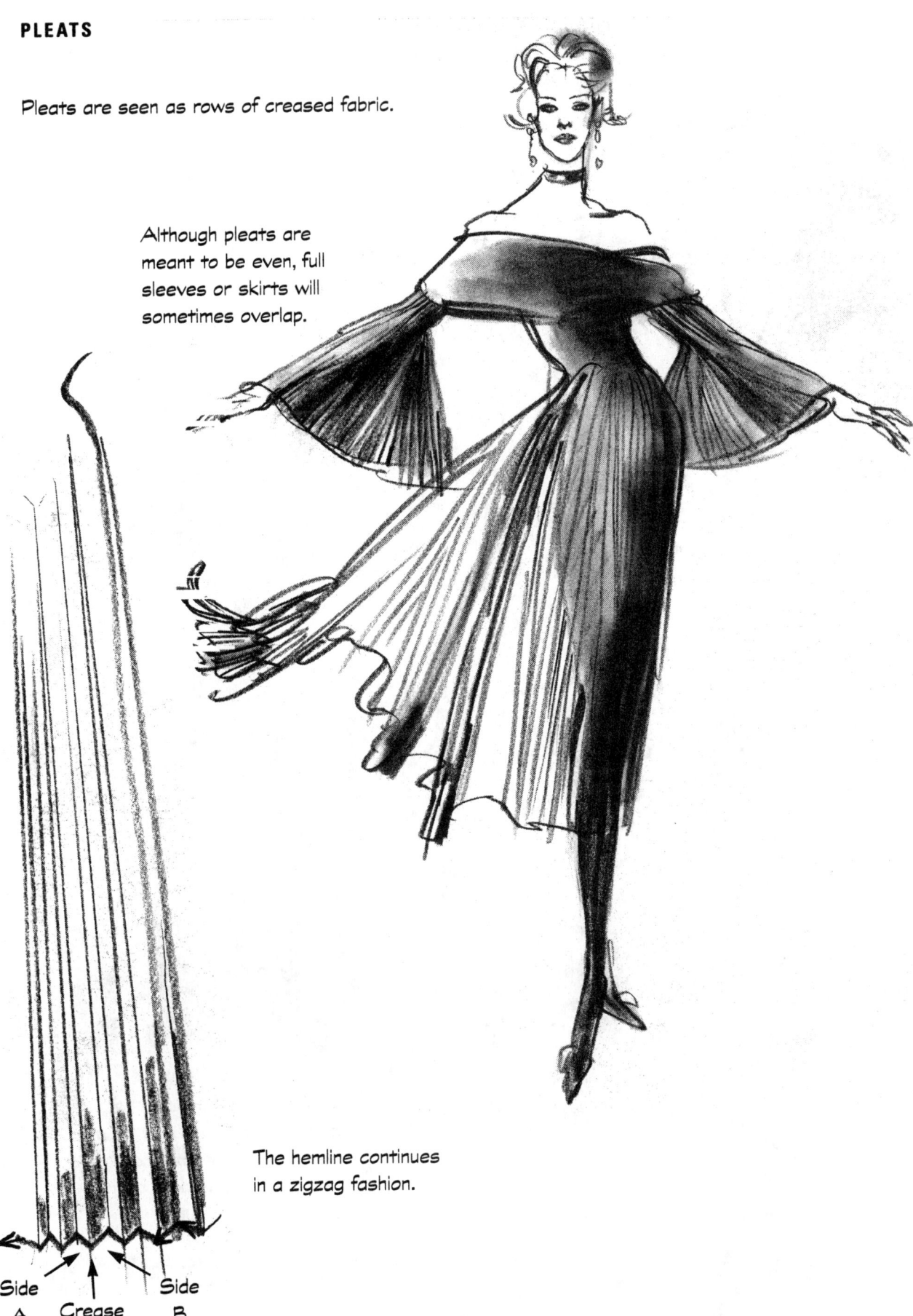

Stripes and seams must follow the slope on which they rest. In this elaborate display of drapery, stripes seem to be running in all directions, due to the placement of the fabric.

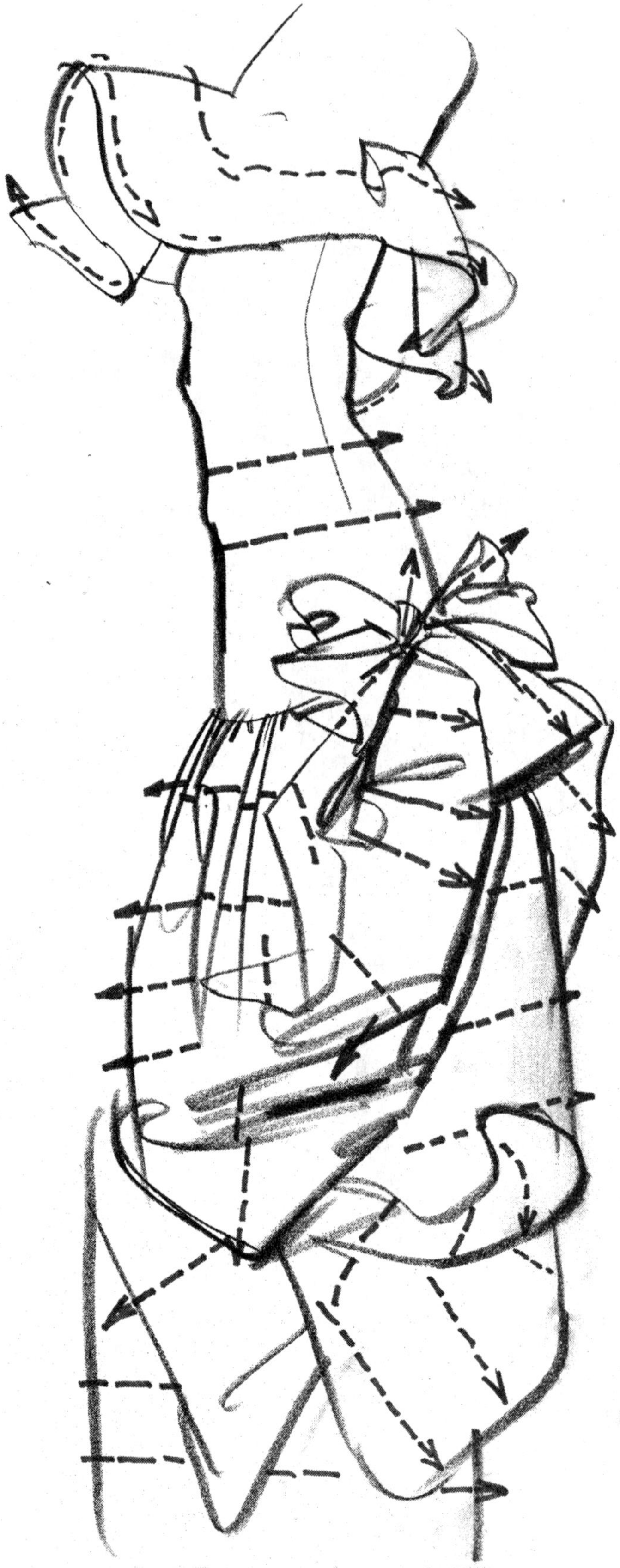

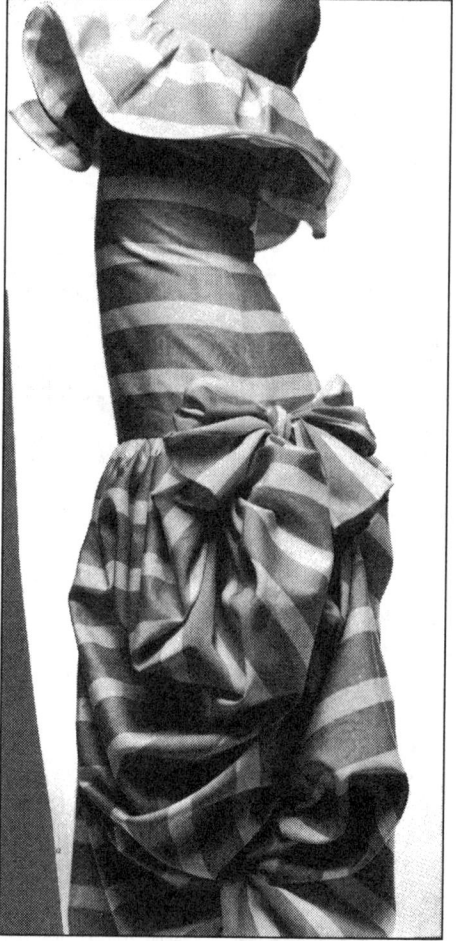

Drape a striped or polka dot fabric—pinned to a wall or on a dress form—and study the play of stripes or polka dots over the folds.

First, sketch in fabric shapes.

BOWS

Bows are an important fashion element and must be illustrated clearly and crisply. There are floppy bows, but they still have the same crisp pieces at the knot, wings, and tails. As in all tied fabric, the knot appears very tight, causing the wings to flair out crisply. This causes both wings to have a teardrop fold.

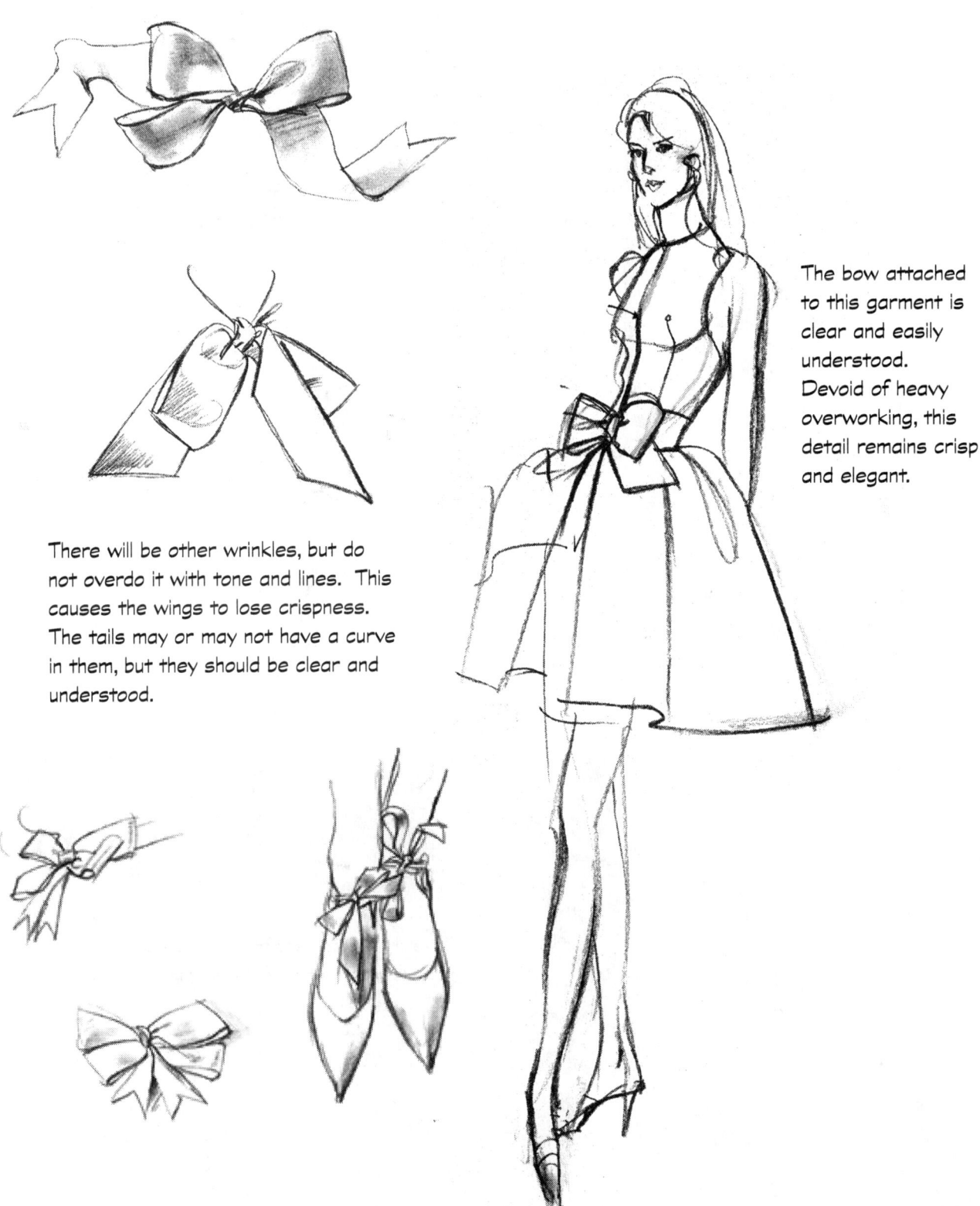

The bow attached to this garment is clear and easily understood. Devoid of heavy overworking, this detail remains crisp and elegant.

There will be other wrinkles, but do not overdo it with tone and lines. This causes the wings to lose crispness. The tails may or may not have a curve in them, but they should be clear and understood.

CHAPTER 7 CLOTHING DETAILS I: FOLDS AND DRAPERY

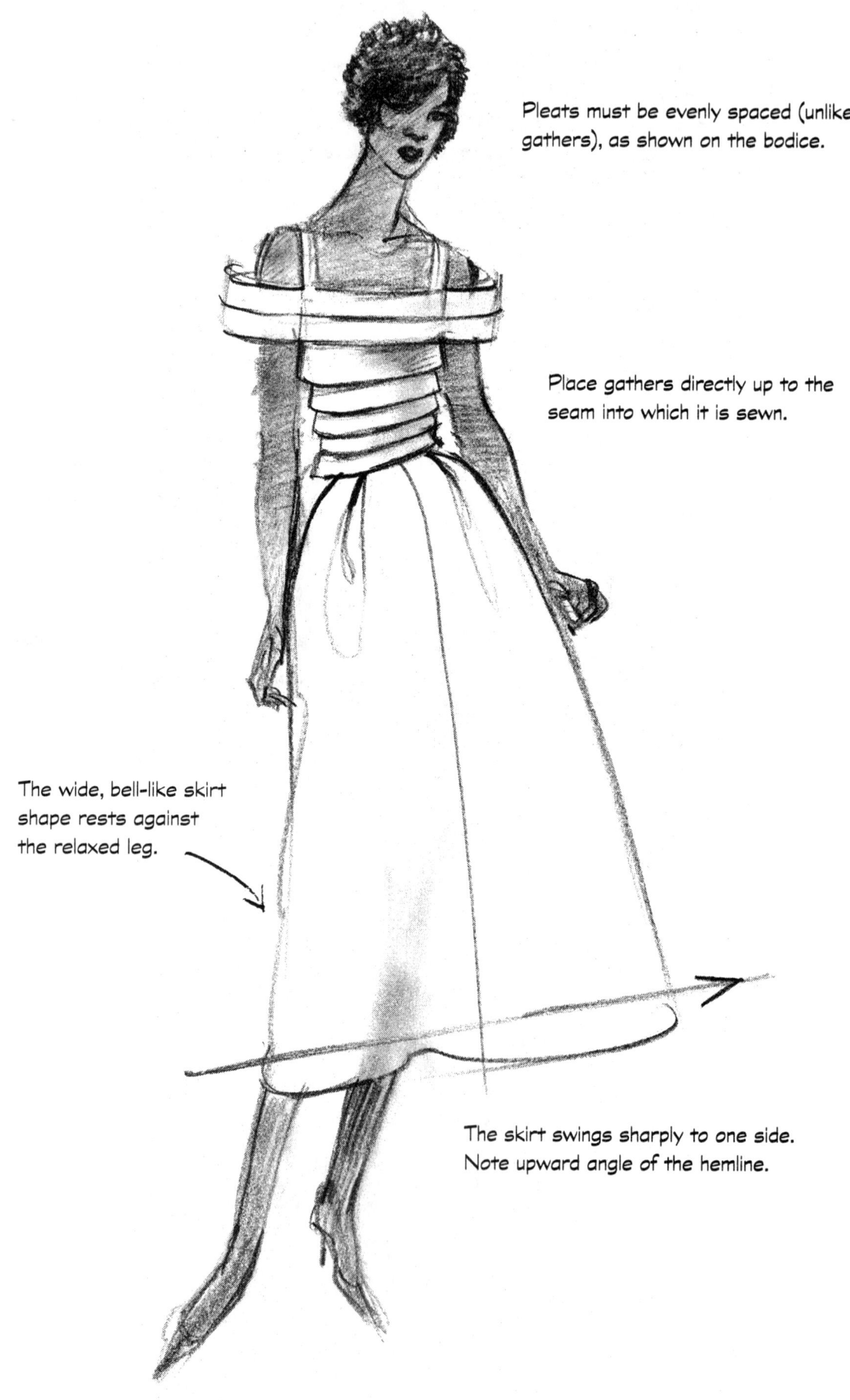

REMINDERS

Check the figure for these important points:

- Slope the shoulders.

- Find the body center to place details.

- The arm hides the body's action, but the hip is clearly being thrust to this side.

- The hemline is accurately placed, just at the ankles.

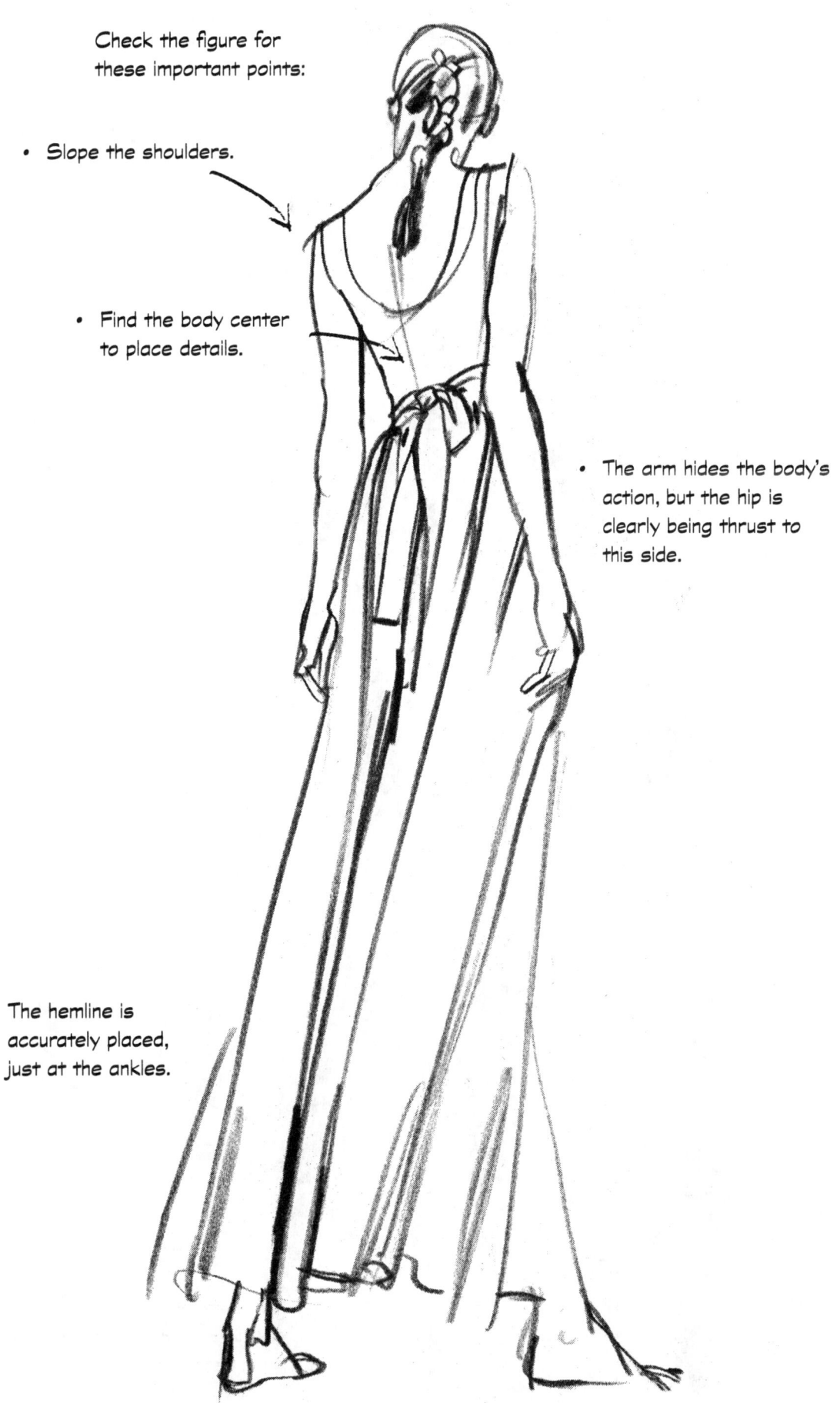

CHAPTER 7 CLOTHING DETAILS I: FOLDS AND DRAPERY

CHAPTER 8
Clothing Details II: Jackets and Hats

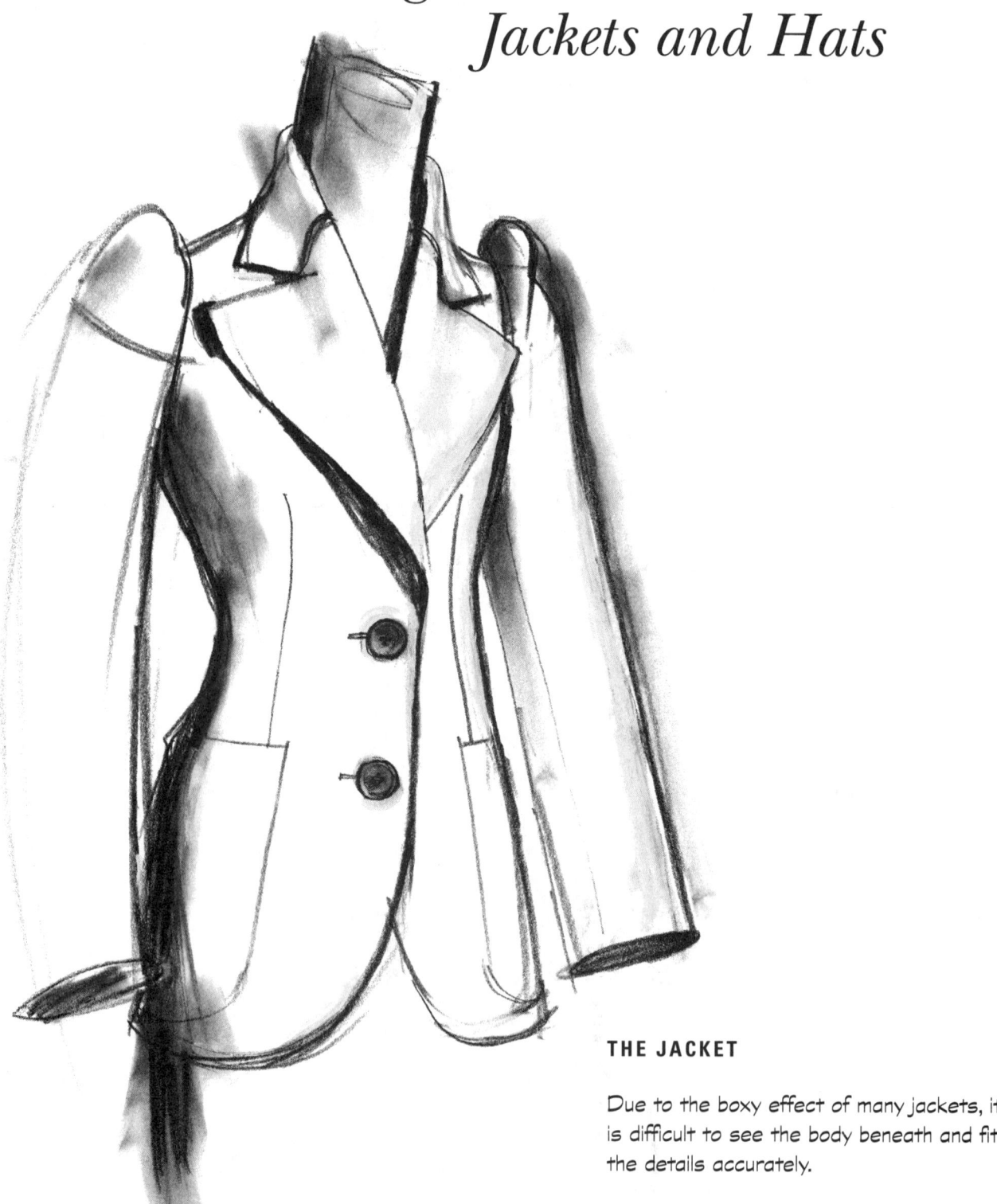

THE JACKET

Due to the boxy effect of many jackets, it is difficult to see the body beneath and fit the details accurately.

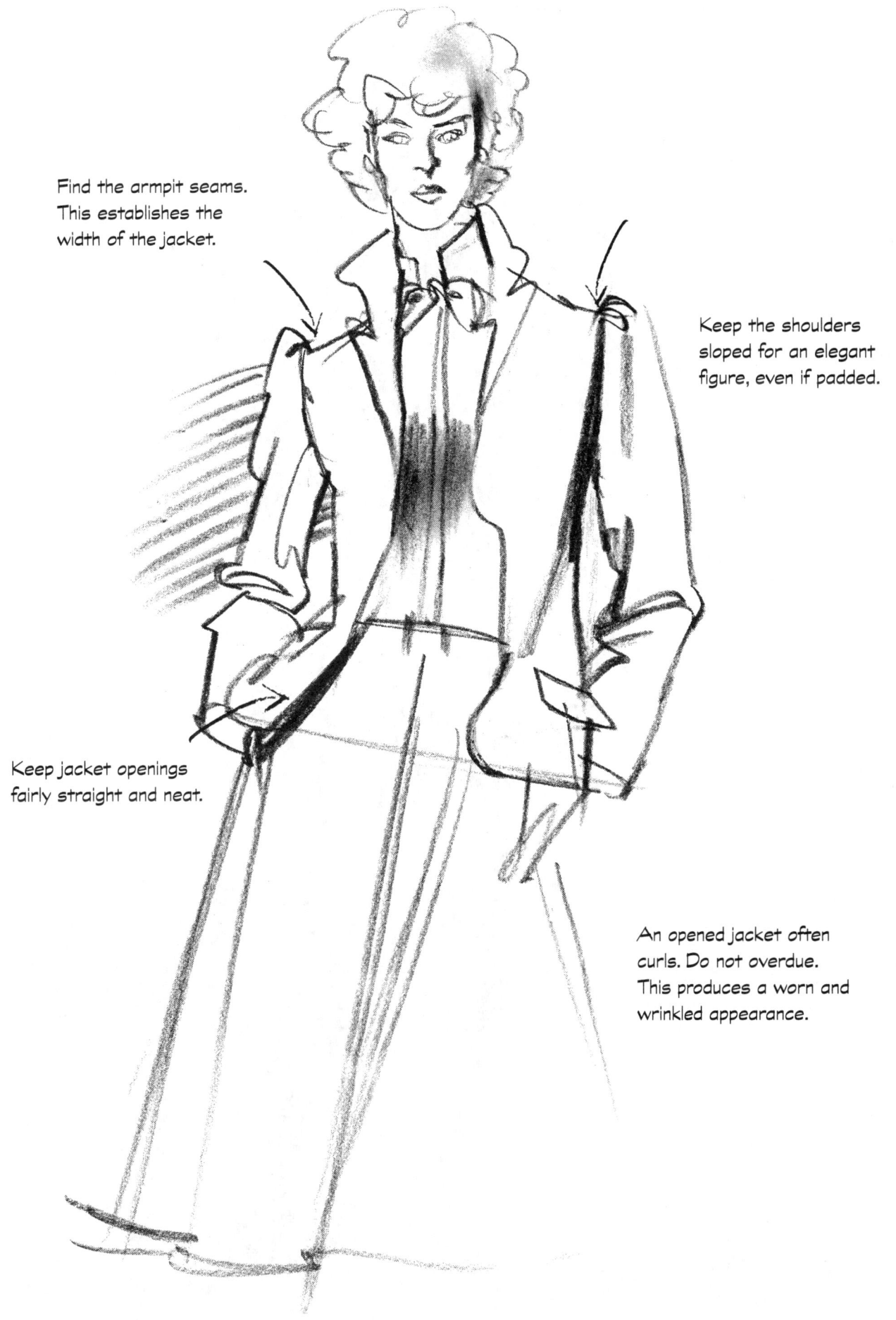

Find the armpit seams. This establishes the width of the jacket.

Keep the shoulders sloped for an elegant figure, even if padded.

Keep jacket openings fairly straight and neat.

An opened jacket often curls. Do not overdue. This produces a worn and wrinkled appearance.

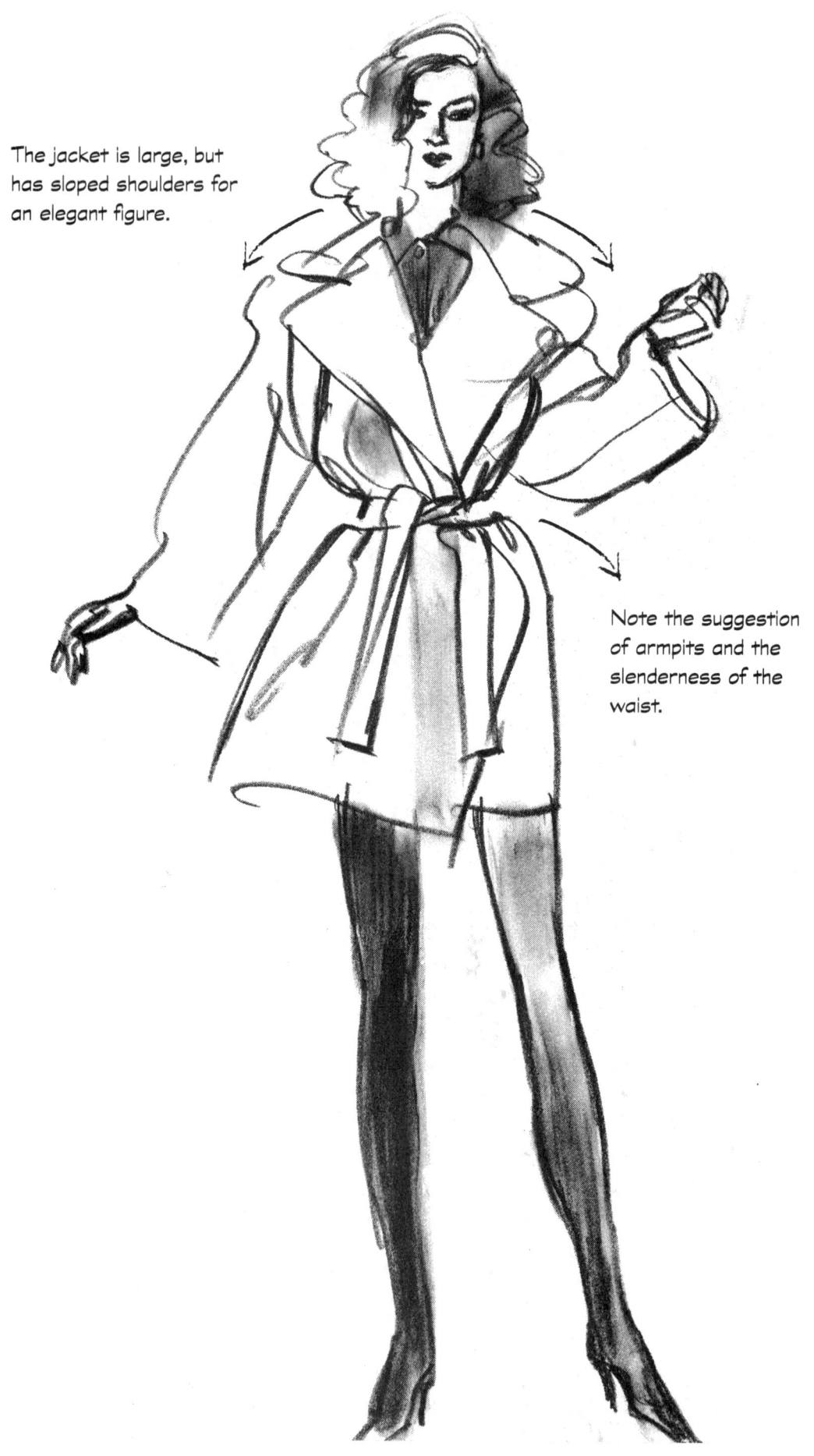

The jacket is large, but has sloped shoulders for an elegant figure.

Note the suggestion of armpits and the slenderness of the waist.

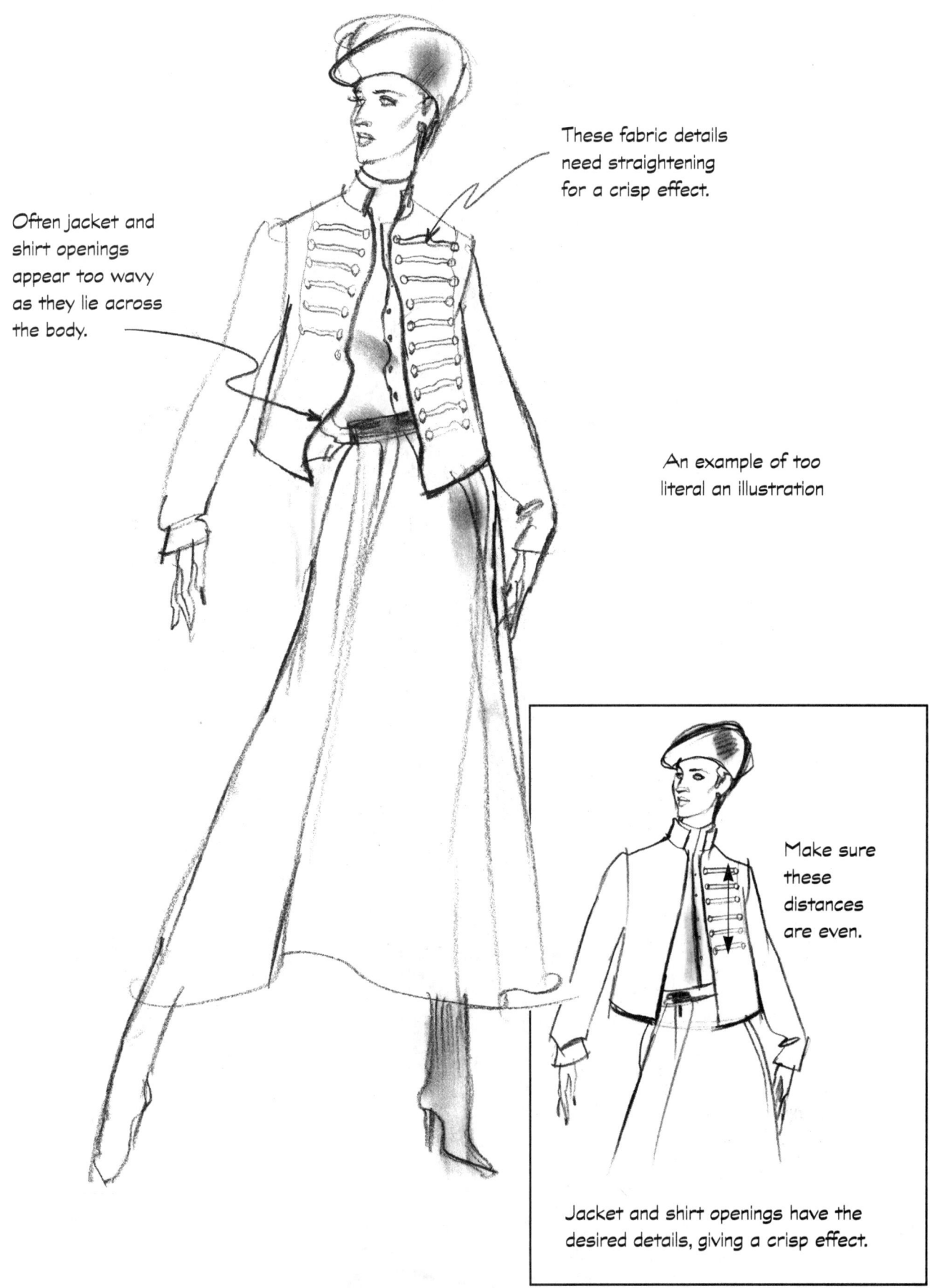

CHAPTER 8 CLOTHING DETAILS II: JACKETS AND HATS

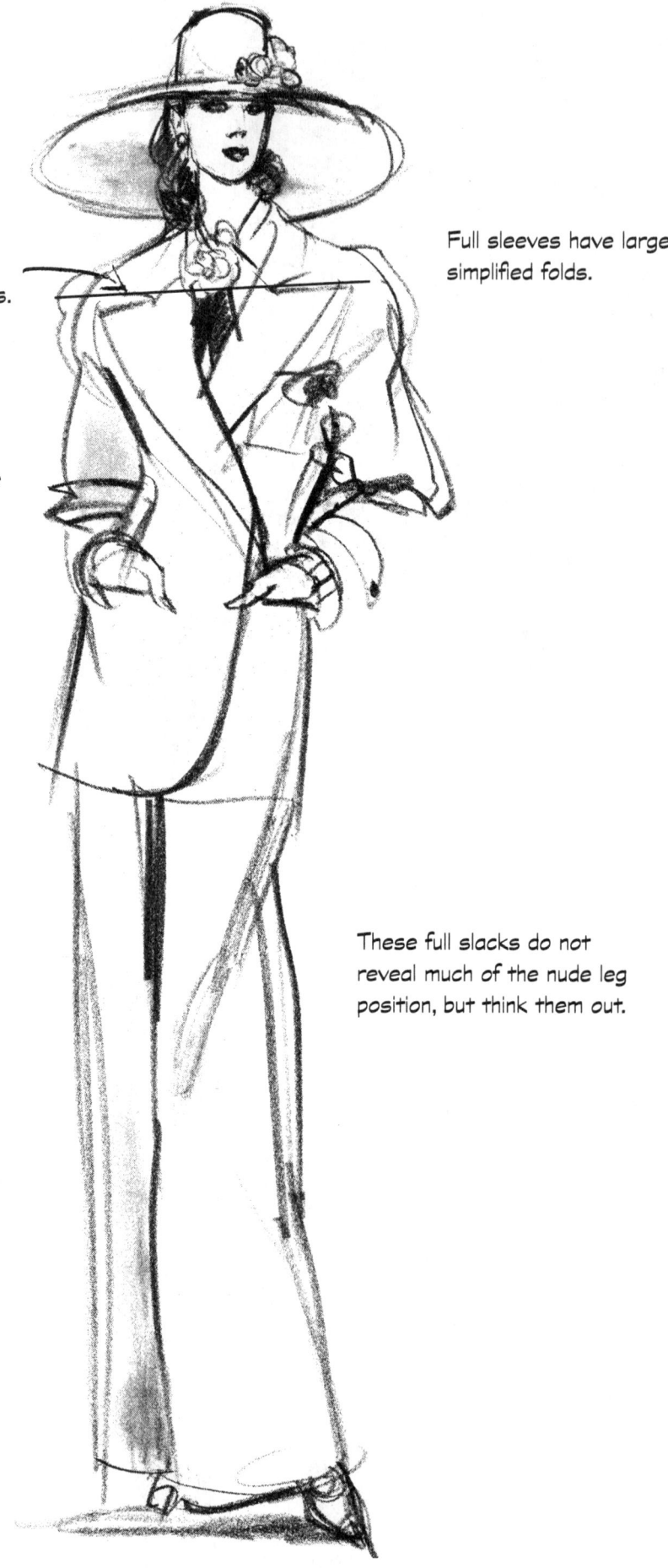

Line up the lapel notches.

Full sleeves have large, simplified folds.

Be clear about the distance of the lapel to the armpit seam and the length of the jacket.

These full slacks do not reveal much of the nude leg position, but think them out.

REMINDER: Think out the action of the body under heavy clothing.

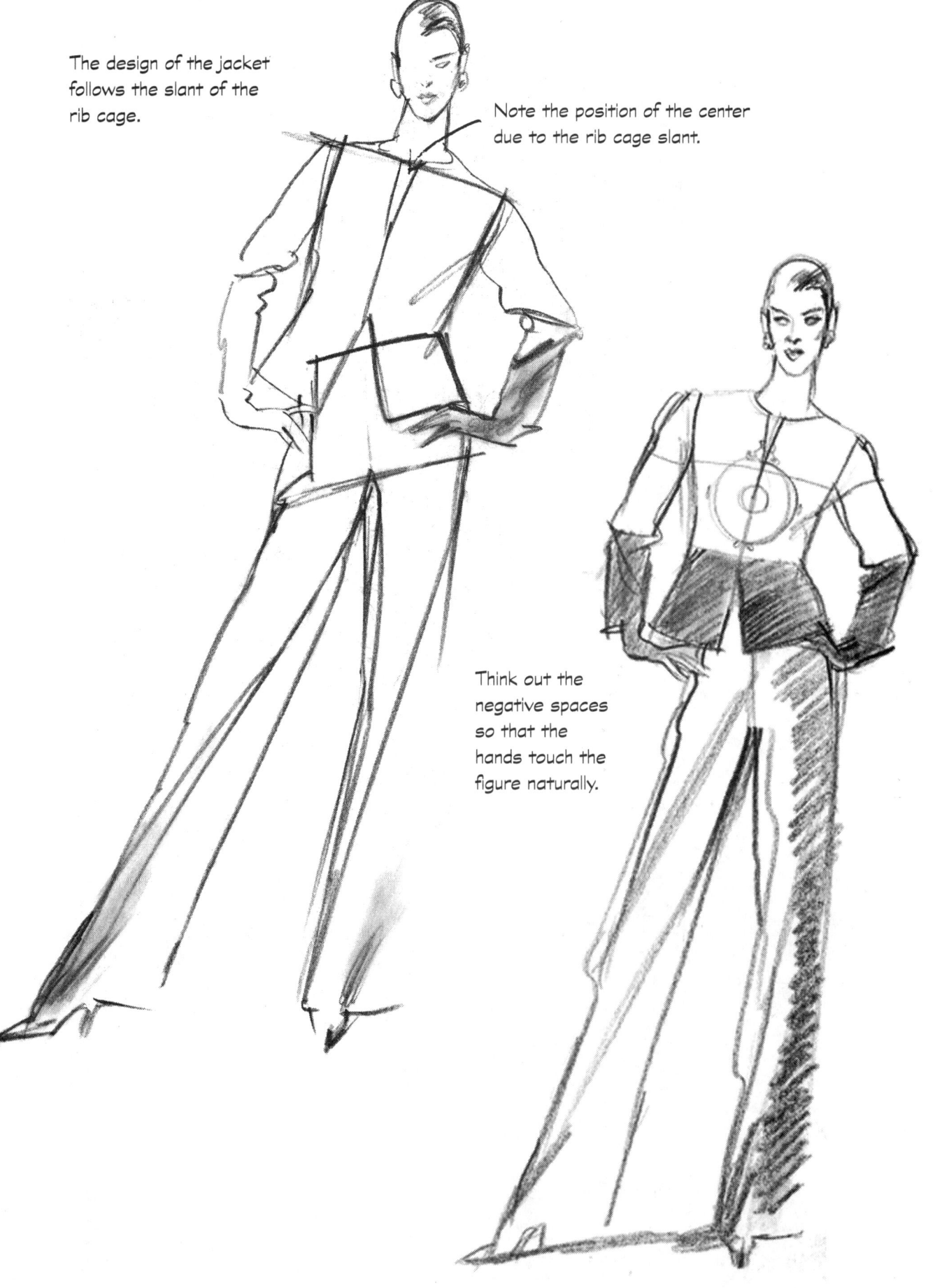

The design of the jacket follows the slant of the rib cage.

Note the position of the center due to the rib cage slant.

Think out the negative spaces so that the hands touch the figure naturally.

CHAPTER 8 CLOTHING DETAILS II: JACKETS AND HATS

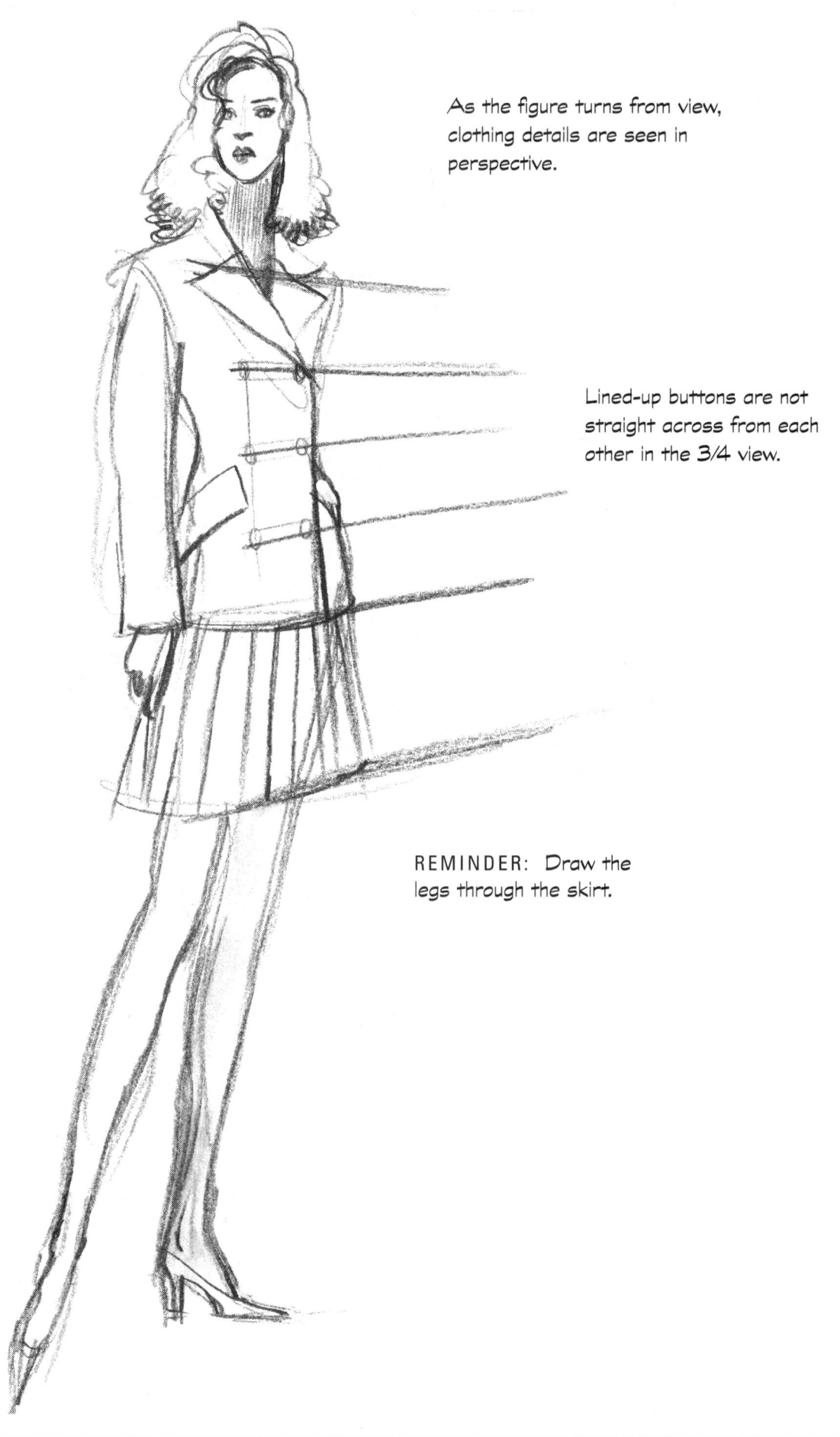

As the figure turns from view, clothing details are seen in perspective.

Lined-up buttons are not straight across from each other in the 3/4 view.

REMINDER: Draw the legs through the skirt.

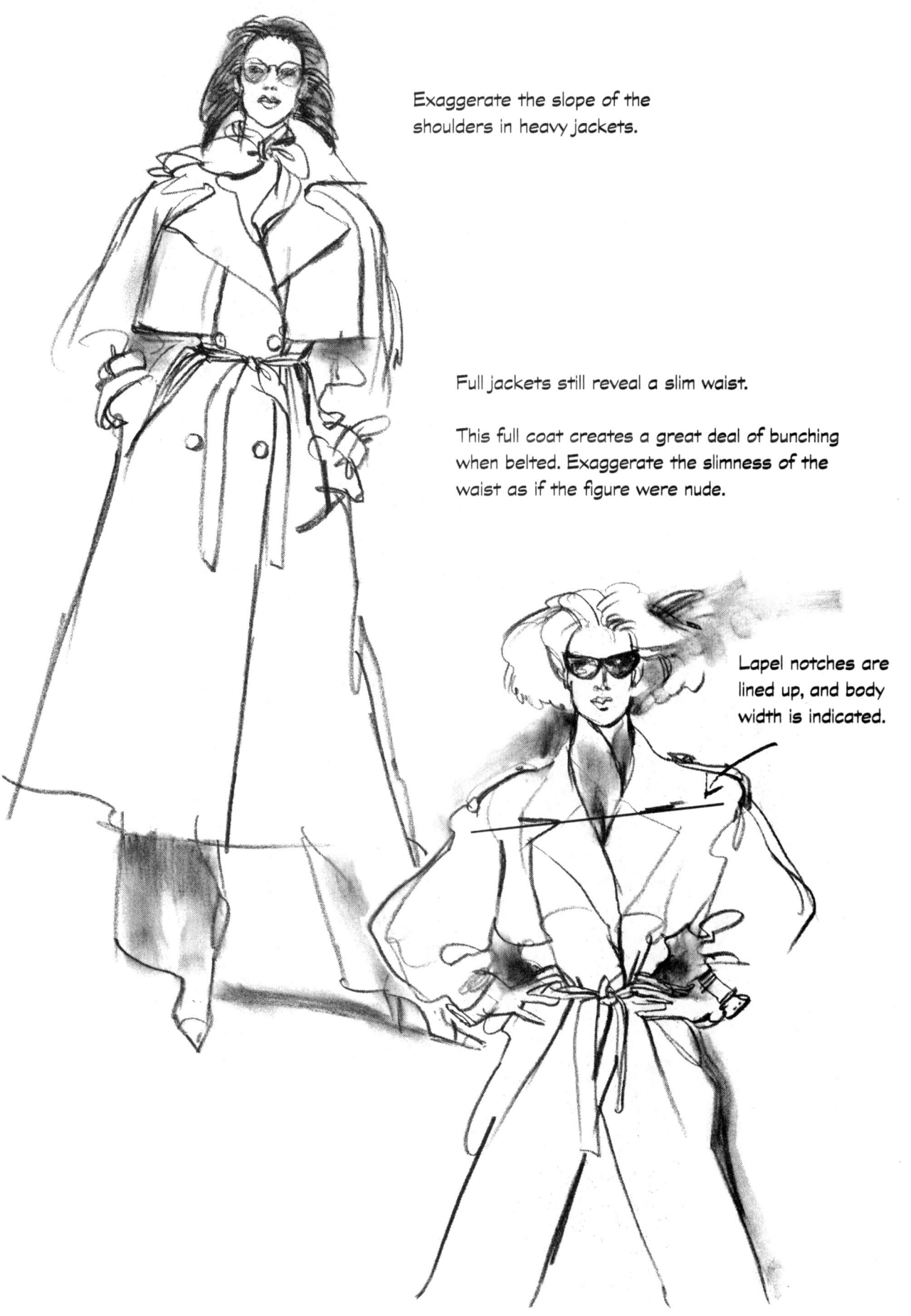

Exaggerate the slope of the shoulders in heavy jackets.

Full jackets still reveal a slim waist.

This full coat creates a great deal of bunching when belted. Exaggerate the slimness of the waist as if the figure were nude.

Lapel notches are lined up, and body width is indicated.

HATS

For any hat, draw the crown of the skull first, then the crown and brim.

Carefully judge the distance between the hat brim and the eye.

Brim widths on hats are important considerations.

122 FASHION SKETCHING

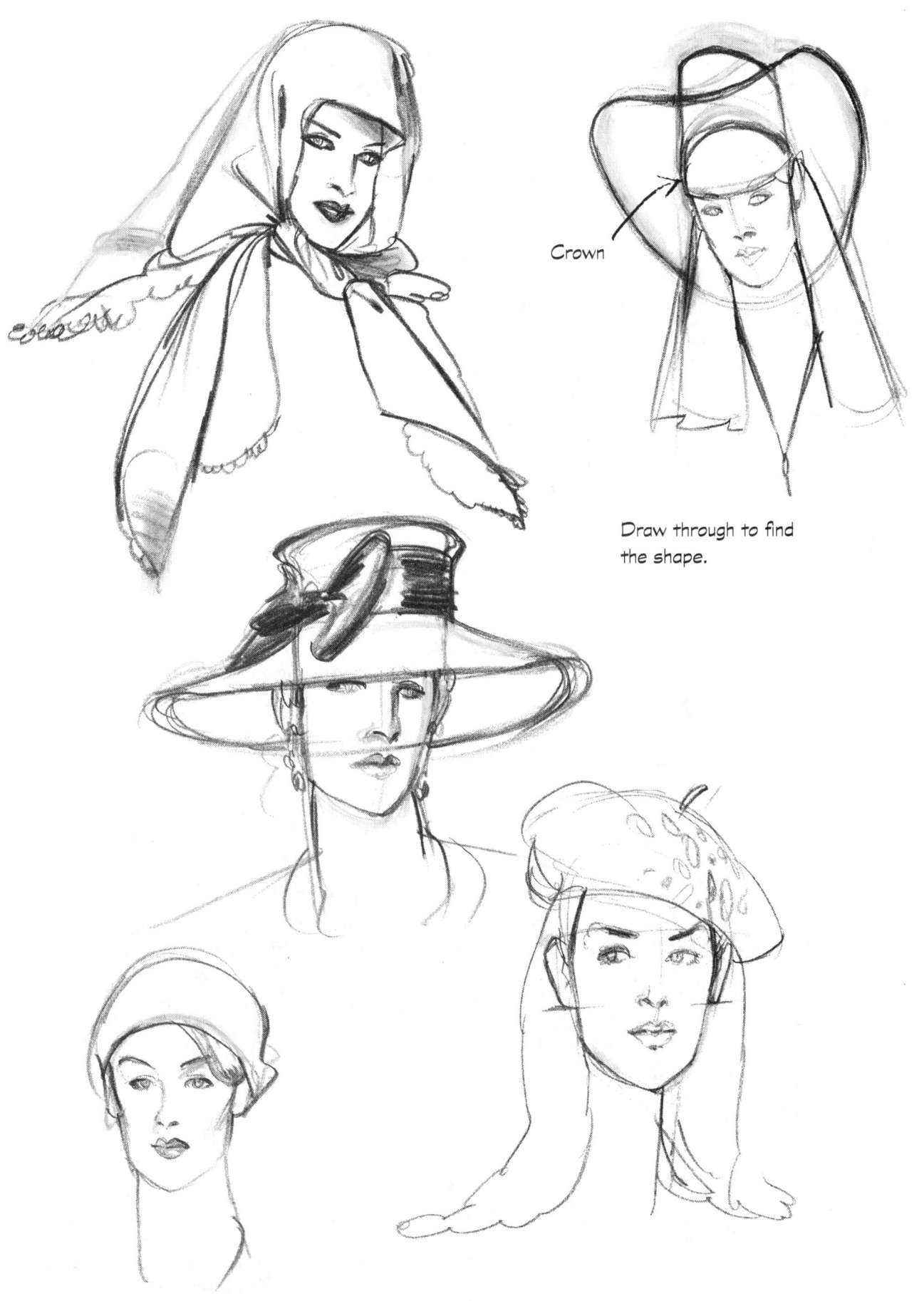

Crown

Draw through to find the shape.

CHAPTER 8 CLOTHING DETAILS II: JACKETS AND HATS

Sketch in the crown shapes to ensure enough room has been left.

The crown is showing. The wreath fits securely on the crown.

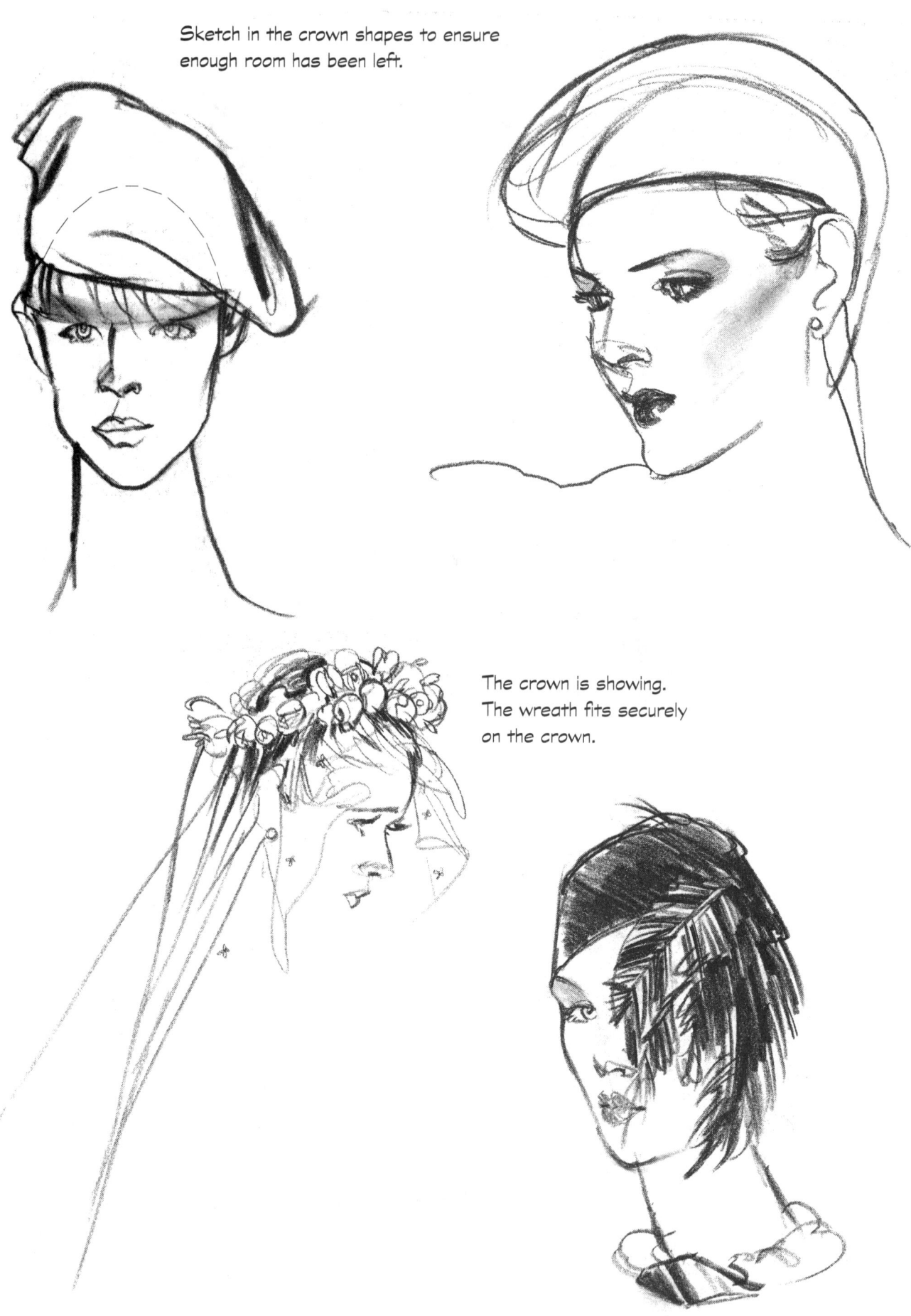

CHAPTER 9
Clothing Details III: Prints and Patterns

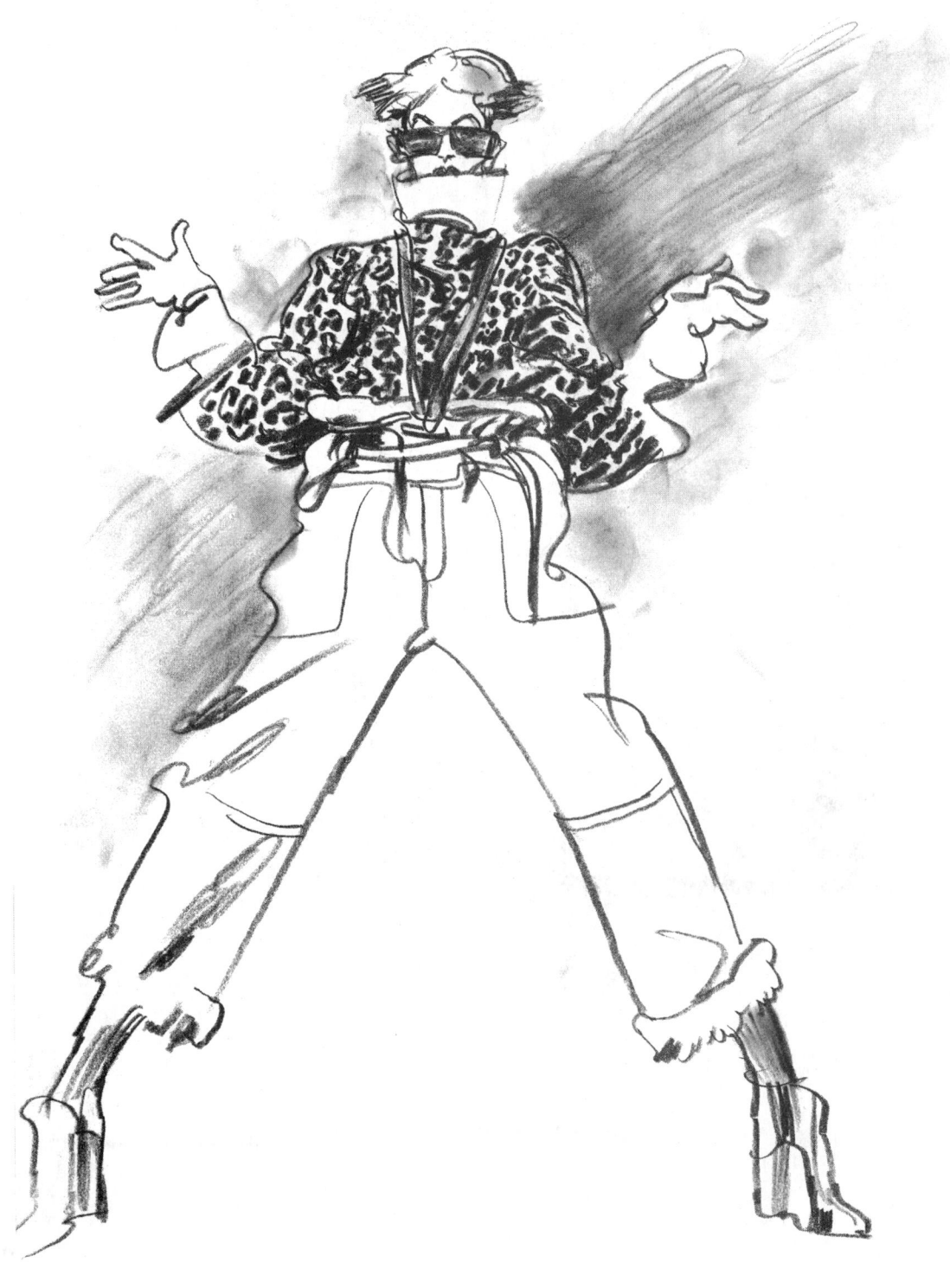

125

With a specific pattern, place a piece of the actual fabric over the dress in the chest area to keep the proportions correct. Copy the print exactly in the area in which the fabric was placed.

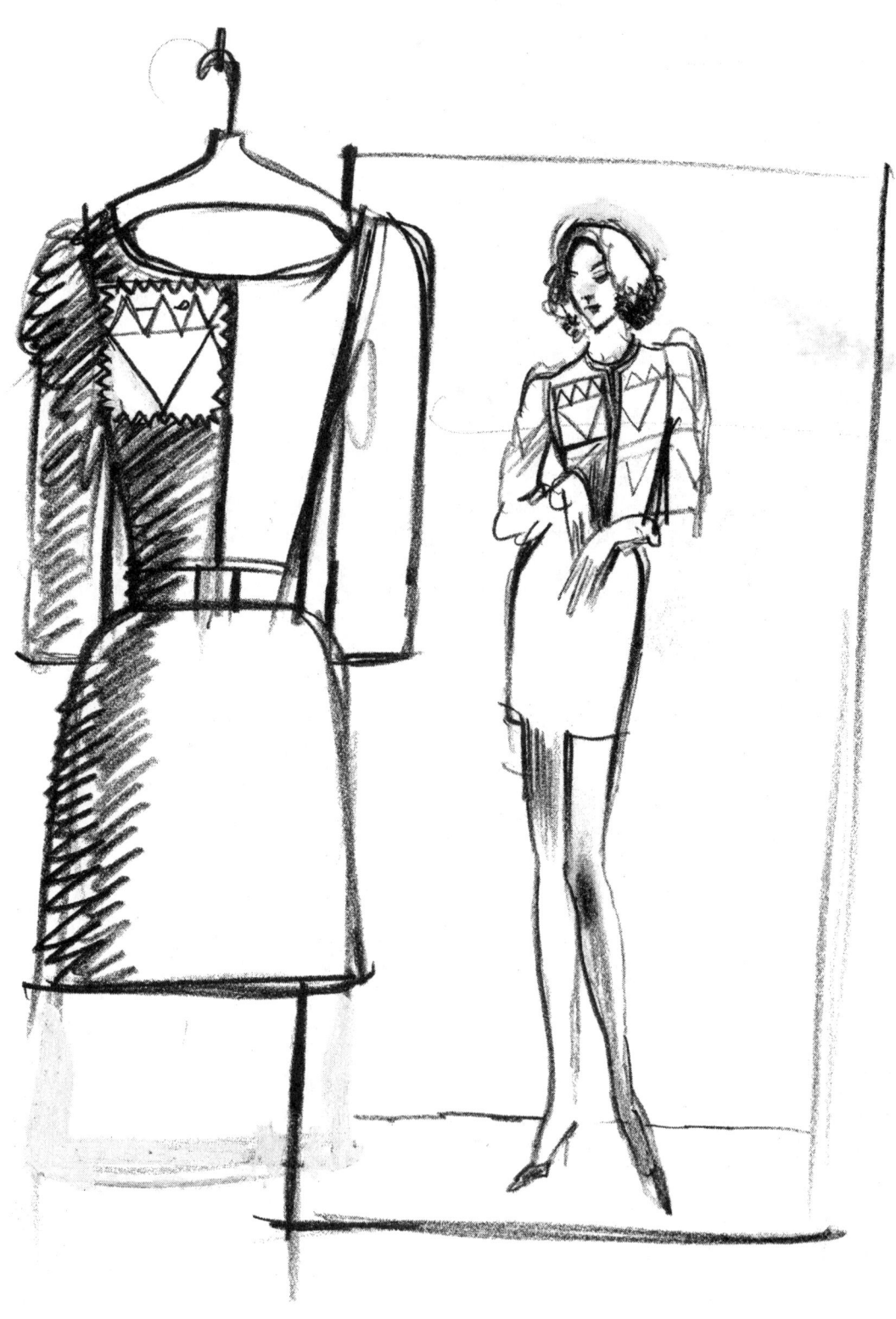

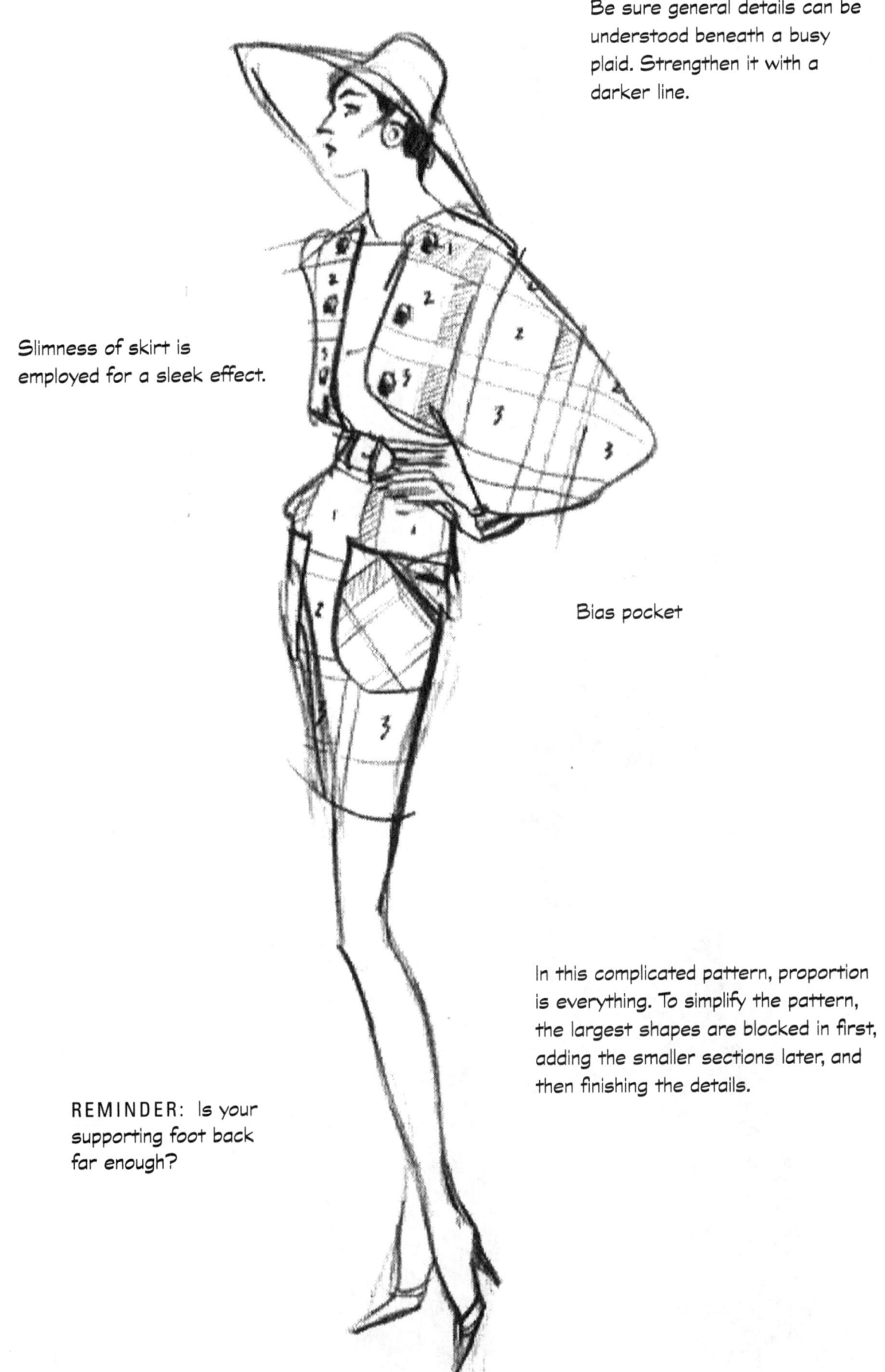

Be sure general details can be understood beneath a busy plaid. Strengthen it with a darker line.

Slimness of skirt is employed for a sleek effect.

Bias pocket

In this complicated pattern, proportion is everything. To simplify the pattern, the largest shapes are blocked in first, adding the smaller sections later, and then finishing the details.

REMINDER: Is your supporting foot back far enough?

CHAPTER 9 CLOTHING DETAILS III: PRINTS AND PATTERNS

PLANNING OUT A PLAID COUNT

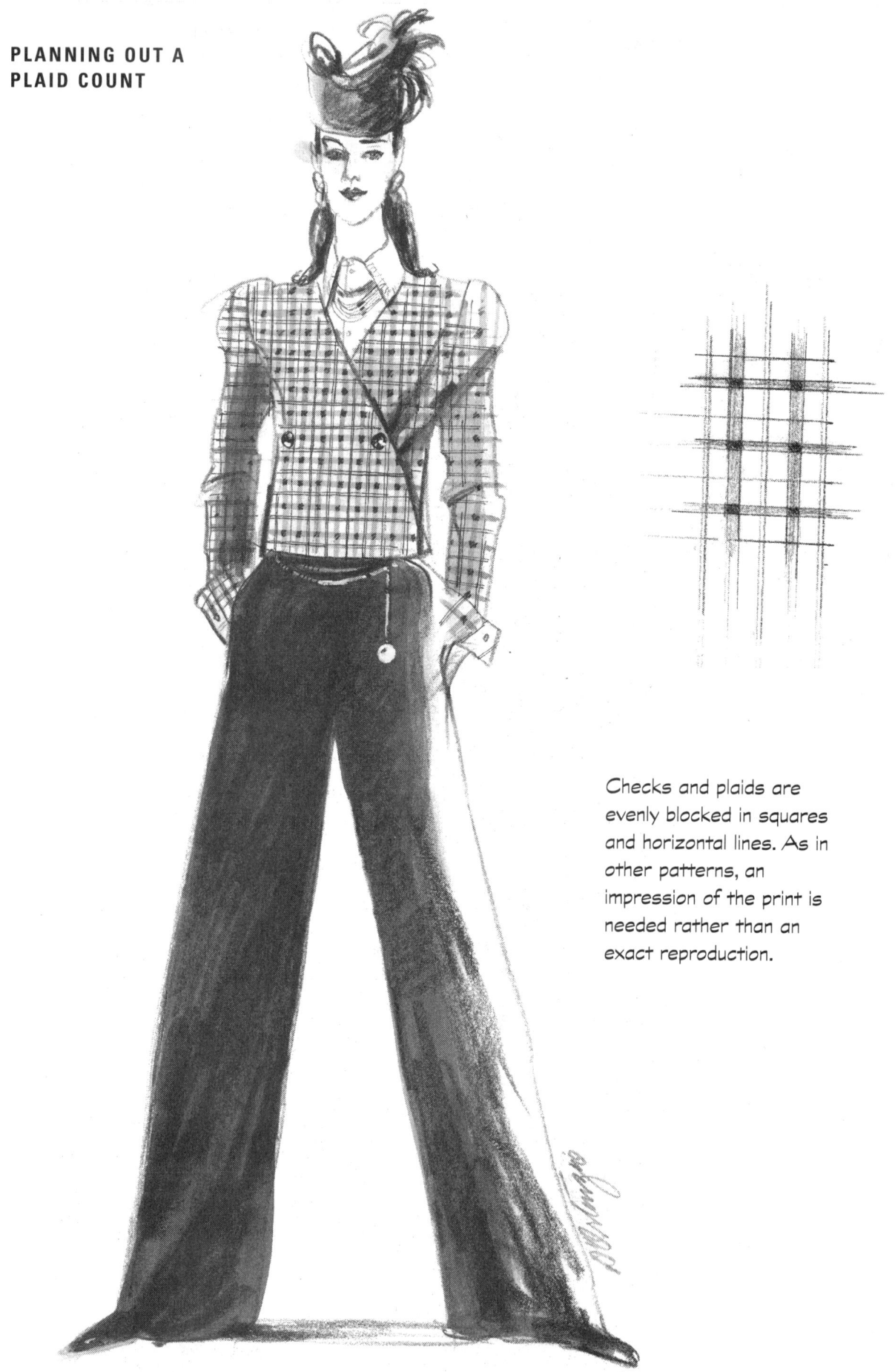

Checks and plaids are evenly blocked in squares and horizontal lines. As in other patterns, an impression of the print is needed rather than an exact reproduction.

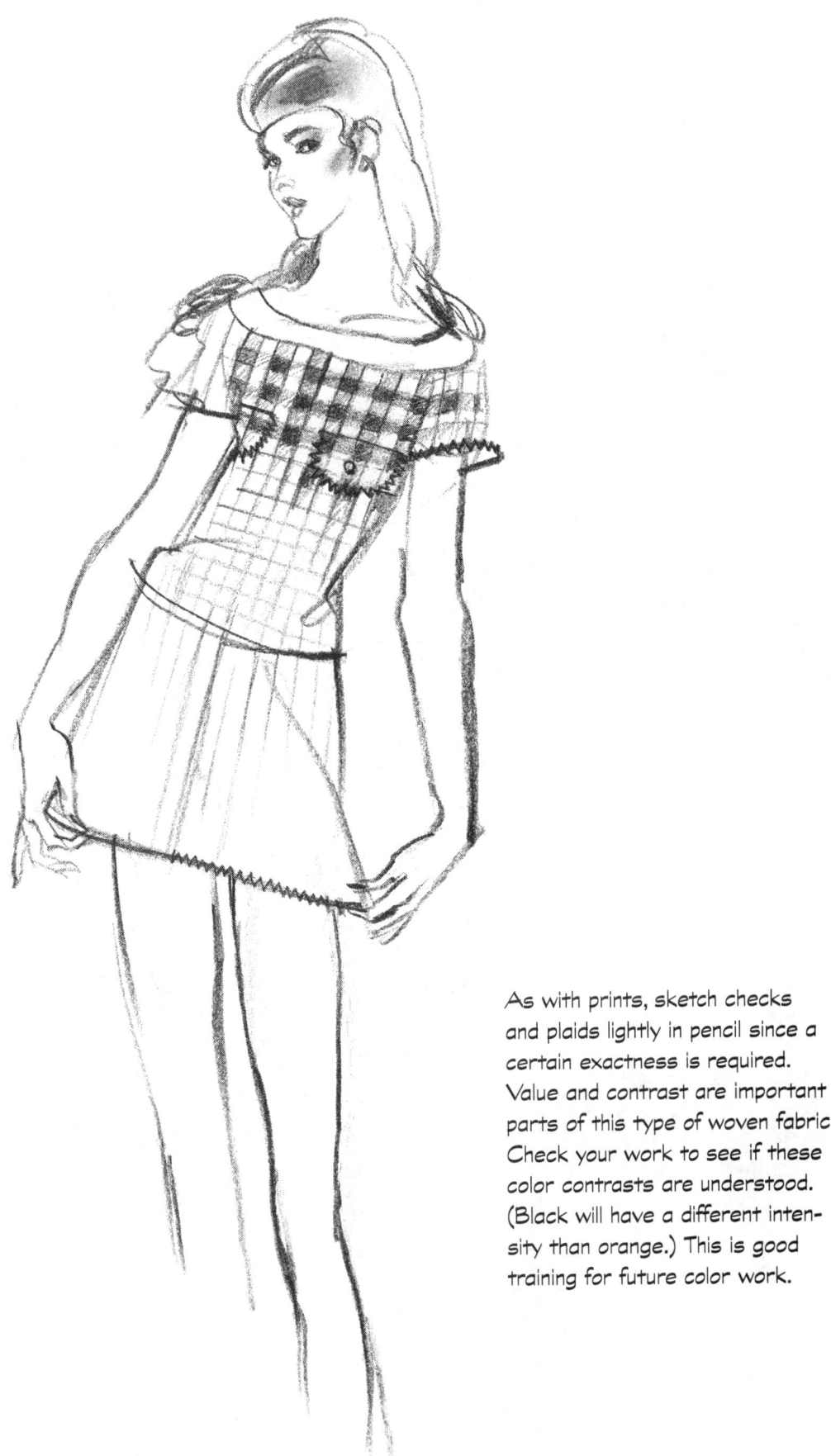

As with prints, sketch checks and plaids lightly in pencil since a certain exactness is required. Value and contrast are important parts of this type of woven fabric. Check your work to see if these color contrasts are understood. (Black will have a different intensity than orange.) This is good training for future color work.

As with stripes, the plaid or print adheres to the movement of the fabric.

Try to see the shape.

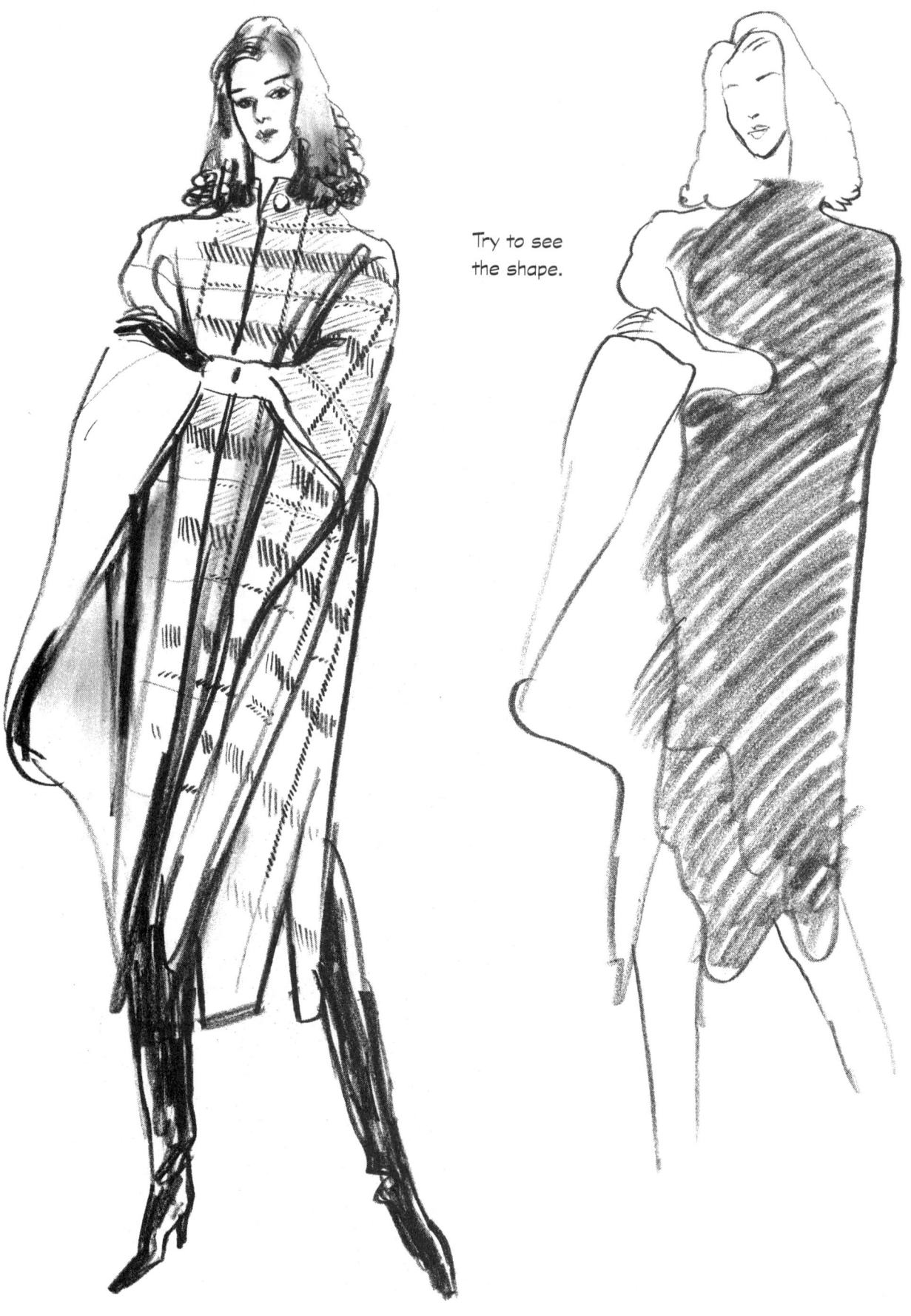

The plaid on the left is carefully measured and planned out.

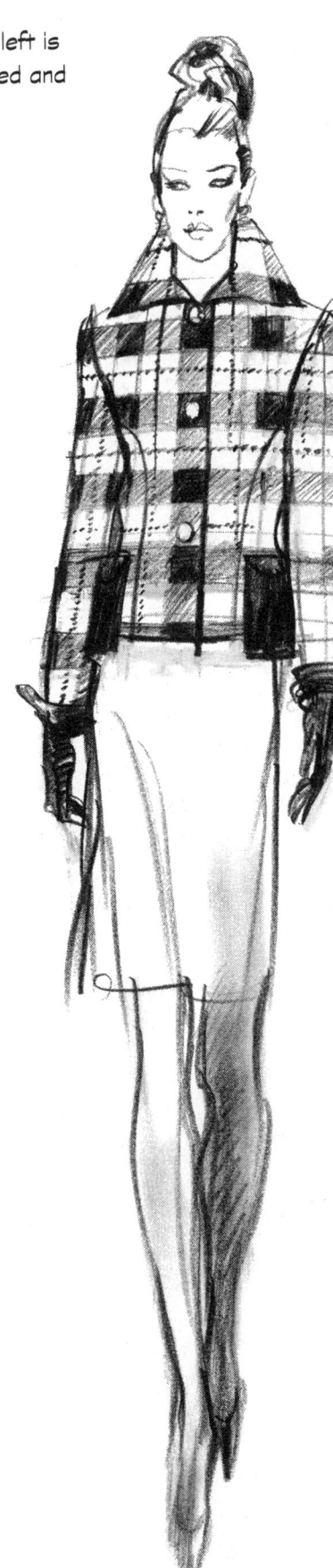

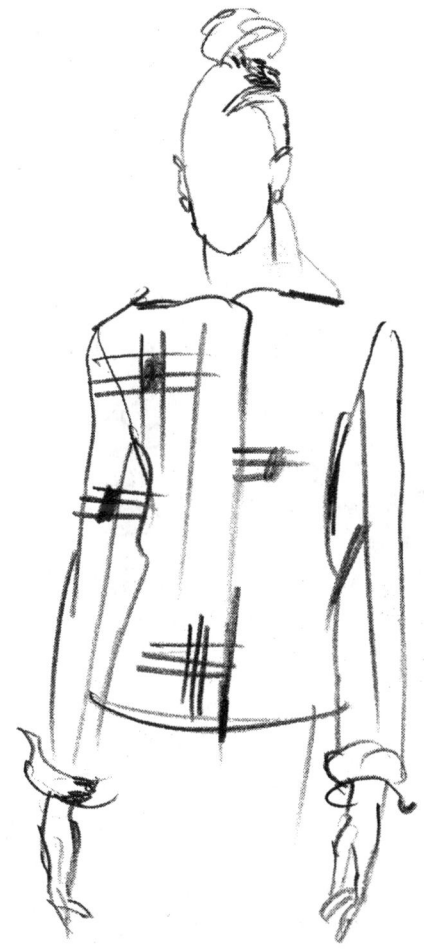

This does not look like plaid. Uneven lines and spotted areas over the jacket suggest a print.

Working within measured distances, plaid can be freely indicated with a great degree of accuracy.

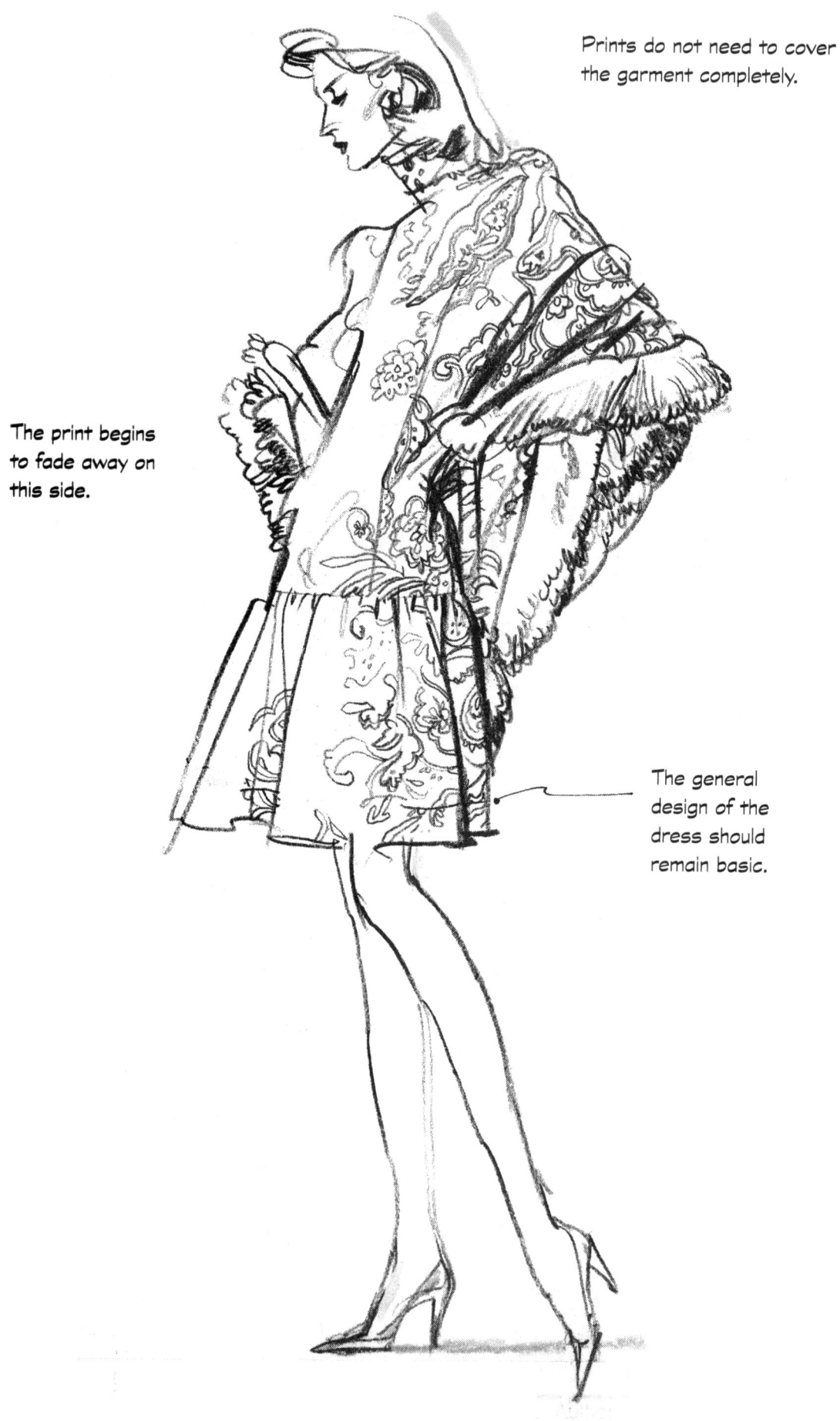

LACE

All lace is built around a basic element of design. Usually it is a flower, specifically a rose. In order to portray a specific pattern, one must count the roses across and down one section of the garment. Often the roses are staggered rather than being symmetrical. The roses are usually connected by a vine of leaves sewn on a background of netting. This can be excessive detail, giving a heaviness to what should be light and airy.

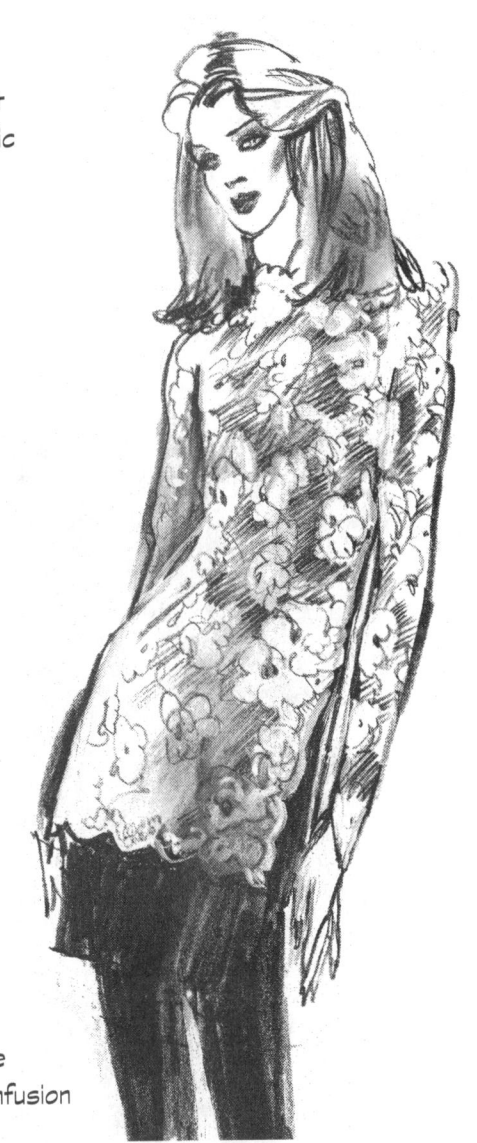

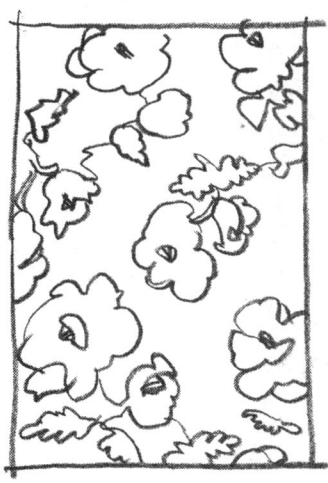

This must be laid out in pencil and in simple shapes before detailing. Unless this is done, detailing takes over, and confusion and false proportions result.

A TYPICAL LACE PATTERN

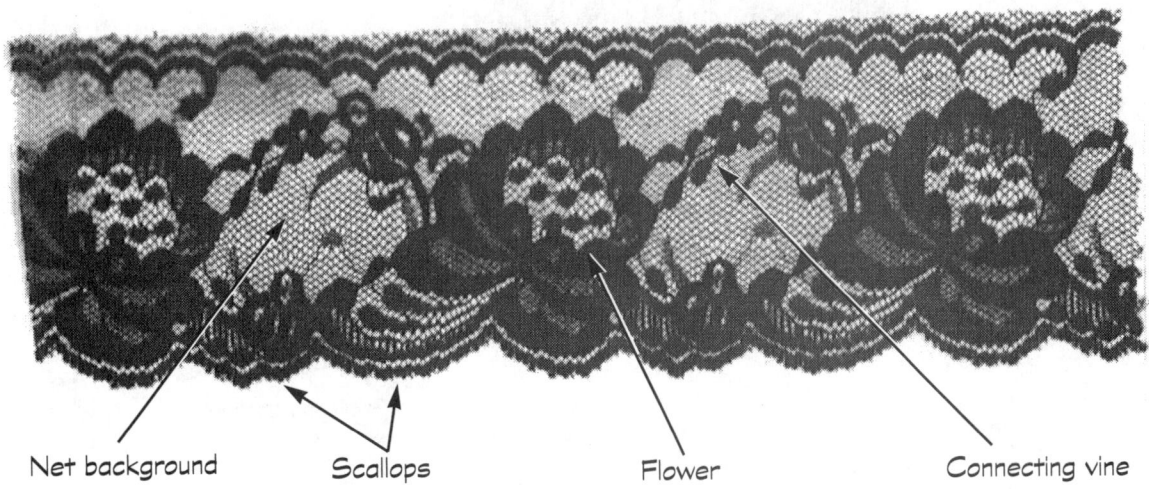

Net background   Scallops   Flower   Connecting vine

CHAPTER 9   CLOTHING DETAILS III: PRINTS AND PATTERNS

LEATHER

Thick, round contours suggest plush, expensive leather.

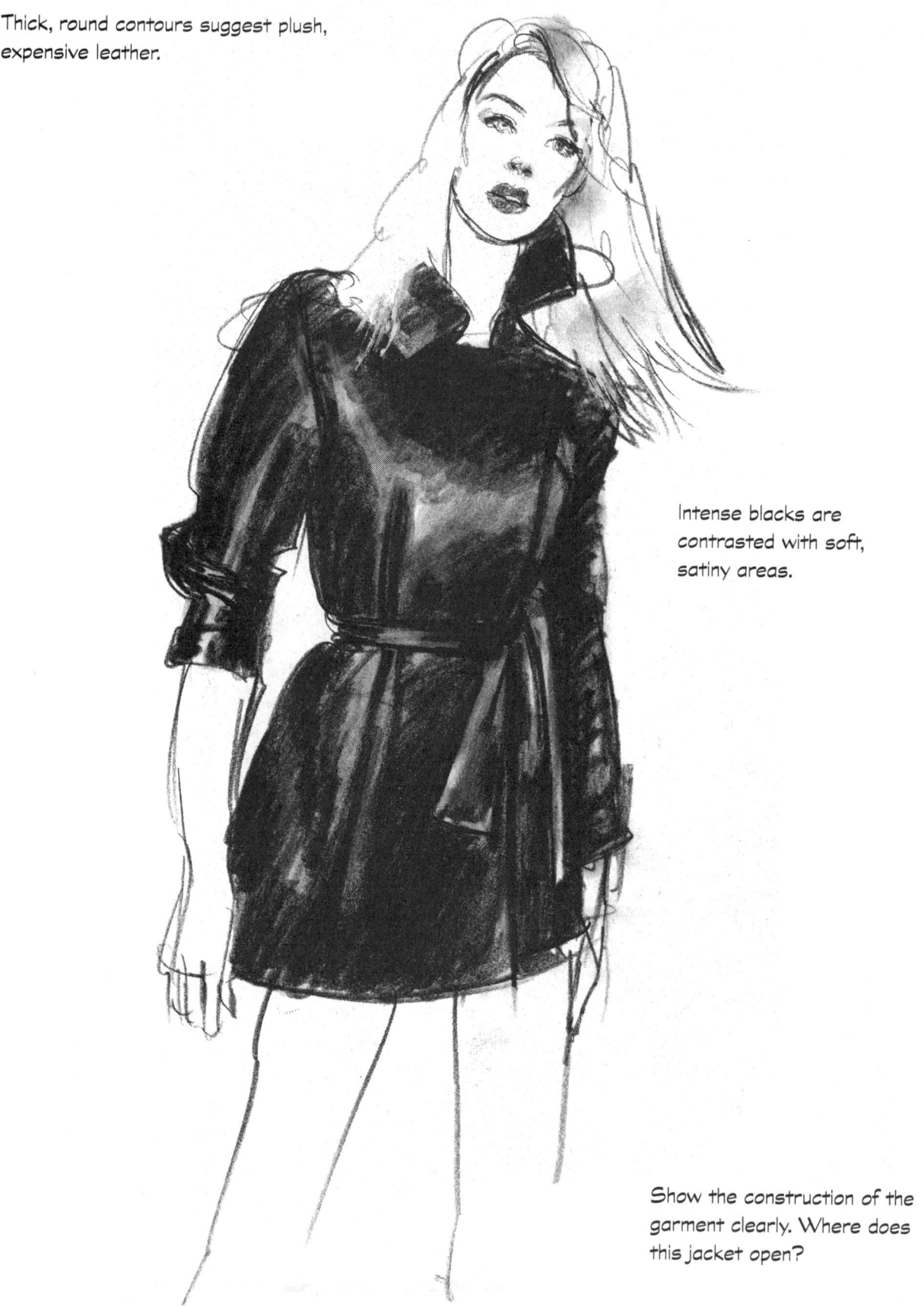

Intense blacks are contrasted with soft, satiny areas.

Show the construction of the garment clearly. Where does this jacket open?

FUR — NATURAL AND FAUX

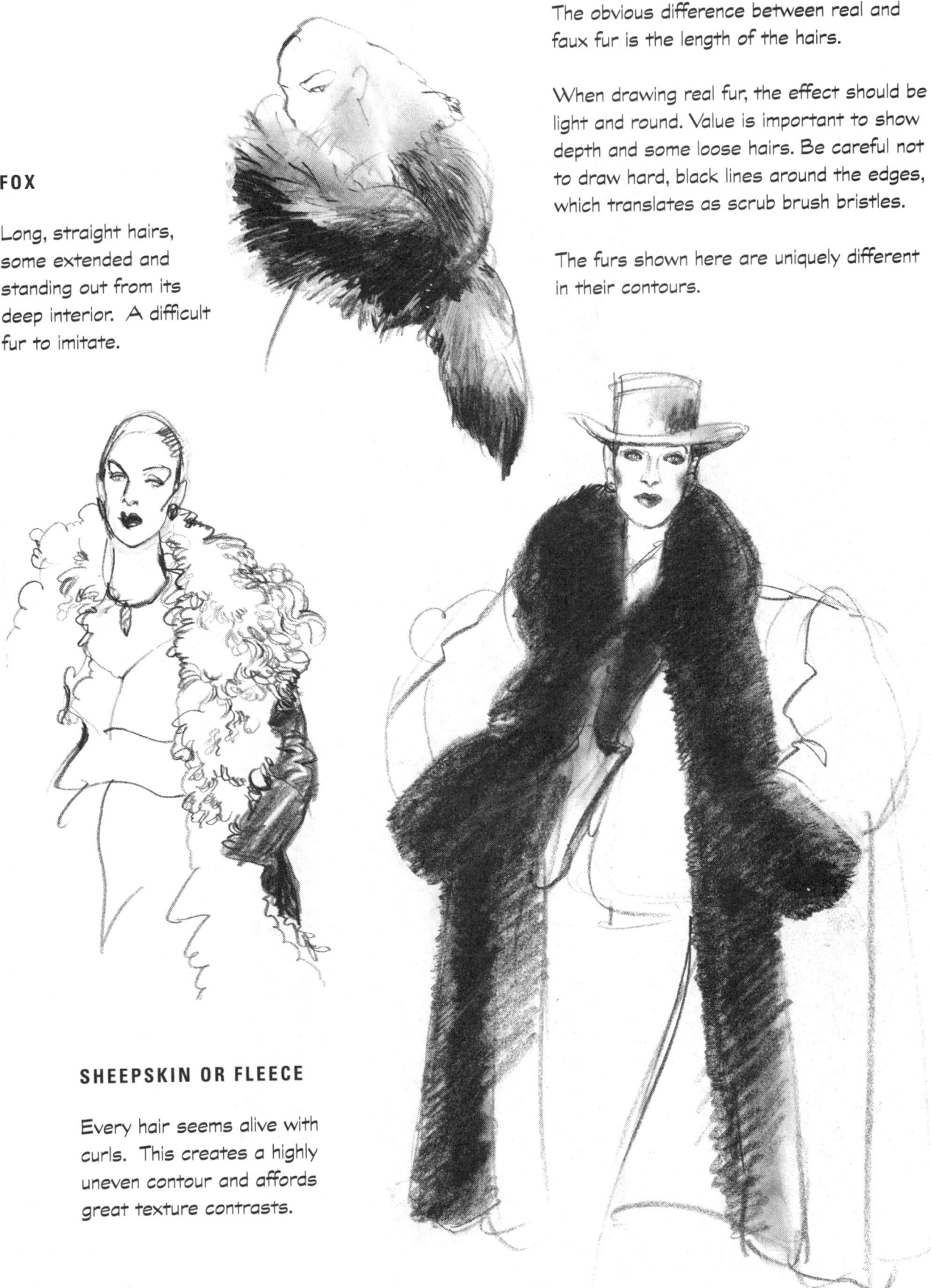

FOX

Long, straight hairs, some extended and standing out from its deep interior. A difficult fur to imitate.

The obvious difference between real and faux fur is the length of the hairs.

When drawing real fur, the effect should be light and round. Value is important to show depth and some loose hairs. Be careful not to draw hard, black lines around the edges, which translates as scrub brush bristles.

The furs shown here are uniquely different in their contours.

SHEEPSKIN OR FLEECE

Every hair seems alive with curls. This creates a highly uneven contour and affords great texture contrasts.

CHAPTER 9   CLOTHING DETAILS III: PRINTS AND PATTERNS   135

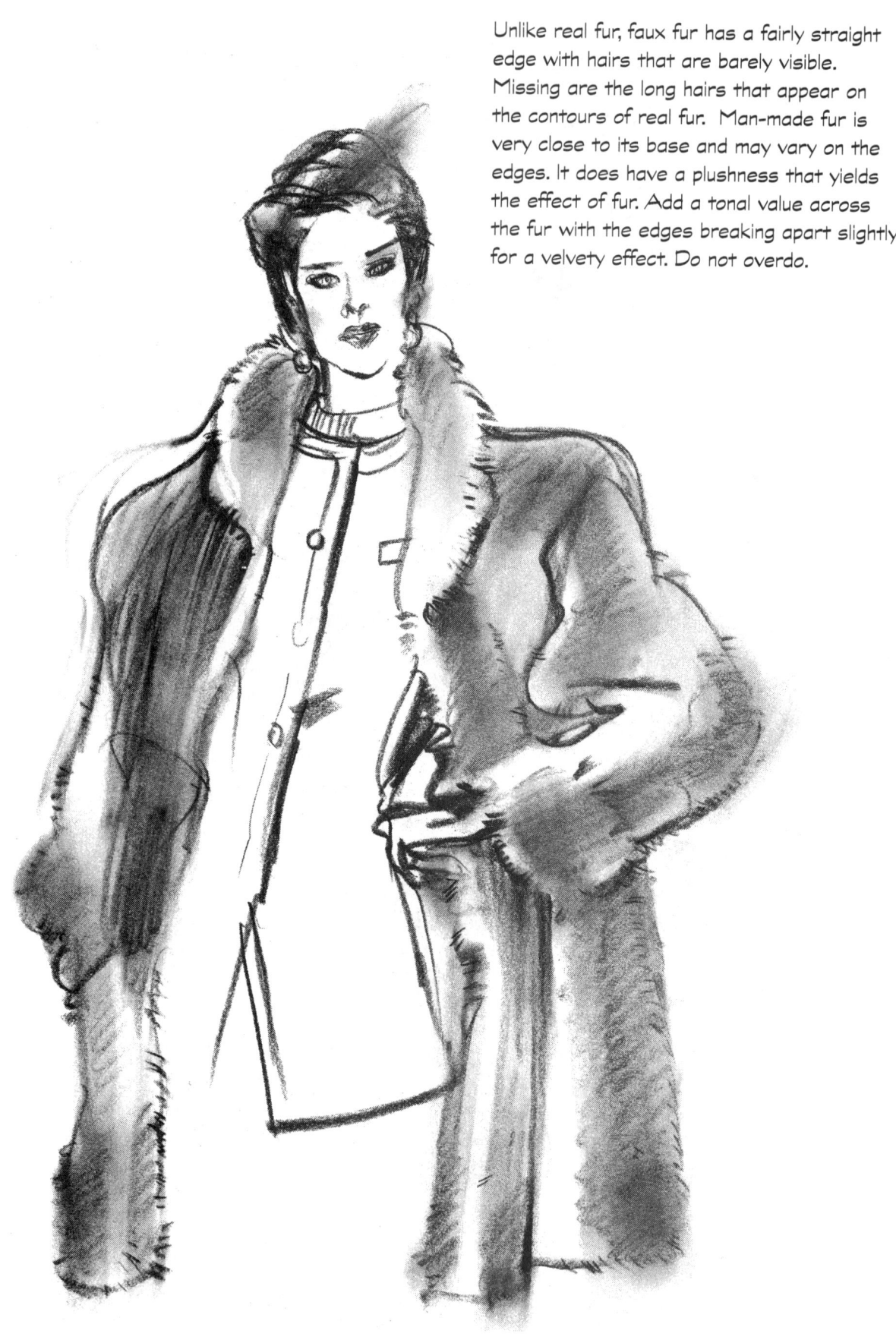

Unlike real fur, faux fur has a fairly straight edge with hairs that are barely visible. Missing are the long hairs that appear on the contours of real fur. Man-made fur is very close to its base and may vary on the edges. It does have a plushness that yields the effect of fur. Add a tonal value across the fur with the edges breaking apart slightly for a velvety effect. Do not overdo.

ANIMAL PRINTS

Due to increased awareness of animal conservation, fabrics printed with animal skin patterns have become popular. As a result, it is important for designers and illustrators to imitate these patterns.

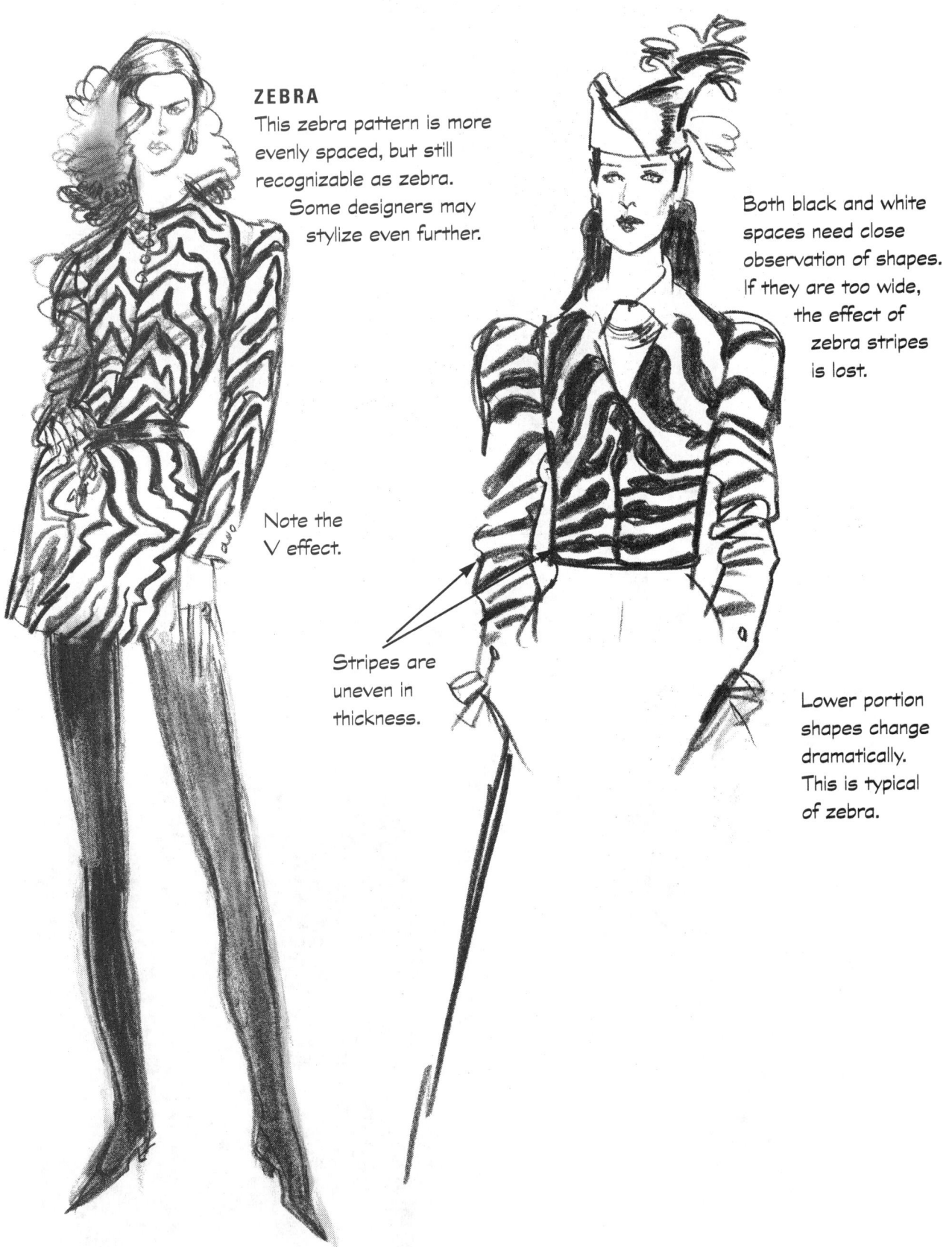

ZEBRA
This zebra pattern is more evenly spaced, but still recognizable as zebra. Some designers may stylize even further.

Note the V effect.

Stripes are uneven in thickness.

Both black and white spaces need close observation of shapes. If they are too wide, the effect of zebra stripes is lost.

Lower portion shapes change dramatically. This is typical of zebra.

CHAPTER 9 CLOTHING DETAILS III: PRINTS AND PATTERNS

One of the most popular prints is the leopard. Often on a white or tan background, the inner spot is a darker tan surrounded by pawlike spots.

Some spots are kidney-shaped. A large area of print gives way to a cluster of smaller black spots.

Tan spot

White areas

Black spots

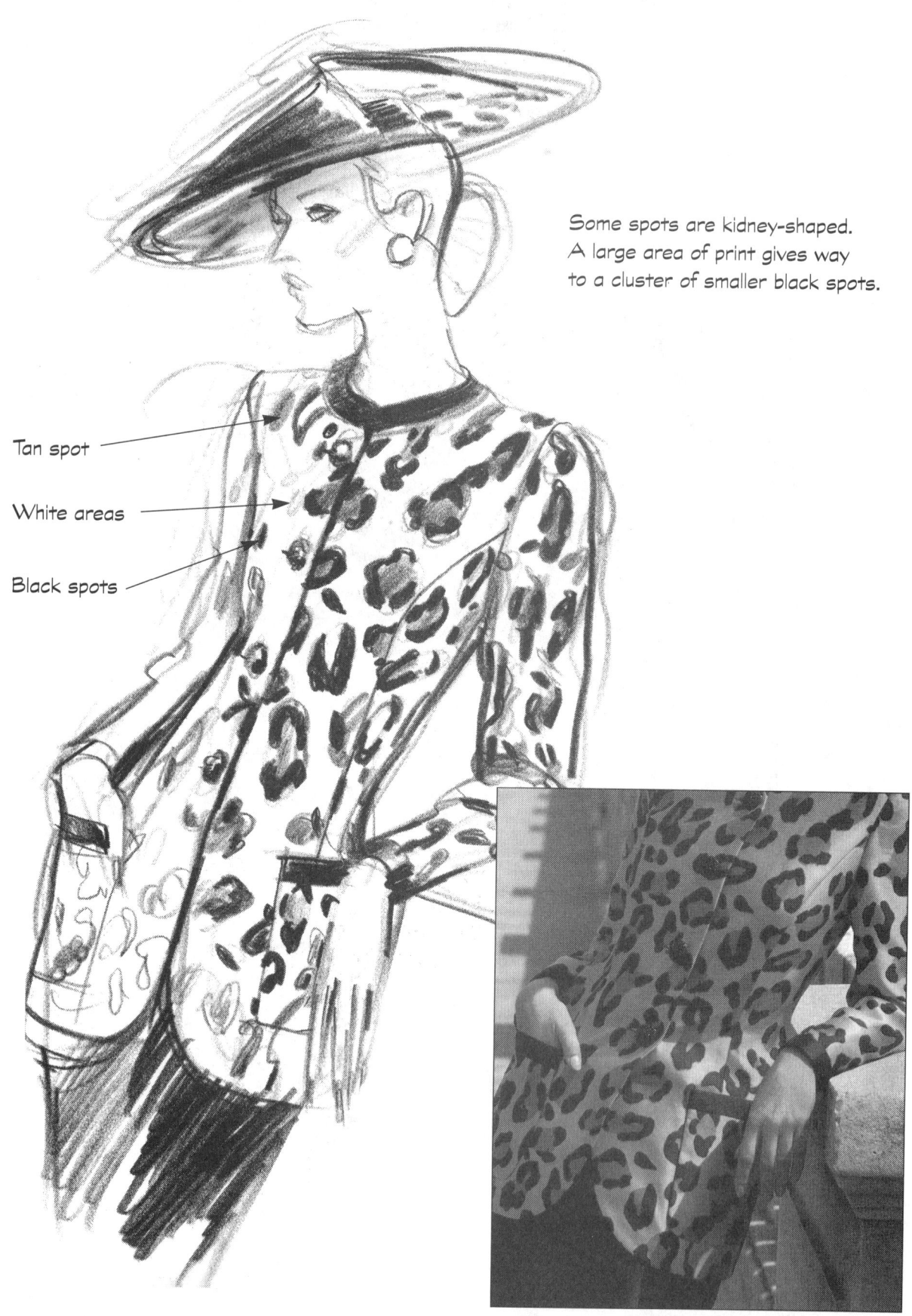

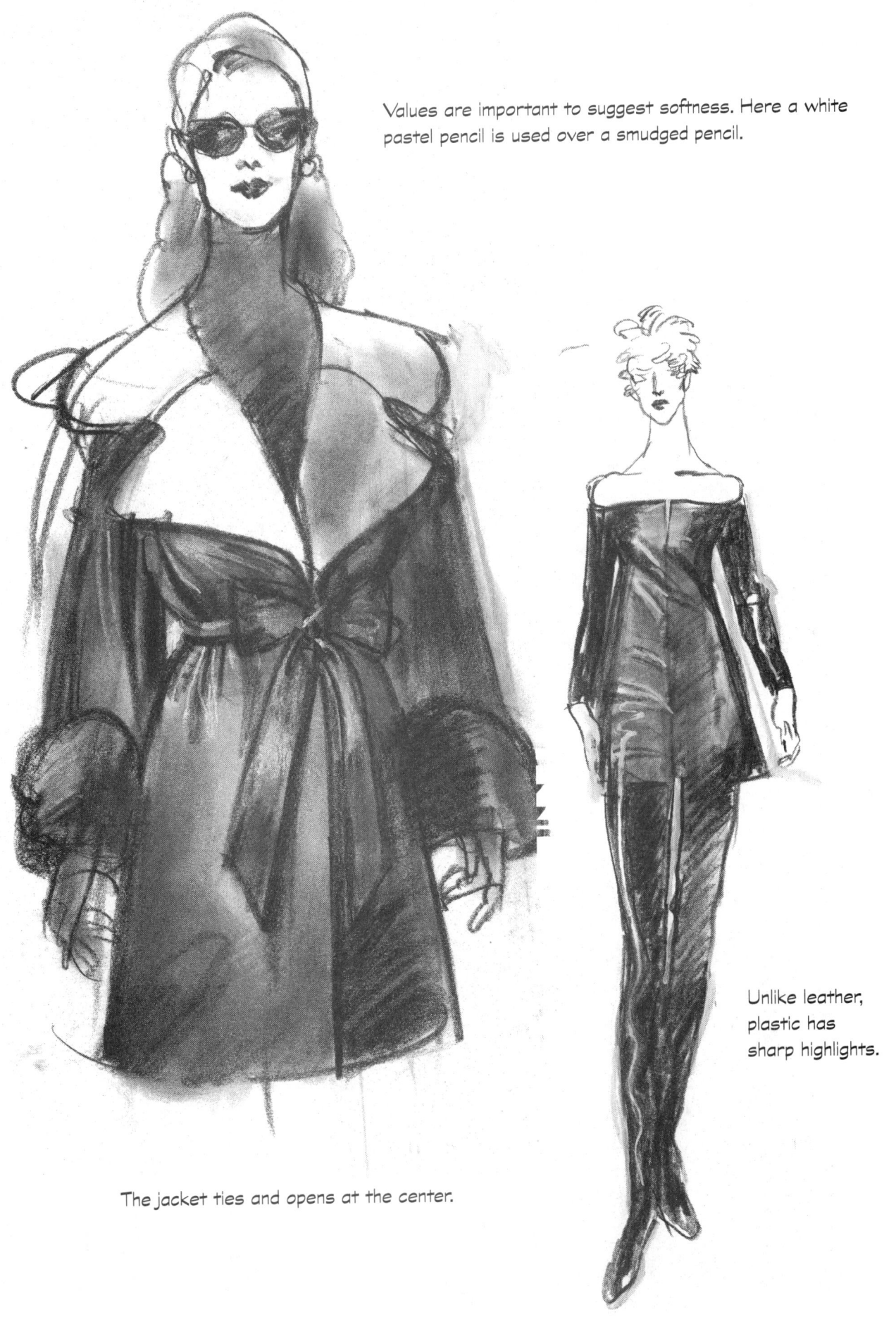

Values are important to suggest softness. Here a white pastel pencil is used over a smudged pencil.

Unlike leather, plastic has sharp highlights.

The jacket ties and opens at the center.

CHAPTER 9 CLOTHING DETAILS III: PRINTS AND PATTERNS 139

CHAPTER 10
Clothing Details IV: Practical Tips and Techniques

SOME PENCIL TECHNIQUES

Use shades of gray to suggest form or value on figures and clothing. Seeing values of gray prepares us to see value in color. Students often see only black as a value. These black holes throw the illustration out of balance.

Use the oblique stroke. Find values by moving the strokes closer and making them thicker as you darken the squares.

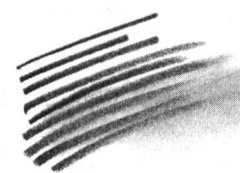

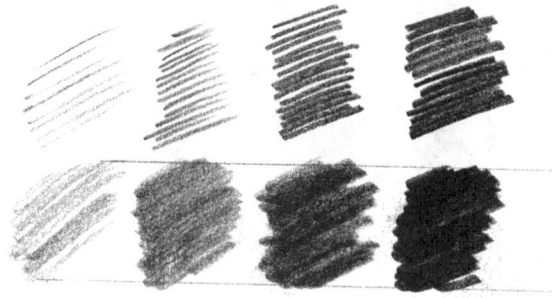

Value chart

Do not use the point of the pencil. Use the side. Keep the spaces even. This helps avoid confusion in the toned area.

LIGHT-TO-DARK

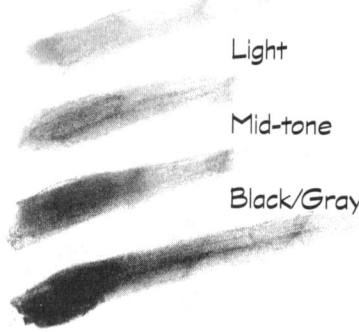

Light

Mid-tone

Black/Gray

Use hand motion to make these strokes. Moving the entire arm causes uneven strokes.

Smudging creates interesting effects when suggesting value. Use your finger to smudge the charcoal pencil to create value.

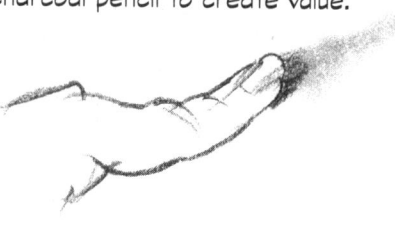

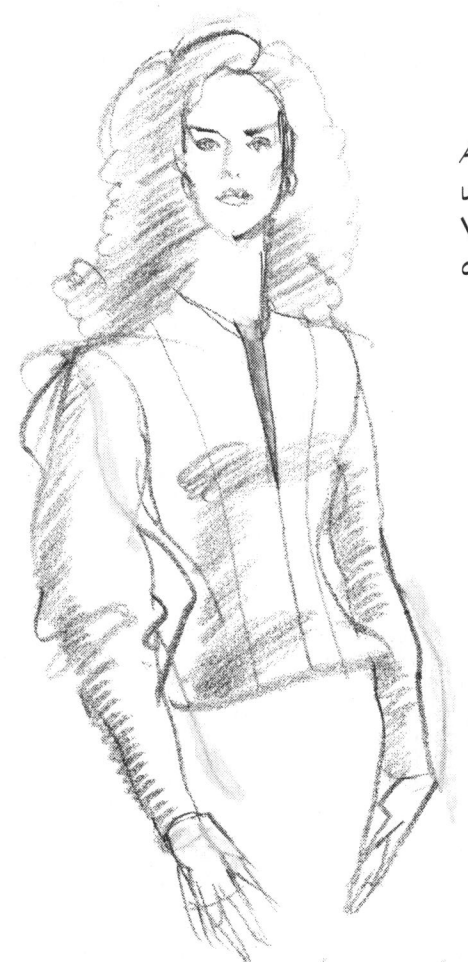

After practicing with still life objects, use a photograph to copy a figure. Work carefully, simplifying the value into one or two shades.

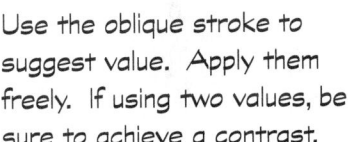

Use the oblique stroke to suggest value. Apply them freely. If using two values, be sure to achieve a contrast.

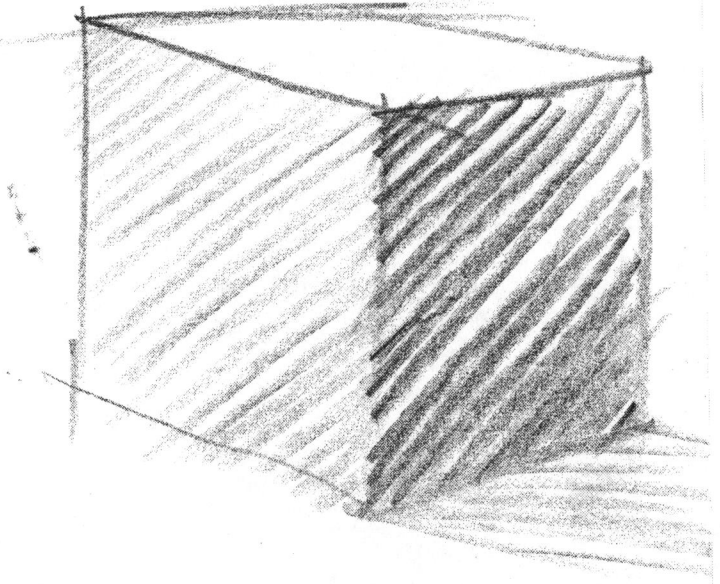

Sketch simple shapes such as a square or rectangular object like a milk carton or box.

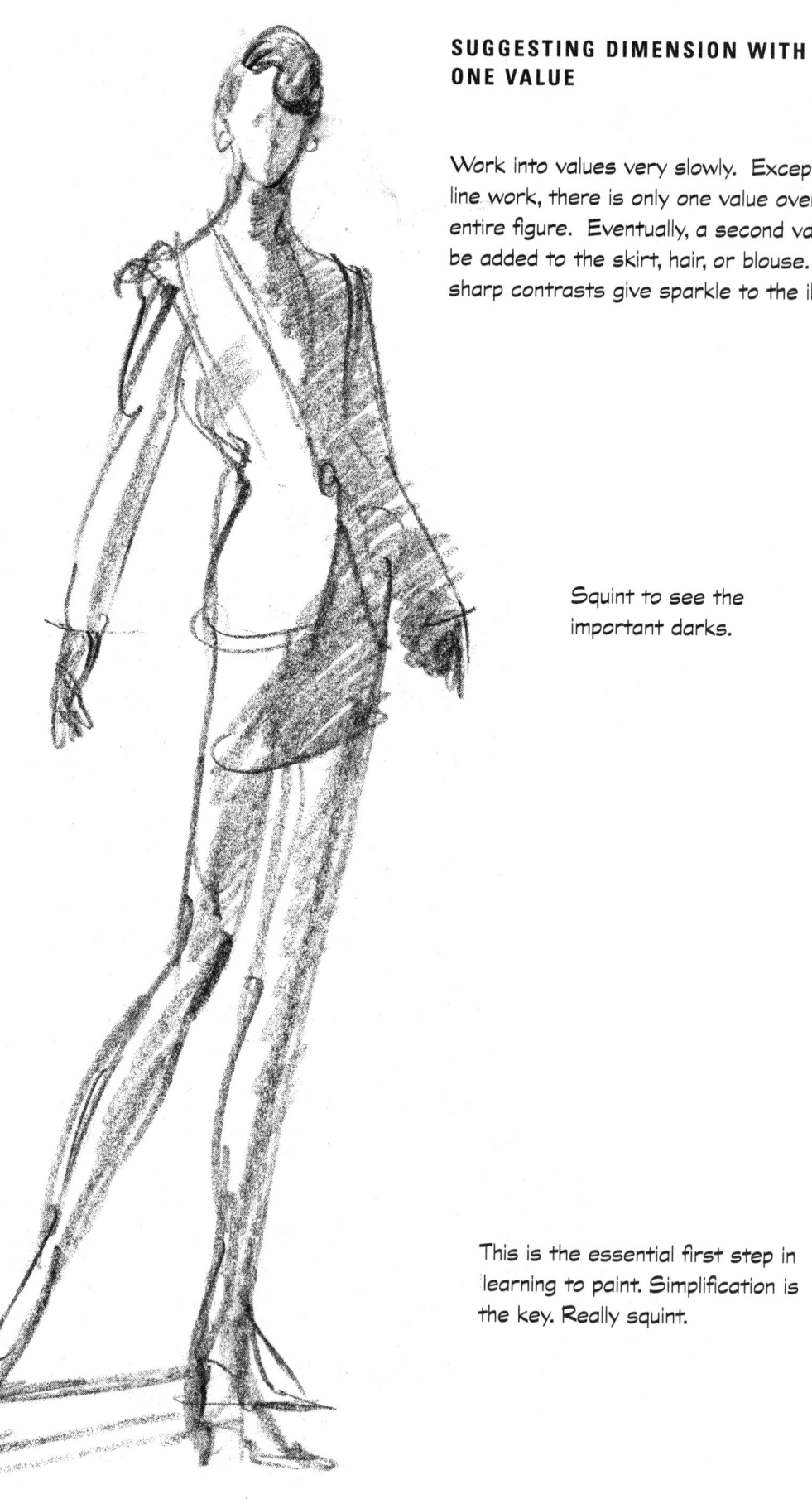

SUGGESTING DIMENSION WITH ONE VALUE

Work into values very slowly. Except for the line work, there is only one value over the entire figure. Eventually, a second value may be added to the skirt, hair, or blouse. These sharp contrasts give sparkle to the illustration.

Squint to see the important darks.

This is the essential first step in learning to paint. Simplification is the key. Really squint.

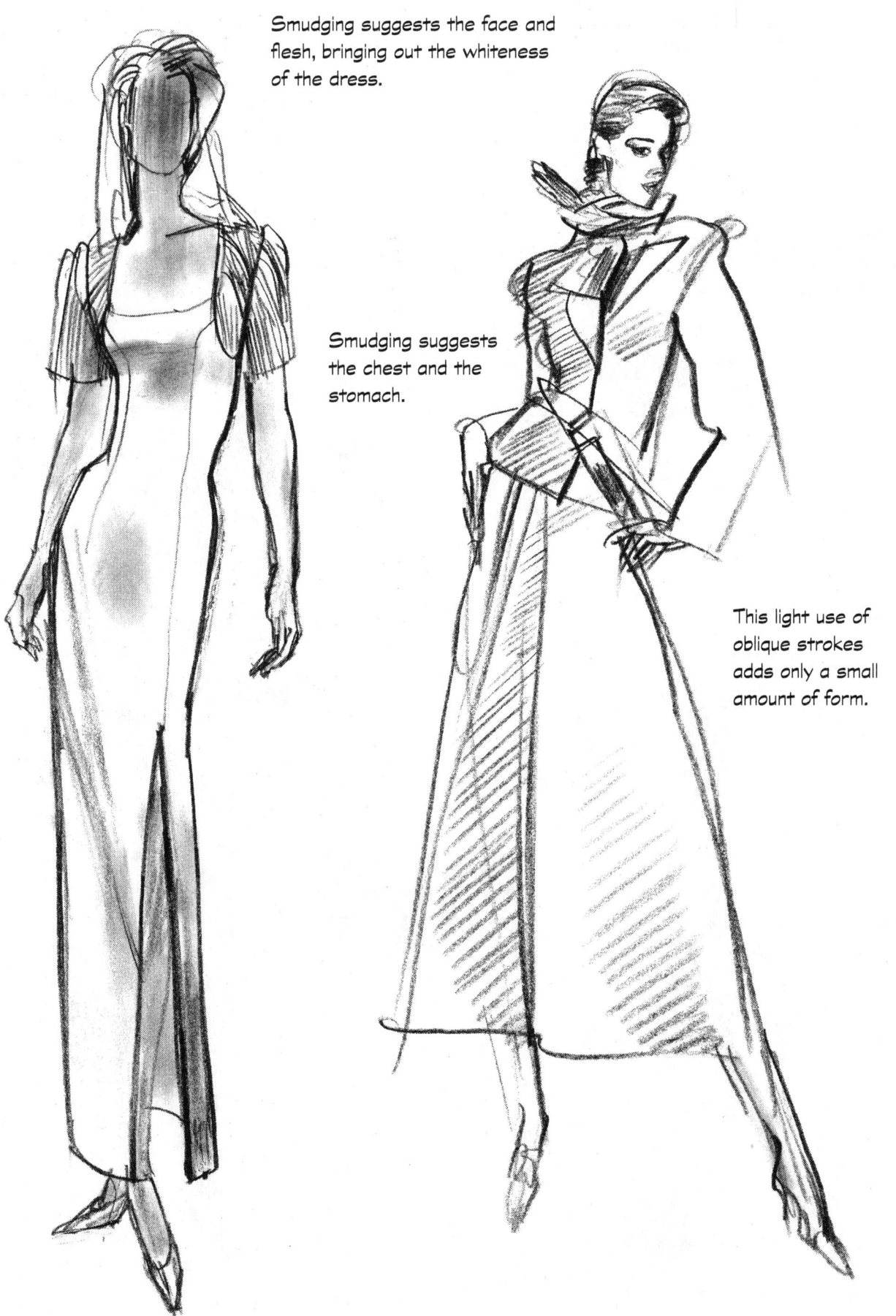

Smudging suggests the face and flesh, bringing out the whiteness of the dress.

Smudging suggests the chest and the stomach.

This light use of oblique strokes adds only a small amount of form.

CHAPTER 10 CLOTHING DETAILS IV: PRACTICAL TIPS AND TECHNIQUES

VISUALIZING BLACK

Avoid the cutout silhouette.

Be sure details can be seen over the value.

This value can now pass as any dark color such as red or dark green.

White paint suggests the gloss of plastic on each button and the belt buckle.

Black lines and shadow areas are enough to give the impression of black.

Even in this quick sketch, value contrasts are defined sharply and establish the effect of this garment.

Visualize the strong shape contrast. A wide hip shape contrasts with the twiglike slimness of the legs.

Seen in the light, black is actually gray. As a value, gray helps us see details of styling and construction.

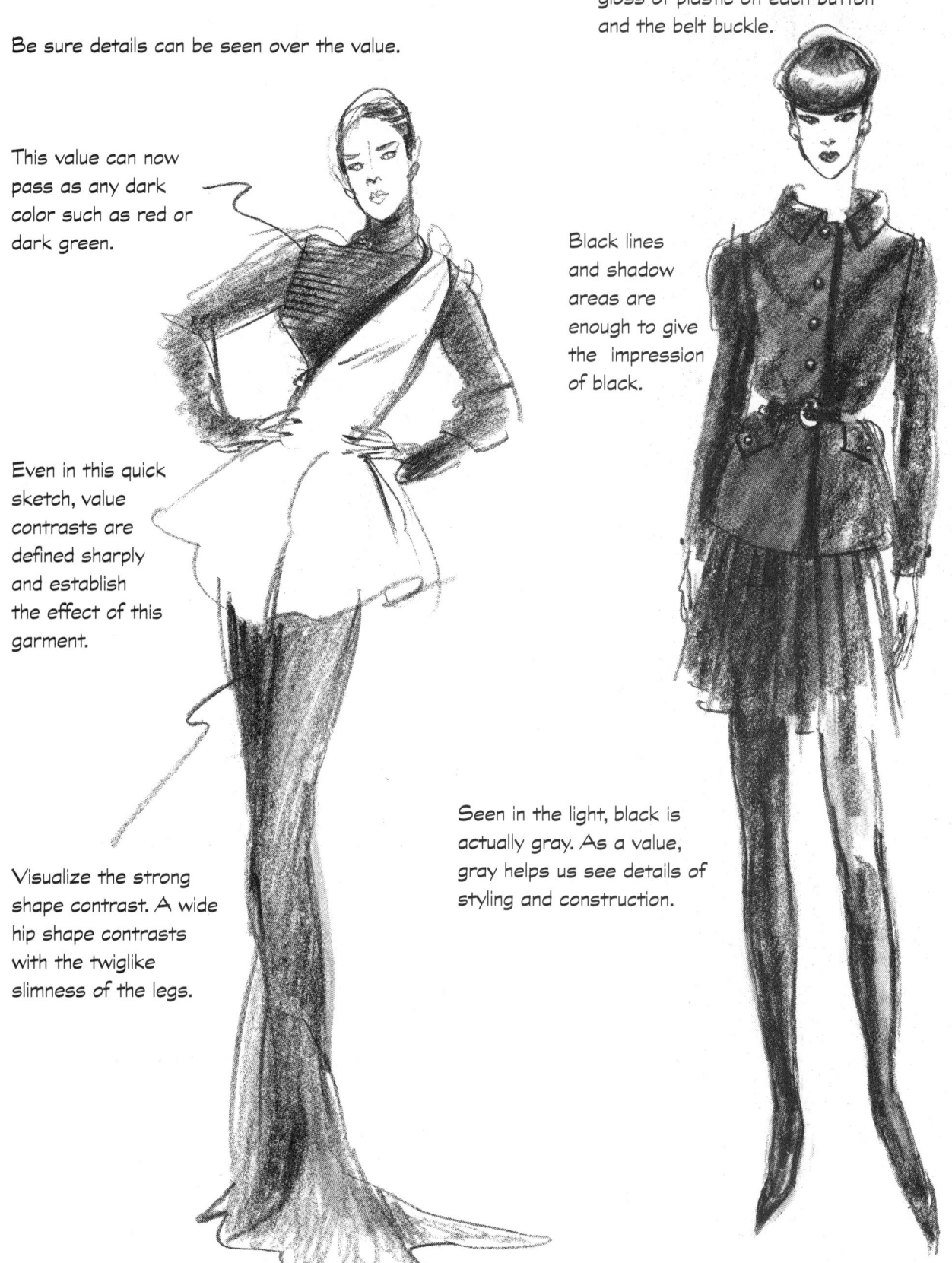

DRAWING SHINE AND BRILLIANCE

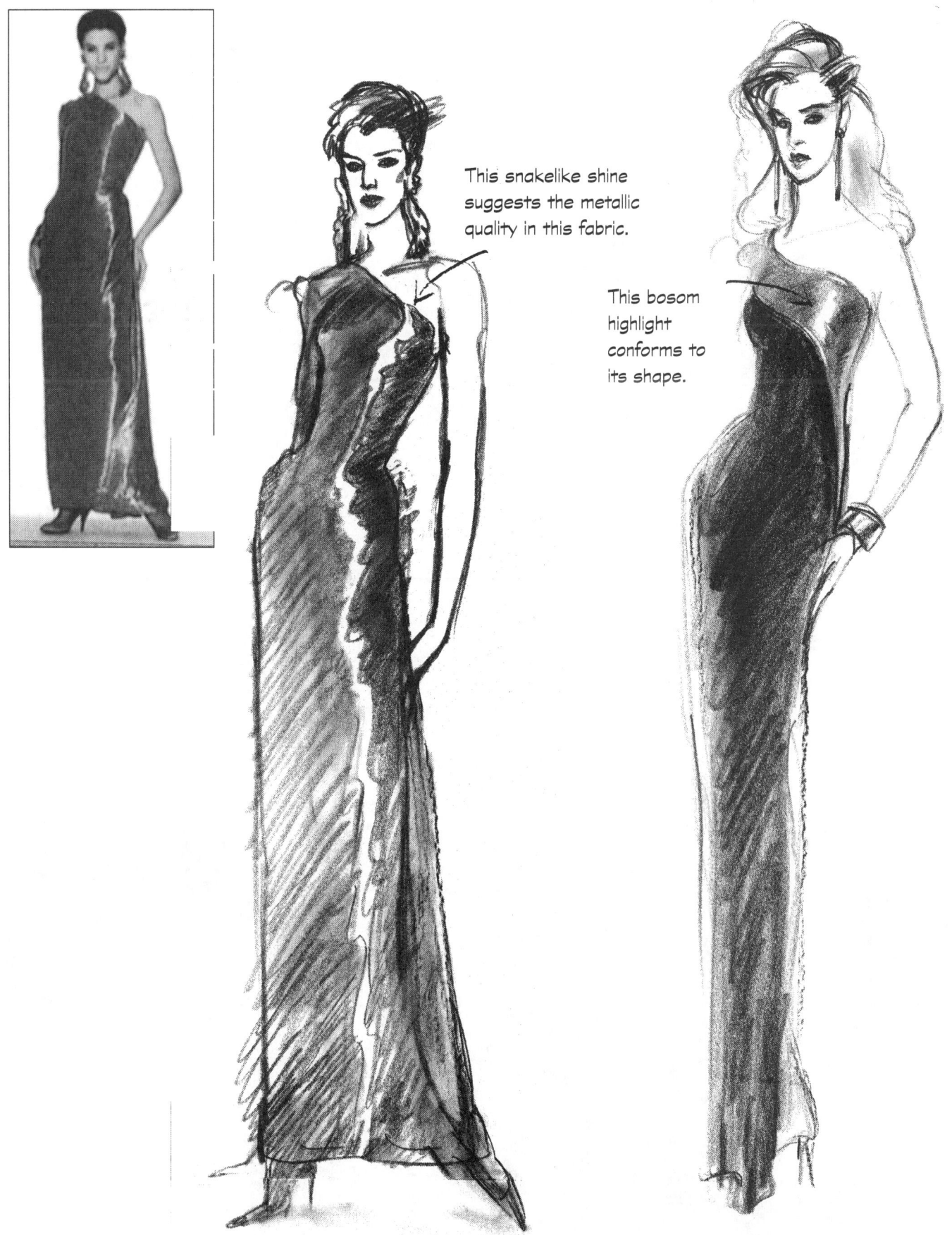

This snakelike shine suggests the metallic quality in this fabric.

This bosom highlight conforms to its shape.

LOOK FOR SHAPES

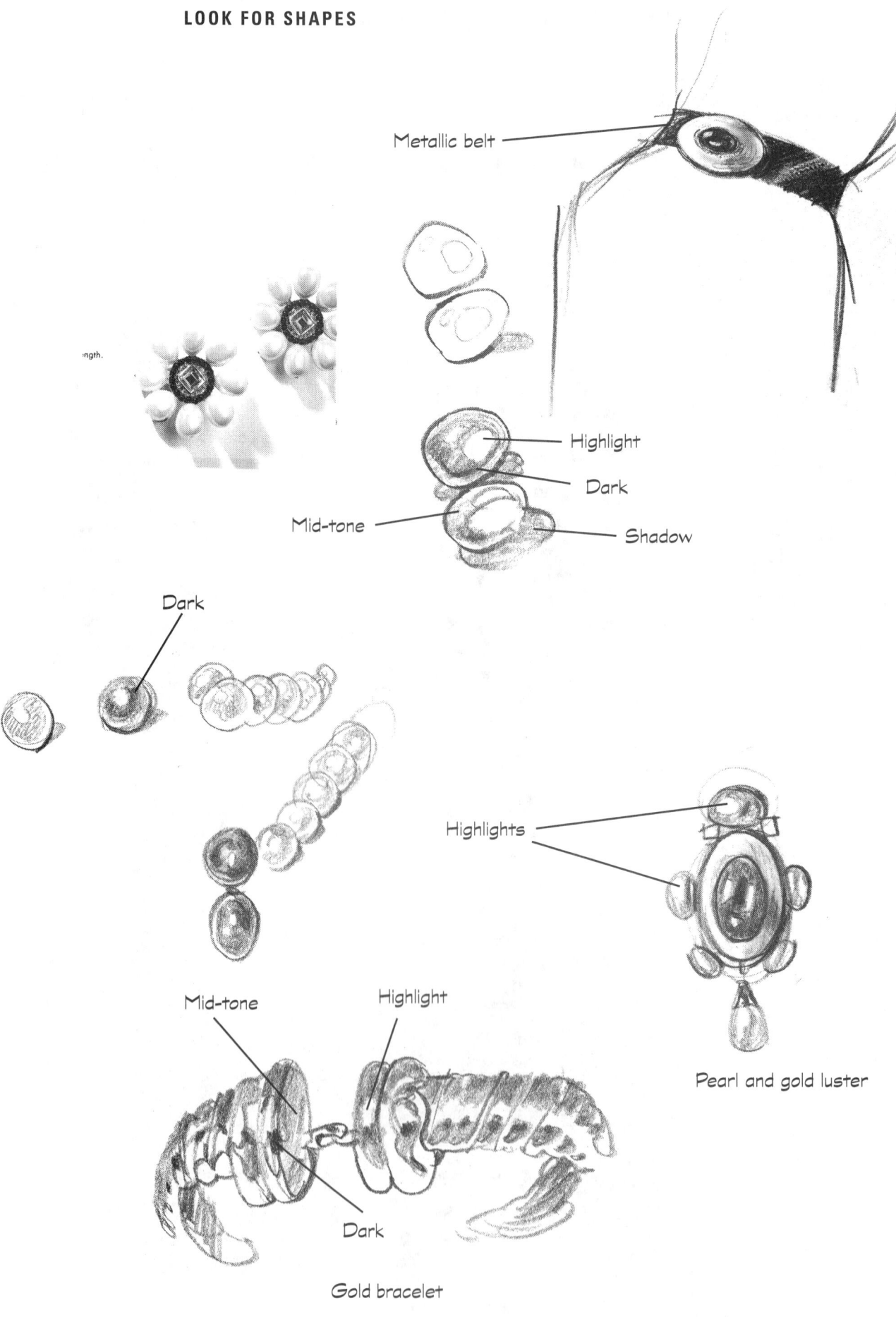

Pearl and gold luster

Gold bracelet

CHAPTER 11

Men's Figures

The approach to men's figures is the same as it is for women—the gesture or foundation sketch. Keep in mind the key differences to be covered: proportions, stance/pose, and facial.

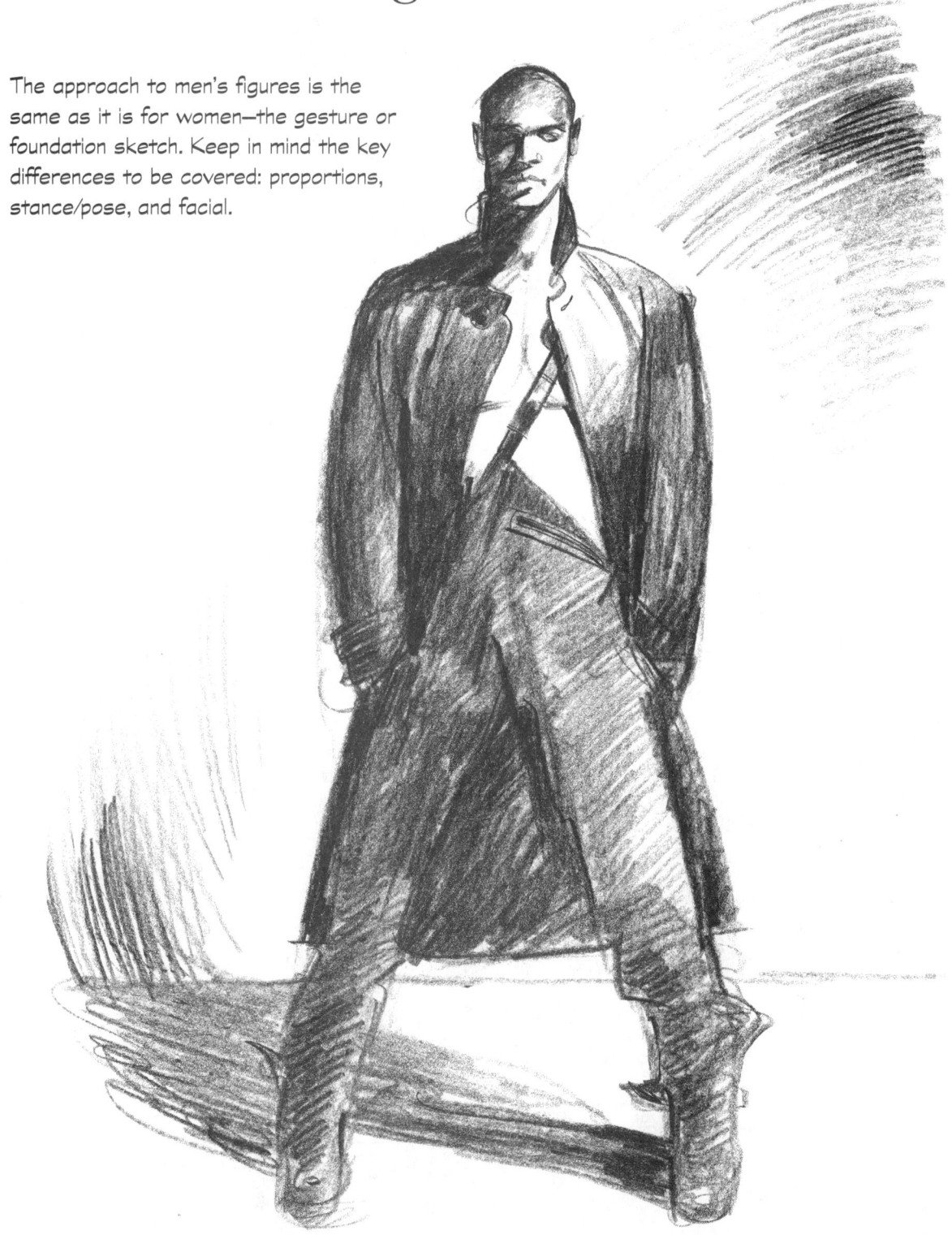

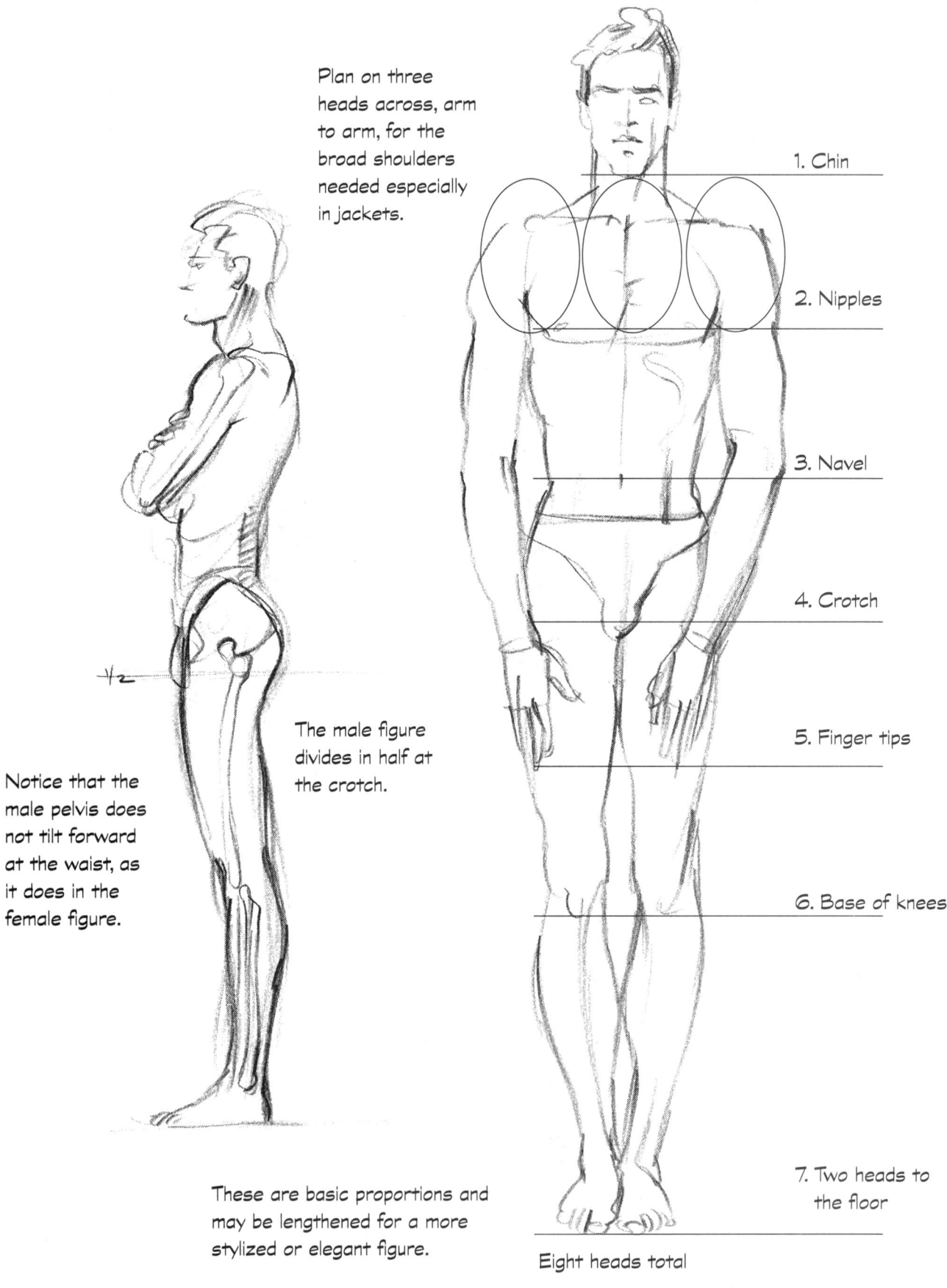

Use head lengths to find the male proportions.

Plan on three heads across, arm to arm, for the broad shoulders needed especially in jackets.

1. Chin
2. Nipples
3. Navel
4. Crotch
5. Finger tips
6. Base of knees
7. Two heads to the floor

Eight heads total

The male figure divides in half at the crotch.

Notice that the male pelvis does not tilt forward at the waist, as it does in the female figure.

These are basic proportions and may be lengthened for a more stylized or elegant figure.

148 FASHION SKETCHING

Leg curves are important.
Try this bowlegged effect.

Curves of the back supporting leg

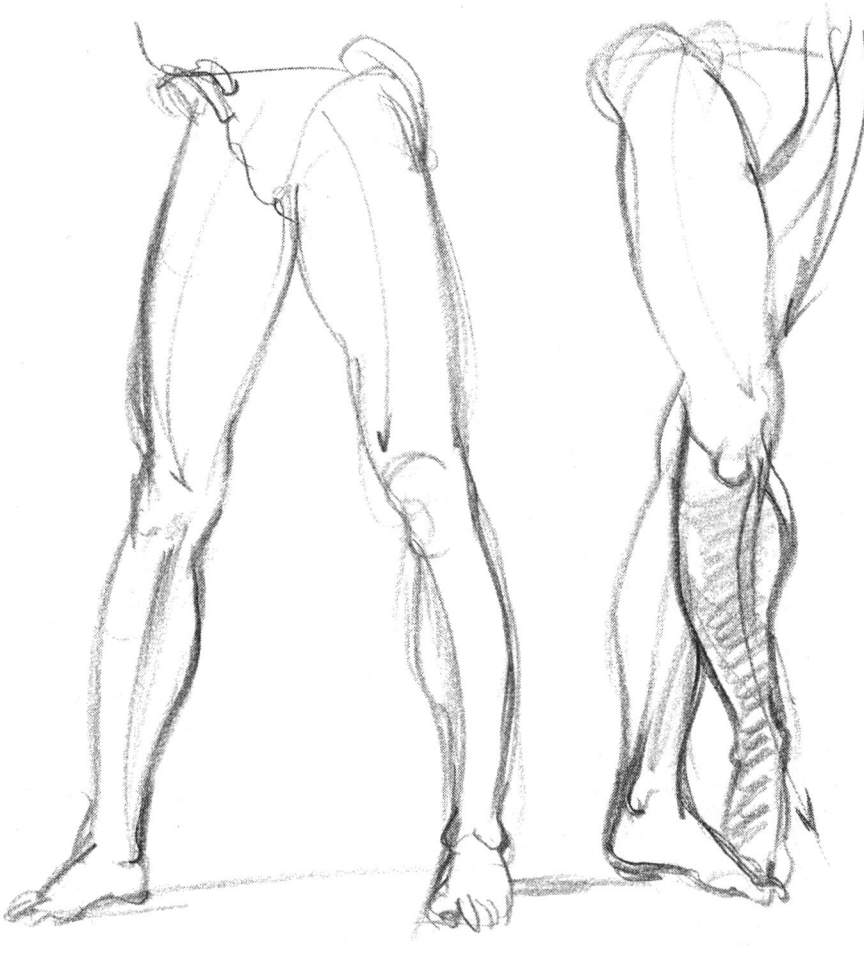

Muscle swells are larger on the male figure.

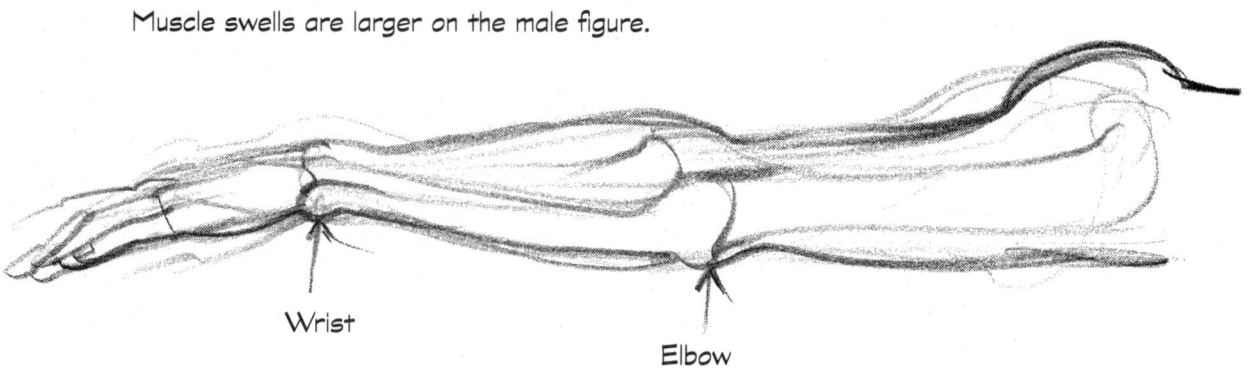

Wrist

Elbow

MALE ACTION

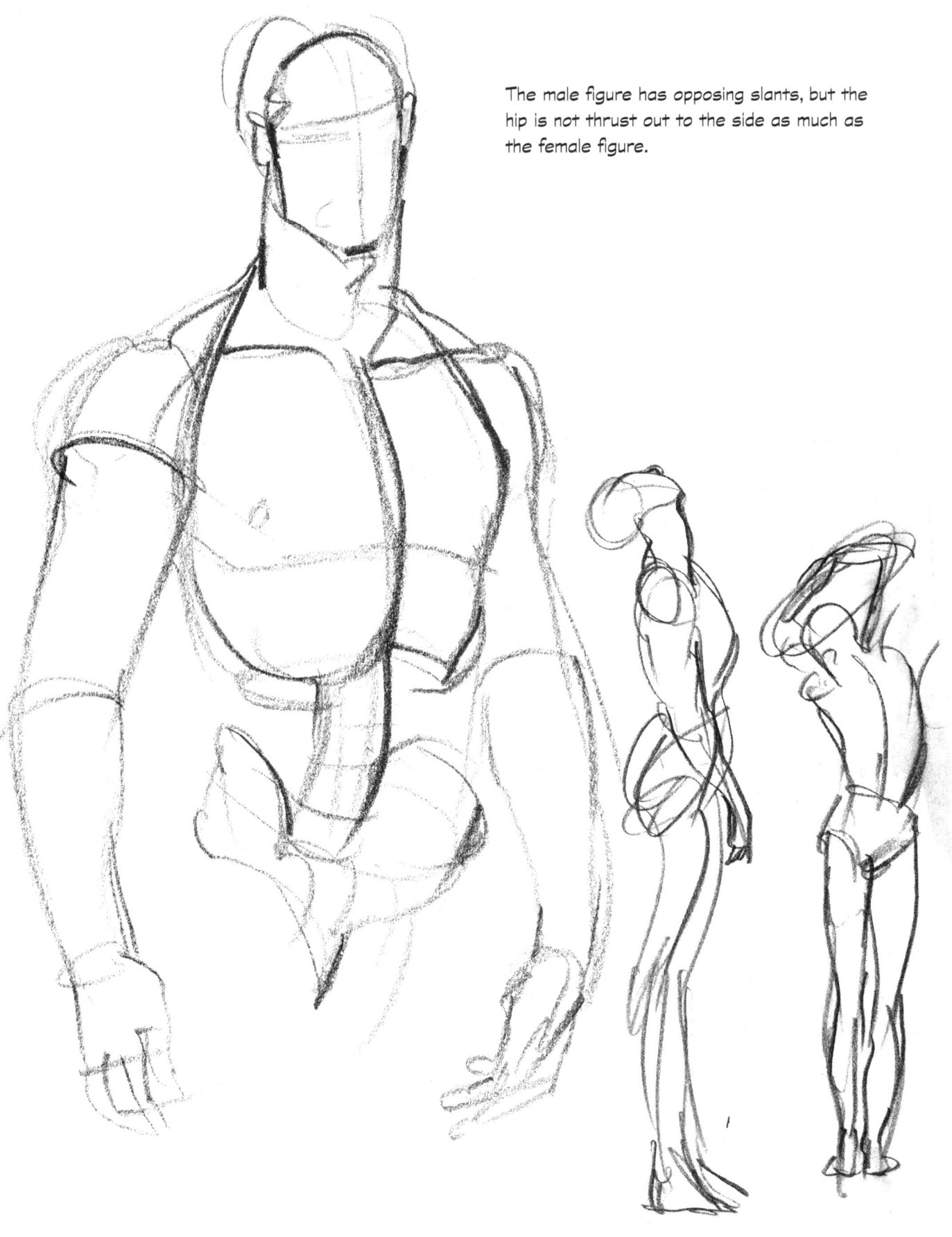

The male figure has opposing slants, but the hip is not thrust out to the side as much as the female figure.

Study these muscle swells carefully. They exist on female legs as well.

Male legs are tall and divide in half at the knee.

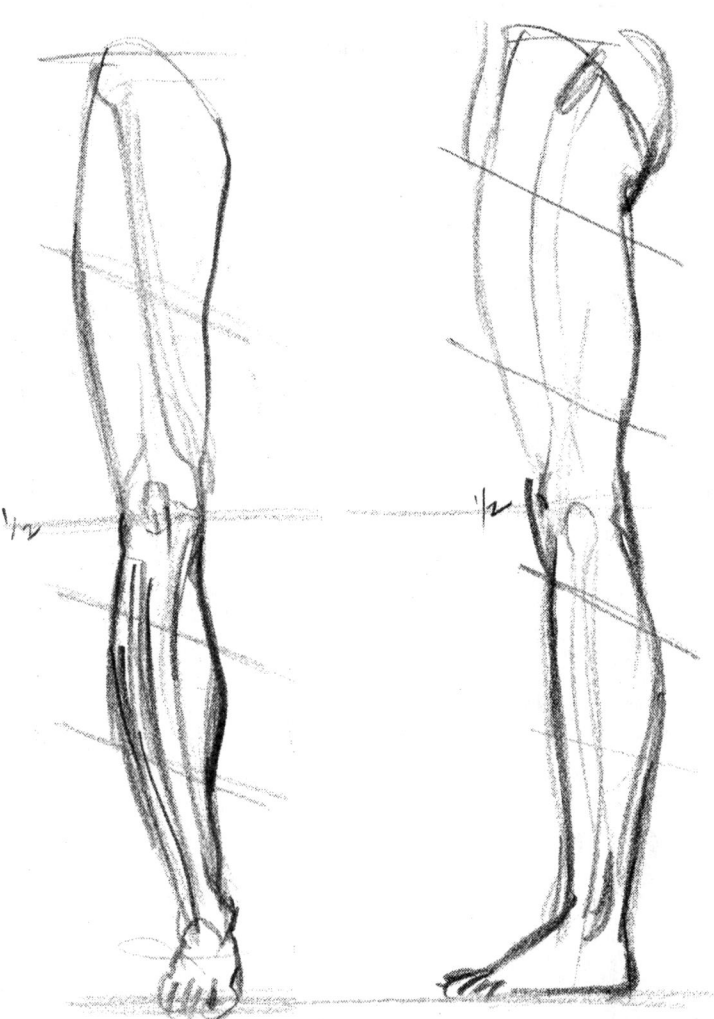

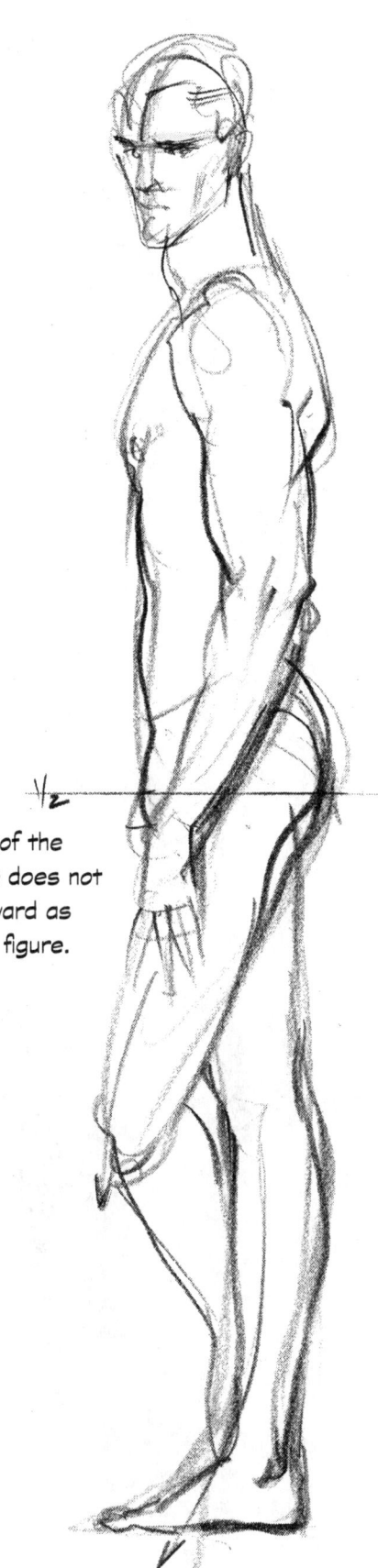

The pelvis of the male figure does not tilt as forward as the female figure.

These muscle swells repeat in the same direction on both upper and lower portions of the leg.

The obvious difference between the male and female figures is the shape of the torso.

The male is wide across the shoulders and narrow at the waist and hips. As shown, waist and hip widths are equal.

Keep the male figure narrow in the hip area, no matter what clothing is covering the figure.

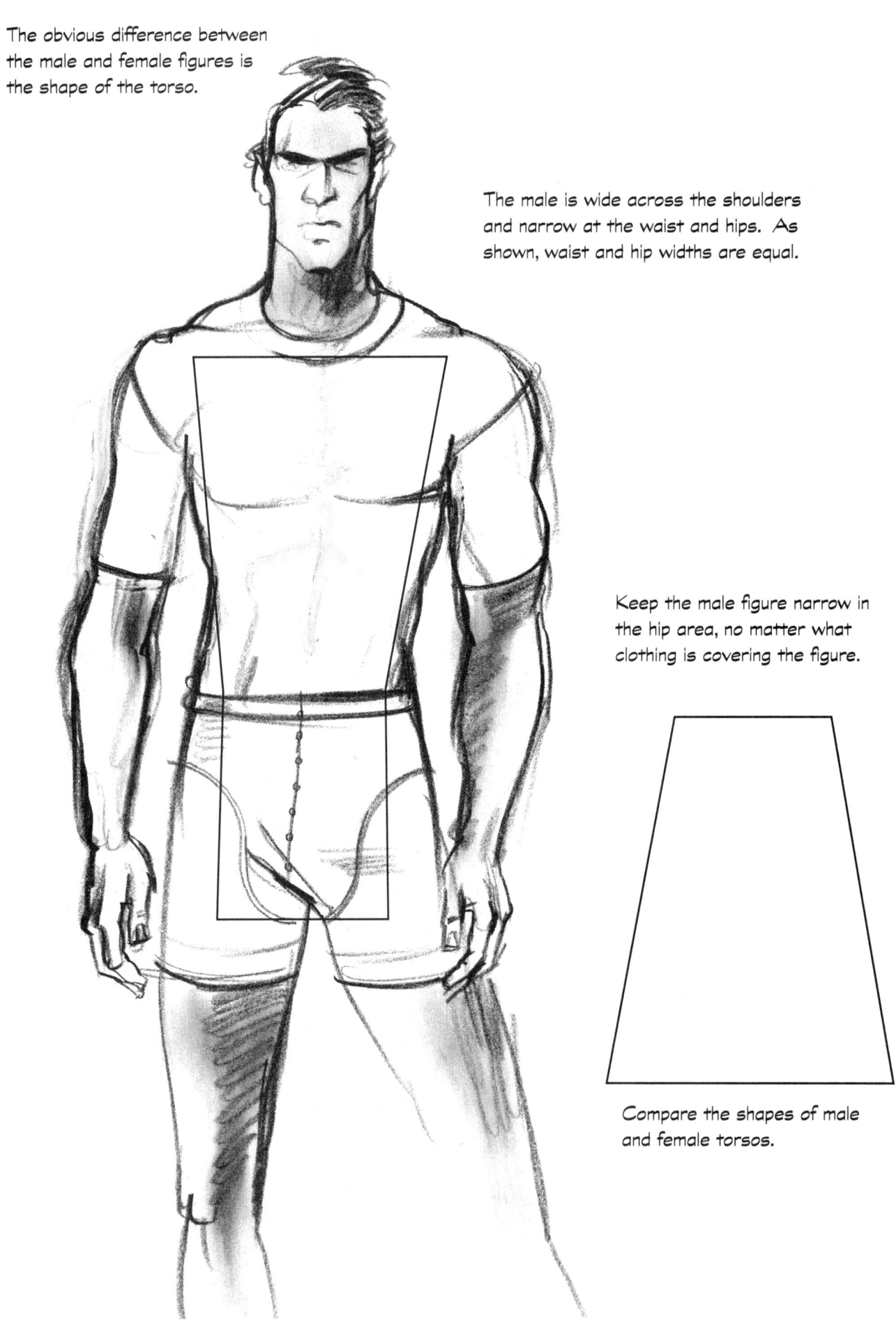

Compare the shapes of male and female torsos.

Use a pastel chalk or crayon to practice the solid forms the male figure needs.

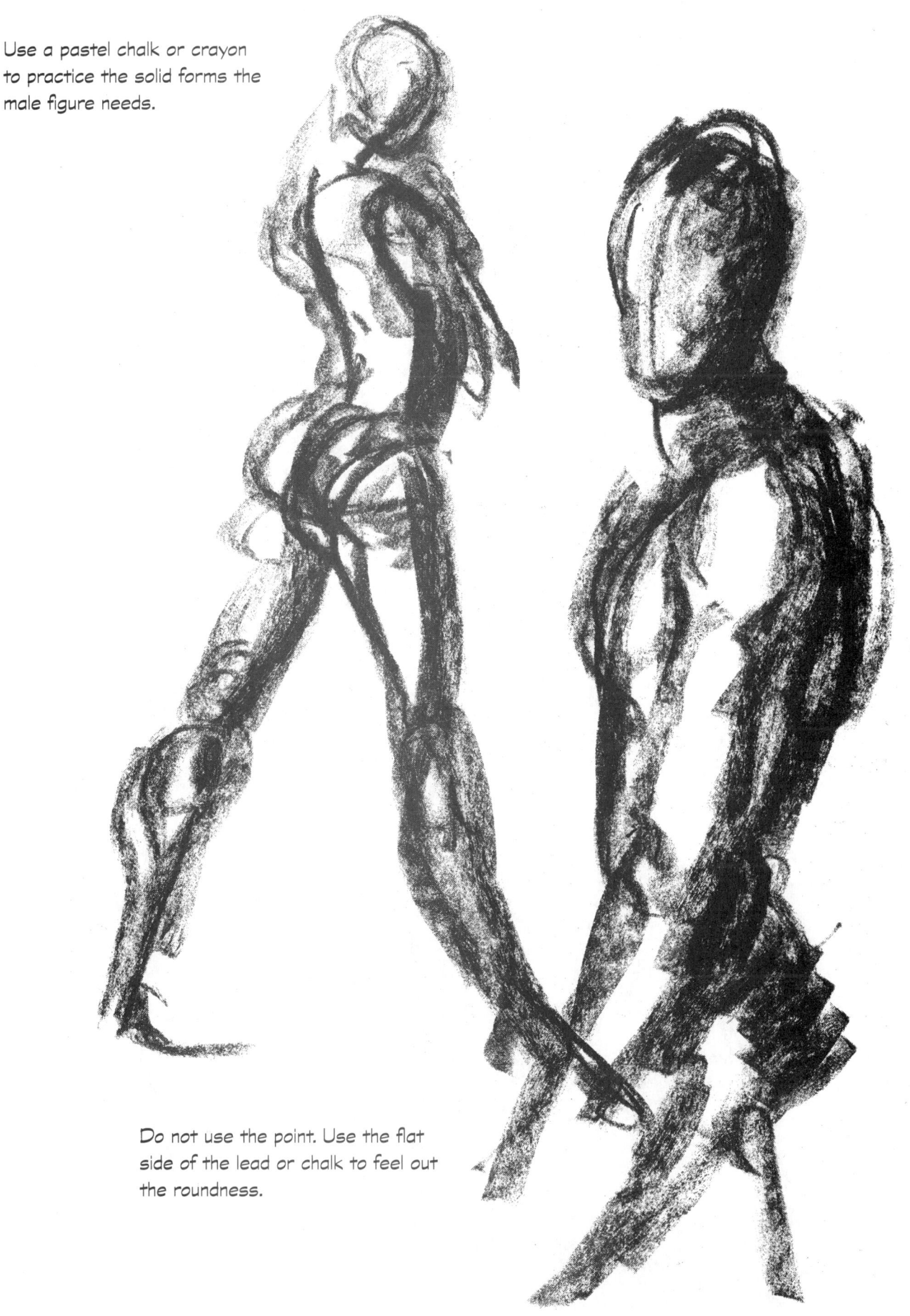

Do not use the point. Use the flat side of the lead or chalk to feel out the roundness.

CHAPTER 11 MEN'S FIGURES

THREE-MINUTE GESTURE SKETCHES

Include the head and the feet in all quick sketches.

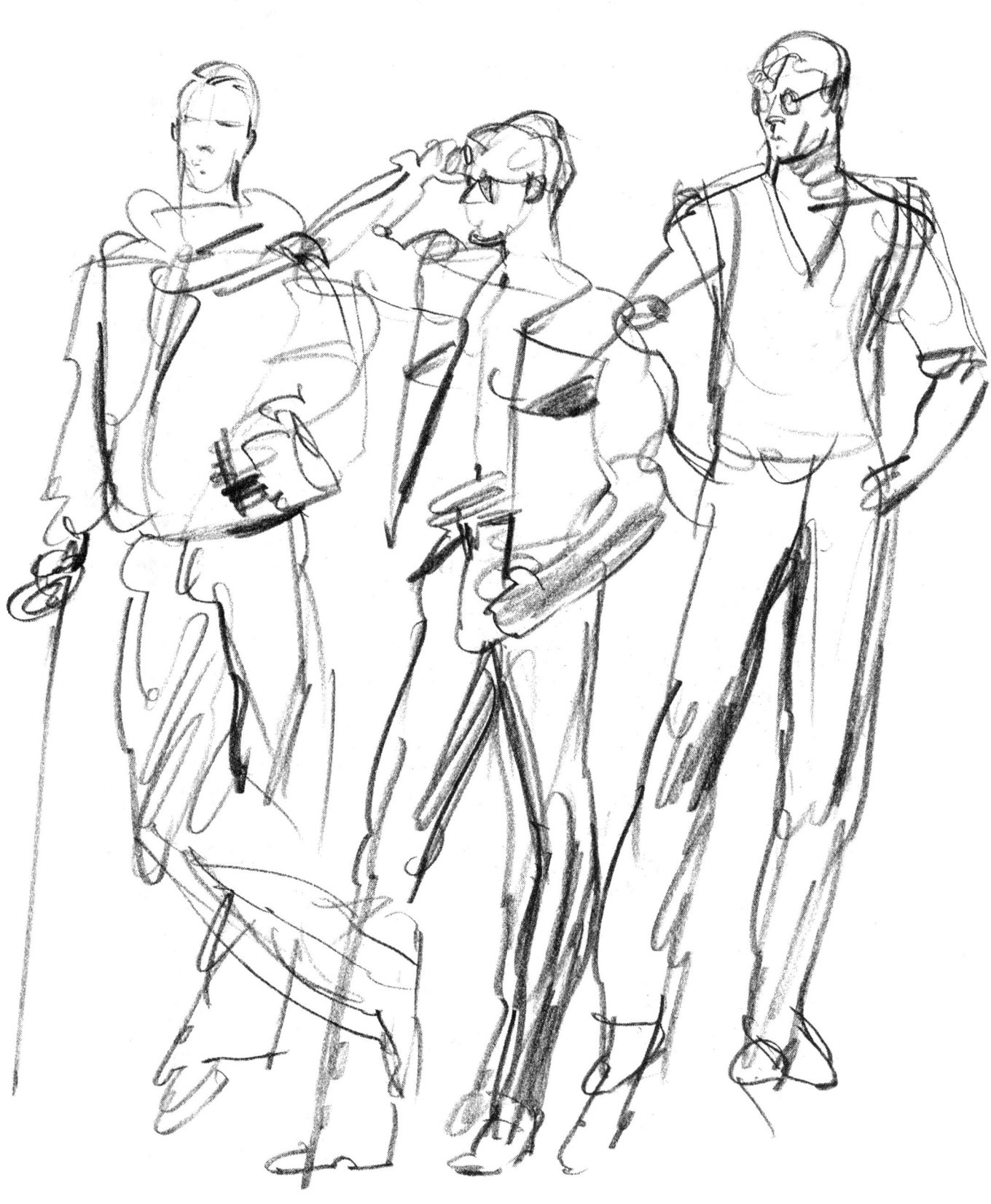

DEPICTING THE MALE HEAD

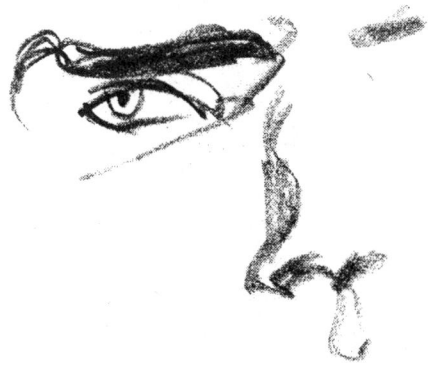

The male nose has strong planes and can be less perfect than the female nose, even hawklike.

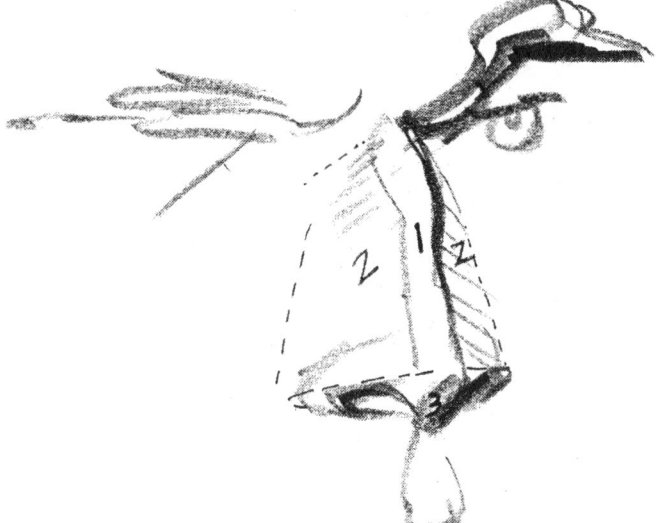

The eyes are not so open. The eye often appears to be touching the eyebrow.

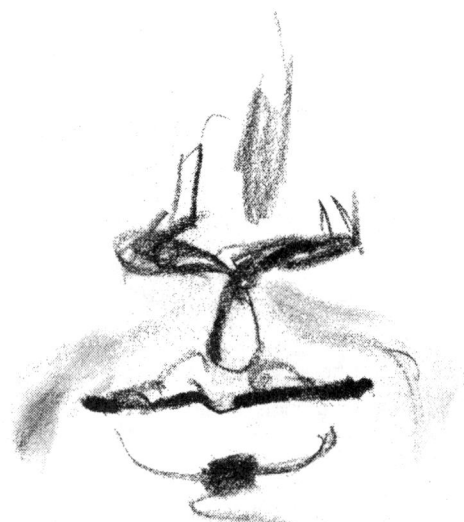

The lips are thin and fairly straight on top, with the lower lip larger. Draw Cupid's bow clearly. Keep this distance long.

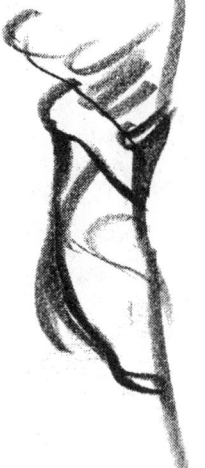

The male ear is larger. Small ears appear out of proportion.

CHAPTER 11 **MEN'S FIGURES** 155

Start with the egg shape. This is the basis of head construction.

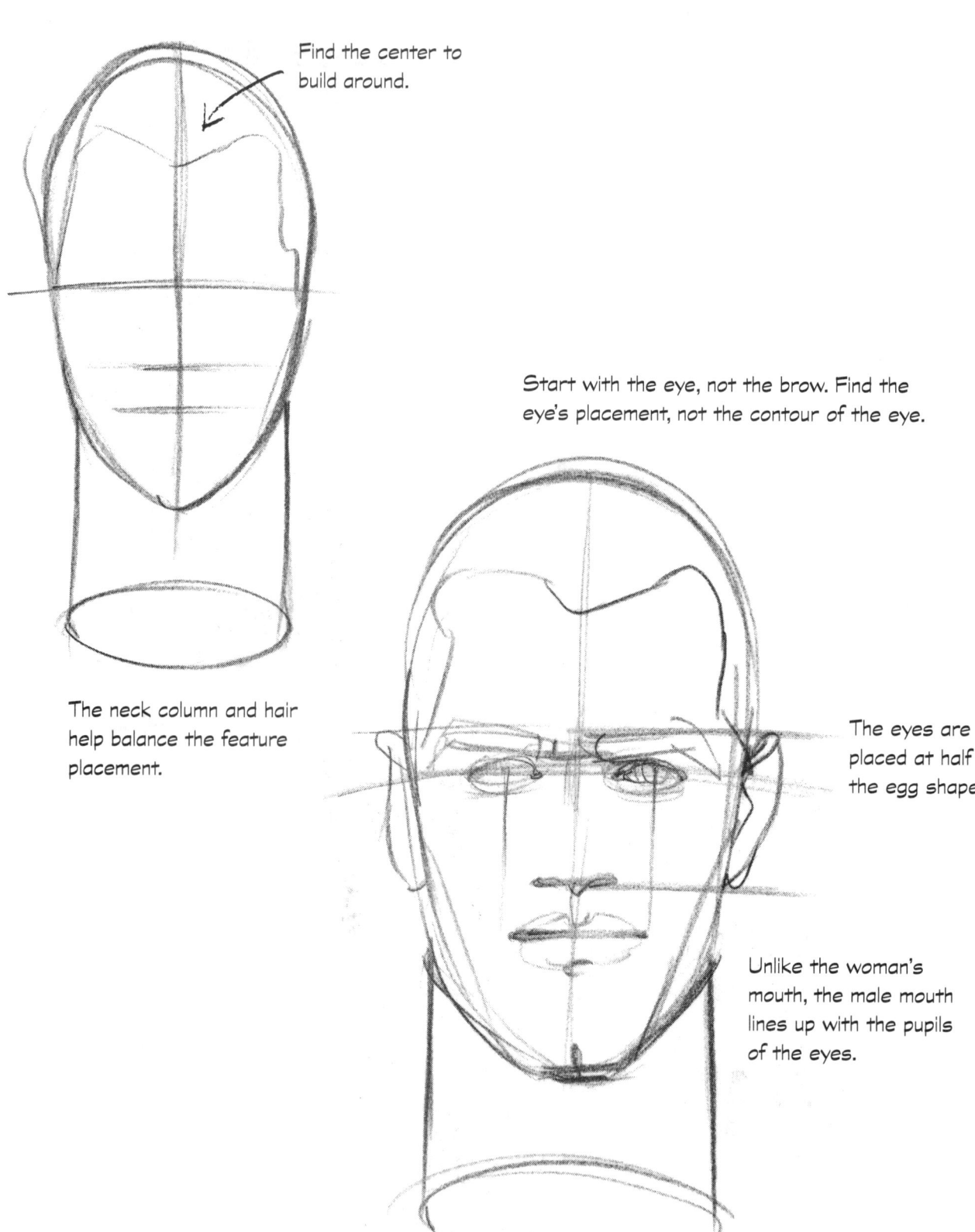

Find the center to build around.

Start with the eye, not the brow. Find the eye's placement, not the contour of the eye.

The neck column and hair help balance the feature placement.

The eyes are placed at half the egg shape.

Unlike the woman's mouth, the male mouth lines up with the pupils of the eyes.

Features are explored gradually and then darkened. The egg shape is now modified into the angular contours of the male head. Note the square jaw.

Parts of the hair line are softened to avoid a wiglike appearance. The male eye's most distinctive feature is a thick brow close to the eye.

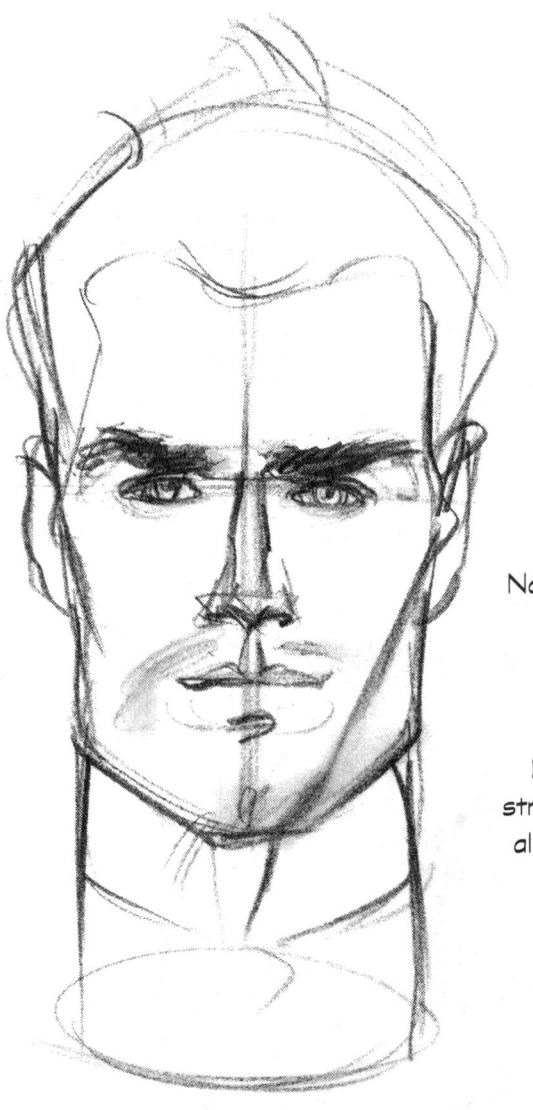

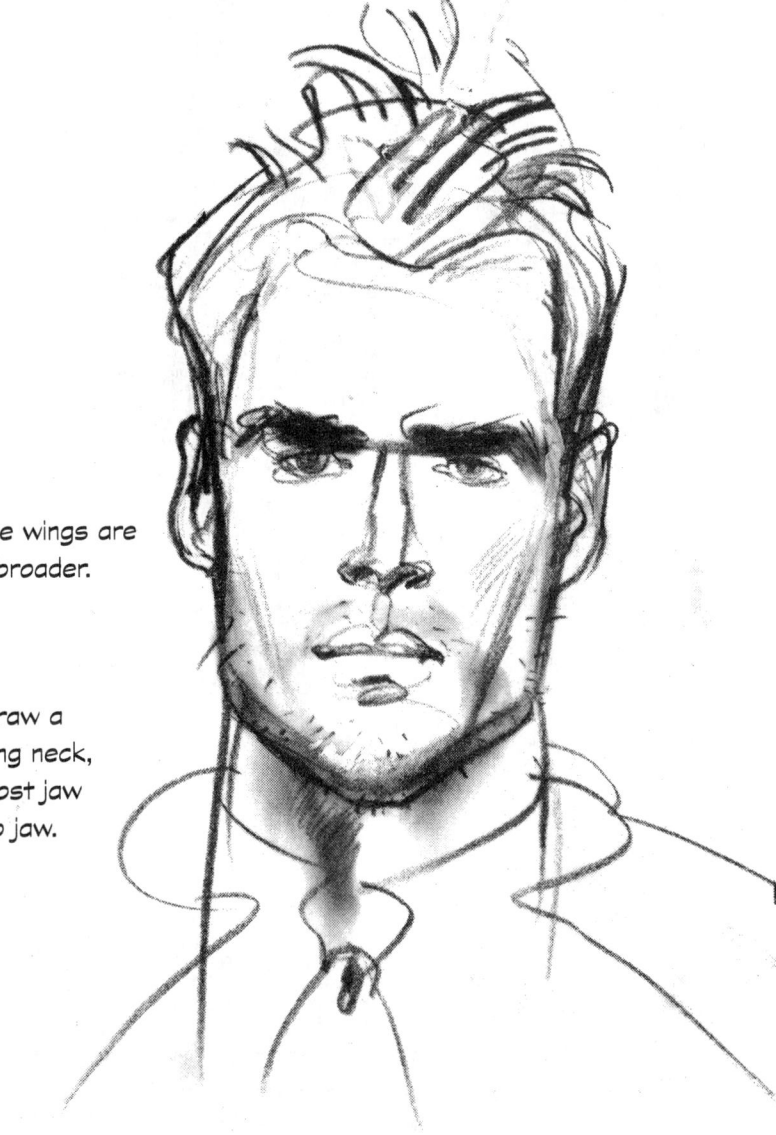

Nose wings are broader.

Draw a strong neck, almost jaw to jaw.

Unlike the female head, surface anatomy is permissible and desirable. The muscle structure of the mouth and pronounced chin are examples.

Do not outline the lips with dark pencil. This gives the appearance of lipstick. The upper lip is thin with a fuller lower lip.

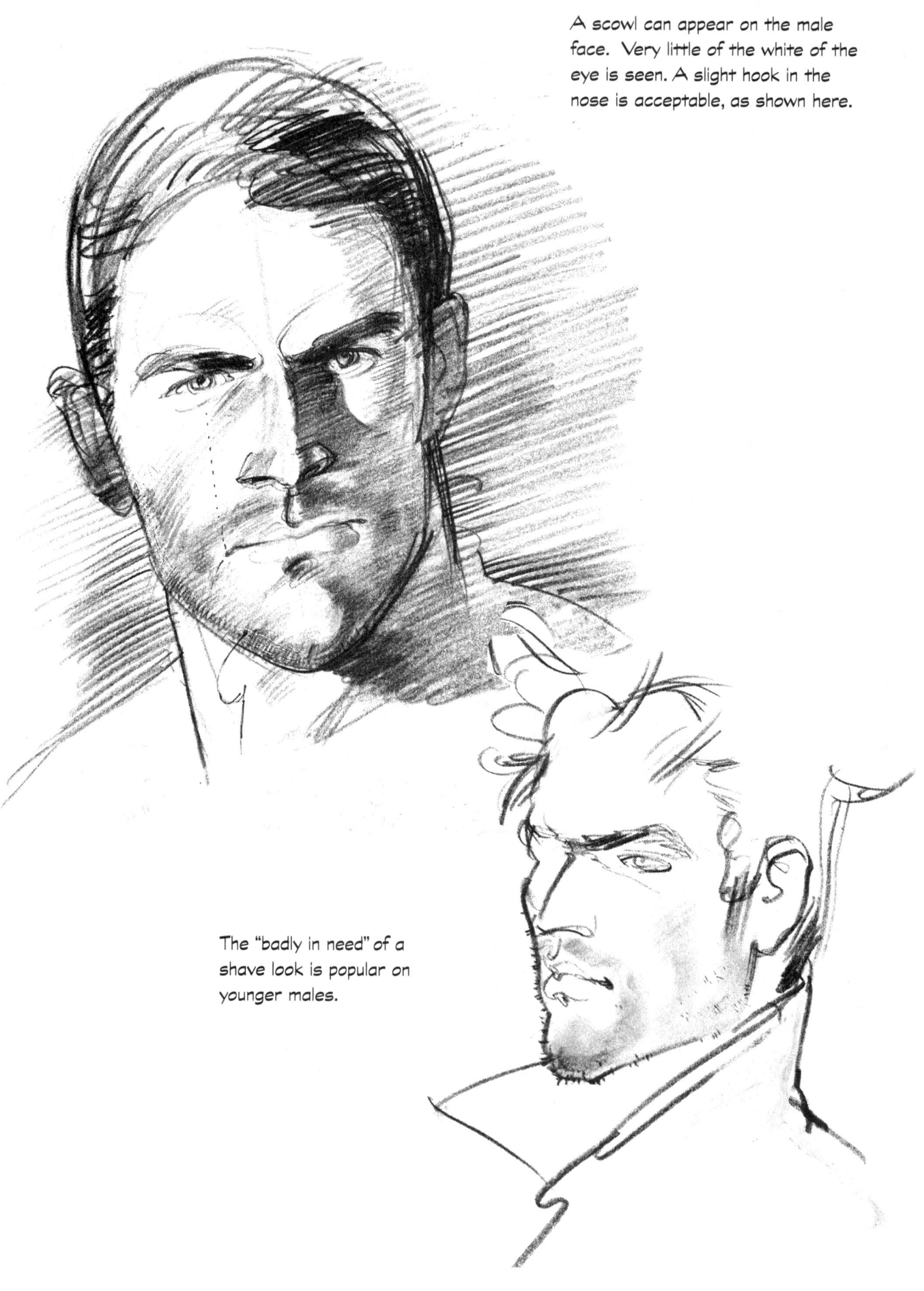

A scowl can appear on the male face. Very little of the white of the eye is seen. A slight hook in the nose is acceptable, as shown here.

The "badly in need" of a shave look is popular on younger males.

158 FASHION SKETCHING

Try out what has been learned about male heads in a series of small studies. Keep them simple and sketchy.

CHAPTER 11 MEN'S FIGURES 159

DRAWING THE MALE HAND

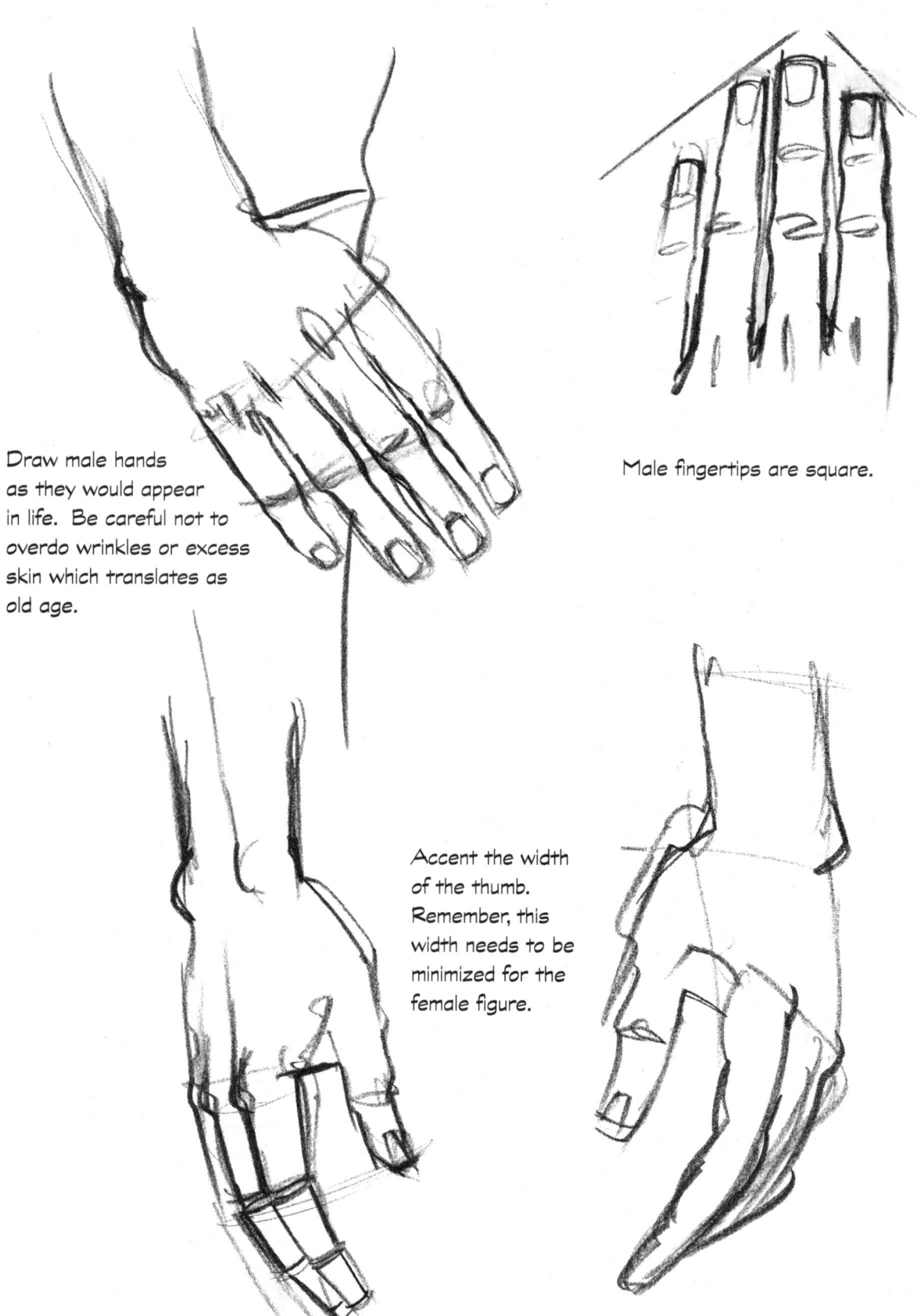

Draw male hands as they would appear in life. Be careful not to overdo wrinkles or excess skin which translates as old age.

Male fingertips are square.

Accent the width of the thumb. Remember, this width needs to be minimized for the female figure.

Keep hand views simple.

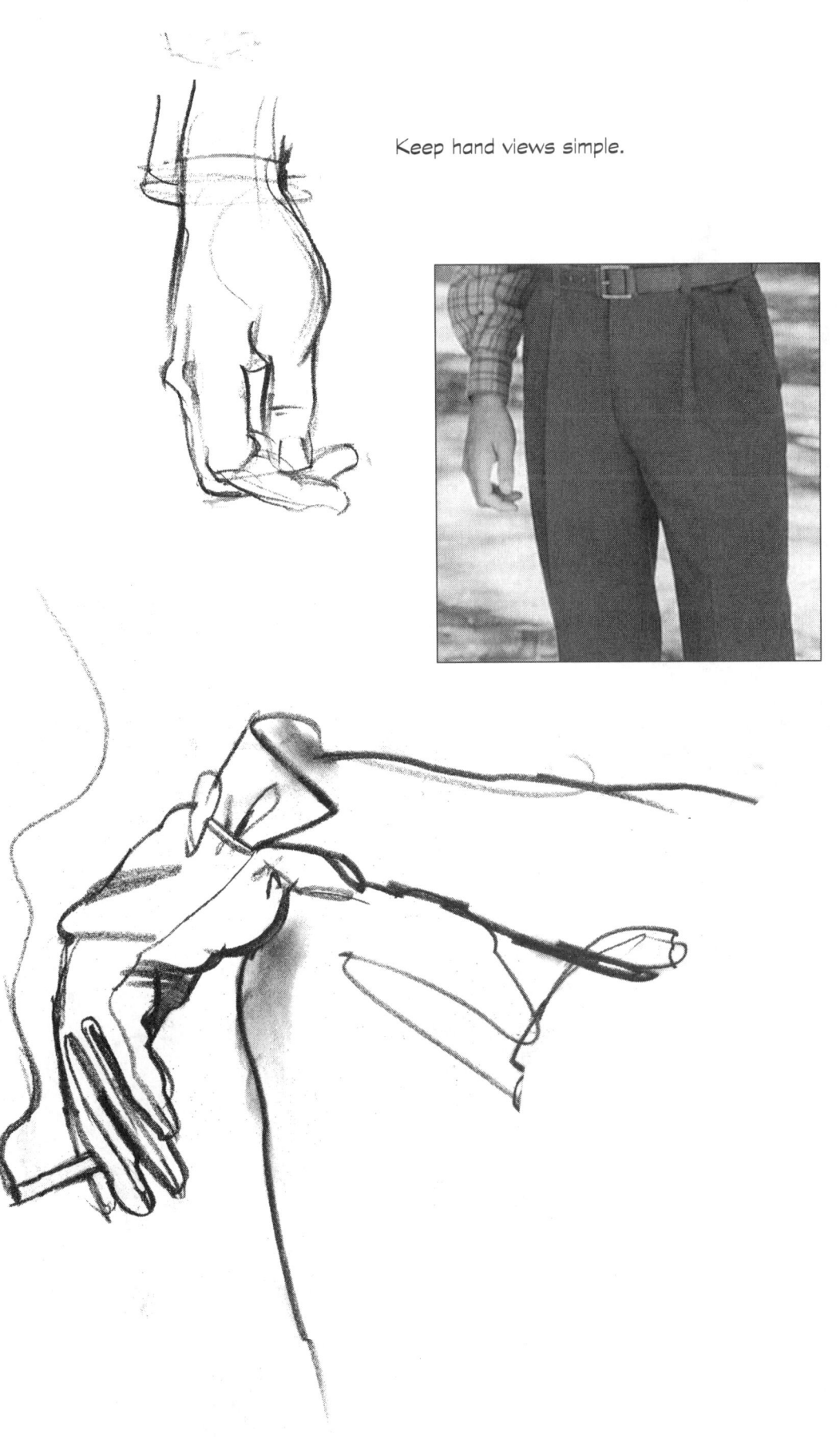

CHAPTER 11 MEN'S FIGURES

THE MALE FOOT

Think of the center so that the foot curves can be divided.

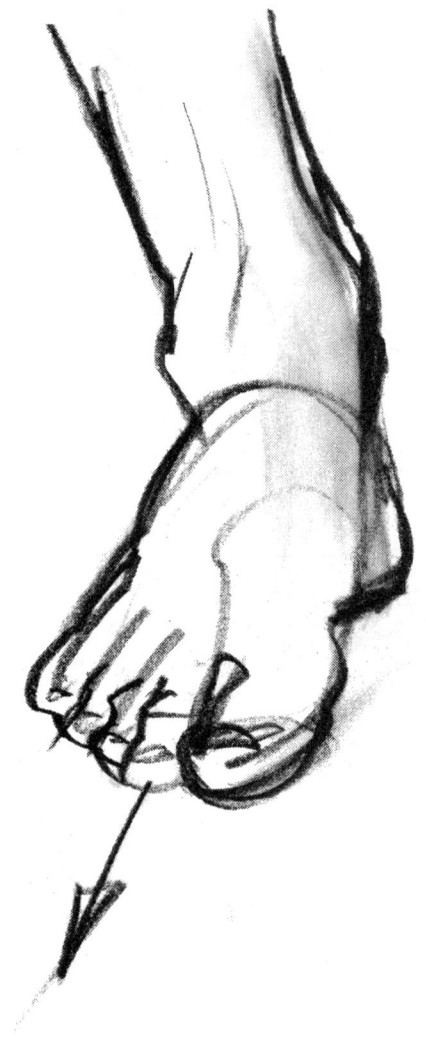

Due to the shape of the male foot, the shoe appears to have two different curves on either side of its center.

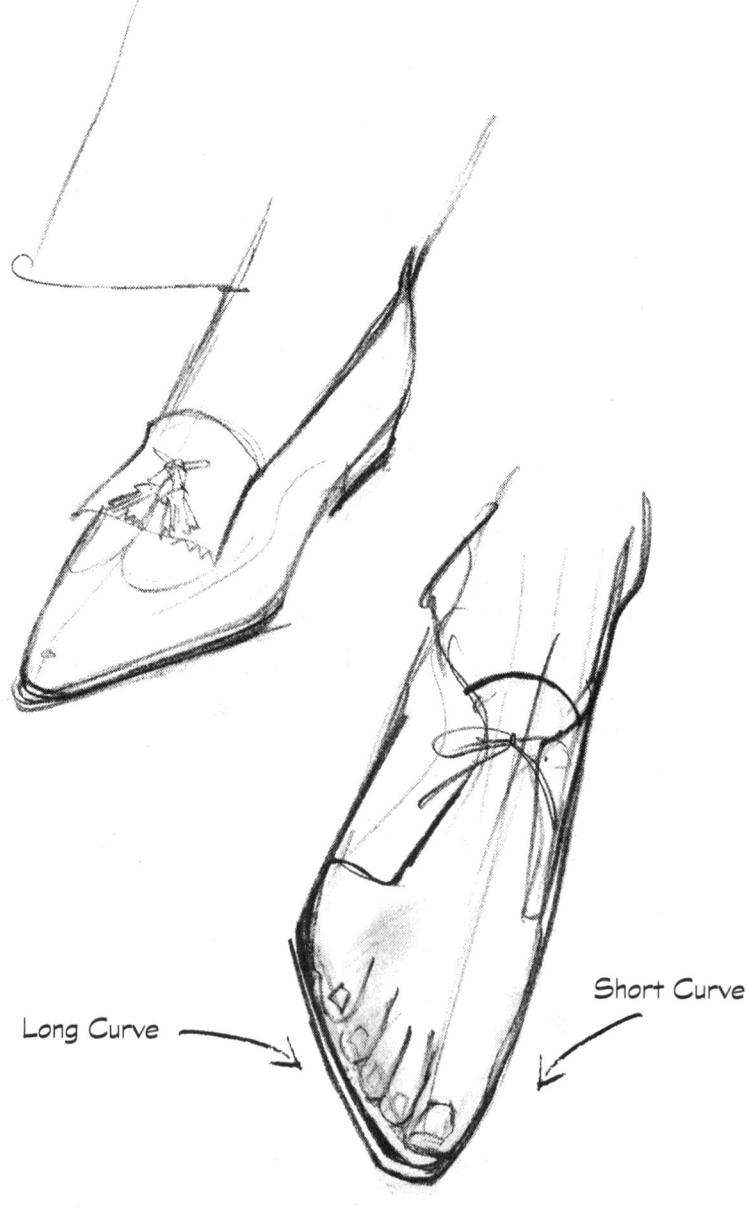

Long Curve

Short Curve

Give width to the foot across the area that is fullest, the point at which the toes begin.

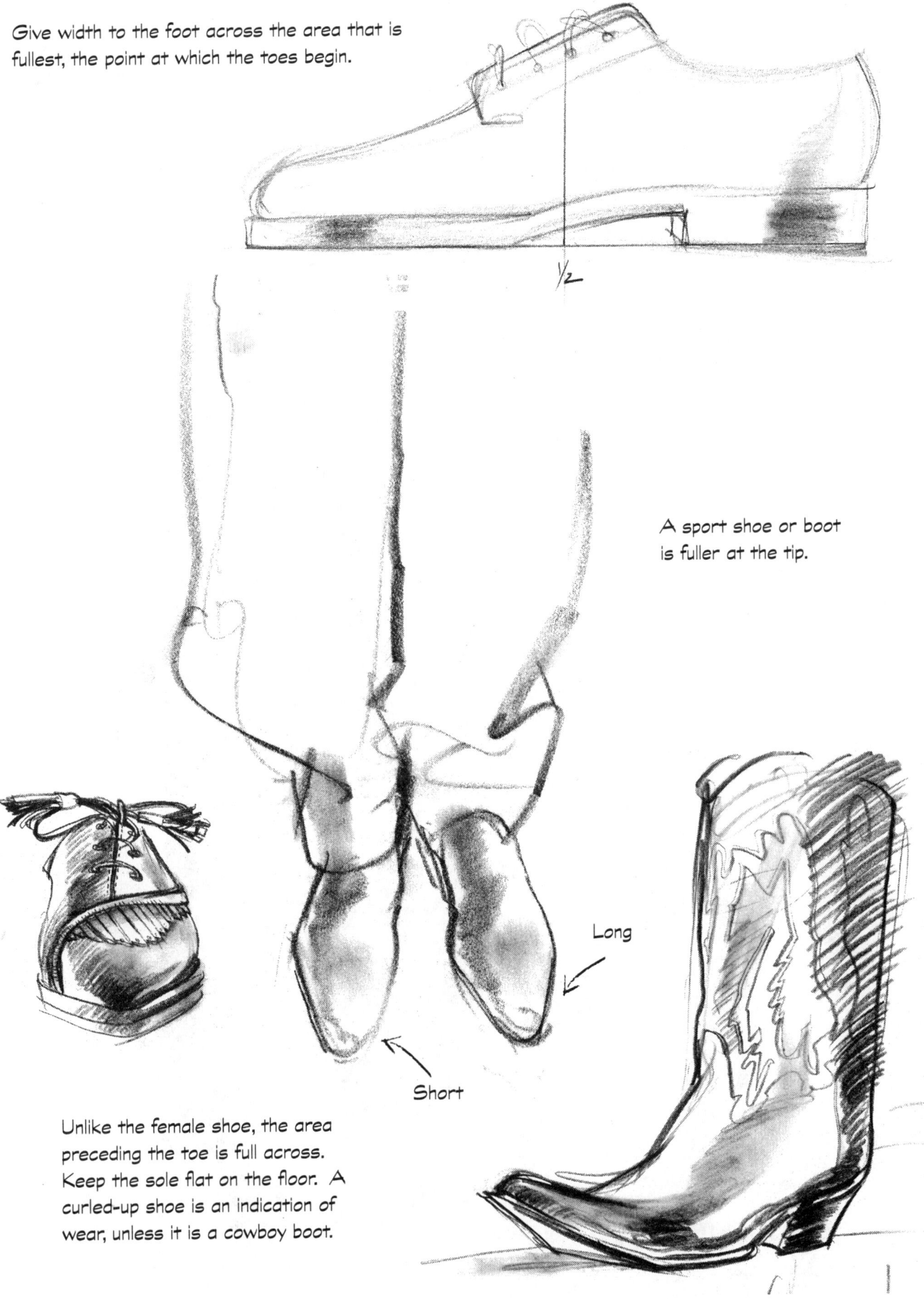

A sport shoe or boot is fuller at the tip.

Long

Short

Unlike the female shoe, the area preceding the toe is full across. Keep the sole flat on the floor. A curled-up shoe is an indication of wear, unless it is a cowboy boot.

CHAPTER 11 MEN'S FIGURES 163

CHAPTER 12

Clothing the Male Figure

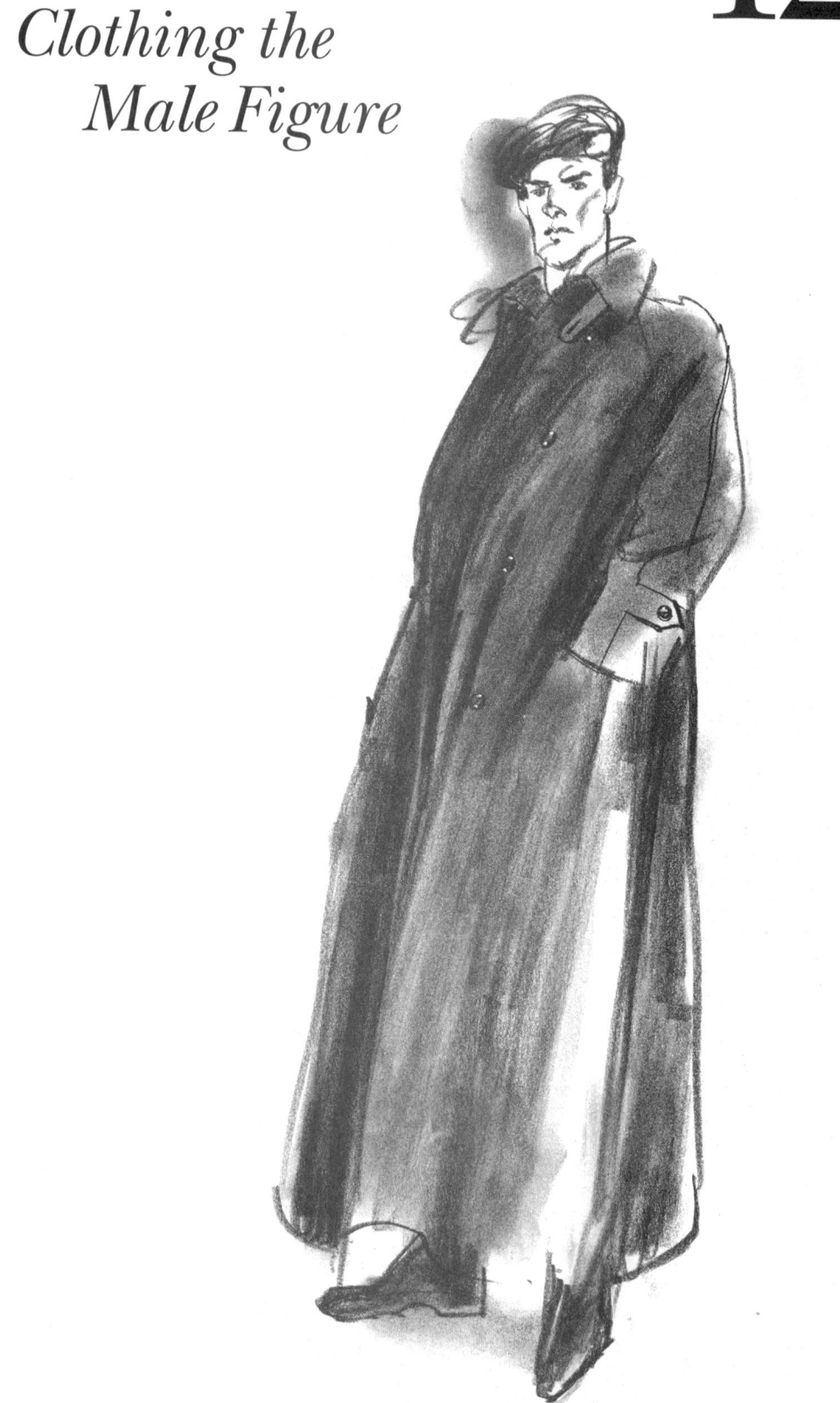

A common fault in drawing the clothed figure is making the arm-to-arm distance too short. This gives the impression of an adolescent.

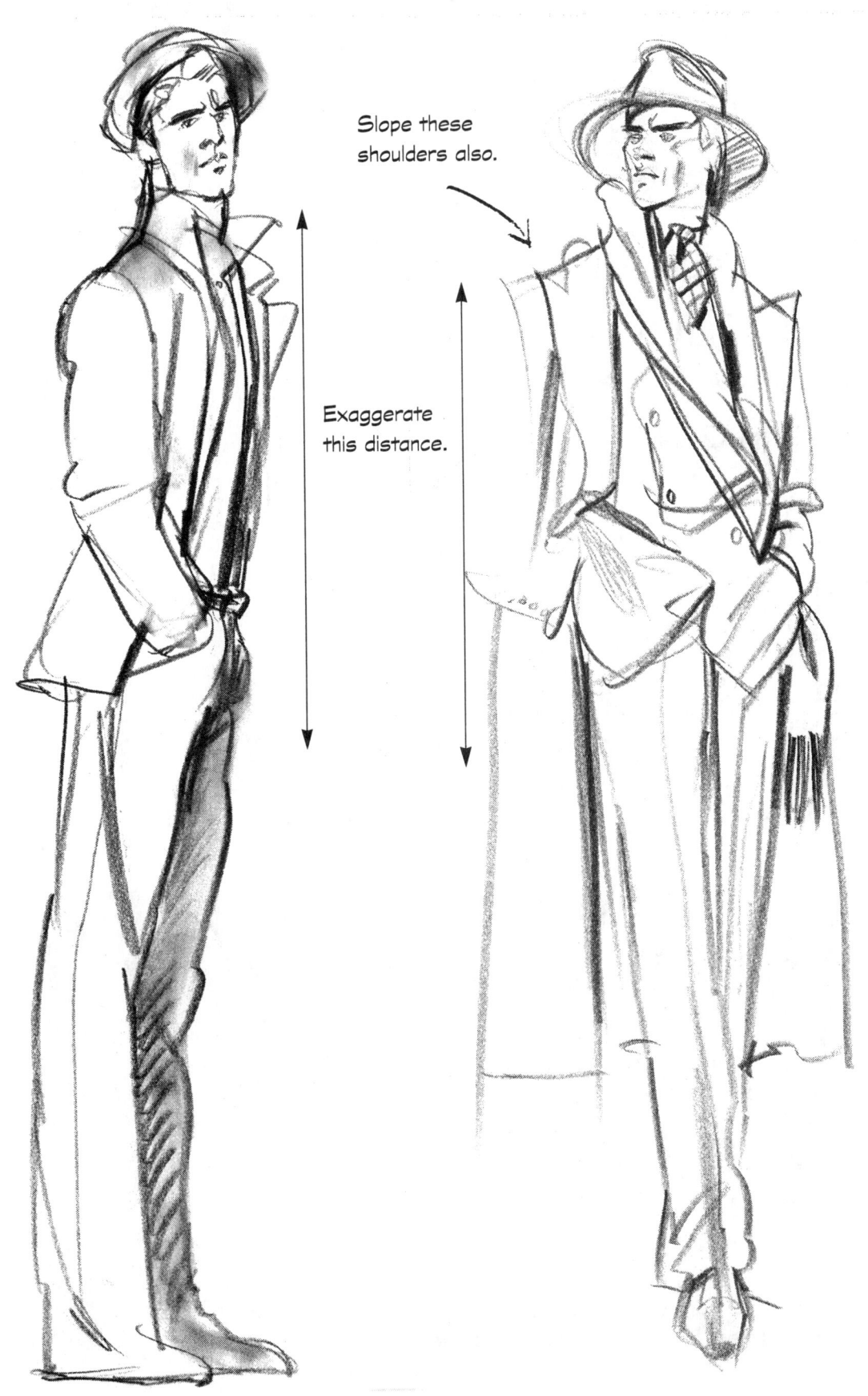

Slope these shoulders also.

Exaggerate this distance.

CHAPTER 12 CLOTHING THE MALE FIGURE

The area from the belt to the base of the pants crotch is longer than that needed for the female figure. This distance is often drawn too short, giving the impression of panties or ballet tights. Draw in the fly front. Without the fly front, the pants look like women's slacks.

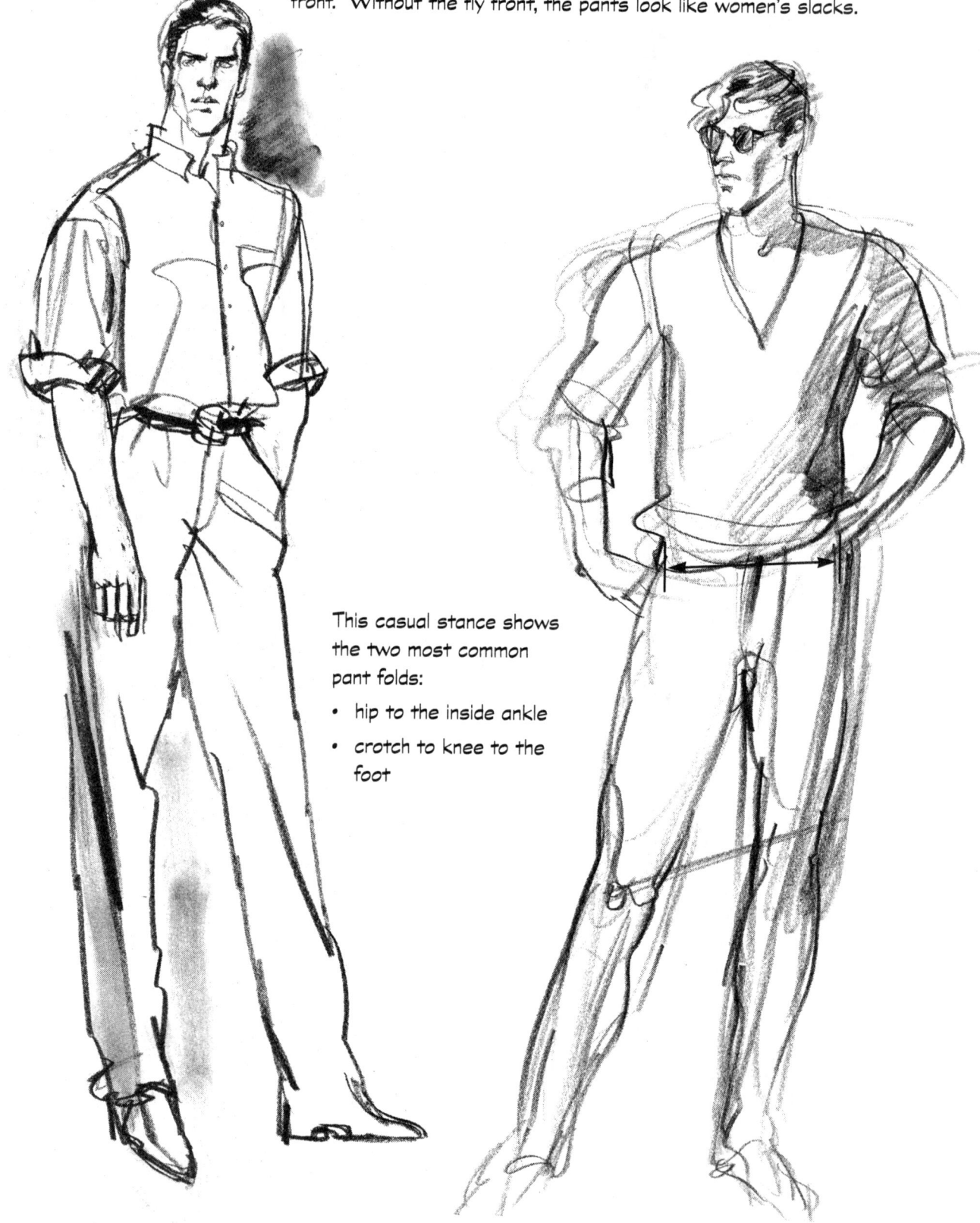

This casual stance shows the two most common pant folds:
- hip to the inside ankle
- crotch to knee to the foot

No matter how full the trousers, keep the male figure slender in the hips. Wide hips suggest middle age.

Seams and tailoring details are clear and easy to understand.

The inverted V effect of the male figure is evident in this suit—broad shoulders and narrow hips.

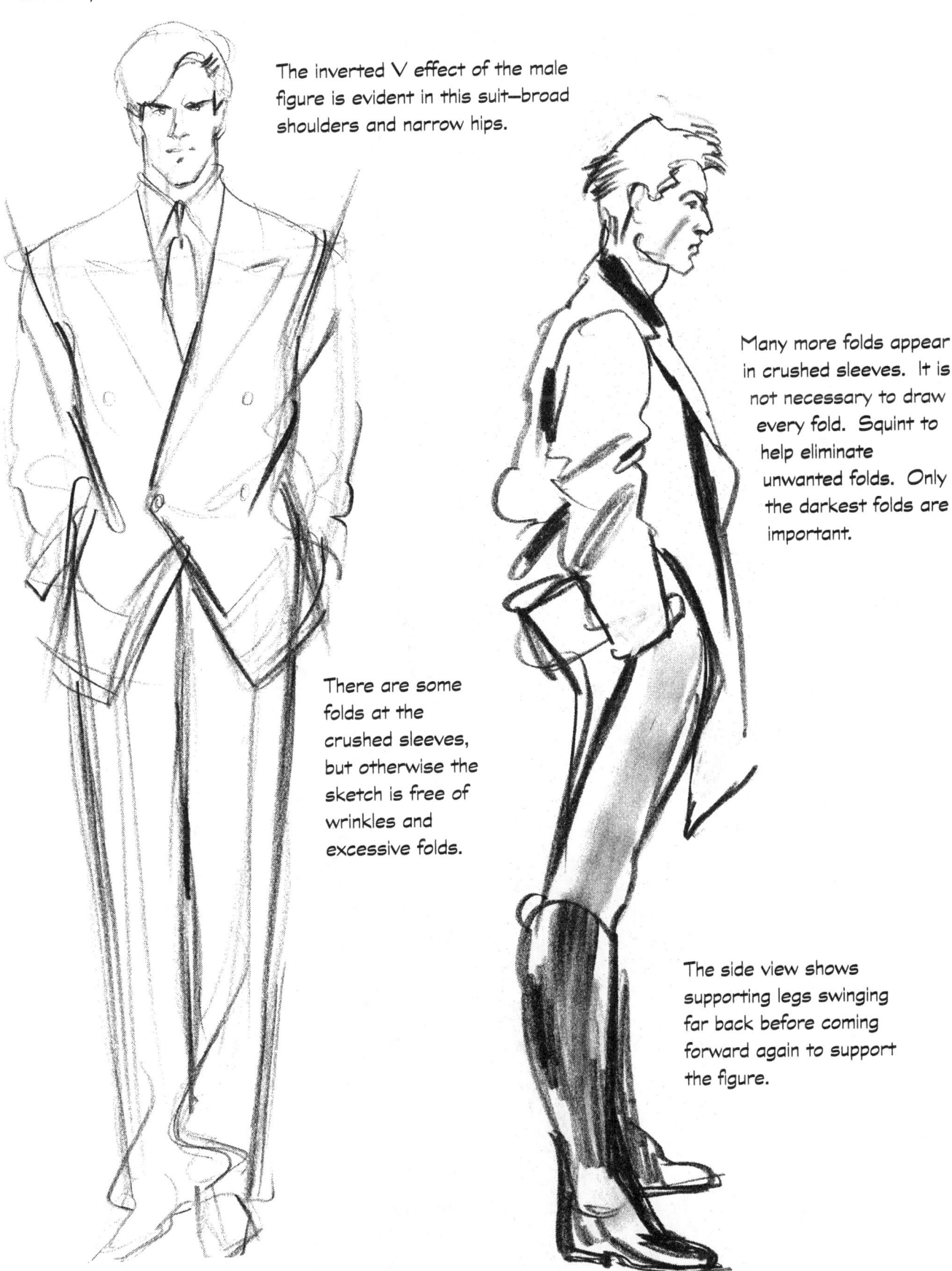

Many more folds appear in crushed sleeves. It is not necessary to draw every fold. Squint to help eliminate unwanted folds. Only the darkest folds are important.

There are some folds at the crushed sleeves, but otherwise the sketch is free of wrinkles and excessive folds.

The side view shows supporting legs swinging far back before coming forward again to support the figure.

CHAPTER 12 CLOTHING THE MALE FIGURE

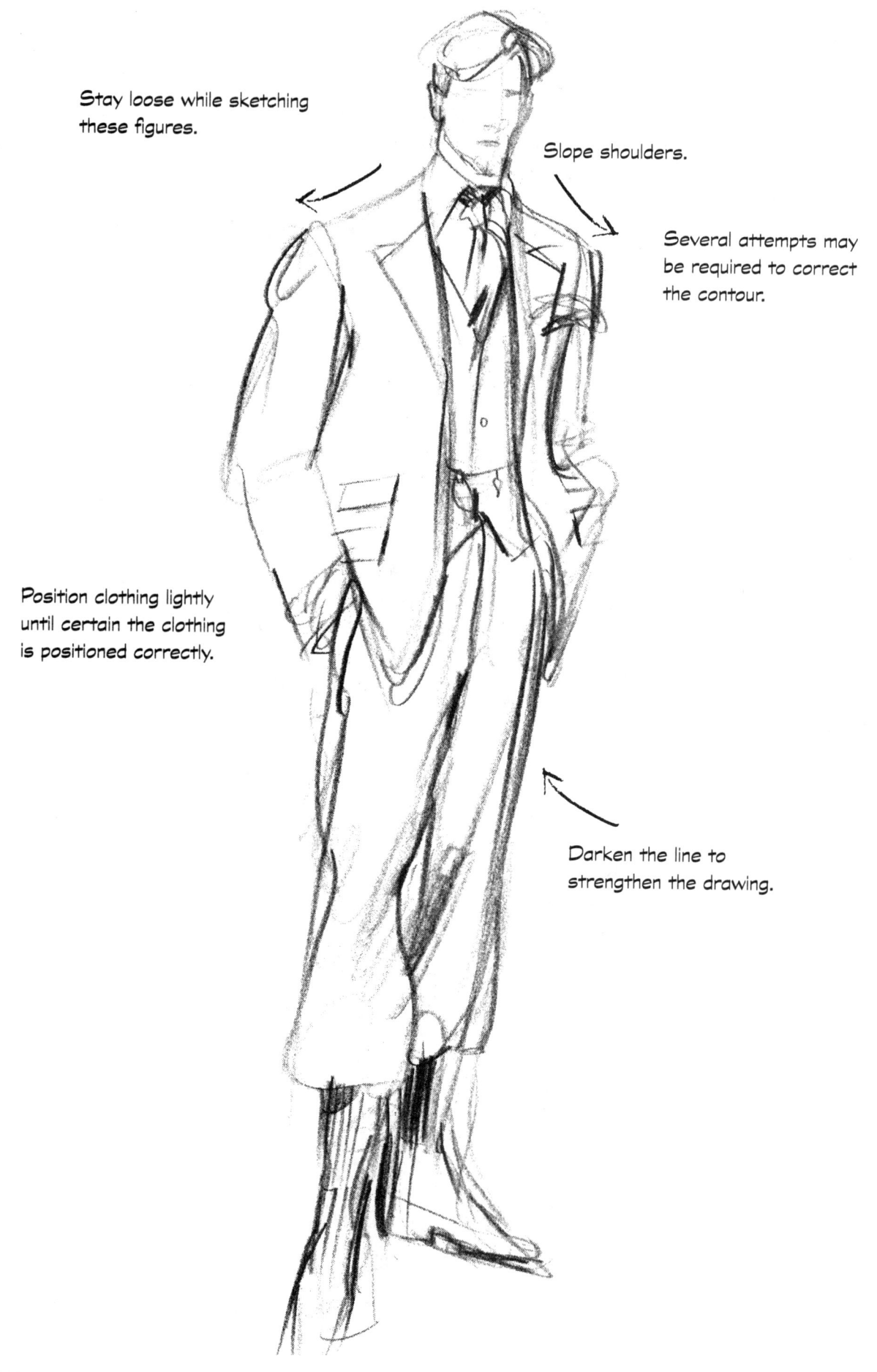

In a bent arm

In side view, jacket sleeves have a forward curve following the natural curve of the arm.

Most jackets are wide at the shoulder, narrowing at the wrist.

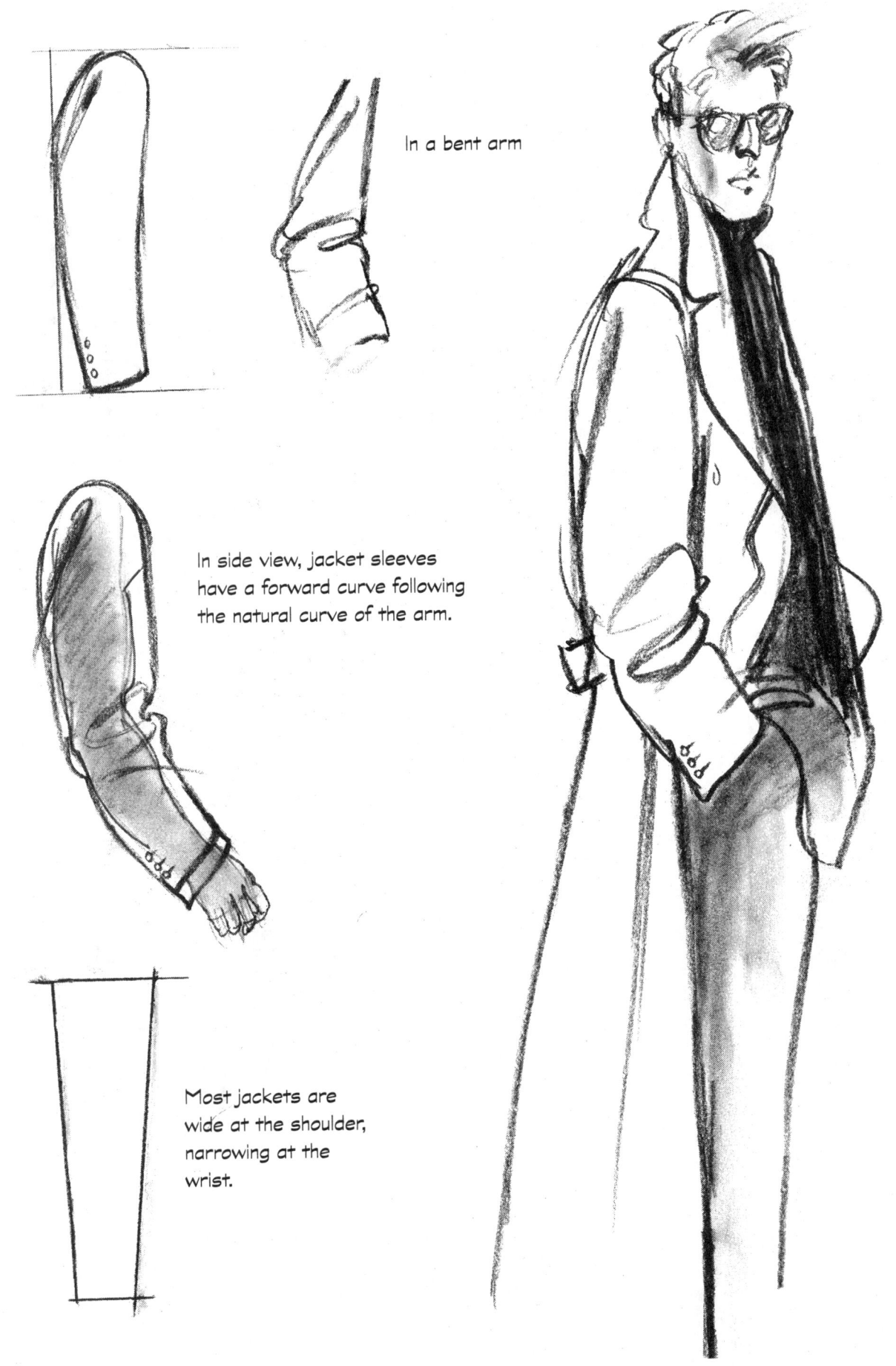

CHAPTER 12 CLOTHING THE MALE FIGURE

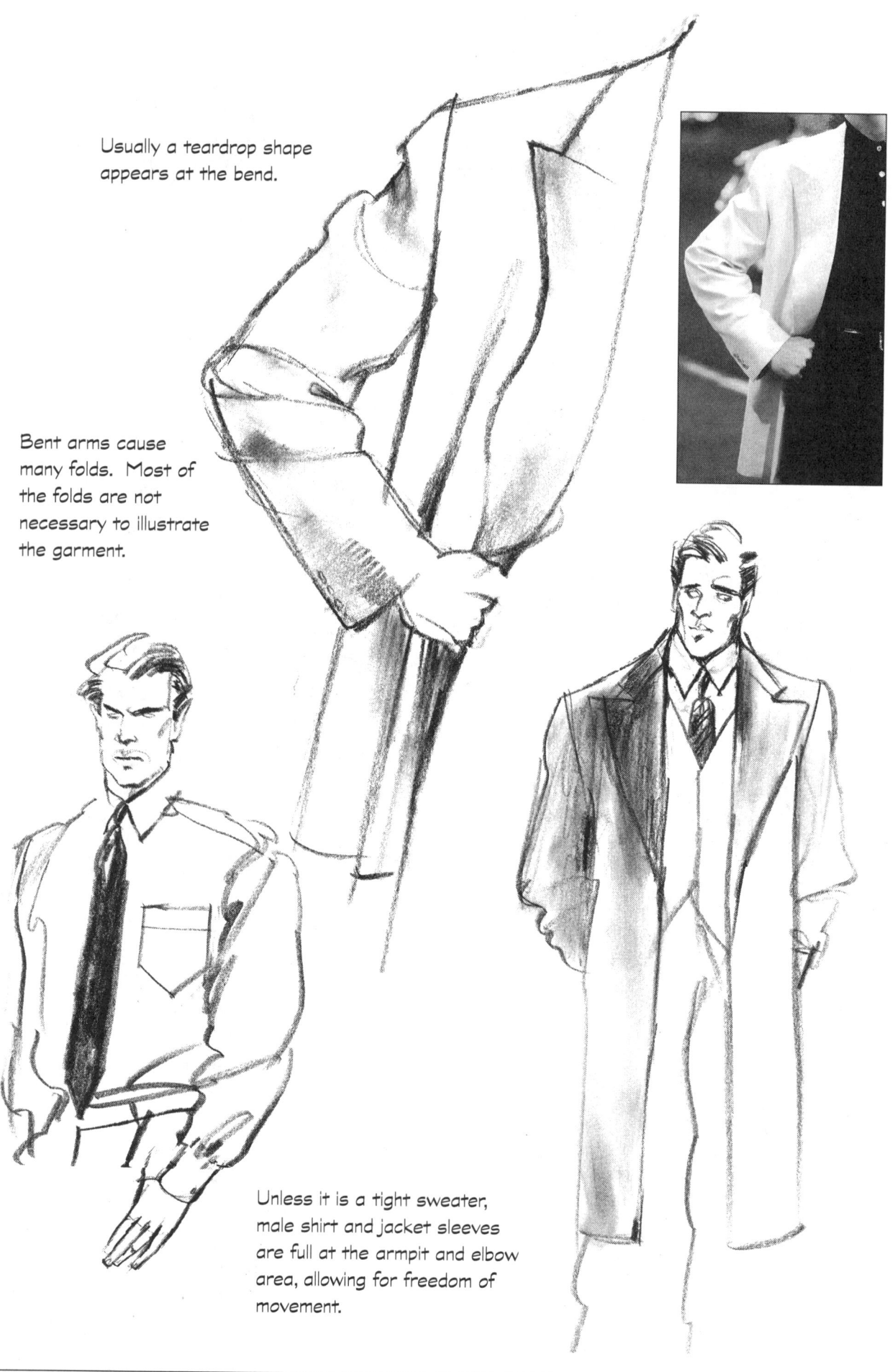

Usually a teardrop shape appears at the bend.

Bent arms cause many folds. Most of the folds are not necessary to illustrate the garment.

Unless it is a tight sweater, male shirt and jacket sleeves are full at the armpit and elbow area, allowing for freedom of movement.

A tight sweater reveals the arm contours. Arm contours are not revealed in dress or sport shirts and jackets that have full sleeves.

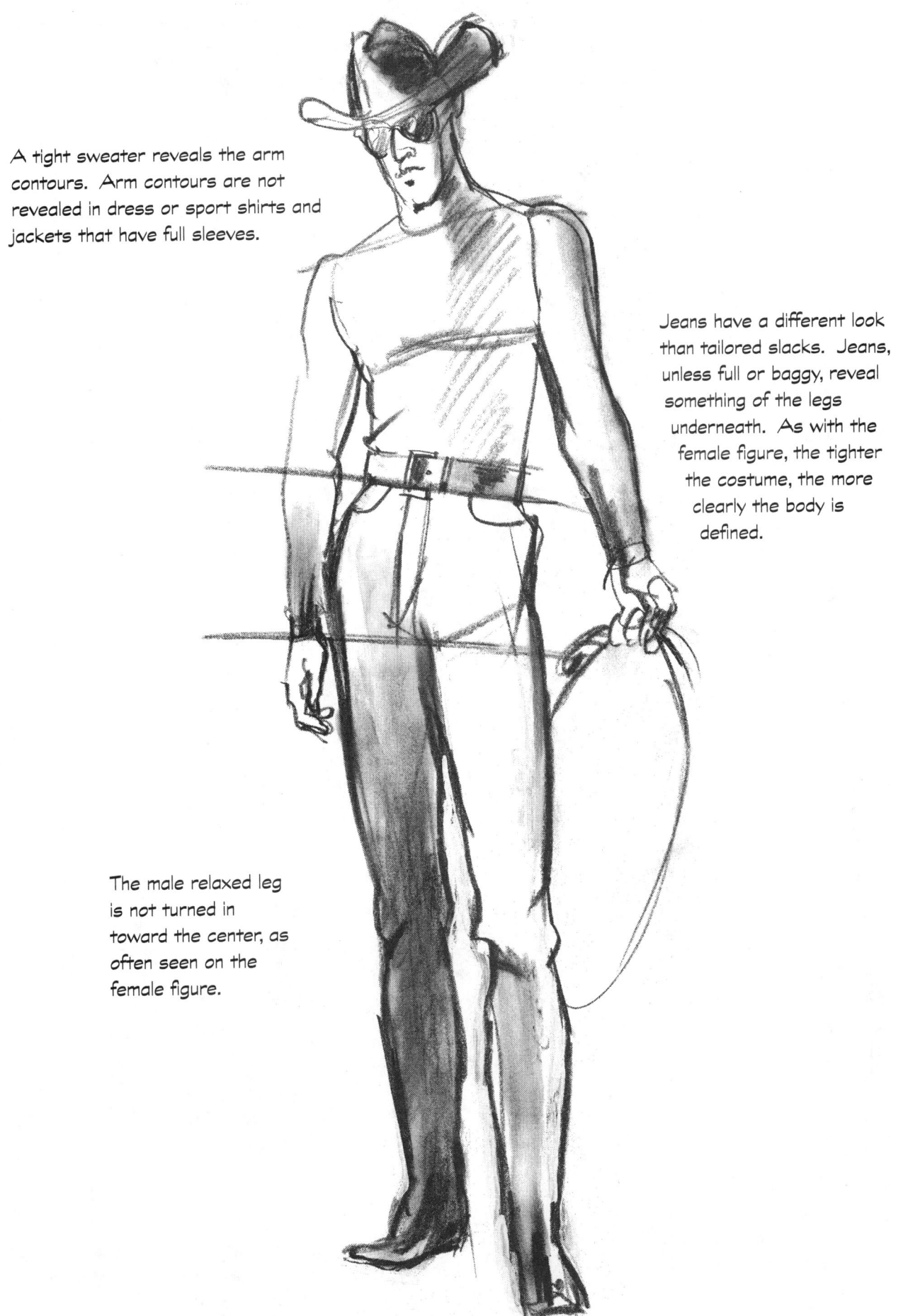

Jeans have a different look than tailored slacks. Jeans, unless full or baggy, reveal something of the legs underneath. As with the female figure, the tighter the costume, the more clearly the body is defined.

The male relaxed leg is not turned in toward the center, as often seen on the female figure.

For pants or slacks, it is important to show where the hem or cuff is, for the effect desired. This varies greatly. Pant legs drawn low on the shoe causes buckling. High off the shoe shows socks. Know which you want to show.

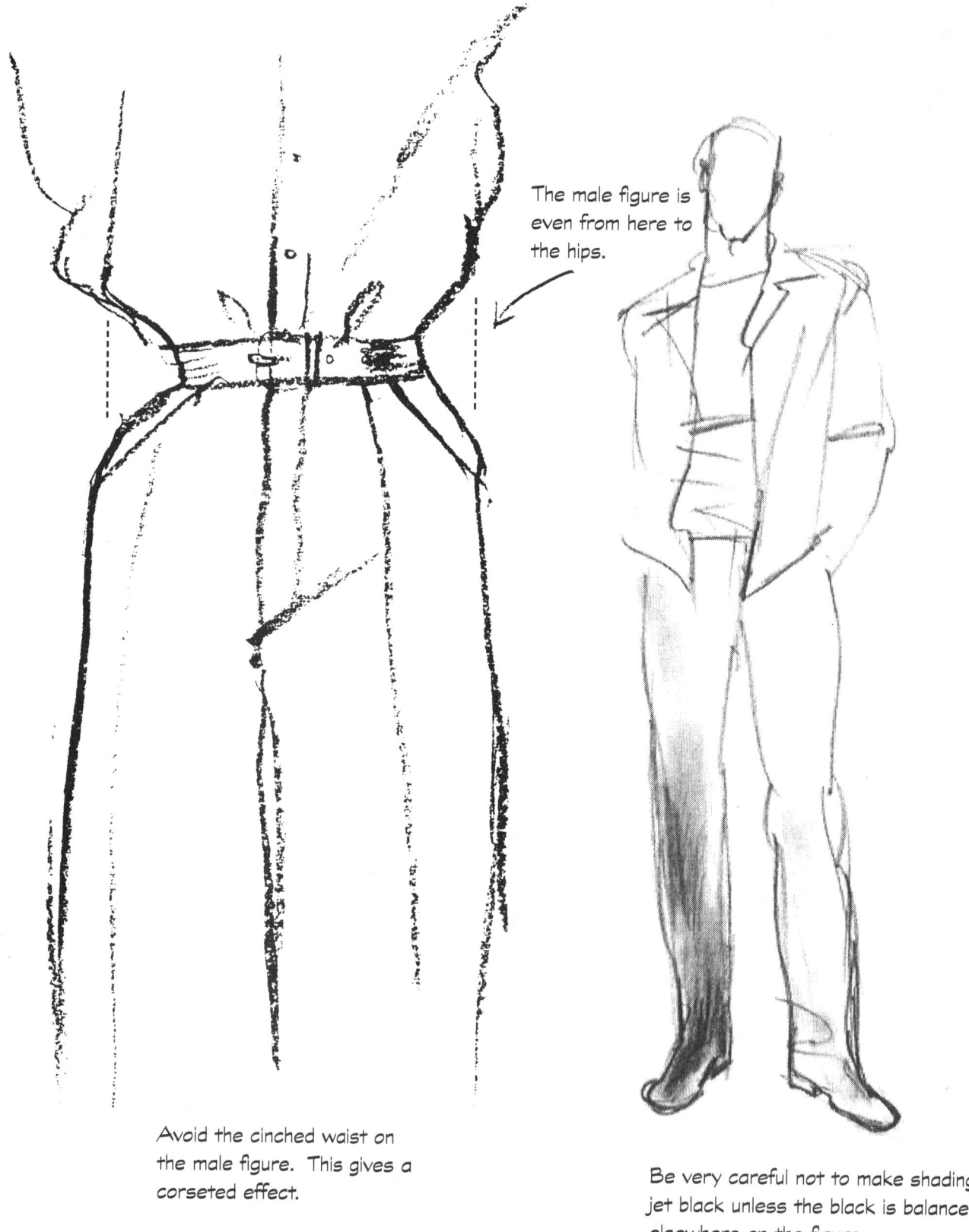

The male figure is even from here to the hips.

Avoid the cinched waist on the male figure. This gives a corseted effect.

Be very careful not to make shading jet black unless the black is balanced elsewhere on the figure.

THE DOUBLE-BREASTED COAT OR JACKET

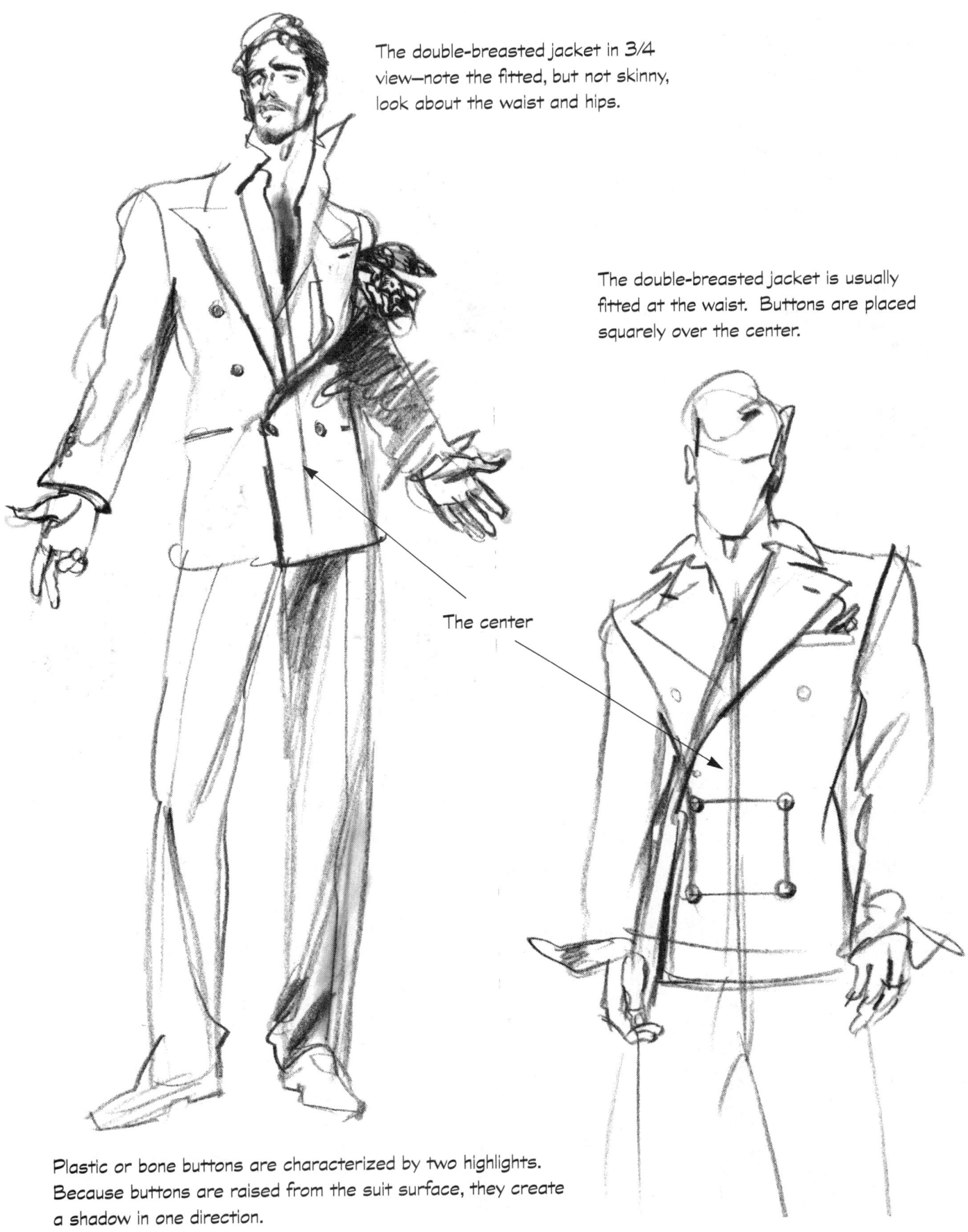

The double-breasted jacket in 3/4 view—note the fitted, but not skinny, look about the waist and hips.

The double-breasted jacket is usually fitted at the waist. Buttons are placed squarely over the center.

The center

Plastic or bone buttons are characterized by two highlights. Because buttons are raised from the suit surface, they create a shadow in one direction.

CHAPTER 12 CLOTHING THE MALE FIGURE 173

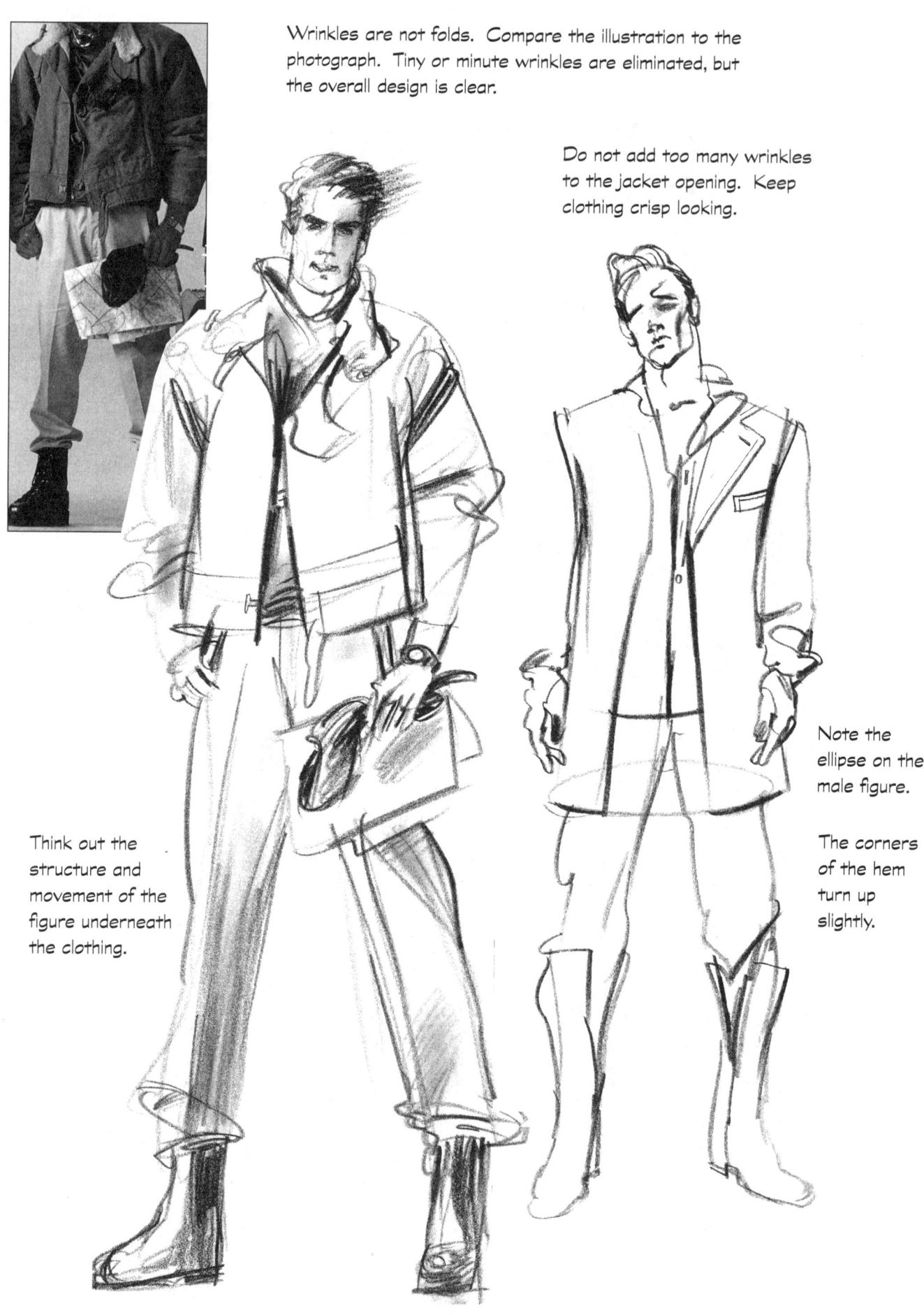

Wrinkles are not folds. Compare the illustration to the photograph. Tiny or minute wrinkles are eliminated, but the overall design is clear.

Do not add too many wrinkles to the jacket opening. Keep clothing crisp looking.

Think out the structure and movement of the figure underneath the clothing.

Note the ellipse on the male figure.

The corners of the hem turn up slightly.

Busy plaids make an interesting contrast on this solid suit.

Explain the tie knot design. The knot shown is very tight between knot and tail.

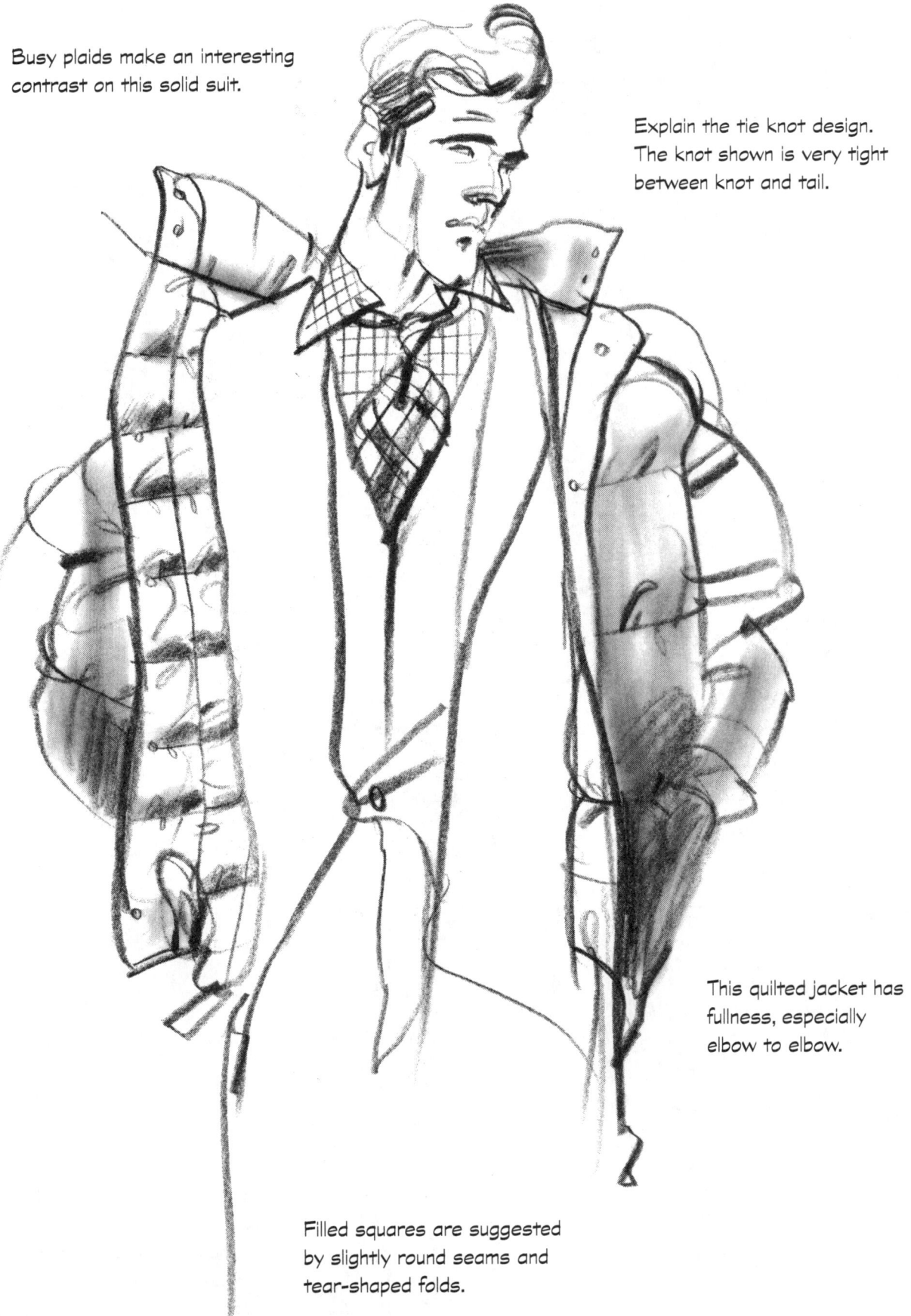

This quilted jacket has fullness, especially elbow to elbow.

Filled squares are suggested by slightly round seams and tear-shaped folds.

CHAPTER 12 CLOTHING THE MALE FIGURE

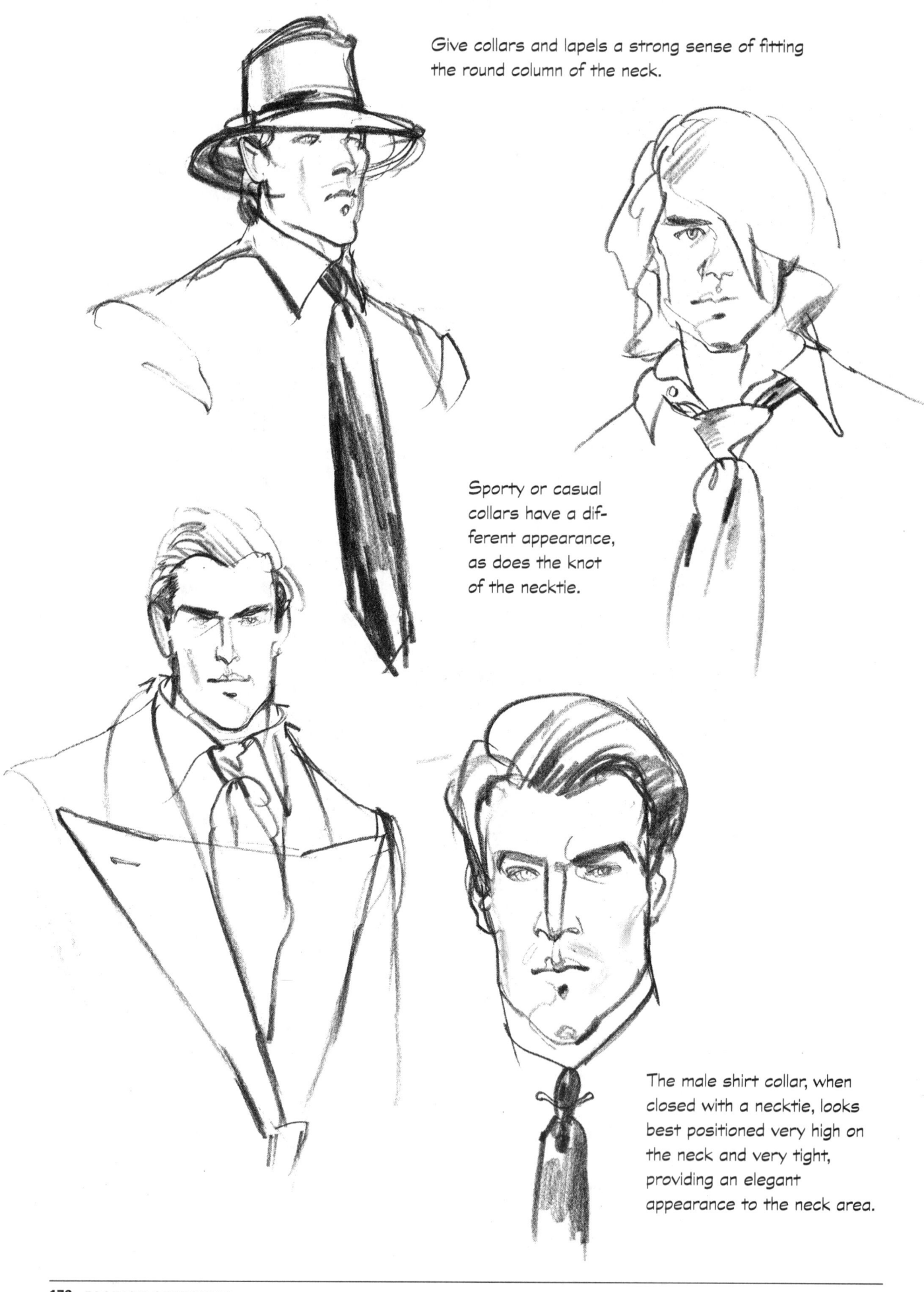

Give collars and lapels a strong sense of fitting the round column of the neck.

Sporty or casual collars have a different appearance, as does the knot of the necktie.

The male shirt collar, when closed with a necktie, looks best positioned very high on the neck and very tight, providing an elegant appearance to the neck area.

This leather effect breaks down into three values: black, dark gray, and light gray with white highlights. Note the bulging contours of thick leather. Pure white is used only for the sharpest highlight. White pastel pencil is used for a soft leather feeling. Shapes are important, as shown here in the look of crushed leather.

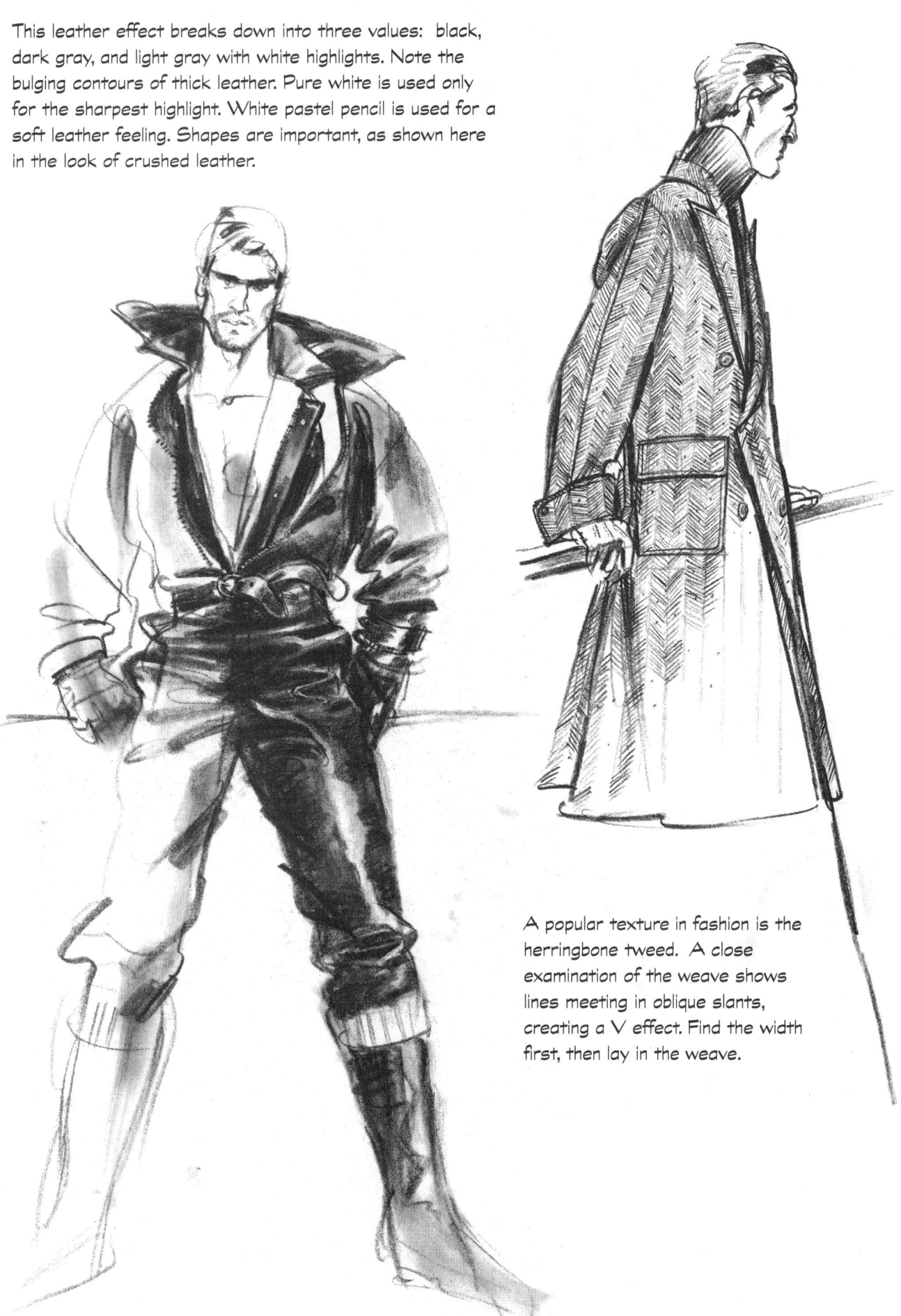

A popular texture in fashion is the herringbone tweed. A close examination of the weave shows lines meeting in oblique slants, creating a V effect. Find the width first, then lay in the weave.

CHAPTER 12 CLOTHING THE MALE FIGURE 177

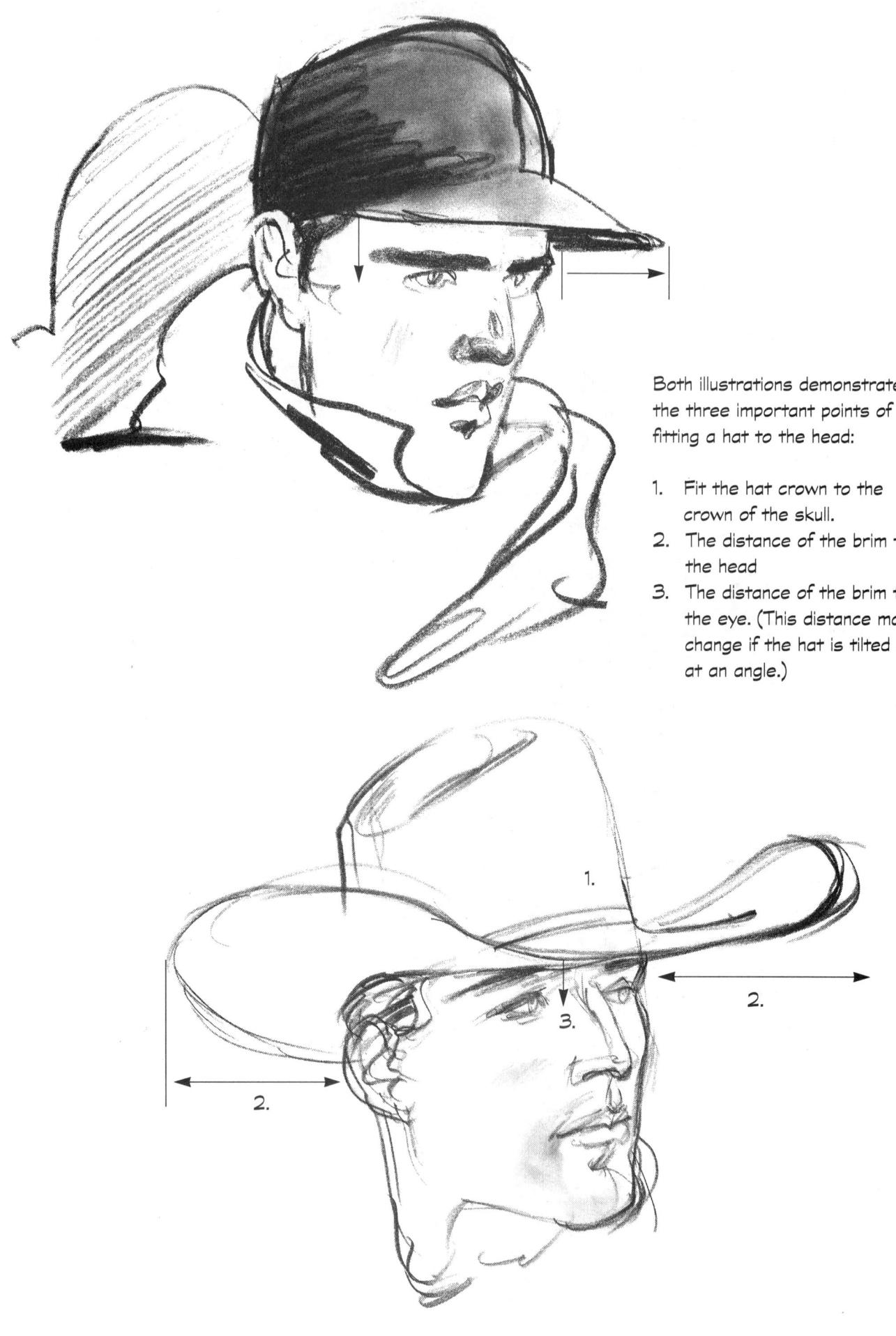

Both illustrations demonstrate the three important points of fitting a hat to the head:

1. Fit the hat crown to the crown of the skull.
2. The distance of the brim to the head
3. The distance of the brim to the eye. (This distance may change if the hat is tilted or at an angle.)

Youthful or children's figures show the age group in the attitudes they assume.

Shorten the proportions to lessen the sophistication. Give expression to the face and lively action to the figure.

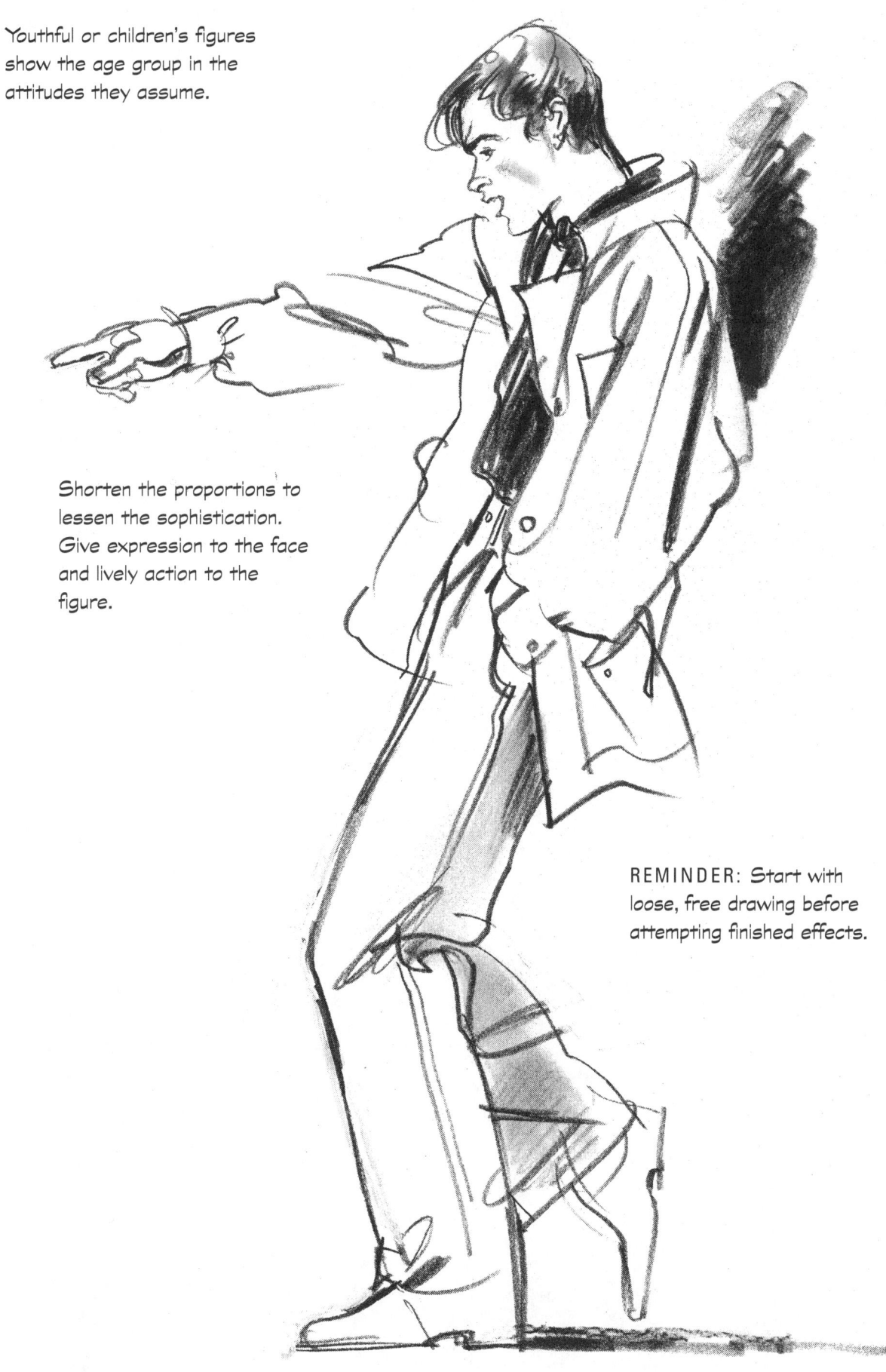

REMINDER: Start with loose, free drawing before attempting finished effects.

CHAPTER 12 CLOTHING THE MALE FIGURE